Where the Party Rules

In most non-democratic countries, today governing 44 percent of the world population, the power of the regime rests upon a ruling party. Contrasting with conventional notions that authoritarian regime parties serve to contain elite conflict and manipulate electoral-legislative processes, this book presents the case of China and shows that rank-and-file members of the Communist Party allow the state to penetrate local communities. Subnational comparative analysis demonstrates that in "red areas" with high party saturation, the state is most effectively enforcing policy and collecting taxes. Because party membership patterns are extremely enduring, they must be explained by events prior to the Communist takeover in 1949. Frontlines during the anti-colonial Sino-Japanese War (1937–1945) continue to shape China's political map even today. Newly available evidence from the Great Leap Forward (1958–1961) and the Cultural Revolution (1966–1976) shows how a strong local party basis sustained the regime in times of existential crisis.

Daniel Koss is Assistant Research Fellow at the Institute of Political Science of Academia Sinica, Taipei. Prior to this appointment, he was a postdoctoral fellow at the Harvard Academy for International and Area studies.

Studies of the Weatherhead East Asian Institute, Columbia University

The Studies of the Weatherhead East Asian Institute of Columbia University were inaugurated in 1962 to bring to a wider public the results of significant new research on modern and contemporary East Asia.

Where the Party Rules

The Rank and File of China's Communist State

DANIEL KOSS

Academia Sinica, Taipei, Taiwan

CAMBRIDGE
UNIVERSITY PRESS

CAMBRIDGE
UNIVERSITY PRESS

University Printing House, Cambridge CB2 8BS, United Kingdom

One Liberty Plaza, 20th Floor, New York, NY 10006, USA

477 Williamstown Road, Port Melbourne, VIC 3207, Australia

314–321, 3rd Floor, Plot 3, Splendor Forum, Jasola District Centre,
New Delhi - 110025, India

79 Anson Road, #06-04/06, Singapore 079906

Cambridge University Press is part of the University of Cambridge.

It furthers the University's mission by disseminating knowledge in the pursuit of
education, learning and research at the highest international levels of excellence.

www.cambridge.org
Information on this title: www.cambridge.org/9781108420662
DOI: 10.1017/9781108354981

© Daniel Koss 2018

First published 2018

Printed in the United States of America by Sheridan Books, Inc.

A catalogue record for this publication is available from the British Library

ISBN 978-1-108-42066-2 Hardback
ISBN 978-1-108-43073-9 Paperback

Contents

Figures

Tables

Acknowledgments

The most enjoyable aspect of researching this book has been the wealth of human encounters on the way. Thinking back to the diversity of acquaintances and friendships over these years, at my home university and in the field – where I spent one third of my graduate career – I feel extremely fortunate and deeply grateful. My dissertation committee chair Elizabeth J. Perry not only incited my scholarly enthusiasm for China, but also went far beyond her duty to advise me on grand issues and crucial detail. The other committee members, Steven Levitsky, Susan J. Pharr, Michael Szonyi, and Adam N. Glynn, also provided steadfast support and continuous inspiration. All participants in my book manuscript workshop – Martin Dimitrov, Anna Grzymala-Busse, Milan Svolik and Andrew G. Walder, in addition to the chair – were generous with their time and helped greatly to transform the manuscript. My colleagues at the Institute of Political Science at Academia Sinica are a truly inspiring community, ideal for finalizing the manuscript; special thanks for their scholarly feedback and everyday cordiality to Chang Liao Nien-chung, Kumakura Jun, Leng Tse-kang, Lin Jih-wen, Lo Ren-yuan, Tsai Wen-hsuan, Wu Wen-chin, and Wu Yu-shan.

Early on Anthony J. Saich and Shinju Fujihira facilitated essential contacts in the field. At Harvard, in addition to Kyle A. Jaros who read all of my dissertation and some of it several times, Timothy Beaumont, Volha Charnysh, Xenia Cherkaev, Sheena Chestnut Greitens, Joan Cho, Aditya Dasgupta, Grzegorz Ekiert, Roberto Foa, Shelby Grossman, Jingkai He, A. Ian Johnston, Jeehye Kim, Małgorzata Kurjańska, Yan Liu, Brendan McElroy, Timothy Nunan, Jennifer J. Pan, Ruxandra Paul, Amanda Pinkston, James Robinson, Daniel Smith, Chiara Superti, Ezra F. Vogel, and Daniel Ziblatt, among others, offered precious comments on parts of this book at various iterations; Li Yunjie provided highly competent GIS research assistance. Participants in the Research Workshop in Comparative Politics, the Cambridge China Politics Research Workshop the Politics and History Workshop at Yale University, and the Conference on Quantitative Studies of the Chinese Elite at UCSD, as well as two conferences at East China Normal University, helped to refine my argument. The librarians of the Fairbank Center and of the Harvard-Yenching Institute, Nancy Hearst, Ma Xiaohe, and Kuniko Y. McVey, as well as M. Lex Berman from the China Historical GIS Project, introduced me to the riches of Harvard's collections. During my time in Cambridge, I enjoyed support from the Karl W. Deutsch Prize, the Richard L. and Faith P. Morningstar Graduate Fellowship, the Samuel Huntington Fellowship, and last but not least from the Harvard Academy for International and Area Studies, where postdoctoral fellows enjoy the welcoming and professional atmosphere created by Timothy J. Colton, Jorge I. Domínguez, Bruce V. Jackan and Kathleen Hoover.

In China, Xiong Yizhi and Lei Ying from Tsinghua University helped me get started. The scholars Liu Ping, Fang Lei, and Lou Suping provided me with a good research base at Shandong University and gave me extraordinary intellectual inspiration. Hu Biliang and Liu Yimeng hosted me for a productive stay at Beijing Normal University, Leng Xiangming and Li Qing let me stay at Central China Normal University in Wuhan, Luo Yanjun brought me to Liaocheng University, and Gao Xiang to Zhejiang University for a talk. Yin Hongbiao from Beijing University helped me to overcome deadlock in my research on the Cultural Revolution. Steven M. Goldstein let me participate in a group of researchers visiting Zouping, giving me an opportunity to develop my own field research techniques. Zhang Wei helped me to access documents that the Japanese had left behind in China after World War II. I am thankful to officials working at the Number One Historical Archives in the Forbidden City (whose documents were used for the dissertation but not this book); the provincial-level archives of Hubei, Hunan, Shandong, and Shanghai; the prefectural-level archives of Jinan, Liaocheng, Qingdao, Yantai, Zaozhuang, and Zibo; and the county-level archives of Lixia and Zouping, as well as the archive at Heilongjiang's Party School and at libraries with strong local collections, for their almost always very polite and oftentimes supportive attitude. Provincial officials from the Propaganda Department and from the Finance Department of Shandong, as well as local officials in Chiping, Gaotang, Jimo, Teng Xian, Mudan, Shanting, Xuecheng, Zouping in

Shandong, and Xianning in Hubei contributed to my research efforts. Du Heng and her family helped me to gain a more personal perspective on historical events in Shandong province. My parents-in-law Li Bin and Wang Yaqing let me represent them on a three-week trip by former Red Guards on a special train to revisit their own revolutionary past in China's "Great Northern Wilderness." My extensive travels in China would not have been possible – certainly not field research for such an extended period of time – without generous financial support from the Harvard-Yenching Institute, the Harvard University Asia Center, the Fairbank Center for Chinese Studies, and, most importantly, from a fellowship endowed by Desmond and Whitney Shum. China's autocratic system is secretive, but thanks to this support it was not impenetrable. Insights gained through citizens committed to truth amply outweigh the obstacles I faced.

At the Institute of History and Philology of Academia Sinica in Taipei, Chin-shing Huang, Hsi-yuan Chen, Cheng-yun Liu, Chen Miao-fen, and Lee Ya-ling were wonderful hosts and helpful advisors, patiently guiding my ventures into China's imperial past. The library staff at Academia Sinica, especially Yu-chien Huang, as well as the archivists at the Palace Museum, provided much-needed assistance. Making possible later discoveries in Japan, the Reischauer Institute of Japanese Studies first provided me with a grant to study Japanese language at Hokkaido International Foundation in Hakodate and with the Hirade family. Hiroshi Sato welcomed me to Hitotsubashi University, allowing me to explore Japanese material on Chinese history. Helped by Linda Grove, Motokazu Matsutani, and Mariko Naito, I learned about the holdings at the National Library, Tōyō Bunko, the Defense Ministry, and Yasukuni Shrine. Conversations with Asahi Shimbun journalists, especially Kenji Minemura's insights into party, elite, and diplomacy and Haruko Kagenishi's ideas on Rashomon, revolution, and relics, have been most inspiring.

The experienced diplomats Tono Eitel, Volker Seitz, and Stefan Biedermann, all belonging to my former employer the German Foreign Ministry, as well as General Lamine Cissé, taught me key lessons in the art of studying politics first-hand in the field. When my collection of Cultural Revolution material aroused suspicions in ultimately understanding Chinese authorities, the official on call at the German Embassy in Beijing helped me to navigate a difficult situation. The staff of the ministry's political archive in Berlin provided me with access to valuable historical material. My wife Jie and our son Anton kept me in good spirits. This book is dedicated to my parents, Anne-Dorothea and Klaus Koss.

PART I

AUTOCRATIC GRASSROOTS POLITICS

1

Introduction: Party-Based Authoritarianism in China

Political parties are pivotal institutions, in democratic and authoritarian contexts alike. Almost all seventy-one nondemocracies, in 2015 governing 44 percent of the world population, have parties. In most of these countries at least one party is tightly controlled by the ruling clique, such as United Russia, the United Malays National Organization, and Turkey's Justice and Development Party.[1] In contrast to other autocratic arrangements, such as military dictatorship and personalistic rule, party-based authoritarianism has proven itself effective in governing modernizing societies and mitigating democratization pressures.[2] But how do parties contribute to effective authoritarian rule? And what are the origins of effective regime parties? The first question calls for a study of contemporary autocratic governance. The second question takes us back to history. The literature provides answers to both questions, but incomplete ones. The case of the Chinese Communist Party (CCP), which is the focus of this book, promises to change the way we think about the functions and origins of effective authoritarian regime parties.

This book demonstrates that an authoritarian regime party can provide the organizational infrastructure that allows a state to project authority throughout its realm. By implication, the book explains why authoritarian regimes are usually more effective in some parts of their territories than in others: The uneven presence of rank-and-file party members makes an important difference for policy implementation on the ground. The CCP's rank and file empowers the state at the local level, precisely because the overwhelming majority of party members is not in bureaucratic positions, but works outside the government. Chapter 2 develops a new theory of authoritarian regime parties, after which the following two chapters test the theory's observable implications for subnational variation in contemporary state-building outcomes, and describe causal mechanisms. To do so, Chapter 3 analyzes the particularly challenging enforcement of the one-child policy, and Chapter 4 turns to the universally relevant state-building task of collecting taxes.

The next two chapters turn to the historical origins of local party strength, arguable found in the Second Sino-Japanese War (1939–1945). Chapter 5 shows that Japanese occupation shielded the Communists from persecution by the incumbent Nationalist government and allowed the party to recruit members behind enemy lines, shaping membership patterns at the time of the Communist takeover in 1949. As Chapter 6 demonstrates, early party membership patterns persisted and shape the party's geographic base even today. The last two chapters bridge the temporal gap between the wartime experience and the post-Mao party era by turning to two important episodes in the history of the People's Republic: The Great Leap Forward with its catastrophic famine (1958–1961) in Chapter 7 and the height of the Cultural Revolution turmoil (1967–1969) in Chapter 8. These cases are important, because they caution us that the party has not always and under all circumstances functioned as a faithful implementer of central policies. Yet even under these rather exceptional historical conditions, party membership patterns shaped variation in local policy outcomes.

The remainder of this introduction is organized as follows. After an overview of the argument, I describe the research process that has led to this book. Next, the empirical portion of the introduction provides impressionistic evidence on the functions of the party as a screening, disciplining, and mobilization device. Rank-and-file party members are at the center of this description. Moving from the micro level of the party to the macro level, the chapter then suggests that a map of party membership density captures crucial aspects of governance in the People's Republic. In addition, geographic membership patterns allow analysis of historical continuities and study of the persistence of historical legacies in a parsimonious way. The introduction ends with an overview of the nine chapters. Overall, this introductory portrait of the CCP provides the intuition for a new approach to regime parties, which is the main contribution of this book.

1.1 THE GRASSROOTS ORIGINS OF EFFECTIVE AUTHORITARIAN RULE

The CCP is an exceptionally important political institution of the 20th and 21st centuries on many counts. It has dominated the world's most populous country since 1949. Its leaders are shaping global politics and its organizational branches are present worldwide, some flourishing in the open, others proliferating covertly. The party's decisions may continue to affect peoples' lives around the globe well into the future. Under the auspices of the party, the People's Republic governs a territory that is roughly equal to the United States, but whose diverse population is five times larger. It has maintained effective rule, while many other countries in the world, and much smaller ones, struggle with anarchy and violence. The emergence of a modern and functional Chinese state in the mid-twentieth century was certainly not a foregone conclusion, if we think of the widespread violence in the nineteenth century and the five tumultuous decades in the twentieth century between the Boxer Uprising in 1900 and the Civil War ending in 1949. This book argues that in addition to existing explanations pointing to the role of the party in mediating elite conflict, the party's presence at the grassroots level of society must be at the center of explanations for the effectiveness of the Chinese state. The party's rank and file allow the state to penetrate local society; its local branches are capillaries that enable the microcirculation of information. Across policy areas, the rank and file of the single party are key to explaining the lasting effectiveness of the regime.

Uncovering the sources of Chinese state strength is important, first and foremost to understand how 20 percent of the world population is governed today. At the same time the country is not as irrelevant for comparative studies as some analysts have us believe, by putting China into a residual classification category comprising the "almost disappeared" species of "unambiguously nondemocratic regime[s]."[3] Like the majority of authoritarian countries today, China is a party-based authoritarian regime.[4] The existence of a regime party is an important characteristic of the regime, since strong parties have been identified as a crucial ingredient for authoritarian regime survival.[5] Yet it is not clear how parties bolster authoritarian regimes, nor how some parties have grown stronger than others. These questions have taken on new urgency now that ideologies have lost some of their force and an instrumental logic has taken center stage. The case of China and the CCP can illuminate the functions and origins of regime parties. To be sure, compared to other regime parties, the CCP may be a particularly sophisticated organization. And yet, notwithstanding differences in the degree of the party's effectiveness, the ways in which party members are deployed in the service of the regime are comparable across nondemocratic regimes. The Chinese case allows investigation of the organizational principles and the causal mechanisms by which party members empower the state. Therefore the case of China

promises to shine a bright light on the functioning of party-based authoritarianism regimes.

This book goes beyond the conventional wisdom in the literature
on authoritarian regimes, according to which regime parties function
as patronage-distribution devices, facilitate political deals at the elite
level, and serve as democratic concessions.[6] Moving from the elite to the
grassroots level, the book sees the CCP as a sharp authoritarian tool to
penetrate the vast and uneven spatial expanse of China's realm. Effective regime parties help rulers elicit accurate information about society
beyond the centers of power. I found ample qualitative evidence that the
CCP fulfills such a role. For example, an internal paper by the Department of Public Security highlights the unique value of information from
local party cells – as opposed to information from the local government
apparatus – for suppressing local protests.[7] For systematic evidence, we
can take advantage of the fact that the CCP is unevenly present throughout its territory. Using a definition explained in Section 1.4.1, China's "red
provinces" with high party membership density look very different from
"pink provinces" where the party is less present:

- In red areas, local governments were more effective at monitoring the
  implementation of the one-child policy. While bureaucrats tend to be
  able to achieve the goal of reducing the number of births, it is much
  harder to avoid the severe side effect of gender-selective abortions,
  which is more successfully achieved in red localities.
- In red areas, local governments extract more taxes. Party members
  help local governments overcome asymmetric information problems
  that plague other tax systems at the grassroots level. They also coerce
  and convince fellow citizens to pay their dues – even if at the same
  time party members themselves have the privilege of being more lightly
  taxed.

In short, the book analyzes the party's role in the information architecture of the authoritarian state, with implications for state capacity and
ultimately for regime durability as well.

The differences between "red provinces" and "pink provinces" were at
least as tangible during the first decades of the People's Republic as they
are now. However, probing the limits of the straightforward argument
that the party functions as faithful implementer of central policy, one finds
cases when the presence of many party members on the ground did not
help to advance the central leadership's policy agenda.

- In the decade after the Communist takeover, some local leaders were still locally connected, deeply committed, and independently thinking revolutionaries. They realized the danger inherent in Mao's Great Leap policies and were willing to drag their feet. Although such leaders were a minority, one would typically find them in areas with the most combatant party members, namely the places most violently contested between the CCP and the Japanese Imperial Army. This small minority of remnant revolutionaries resisted communization policies and alleviated the famine, but this minority of the most committed could not prevent the death of tens of millions of Chinese.
- Party members were also not enthusiastic when their own privileges were at stake during the great turmoil of the Cultural Revolution. When Mao Zedong called on citizens to attack the institutions of the party state, formal party hierarchies ceased to function. Rather than promoting the turmoil, party membership networks contained it. Even when joining in the fray, party members acted in a way that facilitated a quick return of order.

Refining the simple party-as-implementer hypothesis, in these two historical instances the party appears, from the perspective of central leaders, as a double-edged sword. On the one hand, strong party networks slowed down policy implementation, but with the benefit of hindsight we know that it actually helped to achieve larger state-building goals: Great Leap Forward policies happened to be a devastating scheme, so that episodes of resistance now make the party seem like a self-corrective device. Similarly, the party's role in the Cultural Revolution suggests that the institution is self-protective, and thereby ultimately advances the party state's resilience.

Moving back the causal chain, as indicated by the arrows in Figure 1.1, the next goal is to find out why the party is so much more present in some areas of its realm than in others. While the party was founded in 1921, it was only under China's partial occupation by the Japanese army from 1937 to 1945 that party organizers were able to set up a lasting, local structure. Japanese occupation jump-started the party by giving the Communist Party respite from government persecution and by letting it mobilize citizens on patriotic (or xenophobic) anti-Japanese grounds. As my analysis shows, areas formerly occupied by Japan even today tend to remain the party state's power base. Japan's intrusion into the East Asian mainland was a critical juncture in modern Chinese history.

Generic argument	China-specific argument
	Local patterns of the
Historical contingencies	Sino-Japanese War (1937–1945)
(1937–1949)	and Civil War (1945–1949)

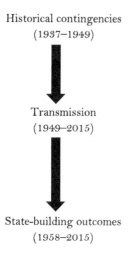

Lasting membership patterns,
because Leninist party carries out
path-dependent recruitment

Geographic patterns of
- Severity of Great Leap Forward famine (1958–1961)
- Degree of Cultural Revolution turmoil (1966–1976)
- Enforcement of the one-child policy (1978–2015)
- Fiscal extraction (ongoing)

Transmission
(1949–2015)

State-building outcomes
(1958–2015)

FIGURE I.I Outline of the argument: history, transmission, contemporary effects

Why can the party not turn all of China from pink to red? In other words, why do formerly Japanese-occupied areas still tend to be red? The overlap can be only very partially explained by Japanese occupiers and CCP leaders sharing similar strategic interests in governing certain localities. More importantly, path-dependent continuities result in regional patterns of CCP membership that reflect contingencies of the Sino-Japanese War from seven decades ago. Since Japan occupied only some parts of the Chinese territory, we can isolate the lasting effect of the Sino-Japanese War on membership patterns today.

Yet one cannot point to historical continuities after the critical juncture of Japanese occupation without at the same time noticing a gradual evolution away from these initial patterns. Following Kathleen Thelen's call to take slow-moving process as seriously as critical junctures, the analysis scrutinizes the evolution of party membership patterns over time.[8] To do so, this book applies formal models of economic growth and convergence to the dynamics of local party membership, pointing to the time periods when membership patterns took new shape and assessing the overall "half-life of history": how long it takes for the initial differences in party penetration to be cut in half. The result shows that the effect of Japanese occupation on party strength disappears over time, but only at a very slow rate. The methodological approach, albeit developed with the example of the CCP in mind, could be applied to all membership-based organizations, as well as other evolutionary processes of political convergence.

The book also argues that different types of recruits self-selected into party membership during this period, depending on the locality where they joined the party. Members recruited in the party's safe havens tended to be more opportunistic than members recruited in dangerous proximity to the Japanese occupiers. To identify safe havens and embattled areas, the book uses fine-grained information from maps and reports, found in Japanese archives, as well as in party organization histories. My claim is that one decade after the Japanese occupiers had left, the more opportunistic recruits readily complied with Mao's communization policies, even as their disastrous consequences became increasingly clear. While overall the CCP failed to stop the Great Leap Famine, in the areas which had experienced the most intense anti-Japanese struggle, local CCP leaders attempted to resist the central policy and thereby dampened its impact. With the aid of fine-grained mortality statistics, I find fewer famine deaths in formerly embattled areas, even after controlling for socio-economic differences.

There are multiple reasons why early party membership patterns persist (see Chapter 6). One important reason is that apparently the Organization Department does not place a priority on evening out the organizational reach of the party. Strategically, it might be advantageous to recruit precisely in the places where the party is most present already, because it is least costly to gather information about new members. In other words, party organizers have good reason to go after the low-hanging fruit first. In addition, there might be certain beliefs and governance techniques inherited from the imperial past, which continue to inform Chinese statecraft. Imperial era techniques, perfected over centuries, remain uniquely suited for a central authority to govern a large and diverse continent in an autocratic fashion and therefore contribute to regime resilience. Whereas other states see uniform control and nationwide standardization as top priorities, China's administrators are unusual in making conscious and explicit choices of how to deploy power resources and enforce authority selectively. For instance, 300 years ago the Chinese imperial court used a standardized coding system to assess governance challenges in its territory and deploy state resources accordingly. While imperial-era governance techniques certainly shape the assumptions that underlie strategic choices today, they are outside the scope of this book.[9]

1.2 FROM FIELD OBSERVATIONS TO A THEORY OF THE PARTY

This book has its empirical roots in China's second-tier cities and hinterland counties. First inspecting politics on-site, talking to elites and citizens, I extensively used the investigative mode of political science before turning to the tools of statistical inference and to the formal logic of models. Moving between localities, whether as a field researcher or a business person, one is bound to encounter the uneven reach of the Chinese state.[10] When I first visited the four counties in Shandong that served as my initial research sites, I was struck by how each of these local governments had its own interpretation of a policy called *New Socialist Countryside Construction* 社會主義新農村建設. Since this policy created visible outcomes, including brick-and-mortar structures, the differences caught the eye. In one county, the government was content to experiment with garbage collection and provide the villagers with fresh paint – choosing a dark-yellowish color, apparently in an attempt to maximize its lifetime. In another county, driven by an ambitious, prefectural party secretary parachuted in from Beijing, the government took a more activist stance, deployed Great Leap Forward rhetoric reminiscent of Maoist times, bulldozed villages, and asked villagers to buy newly built apartments, whose price was not affordable to most locals and whose location and layout had obvious disadvantages. Yet another county had employed researchers from the urban planning department of one of China's leading universities to conduct surveys and select villages, whose villagers would most welcome – or least oppose – resettlement programs.[11] Finally, another county avoided implementation altogether, setting up one fake construction site to show to upper-level cadres (and one foreign Ph.D. student) eager to see *New Socialist Countryside Construction*. Although this particular policy was too multifaceted to be easily amenable to comparison,[12] it motivated the question of what makes the state strong, maybe even strong-armed, in some places, but more soft-spoken in others. Researching this question let me discover the role of the party.

Nothing in the political science literature had prepared me to look for an answer related to party organization at the grassroots. The party used to be of utmost interest to social scientists in the 1960s and 1970s, but is receiving little social scientific interest today.[13] Informed by Lily Tsai's work,[14] I expected local society to play a decisive role in shaping local state–society relations, with homegrown societal organizations giving locals better bargaining positions in some places than in others. Yet it became clear to me that local society was facing[15] different local manifestations of the Chinese state. Moreover, what struck me was the varying nature of local party presence, to which scholars have paid only minimal attention.[16] In the case of the Soviet Union, scholars only became fully aware of the uneven effectiveness of the party shortly before its downfall.[17] More generally, compared to scholarship from the middle of last century,[18] researchers today pay little attention to the party and its grassroots, instead oftentimes studying the party state as if it were a relatively ordinary bureaucracy.[19] As this book demonstrates, it is a fruitful enterprise to explore the variation in the party's presence across the country and its varying impact on the lives of ordinary people.

As with the existing literature, conversations with practitioners also did not immediately point to the importance of the party to explain subnational variation, albeit for different reasons. In conversation with local officials, I occasionally noticed their genuine surprise when I told them about the different ways in which other nearby counties implemented recent directives. But all in all the differences are too enormous to go unnoticed by practitioners. Instead, many Chinese officials are uncomfortable discussing the fundamental heterogeneity of the Chinese state and prefer to hold up the myth of a uniform state. In my first dozen interviews in China, a most frequent expression was Cha-bu-duo 差不多: There is almost no difference! Question to the fiscal department: "Is your county more or less effective than your neighboring counties at mobilizing fees for public projects?" Answer: "Cha-bu-duo." Question to the general office: "Which county in this prefecture is the strictest enforcer of the one-child-policy?" Answer: "Cha-bu-duo." Question to the history office: "During the Cultural Revolution, was your county hit as much as the neighboring counties?" Answer: "Cha-bu-duo." Acknowledging the uneven presence of party members is particularly unwelcome and goes against the propaganda message of China's homogeneity. Asking about differences in the administrative setup is an unwelcome form of splittism: "Has the foreigner come to doubt the unity of China?" With enhanced questioning techniques, one can advance beyond the cha-bu-duo response: Why has party membership grown so quickly in your county, compared to all the other counties in Shandong? One is then confronted with answers related to leadership, historical and contemporary. The perceptions of local cadres could be summarized as a call to "bring the leader back in," the relevant leader in this case being the series of party secretaries that happened to run the locality over time.[20] Other answers, including by Chinese academics, have a flavor of reverse modernization theory: Instead of political development creating a tendency toward political pluralism at odds with the authoritarian state, the authoritarian state may be at its best in most developed places.

What implications do local state-building outcomes have for the overall "strength" of the Chinese state? It is important to understand the opportunities and the limits of the subnational-comparative approach to study a whole country's state strength, whether carried out as field research or data analysis. First, the approach does not provide much analytic mileage if subnational outcomes are very similar and leave little room for comparison. Fortunately, a lack of diversity certainly does not pose any major concern in the case of China. The effects of corruption, nationalism, or Confucian culture are all studied at a subnational level. Second, specific to the study of the state, a more serious problem arises because the state is not so easily disaggregated into its component parts. Something is missing if we conceptualize Chinese state strength as the "product" of local government strengths. A more precise analytic breakdown of state strength to the county level might be written as

$$State\ Strength = \underbrace{\prod_{0}^{2,900} strength\ in\ county\ dx}_{1st\ multiplier} \times \underbrace{strength\ at\ center}_{2nd\ multiplier} \quad (1.1)$$

Factoring in the strength of the state as it is observed in each of China's roughly 2,900 county-level jurisdictions, the first multiplier integrates strength across the realm. The second multiplier captures strength at the center. The equation expresses the fact that Chinese state strength is a combination of strength out in the realm and strength at the center. If local governments had a good grip on society, but elite conflict was rocking the boat, one would not consider the Chinese state to be strong. Inversely, if politics at the core of the state in Zhongnanhai were orderly, but the realm was in chaos, this would also not be a strong state. Just as order at the center promotes order at the local level, so also does order at the local level promote order at the center. This book explores the first multiplier and follows a subnational comparative method by asking why the Chinese state is stronger in some places than in others.

1.3 MICRO LEVEL: RANK-AND-FILE PARTY MEMBERS

The power of the Chinese government rests on a well-organized, nationwide party network. Western eyes, accustomed to the sight of crumbling

Communist parties in the Soviet Union and Eastern Europe two decades ago, tend to see the CCP as an anachronistic leftover from the past. Systemic corruption among its leaders further contributes to the impression that the party is doomed to what Lü Xiaobo calls "organizational involution."[21] If Chinese citizens themselves perceive the party as thoroughly corrupt, so the argument goes, the CCP's legitimacy and with it the regime's authority will evaporate before long. As David Shambaugh demonstrates, views of the party as an outdated component of an ossified Leninist system are misleading. While the party undergoes decay and atrophy in some areas, it is also reinventing and adapting itself in others.[22] Corruption is bound to occur where so much power is concentrated in the hands of a few local officials. In a setting where classic Communist ideology is largely passé and most party members join for non-idealist reasons,[23] the vested interests that come with privileges are part of the glue that holds the regime together, even if at the same time they undermine the party's remaining legitimacy. Moreover, the overwhelming majority of party members are nonelite rank and file party members, with few opportunities to sell privileges.[24] At the end of the day, the CCP remains an indispensable instrument of the regime.[25]

The lifeblood of the party are its 88 million members (as of the end of 2014). This corresponds to "only" 6 percent of the population,[26] but translates into a substantial presence of the party in society. Three reasons stand out: First, multiple party memberships in the same household are rare. In rural areas, among all households with a party connection, more than 90 percent contain exactly one party member, whereas less than 10 percent contain multiple party members.[27] As a result of such dispersion, 23 percent of all rural households have a party connection, even if the household is narrowly defined as a living community of four people on average. Second, members are dispersed through various strata of society. Party cells exist in villages, urban residential communities, companies, government agencies, and schools. In each of these settings, over the past twenty or thirty years, party cells have developed increasingly specialized goals, functions, and operating procedures, keeping up with the challenges of a quickly differentiating society.[28] Organizers make sure that the party is present where it matters most. Recently, tailor-made forms of party organizations have been set up within NGOs of a certain size.[29] Third, tweaking a Leninist apparatus to serve a post-Communist government, membership in the party functions as an effective screening device to identify politically loyal citizens, who are put to work in the interest of the elite. The remainder of the section describes the organizational methods that help the CCP to secure its dominant presence in society.

1.3.1 The Party as Screening Device

For ruling elites everywhere, it is vitally important to identify individuals prepared to support their regime, especially among young people who have no political record and are amid a large pool with many potential protesters. But how to distinguish between "reliable" and "less reliable" groups of people? One important function of the party is to serve as a screening device, helping to assess individuals' readiness to play by the rules of the system. In game-theoretic language, to elicit information about political attitudes, ruling elites design a "strategic game" that reveals otherwise hidden characteristics. Confronting someone with the choice to enter the party or not is such a game. For politically conscious Chinese, as for many people in formerly Communist countries, this moment of choice is a memorable one. Many would recount this confrontation to intimate friends for the rest of their lives. The reliability of the "strategic game" is further enhanced by plain investigations concerning the background of potential party members.

Nowadays, the choice may be less ideological. To the extent that ideology does continue to play a role for some party members, it is nationalist sentiments, not Communist ideals, that motivate people. Many ordinary Chinese are convinced that joining the party is all about privileges, as countless variations of anti-party curses suggest. Comparing corrupt party members to insatiable termites eating up the trees all around them is one of the less vulgar metaphors. Even the party members themselves often downplay their ideological commitment. On the Internet, one blogger asked: "Question to party members: Were you sincere when you took your party oath?" We cannot verify whether the respondents were actually party members, but the answers are similar to those I heard in countless conversations, and give me confidence that people curse the party not only during encounters with foreigners:

– If there are no benefits, who would join the party?
– It's all about career and *renminbi*. Conscience falls flat on the face. (Literally: Conscience turns into a dung-eating dog.)
. . .
– Basically, everyone is currying favors. When in a factory there is downsizing and someone is a party member, then it's no longer about economies of scale, but it's all about scale without economics.

– At the time of taking the oath, I was sincere. But now, actually, . . . sigh . . .
– Yes, generally that's how everyone puts it. Sincere . . . haha, I refuse to believe.
– It was just a task to be completed.[30]

Blog entries such as these indicate that, in many social settings including universities, party membership is not a source of pride. In Chinese universities, especially elite universities with very high proportions of party members, we often hear students downplaying the political significance of party membership: "The academically most outstanding students are offered party membership and naturally do not refuse it." It would be naive to think of party membership among students as nothing more than an academic prize. The undeniable fact is that some outstanding students are not party members. Some students refuse or even revoke party membership. More typically, students are never offered party membership, if their critical mindset is known to their educators. What joining the party signifies is readiness to compromise with the state. Precisely if there is little inner commitment to the party, let alone to ideas of Communism, the act of joining the party reveals that a person is a pragmatist, joining the party for material benefits, better career prospects, or at least to continue a harmonious relationship with one's superior. The new recruit will have to be at least outwardly loyal to the party-state, submitting to party discipline.

The procedure for joining the party has become increasingly elaborate and standardized. During the Cultural Revolution, shortcuts existed to quickly admit new party members without fulfilling the minimum procedural requirements, as stipulated by the party constitution. When the political winds turned and party leaders sought to purge the most troublesome rebels, quick admittance to the party was denounced as "flying over the ocean." To protect the hierarchical integrity of the party, formally correct admittance procedures were emphasized more than ever before. Since then, with each edition of work manuals for basic-level party cadres, the description of how a person is to join the party becomes lengthier and more specific. According to the statutes of the CCP, a person becomes a party member after submitting an application letter; two full party members must support the application, guaranteeing the political integrity of the applicant. Nowadays, the application usually is preceded by two stages. First, a person enters a category called "activist with ambition to join the party." At that stage, two party members are designated to instruct the person about the orthodox party line, and the activist is required to participate in training programs at the local party school. Second, the person turns into a "party development target," during which stage he comes under even closer scrutiny.[31] The process from writing the application to entering the party takes years. As of 2015, standard manuals list as many as thirty stages to full membership, characterized by red tape, forms to be filled out, and reporting up and down the hierarchy.[32]

The most intimidating step in the process of joining the party is an interview with a group of party members, including cadres from the Organization Department. Reading the minutes of such interrogations,[33] one has the impression of a not-so-subtle form of hazing, where the aspiring member is slowly pushed into a corner to be humiliated. After the unpleasant experience of political interrogation, the process of joining the party concludes more ceremoniously, when the new party member is sworn in at a highly ritualized meeting, most of the time along with others. After several speeches, the new party members take a solemn loyalty oath before the party flag, the central stage prop of this event. The party leaders read out the oath sentence by sentence, and the new party members repeat in chorus. When the time comes to insert the individual's name into the oath formula, at least when there are not too many participants, the chorus stops and each person says his own name, going from left to right. The ceremony ends as it began, with the national anthem. The twin purpose of the meeting is to make tangible the political elite status associated with party membership, as well as to stand as a friendly reminder that the mutual deal between the party and the individual requires first and foremost the public display of political loyalty from the new party member. The power of the party is built on the political loyalty of its members.

1.3.2 The Party as Disciplining Device

Strengthening party discipline has been the hallmark of Xi Jinping's tenure as General Secretary of the CCP since 2012. Preparing for more turbulent times, he urges party members to uphold discipline and believes in turning up the heat on them:

> If a furnace is not heated up for a long time, or if it is heated up but not at a sufficient temperature, then it could not produce steel. In real life, if inner-party life slackens for one inch, the party troops will scatter by one inch.[34]

The anti-corruption campaign, in addition to fighting corruption and eliminating political enemies, is an effective tool to intimidate party members into obedience. Like historical campaigns of the Mao era, it serves to keep up "the politicization, the principled stance and the combative nature of inner party life."[35]

The anti-corruption campaign is only one particularly obvious manifestation of a broader process that attempts to transform the party into a more smoothly functioning Leninist hierarchy. Often described as a "return" to a better past, in fact it is not clear whether there ever was a long period of what leaders might imagine to be "perfect" party discipline. So far, an imperfect level of party discipline has been enough to effectively govern the country. Prior to the Communist takeover, local party cells had much autonomy. During the 1950s, a series of violent campaigns combated a perceived lack of party discipline. The Cultural Revolution in the 1960s and 1970s saw an utter breakdown of party hierarchies, and the 1980s was the most liberal era of the People's Republic. Distinguishing between political discipline and economic corruption, which thrived against the backdrop of China's economic rise, from a historical perspective, political discipline in recent decades has been strong and is reaching an all-time high under Xi's leadership.

Even when there is no campaign time, by joining the party, a person submits to a host of disciplining devices. The formal escalation ladder, prescribed in article 10 of "CCP Regulations on Disciplinary Actions" 中國共產黨紀律處分條例, progresses from warning, to revoking a party member's legal immunity, and, in the worst cases, to expulsion. In ordinary circumstances, very few people are expelled from the party. During 2010, only 0.04 percent exited the party for reasons other than death. Even this tiny number is an overestimate, because it also includes people who left the party of their own volition. There are no regular procedures for leaving the party. Some achieve it by leaving the country and by ceasing to pay their dues. One "party member turned opposition" said that she was informed via prison loudspeaker about her exclusion from the party.[36] Only in times of great political upheaval does the threat of expulsion become a tangible possibility. In 1989, the year of the Tian'anmen Massacre, 0.4 percent exited the party under irregular circumstances.[37] The concern of most party members is not expulsion.

Since the Eighteenth Party Congress, the small minority of party members who work in the party state bureaucracy is extraordinarily concerned about disciplinary action, as the prominent display of related books on the shelves of local bookstores reflect.[38] But despite spectacular expulsions of party leaders at all levels of the government, expulsions of rank-and-file party members still remain rare exceptions. For the everyday disciplining of the membership, to make sure that party members show up to the weekly party cell meetings, that they actively participate in party projects, and that they do not post inappropriate messages on the Internet, a reprimand from the party secretary is the most tangible threat. If a party member is invited "to drink a cup of tea with the party secretary," this is usually a euphemism for receiving a small yet dreaded reprimand. It may involve public shaming, as well as an entry into one's record, which is perceived to diminish career opportunities for the rest of one's life, accompanying a person to the grave and beyond.

Xi Jinping has revived Maoist practices of *public critique with self-critique* 批評與自我批評. Reminiscent of the Cultural Revolution, party propagandists work hard to dispel the notion that such forms of criticism are a dangerously anachronistic "leftist mistake."[39] Some local party organizations still preferred to refer to the procedures by more innocuous terms like *public summary and self-summary* 總結與自我總結 and in practice often tended to carry out *public praise and self-praise* meetings instead.[40] To prevent too soft and self-indulgent approaches by local party organizations, the central government decided to let a (carefully chosen) public participate.[41] Even when measures to discipline the party are toned down and softer approaches are chosen by local party organizations, the relentless onslaught of campaigns – including one to hand-copy the party constitution – inspires anxiety among local cadres and rank-and-file alike.

Thought reports are one of the party's evergreens: as a dreaded and effective disciplining device, they have survived the party's many twists and turns and were part of the standard repertoire even at the most liberal moments of the reform era. Aspiring party members must write such reports. Seven months into one's party membership, another report is due. Later on, special occasions such as a political campaign or a trip abroad involve reporting requirements.[42] If a thought report is required after some misstep, it becomes a self-criticism reminiscent of the kind prevalent during the Mao era. Under certain circumstances, a party member becomes subject to a comprehensive evaluation, an occasion at which members of the same party cell – consisting of between fewer than ten to a couple of dozen members – must evaluate the person. Evaluations include achievements at the workplace, political loyalty, level of altruism, and even intimate questions on personal lifestyle. There are not only sticks, but also carrots. If one's relation with the party is going well, it may be a pleasure to receive the party secretary's visit on occasions such as the death of one's relative or one's birthday, sometimes with a nice gift as well.[43]

1.3.3 The Party as Mobilizing Device

Party members also serve as a dependable workforce to carry out specific projects on the ground. During the outbreak of the SARS pandemic in 2002, the government stipulated severe domestic travel restrictions. It is doubtful whether enforcement would have been as effective as it was without a party campaign taking place in the background. Similarly, the Beijing Olympics of 2008 prompted another highly visible campaign that impressed international visitors, and where party organizations played a formidable role to mobilize individuals as volunteers. This kind of party-organized civic activism is by no means limited to extraordinary events, but is an everyday occurrence. In the summer of 2012, on Sundays, an impressive army of volunteers, old and young, flooded the streets of major cities, helping with traffic control at busy intersections. They were sacrificing two hours of their Sunday spare time, suffering from heat and dust. Their flashy uniforms praised the altruist virtues of the model soldier Lei Feng, who had sacrificed his life in a failed attempt to help a truck backing up. The volunteers were (oftentimes new) party members mobilized by their party cells.[44] This campaign may or may not improve traffic safety. It certainly is a bonding experience and socializes party members into a habit of calling their fellow citizens to order. One nationwide campaign asked party member volunteers to "sacrifice their precious blood" in a blood donation drive.

Campaigns including ideological propaganda movements, as well as practical campaigns such as in the health sector, belong to the standard repertoire of Chinese political culture and are critically important for the regime's effectiveness: "Mao's techniques of mass mobilization, born in revolutionary struggle, but adapted to the tasks of post-revolutionary rule, lie at the heart of Chinese exceptionalism," as Elizabeth J. Perry writes.[45] The party is indispensable for campaign-style governance: It is party members who first advertise new mass movements, for example, by writing propaganda slogans on walls or hanging up red banners. "Enthusiastic" party members create the initial momentum needed to get campaigns off the ground. Only through its members can the party achieve the minimum level of coordination necessary for mass mobilization to function properly and fulfill its purpose.

Party cells engage in a broad spectrum of more or less political activities. The minutes of a party cell meeting at an institution of higher education give a flavor of the range of possibilities. To generate ideas for the party cell's new activities, members were asked to brainstorm and made the following suggestions:

Ma: Let's support the school promoting the new energy saving base, encourage some outstanding students to participate in the construction and development of the base.

Ceng: In Xi'an, some citizens and students were recently taken advantage of by people with ulterior motives, they took to the streets and demonstrated. We should start a campaign, explaining to students that unorganized and illegal demonstrations hurt them, the government and the nation and that they should love their country.

Chen: We should link up with the other party cells of this school for some common activities, progressing all together.

Wang: Even if supermarkets are no longer allowed to give out plastic bags for free, many people, when they go shopping, still buy plastic bags, not thinking of the environmental damage. We should go and investigate the problem.

Ma: To make everyone more familiar with the party's thought, line and policy, we can distribute red propaganda fliers, so that everyone understands better "red thinking."

Zhang: The situation in the quiet study room is terrible. Many students put their bags down in the early morning and block up all the space, let's investigate!

Liu: For everyone to fully grasp emotionally what the party's thought, line and policy is, we can organize a tour to the nearby East Big Village and listen to people 80 years and older, reporting about the situation around the time of liberation, and how things have changed over time.

Shi: Our Institute for Astronomy has a Astronomical Science Popularization Team, we can build on our school's specialty and help popularize astronomy, offering courses and giving lectures.

...

Yang: These days in many places throughout the country many people blindly join in demonstrations, with a very negative effect. We can go around the school collecting signatures, appealing to everyone's patriotism and make everyone understand the damage that comes with such blindness.

Jiang: Close to our school, there is the tomb of the patriotic anti-Japanese military leader Zhang Lingfu, we can organize everyone to go visit the tomb, to promote everyone's patriotic sentiment.

Su: Our school is located at the foot of the Qinling mountains, minerals are abundant around here. We can go investigate the national resources.

Bai: Our party cell meetings are missing some dynamism, everyone must be more animated, we can organize a few discussion sessions, debating each other, hopefully this can have an impact on our thinking, like a spark.[46]

This varied collection of ideas reflects the multiple purposes that the party serves. Even the most civic-minded proposal to educate people to share their seats has a bitter aftertaste, since all of these activities are to be undertaken as party campaigns, with the long shadow of the party-state looming large. Policing protest, far from being an unrealistic idea by an over-eager student at a brainstorming session, belongs to the ordinary tasks of party members, who are expected to spring into action when they observe the emergence of protest. The author observed this first-hand while standing with a group of party members at a train station in Northern China when an anti-Japanese protest spontaneously formed. The party members decided to have one of them call his party secretary, tell what was going on, and hear instructions. In this case, the party members were told not to participate and observe passively until further notice. Ranging from more innocent initiatives for promoting environmental awareness to more aggressive suggestions for containing citizen protest, the party is successfully channeling people's idealism to serve public purposes as defined by CCP leaders.

The nationwide network of party cells is a formidable instrument in the hand of the government to sway public opinion and to deliberately dominate public discourse. Regularly trained in reciting the orthodox party line on issues ranging from local history to international affairs, the party members' united voice has an excellent chance of prevailing over less coordinated opinions. Moreover, the Organization Department regularly encourages party members to make themselves familiar with the latest technology to amplify the organization's voice. In the early 1990s, party members learned the use of audio-visual technology.[47] Today, the emphasis is on the Internet. Certain party cells – presumably those with technically more savvy members – in recent years were ordered to become active on Boke, the popular Chinese blog. The minutes of a party cell meeting illustrate how effortless such an operation is for the party:

> This party cell has assigned responsibility for the blog Boke to Comrade Zhang, everyone else supports his work. Mr. Zhang told everyone the new Boke password, and strongly encouraged contributions of articles. Strict regulations: During the first two weeks of our new user profile, everyone must contribute six articles; afterwards, everyone has to write one article a week. That way we will gradually perfect our blog and help build the party's encirclement of the blogosphere.[48]

The resulting quite impressive blog is still online.[49] Similarly, at the outset of 2010, a party general branch[50] of an educational institution started a blogosphere movement, announcing in its internal work plan that at the end of 2010 "the blogs of all professors belonging to the CCP will be investigated and compared."[51] Even if the general public denounces bloggers who follow party instructions as the "fifty cent faction," the great number of well-organized party members at the grassroots have a good chance to make the party's voice heard in public shouting contests on the Internet. The most effective censors are the ones who not only silence critique, but also manage to make people speak out in favor of the government, using "human wave tactics." Flooding the Internet with government-supportive information is an effective way of controlling public opinion.[52] The party apparatus facilitates just that.

1.4 MACRO LEVEL: A POLITICAL MAP OF CHINA

Mainland China does not have liberal blue states and conservative red states. All its provinces are controlled by the CCP, and in that sense they are all dark red.[53] Without competitive multi-party elections, there are no electoral results to rely on as a clue to individual political preference. Yet in the place of voting patterns, party membership statistics provide valuable information for drawing up a political map of China. As long as we guard against too literal an analogy between voting patterns in a multi-party democracy and membership statistics in a single-party system, we can use membership statistics to distinguish geographical areas where the party's grip is stronger from other areas where the party has less of an effective presence.

1.4.1 Red vs. Pink Regions

Until recently, CCP membership statistics were available only in selective and scattered ways.[54] Mysteriously and temporarily,[55] in 2011 a compendium of party statistics, compiled by the notoriously opaque CCP Organization Department, appeared on the shelves of China's National Library. It contains unusual detail, such as the number of members who left the party for reasons other than death, and still carried the designation "strictly secret." The collection includes panel data recording provincial-level membership for 11 points in time between 1956 and 2010, mostly corresponding to the years when the plenum of the Party Congress was convened. The data shows distinct and enduring patterns of party presence. This empirical evidence undermines the propaganda message, according to which the party is equally popular, equally strong, and equally present throughout the country's vast national territory.

   Table 1.1 ranks China's provinces according to the degree of party penetration. Excluded are 5 million party members who are affiliated with the center; among them are the 2 million party members working for the central state organs, as well as other top elites who are different

TABLE I.I *How red are China's provinces? Party presence in 2010*

	Rank	Province	Party members per 10,000 citizens	Compared to the national average
Red provinces	1	Beijing	878	+50%
	2	Tianjin	788	+34%
	3	Shanghai	761	+30%
	4	Liaoning	728	+24%
	5	Tibet	696	+18%
	6	Shandong	634	+8%
	7	Sha'anxi	633	+8%
	8	Shanxi	627	+7%
	9	Hebei	625	+6%
	10	Hubei	624	+6%
Light-red provinces	11	Zhejiang	607	+3%
	12	Xinjiang	605	+3%
	13	Qinghai	602	+3%
	14	Jiangsu	597	+2%
	15	Ningxia	593	+1%
	16	Gansu	590	+1%
	17	Inner Mong.	560	−5%
	18	Jilin	558	−5%
	19	Heilongjiang	554	−5%
	20	Hunan	548	−7%
	21	Chongqing	548	−7%
Pink provinces	22	Sichuan	534	−9%
	23	Anhui	530	−10%
	24	Hainan	516	−12%
	25	Henan	514	−12%
	26	Fujian	494	−16%
	27	Yunnan	488	−17%
	28	Guangxi	456	−22%
	29	Jiangxi	446	−24%
	30	Guizhou	435	−26%
	31	Guangdong	428	−27%

Note: The cutoff points between red versus light-red and light-red versus pink provinces are found by deviding the provinces into terciles according to party presence. *Sources:* CCP members from internal party statistics.[56] Population data from *China Data Online.*

from the CCP's rank and file party members at the center of this book.[57] Even without these elite members, Beijing ranks first, with 878 CCP members per 10,000 citizens in 2010. Guangdong, the economic powerhouse in the South, comes last with only 428 members per 10,000 citizens. The table divides the thirty-one provinces into three equal-sized groups,

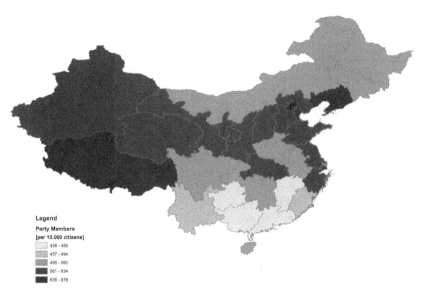

Legend
Party Members
[per 10.000 citizens]
428 - 456
457 - 494
495 - 560
561 - 634
635 - 878

FIGURE 1.2 China's red provinces, China's pink provinces (2010)

defining the quantile as China's red provinces, the middle quantile as
light red provinces, and the rest pink provinces. Neither economic patterns nor geographic features suggest themselves as easy determinants
of party membership patterns. The variation can also not simply be
explained in terms of the emerging scholarly narrative of a collectivist
North and an individualistic South.[58] The map in Figure 1.2 illustrates
the variation of party membership across China. There are no blue
states and red states in China, but some provinces are much redder than
others.

   As this book demonstrates, the number of party members is crucially
significant to understand the varying degree of control that the CCP exercises over different jurisdictions within its realm. Local governments in
"red jurisdictions" with high rates of party penetration achieve better
results in the domain of China's one-child policy, are more effective tax
collectors, and during historical episodes of turmoil have proven more
resilient. Local governments in "pink provinces," with a smaller proportion of party members in the population, are less resilient, less effective
at collecting taxes, and struggle with the unintended consequences of
the one-child policy. Resonating with conjectures that single parties help
authoritarian regimes to maintain order, the book shows that the Chinese
state is most effective in governing localities with a high proportion of

party members. To the extent that China's strength is not merely a matter of elite politics in Beijing, but is built on a strong regional base, regime strength originates with the party membership base.

The three micro-dimensions of membership as a screening device, as a tool of social control, and as a mobilization machine in the aggregate translate into important indicators of political control. The degree of party penetration is a meaningful measure across all levels of aggregation, from the village to the province. Just as individuals with CCP affiliation tend to be politically more loyal, a greater presence of party members marks communities that are politically more loyal, either in return for privileges or out of true conviction. The more party members there are in a community, the more people can be mobilized during campaigns and the greater the chances that campaigns reach their goal. Thus, the density of party networks provides valuable clues about state–society relations in local communities. Comparing two Chinese villages, especially if they are similar in other important socio-economic dimensions, a larger number of party members in one village indicates that the CCP's organizational apparatus has more access compared to the other village. Ever since its foundation, the party has meticulously recorded membership statistics as a basis for decision making. For example, during the Sino-Japanese War and the Civil War, the number of party members in a village could be used as an indicator to gauge how much logistical support could be expected; membership statistics were vital for military planning. Today, the number of party members on the ground continues to hold strategic importance for effective governance.

1.4.2 Interpreting the Political Map of China

Under the circumstances of a one-party state, in the absence of voting patterns, party strength is a good approximation for capturing the political forces across geographic areas in a nation. The choice of becoming a party member is public and generally irreversible, as party members in their oath specifically promise to dedicate their entire life to the party and as there are no regular procedures for leaving the party. Moreover, the individual knows that there will be direct and personal consequences from joining the party, including privileges as well as loyalty obligations. Much is at stake, with tangible consequences for the individual's everyday life, which is why the membership choice is carefully considered. Even if the choice is not ideologically honest, it certainly is not cheap talk, precisely because of its public, irreversible, and immediately consequential nature. In that sense, party membership sends a stronger informational signal than an electoral choice.

While the sheer numerical presence of party members per capita provides a key to China's political geography, it is not a perfect measure. To the extent that the content of party membership varies across space, as a result of distinct, local political cultures, party membership is not entirely comparable across space. For instance, wealthy environments with a strong foreign presence are often said to be more politically liberal; government-critical demonstrations occur more frequently in some provincial capitals than in others, yet this difference does not simply follow the coastal-versus-hinterland divide.[59] Even without taking into account the varying meaning of party membership across space, the sheer number of CCP members on the ground is a pivotal variable of Chinese politics – even that number already varies greatly. In 2010 the standard error of provincial party penetration is plus/minus 18 percent around that mean, as illustrated by Table 1.1. The eight provinces with high party penetration have 52 percent more party members per 10,000 citizens than the eight provinces with low party penetration. In democratic systems, margins of victory above 5 percent are quite formidable. In the political arithmetics of a Leninist party-state, double-digit differences in party penetration point to significant differences in the degree of control by the party over society.

Moreover, party membership statistics share an important shortcoming with voting patterns: the terms of the deal between the party and its local members are not identical across China, just as voting decisions can be differently motivated in different places. Local party historians, speech writers, and party schools make efforts to standardize the political culture inside the CCP.[60] Yet in fact, the party members' duties and privileges vary considerably. Informal rules, such as conditions for joining the party and codes of public conduct for party members, differ from place to place. Party members are said to grow more daring the farther they are from Beijing, and the richer they are.[61] In areas with large minority populations, even the formal rules are adjusted to local conditions. Ethnic politics override standard operating principles of the party. Handbooks for basic-level cadres say that religious believers must not be admitted into the CCP, but places with large minority populations are officially sanctioned exceptions.[62] Membership statistics tell us nothing about the intensity with which party members hold onto their political identity; they tell us even less about the degree of hostility from nonparty members. Membership statistics of provinces with large ethnic minorities, such as

Tibet, Qinghai, and Xinjiang, must be taken with a grain of salt. Both the differing content of party identification and the intensity with which people hold partisan beliefs are familiar problems when interpreting electoral outcomes in democracies. All in all, as this book shows, party membership statistics at various levels of spatial resolution provide an important indicator, because the CCP's rank and file are a dependable workforce for the state.

Even if formal rules apply equally to party units across the country, and even if central leaders have been pursuing standardization, regional differences persist and are just as striking as the similarities. Beijing and Shanghai, the political and the economic centers of the country, stand out for unusually high membership. The politically troublesome province of Tibet stands out as well – presumably leaders are engineering party networks as a counter-force to separatist tendencies. If we focus on the pink provinces, there seems to be some truth to the idea that the party's hold decreases with increasing distance from Beijing.[63] But distance explains only part of the variation and is not a satisfying answer, because it raises the question of why distance hinders the party. For now, it is enough to note that the CCP is a uniform institution only in a superficial sense. Party strength varies considerably across space. For subnational studies of the Chinese polity, this regional variation is fundamentally important.

1.4.3 Mapping Historical Legacies

Party membership patterns also provide a particularly parsimonious approach to studying the effect of history on contemporary political outcomes. Taking advantage of the important implications of membership patterns, this book studies "historical legacies" from one particular vantage point, namely its presence in local communities. The more comprehensive, alternative approach would be to define legacies as culture, focusing on the multiple, competing discourses surrounding history, forming political identities in a more or less conscious way, which help to legitimize a regime. Scholars of Latin America have called for such an approach to discern sources of party strength beyond instrumental patronage.[64] A preeminent example in the study of Asian politics investigates the revolutionary tradition of one key Communist site, demonstrating the central role of historiography in Chinese politics.[65] Instead, this book defines legacies in a narrow, institutional way. Picking only one variable, the ground-level presence of the party, the book demonstrates that even measuring the

variable very literally as the sheer number of party members in the population goes a long way to explain political outcomes. One key characteristic of such narrowly defined institutional legacies, setting them apart
from cultural legacies, is that they are embedded in organization without necessarily being consciously noted by people acting on them. This
mechanical approach brings to light institutional legacies, which are not
salient to political debate, of which political actors are not aware, but
which nevertheless affect the present state-building outcomes.

Party membership patterns are partly inherited from the past and
partly engineered in the present. They shift slowly, as new recruits enter
the party. Recruitment in a given jurisdiction results from "demand" from
citizens and "supply" from the party. CCP organization departments, well
aware of the vital role that CCP members play in the governance of China,
are not only closely tracking, but also minutely planning the number and
socio-economic composition of the party membership in their jurisdictions. Yearly updated membership development plans, drawn up at all
levels of government, indicate strategic goals and tactical measures for
party member recruitment. In a top-down fashion, membership application forms, each carrying a unique serial number, are allocated all the
hierarchical way down from Beijing to individual work units.[66] Yet at
the same time, there are factors that favor recruitment in precisely the
places where the party is already most present: New recruits need rec-
ommenders, which are more easily found in places with existing party
members. Places with few party members are particularly protective of
their status as a small group, where each additional member could challenge the incumbents. By contrast, in places with many party members
the incumbents, thanks to their large numbers, are less weary of newcomers. Moreover, party organizers have a lot more information on potential
recruits in places where the CCP already has a relatively strong organizational presence. In short, path-dependent forces tie current membership
patterns to past membership patterns.

The number of party members in any given jurisdiction is subject to
social engineering by party organizers. Strategic considerations explain
the extraordinary presence of the party in places such as Beijing, or for
that matter Tibet, but they cannot fully account for variation in party
presence across China's territory. One would be hard pressed to explain
the variation in party membership purely based on strategic reasons that
compel the party to cultivate variation of its presence. The party has no
full control over recruitment outcomes, so it would be unwise to seek
to achieve pre-specified outcomes at all political cost. Quick membership

expansion is often followed by major party rectification campaigns, as in the 1950s when the party equalized membership between the North and the South:[67] overly eager admission of new members had attracted insufficiently loyal individuals.

To secure party discipline, party organizers do not make their planning choices blindly, but investigate local party-society relations beforehand. Usually at the end of each year, counties hand up the membership application forms from that year, containing information on the political quality of the candidates in that year. Based on this information, at the start of the subsequent year, prefectures decide on recruitment goals. Counties with a better pool of potential new party members receive a higher quota. In short, the eagerness of politically desirable people to join the party figures into party planners' calculations. Facing trade-offs between quality and quantity, the CCP is likely to require less loyalty and service from members in places where the party is more in need of members. Conversely, in places where the party is flooded with people interested in joining the party, the hurdle for joining will be higher. Yearly recruitment targets reflect the importance that the organization department attaches to recruit new party members, as well as the organization department's assessment as to whether loyal individuals can be identified in a jurisdiction.

1.5 OVERVIEW OF THE ARGUMENT

After this introduction, a comparative theory chapter argues that single parties are conducive to effective authoritarian regimes around the globe, because they allow states to reach deep into society, especially if they have long, historically grown roots. The following empirical chapters explore this hypothesis through the Chinese case. In Part II of the book, Chapters 3 and 4 study how the CCP's rank and file members contribute to contemporary state-building outcomes. Part III investigates the origins of local party penetration (Chapter 5), and how these origins continue to shape the party (Chapter 6). Covering the Mao era, part 4 refines the findings both about the party effect and about the history effect. Along the way, the book revisits crucial historical episodes, key policy arenas, and the arsenal of governance techniques in modern Chinese state-building (see Table 1.2). Each chapter covers not only a different time period, but also a different domain of state-building in a party state. The chapters deal with the one-child policy, tax collection, averting collapse during the Cultural Revolution, crisis management during the Great Leap Famine,

TABLE 1.2 *Chapter-by-chapter roadmap of this book*

Ch.	Topic	Claim	Method and Evidence
Part I: Autocratic Grassroots Politics			
1	Introduction	Party member density is key to China's political map	Descriptive
2	Theory	Effects and origins of strong party visible at the grassroots	Literature, deductive argument
Part II: The Party in Contemporary China			
3	One-child policy	Party members are essential for smooth policy implementation	Multitask model, fine-grained census data
4	Tax collection	Party members enjoy tax privileges, yet are helping extraction	CHIP data, newly available fiscal data
Part III: The Party's Origins			
5	Pre-1949 warfare	Japanese occupation shapes membership patterns of 1949	Maps, recruitment data
6	Persistence	Membership patterns are extremely persistent	Convergence model, original membership data
Part IV: The Party in the Mao Era			
7	Great Leap Forward	Still committed to revolution, party strongholds resisted, suffered less	GIS, county-level famine data
8	Cultural Revolution	Putting self-interest first, party members contained turmoil	Archival and, other primary documents
9	Conclusion	Subnational-historical analysis is key for political grassroots and parties	Summarizing

party organization building, and CCP recruitment during wartime. Taken together, the book portrays how state-making and state-remaking have resulted in the structures of one of the world's most resilient party-based authoritarian states.

1.5.1 Contemporary Effects of a Strong Rank and File

Chapters 3 and 4 demonstrate that party membership patterns go a long way to explain important governance outcomes today. In the People's Republic of China, the degree of party saturation leads to fundamentally different governance outcomes at the local level. This result might not hold true for all policy areas, especially not for routine implementation and public goods provision by the bureaucracy alone – but it does hold for areas where it is most difficult and most important for the Chinese regime to deploy its authority.

Chapter 3 studies the ambitious one-child policy, which has shown the extraordinary effectiveness of the Chinese party state as a policy enforcer. Based on a modified version of a standard game-theoretical model, it clarifies the distinct functions of the party vs. the bureaucracy. Thanks to newly available, unusually fine-grained census data, it is possible to quantify empirically the distinct impact of bureaucracy and party on the effectiveness of one-child policy implementation. While the presence of government officials was enough to reduce surplus births, only the presence of grassroots party members outside the bureaucracy could contain the detrimental, unintended side effect of uneven sex ratios at birth. Red localities are better at avoiding sex-selective abortions. This illustrates that state strength is not always a result of institutional arrangements at the top-level political center, but in this case is a result of local government effectiveness, achieved by the symbiosis between party and bureaucracy at that grassroots level. In places where the regime party is more present, we see a better-informed government and a more effective implementation of the one-child policy.

Moving from the distinctly Chinese one-child policy to the universal state-building task of tax extraction, Chapter 4 shows that the party's rank and file assist the state in raising resources. The empirical analysis of tax extraction in rural areas demonstrates the quid pro quo between the party and its members. A difference-in-differences approach for the most voluminous taxes, primarily collected in urban areas, allows the establishment of a close relationship between the presence of party members and resource extraction. The chapter is the mirror image to the well-established notion that parties function as expensive rent-distributing machines, demonstrating how a successful party collects revenues. Authoritarian parties are costly, but strong parties provide fiscal gains that more than offset such costs. The case of the CCP demonstrates that the provision of patronage can be compatible with a more constructive role of a regime party. In exchange for material benefits to its members, the party not only gets political loyalty, but increases extractive capacity. Places with greater party presence have significantly higher taxation rates, even if party members themselves are more lightly treated. In red areas, the government extracts more taxes than in pink areas, because party networks help to overcome asymmetric information problems usually associated with tax collection in rural areas.

1.5.2 Historical Origins of a Strong Rank and File

To explain today's membership patterns, which are so consequential to understand the contemporary reach of the Chinese state, we must go back several generations in history to the formative period of the party. The origins of today's local party organizations fall in the late 1930s, the era of the Sino-Japanese War, when from a situation of near-defeat the CCP returned and established a lasting presence in some parts of China. Chapter 5 analyzes this process. War contingencies are key, especially contingencies during the formative period of the party, namely the time between 1937 and 1945 when large parts of China were under Japanese occupation. Battle fronts in 1937 continue to matter for the enforcement of the one-child policy seventy years later. Even today, the party tends to have a more sizable local presence in places previously occupied by Japan.

The Leninist party apparatus is a strong link that ties governance outcomes in the present to events of the past. Chapter 6, while identifying recent trends for the party to grow fastest in urban areas, points out that party patterns at the time of the Communist takeover go a long way in explaining party patterns today. There is great persistence in the geographic shape of the CCP's power base. To understand why the party has more of an organizational infrastructure in some areas of China, but not in others, one cannot avoid historical investigations. A formal model of party membership growth describes the membership dynamics and allows an empirical test, which demonstrates that legacies of the past do disappear, but only very slowly.

1.5.3 Mao Era Effects of a Strong Rank and File

While this book emphasizes continuities across momentous historical events, the party's history can be divided into three periods, each lasting roughly three decades: the party's ascent until 1949, the Mao era until 1976, and the era of rising prosperity. Having investigated the contemporary CCP (Part II) and its origins (Part III), the book then turns to the Maoist period in between (Part IV). The Mao era is essential because the traumatic yet idealized experiences of this era are at the core of constitutional debates in China about the nature of the party and the political system writ large. It also provides opportunities to refine the theory and expand its temporal and substantive scope. The goal of including historical cases in particularly tumultuous times is not simply to proliferate examples of the party's rank and file serving state-building interests. In addition, the historical cases bring to light different types of mechanisms, not discernible in the contemporary cases. Most importantly, the Mao era allows us to discover circumstances under which party members work at cross-purposes with the country's top leadership, though ultimately and paradoxically still in the interest of the state.

Chapter 7 studies the Great Leap Forward (1958–1961), along with the ensuing famine. When recognizing the devastating effects of the policies, committed party members were torn between loyalty to the People's Republic and its leader Mao Zedong on the one hand, and their commitment to the cause of the country's destitute peasants, which they had risked their lives for until less than a decade before. Only the most committed party members, found in places where the party was most directly born out of the anti-Japanese struggle, took the great personal risks of dragging their feet, so that people in their surroundings suffered less from the famine disaster. Surely the overall impact of foot-dragging party members was limited. The kind of action they took, by violating party discipline, turned the party into a self-corrective device, prevented deaths, and contributed to state legitimacy.

The height of the Cultural Revolution (1967–1969), when the party hierarchy clashed with Mao Zedong's personal authority and when the People's Republic of China stood at the brink of anarchy, is the topic of the final empirical Chapter 8. Recognizing that one can best assess the defensive capacity of a regime when it is under stress, the chapter demonstrates how a strong local party presence mitigated the impact of the crisis. The chapter provides a thick description of how the party informally continued to function in crisis mode when its hierarchy had collapsed.

As in the case of the Great Leap Forward, the party did not faithfully implement central commands, which would have been tantamount to self-destruction, but took a different course that ultimately was in the interest of state-building. For the contemporary period, rank and file party members help state-building, narrowly defined as effective implementation. During the Mao era, this narrow definition was misleading, because of the disjuncture between Mao Zedong's policies and constructive state-building goals. Helping implementation under such circumstances hardly qualifies as state-building, whether Mao ignored famine deaths and internal violence or whether he thought of them as worthwhile sacrifices in the interest of building a Communist state. The core hypotheses of this book hold water also for the Mao era: the party's rank and file empowered the state at the local level, also in the past and under different circumstances; and prerevolutionary war contingencies affected important postrevolutionary outcomes.

Each chapter is self-contained, but ultimately the goal of the book is to bridge the different historical layers to provide a comprehensive view of the sources of Chinese state strength. By analyzing the spatial patterns of Chinese state effectiveness, the book illuminates the sources of the People's Republic's effectiveness throughout its realm. It draws attention to the organizational power base inherited from the revolutionary wars, and to a variety of tactics to foster state-building, extractive capacity, and implementation effectiveness of China's party state. From the perspective of authoritarian rulers, the Chinese case demonstrates what a regime party can do for authoritarian governance.

2

A Theory of Authoritarian Regime Parties

Political parties are most efficacious instruments for autocrats to govern modernizing societies.[1] As socioeconomic development puts increasing strains on nondemocratic systems and as episodes of economic downturn can quickly throw regimes into disarray, authoritarian leaders have a better chance to maintain order if they rely on a party apparatus, rather than on personalistic arrangements or military cliques.[2] Maintaining order is not merely a question of sheer regime survival, but also of effective governance on an everyday basis, which reflects the strength of a regime.

Recognizing that parties make such a big difference for authoritarian strength, the literature on authoritarian parties is now among the most vibrant fields of political science inquiry. This literature has pinpointed two important questions: How exactly do authoritarian parties contribute to political order? And what makes authoritarian parties strong to begin with? To both questions answers are emerging, but they do not sit well with the case of the Chinese Communist Party. Therefore, by introducing into the debate the case of China, this book contributes to improving the answers to both questions.

But before delving deep into the case of the CCP, this chapter develops elements for a new theory of authoritarian regime parties, which could plausibly apply to many other undemocratic governments as well, including historical ones. The theory first addresses the question of how exactly parties help effective governance, focusing on the maintenance of political order in ordinary times and in times of crisis. It has implications for, but does not directly speak to, questions of regime durability. Existing answers revolve around three central ideas, which the following section spells out in detail. Each idea captures important aspects of contemporary regime parties, but the focus is too narrow and misses other important aspects of what authoritarian parties are, what they do, and how they make regimes strong.

- According to conventional views, authoritarian parties moderate elite conflict at the central commanding heights of power. In fact, regime parties operate not only at the centers of power, but also at the periphery. Often the distinct strength of parties is precisely their deep penetration of society and their nationwide projection of authority based on their local presence.
- Conventional views emphasize that authoritarian parties dispense patronage. In fact, regime parties do many other things as well, and the ability to manage patronage provision may not be their most decisive strength. Patronage systems are costly and prone to malfunctioning in times of economic downturn. In the long run, corruption undermines regime legitimacy, whereas the stronger kinds of regime parties play a genuinely constructive role in state-building.
- Some authors conceptualize authoritarian parties as essentially democratic institutions in an authoritarian setting. They are said to function as input institutions, as liberal concessions, and as tools to control electoral and legislative processes. Most political parties do in fact display certain democratic features, but authoritarian regime parties are notable for their fundamentally authoritarian functions. Membership recruitment provides a signal of loyalty, party hierarchies exercise tight control, and party members are at the heart of top-down mobilization of society, especially in times of crisis.

This book intervenes in the literature to redirect attention from the center to the grassroots, from patronage systems to a broader set of functions, and from a democratic to an authoritarian interpretation of parties. The second question asks where effective parties come from in the first place. Research on the origins of strong regime parties has been underway for decades, but takes on greater urgency now that authoritarian parties appear to be more than a transient phenomenon, still remaining powerful institutions of the 21st century. This book moves the debate forward on two fronts.

- A prominent argument holds that strong parties are born of violent, revolutionary struggle. But the existing, cross-national comparisons are inconclusive. The book provides a subnational analysis of whether in China the violent legacy of the anti-Japanese struggle shapes party strength at the local level. It turns out that the party tends to be stronger in places occupied by Japanese forces during the wartime period.

- The Chinese case also allows us to address empirically a question that has been discussed theoretically, but has barely been addressed empirically, namely, whether the effect of violent revolutionary struggle gradually disappears over time, and if it does disappear, how fast?

The Chinese example is a paradigmatic case of a regime party that is strong thanks to a particular legacy of revolutionary struggle. The case illuminates the transmission mechanism through which a cause that is already three generations away can still affect present outcomes.

By and large, the theory addresses the question about the party's functions separately from the question about its origins; the different parts of the book also treat them sequentially. Partly, this is for expository reasons of presenting material from different eras, with the foundational moment of many parties, including the CCP, situated in the early twentieth century. Partly, analytical considerations also call for a separate analysis. Analyzing the micromechanisms by which regime parties contribute to authoritarian regime effectiveness amounts to specifying key causal pathways that connect the local presence of the regime party to governance outcomes. Here party presence is the explanatory variable. By contrast, probing into the origins of the party's strength, party presence becomes the dependent variable. Nevertheless, one must keep in mind that there is added value in considering both questions simultaneously, as recent work by Steven Levitsky and Lucan A. Way demonstrates: Ideologically driven conflict makes authoritarian parties strong, and it is precisely this same ideological endowment that provides a nonmaterial mechanism by which strong parties sustain authoritarian regimes.[3] Thus the two questions are largely treated separately, but as parts of the same overall theory.

This chapter identifies current frontiers in the research on authoritarian parties and then moves into theoretically less well charted territory. Building on existing literature, the chapter's purpose is to prepare the ground for testable hypotheses. This means developing a paradigm that can be translated into falsifiable hypotheses, to be successively presented in the empirical chapters. The remainder of this chapter is organized as follows. The following Section 2.1 reviews the literature and points out that existing research on regime parties is too narrowly focused on a small set of functions. Correcting what could be called a democratic bias in the research on authoritarian parties, Section 2.2 calls for an analytical move away from the centers of power and claims that parties make the state strong at the grassroots level. Reversing the characterization of parties as patronage distribution machines, the section argues that strong parties also help the state with tax collection and policy implementation. Section 2.3 provides an overview of the universe of cases to which the theory of regime parties applies. Section 2.4 revisits findings about the origins of strong parties. The case of China provides unique possibilities for testing, at a subnational level, hypotheses on the origins of strong parties. It also suggests institutional dynamics of gradually disappearing historical legacies. Taken together, the amendments laid out in this chapter are suitable to bridge the gap between the literature on authoritarian parties and the case of China, allowing the theory of authoritarian parties to sit more comfortably with authoritarian realities.

2.1 THE LITERATURE ON THE FUNCTIONS OF REGIME PARTIES

What makes regime parties so useful to authoritarian rulers? Famously arguing that traditional modes of governance are inappropriate to preserve political order in modernizing societies, Samuel Huntington suggested that political parties may be able to live up to the challenges of political modernity and preserve political order not only in democracies, but also under authoritarian conditions.[4] Since the collapse of some authoritarian regime parties, but not others at the end of the 20th century, specifying the link between effective regimes and authoritarian regime strength has been high on the research agenda of comparative politics. While Huntington is notable for his broad vision of political parties, research three decades later has taken a more narrow view of their functions. Highlighting parties' ability to defuse elite conflict and to distribute patronage, the predominant approaches study two related functions of authoritarian parties, namely a "bargaining function" and a "mobilizing function," both revolving around the exchange of material benefits for political loyalty.[5] The existing arguments are compelling, but incomplete. As the Chinese and other cases of authoritarian regimes remind us, the literature on authoritarian parties overlooks a range of important political functions that regime parties fulfill.

2.1.1 Regime Parties as Mediators of Elite Conflict

In the quest for understanding the function of regime parties, analysts have directed much attention to the centers of power. This is curious, because it is precisely at the pinnacle of authoritarian power that even highly institutionalized single-party regimes look most similar to personalistic regimes. The recent surge of interest in the functions of authoritarian parties began with an influential article published by Barbara Geddes in 1999, empirically vindicating Huntington's earlier conjecture and presenting evidence that the survival of authoritarian regimes depends on the type of regime, with single-party regimes being the most durable type.[6] The article gave new impetus to research on what makes party regimes so different from other types of regime and on why parties are so uniquely helpful not only for regime durability, but more generally for authoritarian governance outcomes. Geddes' article also set a trend by directing scholars' attention to the role of parties in improving elite cohesion and avoiding political defection.

By now, there is a growing consensus among political scientists that regime parties contribute to authoritarian durability by helping to defuse elite conflict. Jason Brownlee summarizes the gist of this research when he writes: "In a context where elite differences appear irresolvable, parties mediate conflict and facilitate mutually acceptable solutions. They do so by generating political influence that reduces individual insecurity and assuages fears of prolonged disadvantage."[7] In a similar vein, Beatriz Magaloni describes the dictator's dilemma, as he tries to commit himself for the long term to sharing the fruits of power with the members of his elite coalition. Political parties institutionalize power-sharing agreements, thereby helping dictators to overcome severe commitment problems.[8] In short, political parties transform conflict among authoritarian elites, leading to cooperation rather than defection.

To be sure, while the focus on elites unifies much of the research on authoritarian parties, some important debates remain unresolved. There is doubt whether effective parties cause elite cohesion or vice versa. In Dan Slater's arguments about authoritarian durability, elite cohesion is a central variable, yet the party is not a cause, but rather a result of elite cohesion.[9] Moreover, questions arise as to whether authoritarian parties alone contribute to regime durability, or whether parties are better seen in conjunction with other regime characteristics, such as legislative assemblies and elections.[10] This harks back to the "functionalist challenge," asking "why autocrats frequently use parties instead of using other institutional structures that could serve similar functions."[11] In search for an answer, Milan Svolik argues that party institutions are superior to other kind of institutions, because party nomenklatura systems are most effective at enforcing term limits and other power-sharing arrangements.[12] When Charles Boix and Milan Svolik translate the logic of elite-unifying institutions into a formal model of the "foundations of limited authoritarian government," they highlight that at the end of the day, it is only a threat of rebellion that can enforce limits on the authoritarian ruler.[13] Since elite factions would seek to maximize their threat potential and mobilize citizens outside the elite in the event of a rebellion, at least implicitly ordinary citizens play a role in the argument. Overall, the unifying thread running through this research is that elite conflicts take center stage to explain the durability of single-party systems.

The prominent attention given to the role of regime parties in alleviating elite conflict is warranted to the extent that elite fractionalization – a split between "hard liners" and "soft liners" – is a frequent factor contributing to regime breakdown.[14] As a paradigmatic example, in 1986 the Marcos regime in the Philippines fell after large segments of the civilian and military elites had allied against the dictator, who had not thought it necessary to invest in creating an effective party.[15] The overall record of single parties to ward off elite splits is mixed. Analyzing 227 elections in competitive authoritarian regimes, Ora Reuter and Jennifer Gandhi report that in 19 percent of the cases they find the most serious form of elite defection, namely, a member of the hegemonic party running against the regime's official candidate.[16] The singular focus on the centers of power also raises concerns, because it resembles the proverbial search for a lost key under the lamp post. In tumultuous political crises, elite divisions are among the most visible aspects of day-to-day political developments. To make short-term predictions about stability and chaos, diplomats usually report on elite conflict as the most proximate predictor for outcomes of the crisis. Similarly, for the sake of weaving together consistent narratives of convoluted crises, journalists personalize conflict as competition between individual leaders. Surely one should not ignore the area under the lamp post. But what if elite conflicts are a symptom of more fundamental difficulties of the ruling elite to sustain its control over society – that is, that defectors are in fact leaving a sinking ship? After all, if a hegemonic party has steadfast control over society, who among the elites would place his bets against it? Too exclusive a focus on parties as mediators of elite conflict distracts attention from a much wider range of functions that parties fulfill.

Elite Conflict in China
China has served as an exemplary case to illustrate formal models of authoritarian durability based on a strong regime party as guardian for institutional norms.[17] Yet the Chinese case also demonstrates that the

salience of elite conflicts, as well as the ability of party institutions to contain them, can change abruptly. The dramatic events accompanying the democracy movement of 1989 exposed the delicate and tenuous nature of elite cohesion. Within months, sharp disagreements between conservatives and liberals inside the Standing Committee of the Politburo escalated. At the end of the day, it was the authority not of institutions but of one individual, namely party elder Deng Xiaoping, which determined the course of action and unified the CCP's top leadership – much in the fashion of a personalistic regime.[18] If Deng Xiaoping is sometimes held up as a champion of institutionalization, we should not forget that he was the paramount ruler without holding formal office, an extreme manifestation of the observation that China remains under "rule by men and not by law."[19] As long as the party's supreme power is vested in a small group of leaders, despite advances in institutionalization, much depends on the ability of these individuals to reach compromise. Despite strong incentives for accommodation, political brinkmanship and personal idiosyncrasies of a single leader can threaten the strategic equilibrium holding the regime together.

To be sure, at several occasions the institutions of the CCP have mitigated the type of elite conflict that would typically accompany leadership successions. The 2002 power transition from Jiang Zemin's third generation of leaders to Hu Jintao's fourth generation was remarkably smooth. As Andrew J. Nathan and others have argued, this was the result of "norm-bound succession politics," reflecting the gradual institutionalization of the CCP.[20] This interpretation corresponds to broader historical narratives of political developments in the People's Republic of China. After the official end of the Cultural Revolution, under Deng Xiaoping's lead, the empowerment of institutional procedures over the role of personal influences became an official goal of the CCP.[21] Spending time in exile during the Cultural Revolution, Deng Xiaoping had "time to ponder" about ways to achieve lasting political order, with conclusions that called for some degree of institutionalization.[22] Even when advertizing an ideal of institutionalization and introducing institutions such as a strict retirement norm for party officials,[23] factional and personalistic politics remained a part of Deng's tactics. Seeking institutionalization, Deng Xiaoping nevertheless claimed an exception for himself and held onto his position above the institutions.[24] At a second look, even the smoothness of the 2002 transition might be deceptive. Some claim that it "had more to do with the powerful legacy of patriarch Deng Xiaoping than it did with institutionalization."[25]

Moreover, the 2002 transition was exceptional. Heated factional power struggles determined all three preceding power transitions, as well as the following power transition from Hu Jintao to Xi Jinping, which turned the year 2013 into "one of the most dramatic years in recent Chinese politics" and demonstrated the "limits of institutionalization."[26] A group around the powerful and popular princeling Bo Xilai had tried to challenge Xi Jinping's faction.[27] Bo Xilai's faction lost out, and purges in the disguise of an anti-corruption campaign soon rocked the country. Putting into perspective the assertion that the stakes for the leaders involved in competition are more moderate than in the past, the outcome of the power struggle still retains the character of winner-takes-all payoffs. While Xi Jinping is quickly centralizing power in his own hands, Bo Xilai's supporters are persecuted on corruption charges. Bo Xilai and his closest ally in the Politbureau of the Standing Committee, Zhou Yongkang, were sentenced to life imprisonment. His wife received a suspended death sentence. Many others are under arrest and awaiting trial. In short, internal power struggles among the elite continue to characterize the regime, despite the existence of a single party. Keeping in mind that most internal disagreements remain hidden from the eyes of outside observers, the track record of volatility makes it doubtful whether even a strong regime party such as the CCP immunizes the leadership against conflict and defection. There is always the risk that one faction, using unconventional tactics, will threaten the stable, strategic equilibrium. Even in the absence of major economic crisis, this risk materialized in 2012 when two competing leaders twisted the rule of the leadership competition game – one by rallying the public and the other by selectively cracking down on corruption. Looking toward the next succession, knowledgeable observers of Chinese elite politics reckon with the possibility of Xi Jinping hanging onto power beyond his second term, in blatant violation of party rules.[28]

Elite Conflict Elsewhere

In other countries as well, the historical record of authoritarian parties in alleviating elite conflict is mixed. Even regimes that yesterday appeared as compelling examples of elite conflict-defusing parties must be reevaluated today. Take, for example, the United Malays National Organization and the National Democratic Party of Egypt. Based on careful analysis, Jason Brownlee found that the two parties were able to defuse elite conflict and to solidify their countries' regimes, as they "curbed elites' incentives to exit the regimes or push for change from outside."[29] In both cases, however, recent political developments weaken this line of argument. The problem is not so much the fact that the party in Malaysia is losing power and that there was a revolution in Egypt, since it is inherently difficult to accurately predict regime survival. What is problematic is that in both cases the regime party unraveled in precisely the way the theory would least predict, namely with elite defection.

In Malaysia the regime party continues in power, but finds itself in a markedly more precarious situation than ten years ago. It still holds a majority, but no longer the supermajority of the past. Over the past decade, the opposition party Pakatan Rakyat has risen quickly and has turned into a political force to be reckoned with, now in charge of several state governments. What is remarkable is the degree to which the political competition in Malaysia has evolved out of an intra–party elite conflict. In the wake of the Asian Financial Crisis in 1998, at a time when the regime was most in need of elite cohesion, a sharp conflict tore apart the ruling *United Malays National Organization*, led to the defection of Vice Prime Minister Anwar Ibrahim, and laid the foundation stone for the opposition party.[30] Today, Anwar Ibrahim has become the figurehead of the growing opposition party. The substantive influence of the opposition party can be traced back to the 1998 elite split. The erosion of the Malaysian regime began with an internal conflict within a party that is considered to be among the strongest in Southeast Asia.[31]

The Egyptian dictator Hosni Mubarak fell in 2011. The authoritarian regime's National Democratic Party of Egypt survived him only by a few months and was dissolved later the same year, despite its previous strength. When the Arab Spring struck Cairo in 2011, the regime party was in unusually bad shape. Since the 2005 elections, the party had experienced unprecedented infighting, as competing factions were vying for influence, in view of Mubarak's impending succession.[32] In light of these developments, it seems more than questionable whether a strong regime party is a reliable shield against elite defection. Just as with the *United Malays National Organization*, intra–party elite conflict turned out to be the Achilles heel of the National Democratic Party of Egypt. These two examples are enough to raise doubts: is it really the immunity against elite defection that makes regime parties so useful to authoritarian leaders?

2.1.2 Parties as Patronage Distribution Machines

Research on the contribution of political parties to authoritarian regime durability also revolves around a second theme, namely the distribution of patronage. To survive in office, authoritarian regimes must juggle the material interests of their population. At the macro level, compelling models describe how authoritarian durability and democratic transition result from the nature of distributive conflicts over political power and economic resources, with democracy and dictatorship appearing as alternative distributive arrangements.[33] Studying dictatorial regimes ranging from the Roman Empire to the apartheid system in South Africa, Ronald Wintrobe explains the particular institutional setups that dictators adopt as the solution to an essentially distributive problem.[34] Following in this tradition, authors explain the value of regime parties to authoritarian regimes as part of an institutional solution to managerial micro-level problems that arise with the distribution of resources to large numbers of people beyond the elite's inner circles.

Most authoritarian regimes engage in redistributive schemes, many on an extraordinary scale. Even in rentier states, which can distribute without first extracting resources, distributing rents is not a trivial task, since it requires dealing with more or less covetous citizens. To understand the political stakes of distributive schemes in developing countries, one must put the volume of the transactions in relation to the resources available to ordinary citizens. In Equatorial Guinea in Africa, thanks to natural resource revenues, even after money is siphoned off into private accounts of the ruling clan,[35] the regime still has at its disposition USD 7,000 per citizen per year (USD 20 per day) in the government budget, which is an extraordinary amount of money in a country where 75 percent of the population live off less than USD 2 a day.[36] In short, even when the resources at their command are extraordinary, especially compared to general income levels, it is not a trivial task for authoritarian rulers to manage the material appetites of their citizens in a way that strengthens their hold on power.

Political parties are adept at carrying out the allocation of resources in a way that stabilizes the authoritarian regime. On the one hand, they provide privileges to foster ongoing support from members of the elite coalition. On the other hand, they keep in check the price tag of these privileges for ordinary citizens, to prevent popular rebellion. This kind of redistribution creates vested interests in the regime. Most studies of this phenomenon describe how parties function in conjunction with elections as vote-buying machines. In Beatriz Magaloni's view, the ruling *Partido Revolucionario Institucional* stood at the center of Mexico's patrimonial politics before the democratic transition.[37] Lisa Blaydes, while confirming that Mubarak's *National Democratic Party* took part in Egypt's political corruption, reminds us that personal patronage networks played a key role as well.[38] Arguments like the ones by Magaloni and Blaydes presume elections and do not directly apply to political systems where elections do not play a significant role. For such systems, Milan Svolik argues that parties facilitate patronage distribution to party members. By distributing according to the seniority principle, authoritarian parties create incentives for party members to provide enduring support for the regime.[39] The function of parties as mediators of elite conflict and as distributors of patronage overlap. Both functions revolve around material resources, with the elite approach highlighting the difficulty of authoritarian leaders credibly committing themselves to continue to share the fruits of power, and with the patronage approach highlighting the organizational problem of dispensing patronage. As the authors observe, parties are only one of several institutional arrangements to achieve the same goal.

Limits of the Patronage Approach

Regime parties around the world deploy substantial material resources to buy support and co-opt potential dissenters. Certainly in China, the privileges of party membership have taken on new importance since the system has moved beyond its erstwhile Communist ideology.[40] What is questionable, however, is whether money buys stability; whether patronage systems put the regime on a good footing; whether parties rather than, say lineages, are particularly good at administering neo-patrimonial networks – in short, whether the role of authoritarian parties in the realm of patronage provision really is their most important contribution to regime durability. The opposite argument carries much weight, especially in the case of China. The omnipresence of patronage networks and privileges threatens to bring about the CCP's "organizational involution."[41] The Chinese regime has been aware of this threat for a long time and has been taking measures to curb corruption. Some scholars suggest that the measures seem effective,[42] although even Xi Jinping's strong-armed crackdown on corruption does not prevent most people in a major opinion poll from stating that they think corruption had been on the rise since the new President came to power.[43] Rather than a strength, the more a political system depends on patronage to hold together, the more unstable it may actually be.

Parties seem dispensable to the extent that resources to buy political support can very well be distributed through impersonal schemes. Dissecting agricultural policies in postcolonial Africa, Robert Bates shows how coercive and sophisticated schemes, such as price controls, have redistributed resources from rural to urban areas, to ward off discontent among the urban middle class, whose rebellion would have been most threatening to the regime.[44] Alternatively, in a neo-patrimonial fashion, authoritarian regimes provide material resources in exchange for a personal pledge of loyalty to the regime. Given the size of modern nation states and the impossibility of the ruler cultivating personal relationships with his subjects, such a strategy requires a sophisticated organization of personalized relationships; regime parties can perform the function of such a patrimonial network. In Iraq under Saddam Hussein, we could observe a neo-patrimonial attempt by the dictator to personally hand out privileges to his subjects "like a mayor," even when at the end of the day Saddam Hussein did recognize the need to administer privileges through the Ba'ath Party, delegating decisions to investigation committees and to the ordinary party-state apparatus.[45] Looking for regime parties that are not systematically involved in neo-patrimonial practices, one might think that the best candidates are the most deviant and fervently ideological cases, such as Germany's Nazi NSDAP. But even there, research on the party at the district level has discovered that local party officers were also "dispensers of patronage."[46] While parties are not the only channel through which regimes distribute privileges, all regime parties seem to be involved in neo-patrimonial practices.

Other authors have questioned the effectiveness of patronage as a source of regime durability.[47] Competitive authoritarian systems often disintegrate when economic downturn coincides with general elections, suggesting that patronage networks fail to sustain the regime precisely when the regime most needs them, namely, in times of (even mild) economic turmoil.[48] Taking a second look at the formal theory of patronage-based elite cohesion, one cannot be overly surprised. The game theoretical model by Carles Boix and Milan Svolik, while providing a compelling rationale for the existence of parties, at the same time points to the fragility of these very arrangements. As the authors emphasize, the resulting elite cohesion hinges on the continued existence of a "credible threat of a rebellion by the dictator's allies."[49]

Last but not least, patronage-based systems are prone to failure when the rulers run out of fiscal resources. Distributing patronage is one thing, raising resources another. Dan Slater draws attention to the lack of sustainability of systems built on patronage alone. To achieve sustainability, regimes need good reason for people to contribute: Provision pacts are doomed, protection pacts are resilient.[50] Authoritarian regimes must come up with a strategy for extracting resources in order to balance their budgets and avoid bankruptcy. Few regimes have the luxury of easy access to plentiful state coffers, except for affluent rentier states, which comfortably live off of natural resource revenues. For most, the task of extracting money seems incomparably harder than the task of spending money. Like patronage distribution, tax collection creates sharp distributional conflicts over the question of who will foot the polity's bill. Moreover, overdistributing patronage beyond what the recipient would be content with will not create opposition, whereas overextracting beyond what the contributor finds tolerable may unleash rebellion. If the party were only to solve the easy problem of patronage distribution, the task of solving the harder problem of collecting tax revenues would fall to the state. Under such a division of labor, the party would be giving and the state would be taking away. It is curious that the relatively easy task of distributing patronage is cited as the main contribution of the party to the durability of authoritarian regimes, whereas the hard task of extracting resources is not even discussed in the context of the party's contribution to regime durability. Empirically, it might well be true that some parties spend money without raising it. But that would raise serious doubts about the contribution of such parties to authoritarian durability.

2.1.3 Authoritarianism through a Democratic Lens

The literature on parties, from its inception, has made conscious efforts to include within its purview both democratic parties and authoritarian parties. As a result, the label "party" assembles an astounding variety of institutions. In his foundational work on political parties, Maurice Duverger, whose own biography transitioned from fascist to communist affiliations and later from totalitarian to democratic sympathies,[51] aims for a general theory of parties, analyzing pluralistic parties alongside dictatorial ones.[52] The notable volume on political parties and political development by Joseph LaPalombara and Myron Weiner includes political parties from around the world and opens up debate among scholars working on different types of political systems, in a conscious effort to arrive at more generalizable conclusions.[53]

Similarly, analysts in China study the CCP with reference to both authoritarian and democratic parties. The Communist Party of the Soviet Union served as a (contested) model for effective party building until its dissolution, at which point the CCP pivoted to learn useful lessons from its cousin's failure.[54] Since the demise of the Communist Party of the Soviet Union, political scientists in China have been looking for more positive examples that might suggest ways to improve the CCP, analyzing both single parties and pluralistic parties.[55] Similarly, the leaders of *United Russia*, in initiatives such as the "world experience project," are incorporating lessons from parties in Western democracies.[56]

Scholars have approached regime parties primarily by studying them in the context of competitive authoritarian states, where they are involved in electoral and legislative processes.[57] Few authors address head-on the role of parties outside the realm of competitive politics.[58] The less competitive a regime, the less relevant the party's role in electoral and legislative processes is for explaining authoritarian regime durability: When there are no elections and no parliament worth mentioning, regime parties do not function as a "democratic concession," as which they are often characterized.[59] This critique is reminiscent of a critique of the scholarship on the legal system in China. Laws in China may not be the concession to democratic pluralism as which they are described, because a pragmatic and partial implementation of the rule of law advances regime interests.[60]

The problem with a universalistic perspective on parties is that the authoritarian nature of authoritarian parties becomes an afterthought. The literature on democratic parties, borrowing from and building on research on American politics, is so developed that it is tempting to begin by exploring those aspects of authoritarian parties that look most like the democratic prototype. Since most authoritarian parties operate under conditions of hybrid regimes, studying the democratic aspects of authoritarian parties is a meaningful pursuit. However, the more authoritarian a regime is, the more the democratic approach leaves out. Jennifer Gandhi's research on authoritarian parties conceptualizes parties as "partisan institutions" and "concessions" designed to provide renewed legitimacy and function in an essentially democratic fashion.[61] In their review article on authoritarian parties, Beatriz Magaloni and Ruth Kricheli see single parties as one of several "pseudo-democratic institutions to appease potential elite challengers and enhance their longevity."[62] Similarly, Carles Boix and Milan Svolik study parties as instruments to sustain effective "authoritarian power-sharing."[63] Dawn Brancati summarizes current research efforts as studies of "democratic authoritarianism," particularly concerned with the "mechanisms by which authoritarian states arguably use nominally democratic institutions in order to maintain power."[64] It is unfortunate that theories of authoritarian parties turn into theories of pseudo-democratic parties. Authoritarian parties are seldom analyzed on their own terms.

Where do Saddam Hussein's Ba'ath Party, the Leninist parties of the Soviet Union and Eastern Europe, or the NSDAP in Hitler's Germany fit?

We need to keep in mind entirely undemocratic parties, those that are by no stretch of the imagination concessions, but sharp dictatorial instruments. Parties are often associated with civic virtues, but there are also parties that stifle civic debate, block political participation, and prevent public accountability. Yet parties are at the heart of politics not only in liberal democracies, but also in authoritarian systems. Parties can be instruments that give citizens a voice, but they can also be instruments of authoritarian control. By and large, authoritarian ruling parties are not democratic concessions in an authoritarian context, but powerful instruments in the hands of authoritarian rulers. What both aspects of the authoritarian party and the liberal party have in common is that they create order, but they do so in very different ways. The theory of party-based authoritarianism presented in this chapter breaks with the prevailing democratic bias, addressing the question of how parties stabilize authoritarian rule and make authoritarian government effective.

It is rare to find ideal-type authoritarian parties: ruthlessly cruel, centrally commanded, completely unaccountable, and made to promote the leader, such as the *Partido Democrático de Guinea Equatorial*. Yet all authoritarian regime parties display some authoritarian characteristics. Opposition parties and opposition movements under authoritarian systems may display authoritarian characteristics because they may have a natural tendency to take on some tactics and strategies of their oppressors.[65] In hybrid regimes, the democratic aspects of the regime party are only part of the picture; for a complete picture, one has to take into account the authoritarian aspects as well.

The CCP is not a democratic concession, but an indispensable instrument of China's authoritarian regime and at the core of the current leadership's governing strategy. The democratic lens has misled researchers to spend an extraordinary amount of energy studying intraparty democracy, or rather, the potential for intraparty democracy of a party that at the present time does not remotely resemble a democratically ordered institution. Without denying occasional and surprising experiments with democratic procedures, such as when certain positions in Guizhou province were filled through party-internal relatively competitive elections,[66] studying the CCP as a pseudodemocratic institution is misleading. The party is not even the primary input institution through which the state learns about and takes into account popular sentiment. The most well-known input institution, with a long historical pedigree, is the petitioning system.[67] Petition offices collect complaints from older citizens. Local People's Congresses come closer to representing the interests of certain economic groups. Internet surveillance also provides leaders with information, as do "democratic appraisal meetings" where citizens evaluate their local leaders.[68]

As a corrective to these shortcomings of the existing theory, this section proposes to adopt a new theoretical perspective on regime parties. First, the new approach sees parties through an authoritarian lens as potentially beneficial to the interests of the regime, a viewpoint with clear analytic consequences: For instance, perceiving parties through an authoritarian lens means to focus on regime parties, rather than on opposition parties, if such opposition parties even exist. It also means to study parties not only with reference to a future regime breakdown, but with an awareness of their functions for effective governance under the existing regime. Second, the new approach moves away from the pinnacles of the state, which receive most attention from foreign observers, to governance at the grass-roots level, which necessarily is an everyday concern of any functioning regime. Third, in addition to the distributive side, the approach highlights how parties contribute to the regime, rather than merely consuming privileges. Finally, this section points out that a theory of regime parties, which takes these aspects into account, can still be analyzed using concepts and tools from information economics.

2.2.1 Authoritarianism through an Authoritarian Lens

A gulf separates the ideal-type democratic system from the ideal-type authoritarian system. Yet in a world dominated by hybrid regimes,[69] it is desirable to build theory that bridges the gap between the two regimes. It is the distinctive strength of the literature on political parties that its subject of study is an institution at the heart of both democratic and authoritarian systems. Unfortunately, as a result of this overlap it is easy to succumb to the fallacy of "idealizing" authoritarian parties and of searching out their democratic aspects – a mistake that the study of less ambivalent institutions such as the coercive apparatus[70] would not make: Theories developed for democratic parties are applied too literally to the study of authoritarian parties. Studying authoritarian parties equipped with concepts and intuitions about democratic parties is enlightening, but it also obscures important aspects that are distinctive for authoritarian parties. Because of the dual-use nature of many parties, and because of the existence of highly developed theories on democratic parties, all too often authoritarian parties are perceived through a democratic lens. Studies of authoritarian parties and their distinctively autocratic functions promise to shed light on the underappreciated autocratic functions of parties in hybrid and imperfectly democratic regimes, where these functions are harder to discern.

The inquiry begins with an analytic distinction between authoritarian *regime* parties on the one hand and authoritarian *opposition* parties on the other. While a democratic lens is focused on the opposition parties as harbingers of democracy, the following theory deals with *authoritarian regime parties*. For a political party to fall within the scope of this theory, it must fulfill three criteria:

(i)   The party must exist within an authoritarian regime setting. For the definition and classification of regimes as authoritarian, this book follows the *Polity IV Project*:[71] What the authors call "autocracy" or "anocracy," I call "authoritarian."[72] In 2013 there were seventy-one authoritarian regimes.

(ii)   The term authoritarian party refers only to parties that stand firmly on the side of the regime. They share the preferences and work in the interest of the regime. The theory does not deal with authoritarian opposition parties. Such opposition parties have a dual nature. On the one hand, they are unwelcome democratic concessions existing in opposition to the ruler, but on the other hand, they can make the regime more resilient, because they allow leaders to strike deals and thereby appease the opposition.[73]

(iii)   The party must be the most politically significant party within a regime front. This means that by definition in any given country there can be at most one authoritarian regime party. Many authoritarian regimes work through a multiparty regime front. In North Korea, the regime front consists of three or four parties, depending on how one counts. The minor parties have a fascinating history going back to the founding of the regime, but have experienced *Gleichschaltung*, that is, they have lost their independence as a result of a coerced synchronization to achieve totalitarian control. By now, as far as one can tell from outside, the only significant party is the *Korean Worker's Party*, which would count as the authoritarian regime party. In Ethiopia, we find almost one dozen ethnic-based parties that belong to the regime front. Yet four of these parties have joined together and are now subparties forming a superparty, the

Ethiopian People's Revolutionary Democratic Front, which would be the organization counting as the authoritarian regime party.[74]

As the overview in Section 2.3 shows in detail, by the preceding definition there are currently about fifty authoritarian regime parties. Despite their relatively small number, these parties shape the political experience of a large share of the world's population and are of utmost relevance, intervening and governing their lives in ordinary times. This book questions the uses and origins of authoritarian regime parties, investigating two related questions: How do regime parties contribute to authoritarian regime durability and what makes a regime party effective in the first place?

As important as the distinction between regime party and opposition party is the distinction between party and state. The term party state, albeit correctly characterizing the domination of the state by the party, tends to blur this distinction. As a result, the "unstately" rank and file of the party is discounted and the statelike bureaucratic apparatus of the party (where typically only a fraction of the party's membership is employed) is overemphasized. In the search for institutional characteristics of authoritarian regime parties that contribute to a regime's efficiency, one must distinguish between the state and the party, to avoid seeming tautologies. The efficiency of the regime is defined as the ability to implement policies, ideally in a way that also improves regime durability, that is, the ability of the ruling elite to survive in power even when faced with exogenous shocks. In contrast to some definitions in the existing literature, party strength does not refer to characteristics at the elite level, but is defined as an effectively organized and active rank-and-file membership network. The book argues that a strong party, with its grassroots presence as well as its ability to engage in constructive state-building tasks, will help the regime elite to enforce even less popular policies on the ground. This proximate explanation for the efficiency of the Chinese state begs the question where the strong grassroots presence of the party comes from in the first place, a question postponed to Section 2.4.

There is a perception bias against thinking of a regime as resilient if it perished more or less spectacularly. Consider the example of Egypt. For a long time, scholars tended to agree that Mubarak's regime was among the most resilient in the world. Lisa Blaydes provided a careful analysis of the power mechanisms at the heart of Egyptian regime durability.[75] The only "problem" with her book is that it arrived in the bookstores in 2011, precisely at the time when the world saw the Egyptian party and Mubarak's regime collapse. No matter how well-founded her argument might be, it is hard to overcome the images we all have of Tahrir Square. Overnight, Egypt turned from a picture-book example of a stable dictatorship into a case of authoritarian breakdown. Scholars of the Middle East began to intone the familiar *mea culpa* of political scientists, whose country of expertise had just experienced a regime transition.[76] What was in demand then were explanations for regime breakdown, not explanations for regime durability. Objectively approaching the subject, one might still argue that Mubarak's regime was durable, yet faced an extraordinary challenge. Instead of going with the fashion, a more rational way of looking at Egypt may go against the grain and continue classifying Mubarak's regime as strong, since it survived the Third Wave of democratization, defied a number of socioeconomic challenges, and only fell when by coincidence a number of factors simultaneously put unusual strain on the regime. All we have learned is that facing the jasmine revolution, Egypt turned out to be less than perfectly resilient. The point is that after a long-serving regime that survived many perils suddenly becomes history, there is nothing wrong with investigating its erstwhile durability.[77]

Just as it is deceptively easy to think of fallen regimes as weak and surviving regimes as strong, it can also be misleading to interpret regime duration as a sign of regime strength. One must guard against post-hoc rationalization: If a regime fell, one says that the party was weak.[78] As Anna Grzymala-Busse points out, "duration alone is not the best measure of regime durability, since it tells us little about the stability of the regime, or its ability to meet and overcome potential crises."[79] The problem with such heuristics is that weak regimes might survive in the absence of a significant challenge. The *True Whig Party* ruled Liberia for more than 100 years from 1878 to 1980. Taking seriously the modern theoretical notion of regime survival becoming more difficult over time, one might assign greater weight to survival at later times in history and therefore discount durability in an era of colonial rule.

To accurately determine regime strength is extremely difficult, if not impossible, at least if durability is defined as the ability of an authoritarian regime to survive hardships, such as economic shocks and social upheaval. Maybe the most practically promising approach could follow a methodology similar to that of Ora Reuter and Jennifer Gandhi. They begin by defining a "challenging moment," namely an election, and then analyze the ability of regimes to survive this challenging moment.[80] In the spirit of this approach, one could measure durability as an error term:

First one runs a regression that explains regime survival as a function of "challenges" that are known to favor regime collapse, such as economic conditions or rebellion in a neighboring country. If a regime survives despite many factors that would usually lead to regime collapse, the regime can be called "resilient." Yet a fundamental problem remains: A strong authoritarian regime may not even have had an opportunity to prove its durability, simply because it was not faced with any formidable crisis. A young regime that has not faced the slightest challenge would necessarily count as weak, even if it would be able to master the most formidable challenges. In the case of China, we know that the regime has been resilient enough to survive the collapse of the Soviet Union, the Asian financial crisis, and popular challenges from Hong Kong, to mention just some of the challenges. We also know that its economic planners have been successful in warding off deep economic crisis. But we do not know if post-Mao China is resilient enough to survive a sustained recession, precisely because it has only experienced one transient recession in 1989.[81] It is hard to disprove those who say that China's stability hinges on maintaining a GDP growth of at least 8 percent.[82] <u>Strictly speaking, only when the Chinese regime falls will we know exactly how resilient it was.</u>

2.2.2   A Regime Party's Role beyond the Power Center

It is at the grassroots level where party regimes and personalistic regimes look most distinctive, as local cadres in party-states tend to be tightly constrained by institutional regulations. Certainly in a Leninist-type party-state like China, institutions tend to be more constraining as one moves down the party hierarchy. The theory of authoritarian regime parties presented in this chapter differs from conventional approaches, because it takes the analysis from the center of power all the way to the periphery. <u>In this account, party regimes are strong, not primarily because they prevent elite splits, but because they are highly effective in achieving the territorial reach of the state.</u>

A distinctive characteristic of political parties is their territorial expansion. Sending out their organizational tentacles from the centers of power to the periphery, regime parties typically make strong efforts to achieve countrywide coverage. If successful, authoritarian parties penetrate society throughout their realm, developing intimate familiarity with all the important sectors of society. At an ideal point of saturation,[83] party organs provide a tool to reach into every nook and cranny of society. These particular institutional arrangements are not primarily designed to mediate elite conflict, say, in a succession crisis. One might say, however, that the ability of a regime party to effectively mediate elite conflict depends on its success in achieving territorial control first: Potential contenders for power need to take into account the territorial expanse of the party machine. What a leader gets in return for competing within the party and abiding by the party rules, rather than attacking the regime party from outside, is a nationwide party support network. The greater the regime party's territorial reach, the higher the price for attacking the party from outside. If a party loses its ability to dominate the entirety of the national territory and is no longer able to hold the country together, it also loses legitimacy, signals weakness, creates expectations of party decline, and makes defection more attractive. In short, one cannot ignore the territorial nature of the party, which allows it to project authority to the grassroots level. A party regime's distinctive comparative advantage over a personalistic regime is that a party apparatus can achieve a presence throughout the entire realm, thanks to organization.

The political power that resides in a countrywide organization becomes apparent during election times, even under authoritarian rule. Despite significant democratic concessions, in Tanzania the regime party *Chama Cha Mapinduzi* has consistently been able to win elections by an astoundingly wide margin. One study of a local community in rural central Tanzania analyzes "nation-building from the hinterlands" and describes the micromechanisms of the ruling party's success: Local party organizations are extremely effective at mobilizing rural citizens, making sure that party apparel like "t-shirts, hats, kangas, and scarves circulate widely"; not only as a form of vote-buying, but also, and at least as importantly, as a way to achieve a powerful propaganda effect, testifying to the potency of the party.[84] It is remarkable how vigorously and how successfully the party fights for leadership positions at the grassroots level during apparently inconsequential neighborhood, hamlet, and village council elections.[85] For now, the opposition forces have a hard time projecting power beyond the confines of Dar es Salaam. It is *Chama Cha Mapinduzi's* effective penetration of local communities that until now has sustained its power monopoly.

The presence of the party beyond the center down to the grassroots level is just as crucial to sustain regime power in ordinary times, when there are no elections. In the 1990s, Russia under Yeltsin was a notable example of a regime that ran the country without a regime party. While top leaders sought to convince Yeltsin of the necessity of establishing a regime party, he consistently steered away from close entanglement with parties.[86] The lack of a regime party aggravated the difficulty of integrating the Russian polity. The central challenge for Russia in the 1990s was to hold the state together, since strong centrifugal forces were tearing the country apart, so that "the center lost an effective governing presence in many Russian provinces."[87] Although it is impossible to know the counterfactual had Yeltsin's Russia had a regime party, the contrast to Putin's Russia is remarkable. While Putin's government has adopted a whole new set of oppressive governance tactics, the country-wide deployment of United Russia as a regime party has also made an important difference. Analyzing how Putin systematically constructed his party of power, Thomas Remington attests that United Russia now serves as the "premier political institution linking executive and legislative branches, and central government with government in the regions."[88] The regime party's organizational presence is found to be an integrative force all the way down to the local grassroots level.[89] A telling statistical indicator reflects the role of the regime party in integrating the Russian polity: Under Yeltsin, most local leaders won elections as independent candidates, and only a tiny percentage of them, fewer than 5 percent, were affiliated with a party. By contrast, in local elections under Putin, almost 20 percent of local leaders won elections as candidates of a party, normally United Russia.[90] Under Yeltsin local politics were almost disconnected from national politics; under Putin local politics are increasingly drawn into national politics.

Historical evidence suggests that in times of crisis, the regime party's territorial reach and its penetration of society are essential for authoritarian rulers to remain in office and to be treated lightly even after leaving office. The fall of Ferdinand Marcos in the Philippines demonstrates that in the absence of a party organization, a dictator can retain support in a limited home base, but lacking a robust organizational apparatus can hardly achieve countrywide support.[91] Comparing Indonesia and Iran, two populous, oil-rich Muslim countries, Benjamin Smith explains why Suharto's regime survived through 1998, whereas the Shah's monarchy was overthrown in 1979. He traces the different outcomes to Suharto investing the windfall gains from the 1973–1974 oil boom into a "new program of central investment in local political institutions, which tied them closely both to late development and to the Golkar party apparatus," whereas the Shah kept these windfall oil revenues in urban industrial projects.[92] Golkar, although unevenly powerful in different parts of the country, nevertheless achieved a remarkable presence down to the grassroots level. Even after Suharto finally resigned in 1998, the Golkar party remained a significant political force and in the elections of 2014 was still able to gain 15 percent of the vote. The remarkable survival of the *Golkar* party into Indonesia's democratic age might explain why new governments were hesitant to prosecute Suharto and his family members on corruption charges. The strong presence of a regime party at the grass-roots level might not only contribute to regime effectiveness, but also help the regime party to survive well into the democratic era. Arguably, the regimes in Cuba, Malaysia, Mozambique, and Vietnam were able to hold onto power because their regime parties were "cohesive mass organizations."[93]

Historically, political crises in China have displayed important territorial dimensions. The fate of the country's last dynasty was sealed when in late 1911 one province after the other declared independence from the imperial court, thereby quickly reducing the territorial reach of the central government. During the democracy movement of 1989, the eyes of the outside world were glued to events in Tian'anmen Square. Although shaken by the protests unfolding just outside the leadership compound, Chinese leaders were particularly disconcerted by the fact that protests were spinning out of control in many provincial capitals and even beyond.[94] Observing the leadership transition crisis of 2012, one is struck by how regionally based Bo Xilai's bid for power was. His efforts to put together a coalition at the elite level were accompanied by a popular mass movement in the provincial-level city of Chongqing. Yet at the end of the day, even in the era of mass media and Internet, elite factions like the one of media-savvy Bo Xilai found it hard to compete with the official party line at the grassroots level and could scarcely build a nationwide base. More than in other countries, losing control over territory in China would quickly undermine regime legitimacy and lead to expectations of regime decline. The Chinese party-state cannot allow any area of its territory to slip away from government control.

<u>In China, the reach of the party is greater than the reach of the state</u>. The organizational hierarchy of state organs ends at the township level, whereas the organizational hierarchy of the party reaches further down to the village level. The state organs have offices in townships and, if need be, make visits to villages. By contrast, the party has a permanent presence in the majority of villages. The empirical chapters will test the hypothesis that local party organization contributes to regime strength by leveraging the unevenness of the party's presence. What difference does it make if the party is present in any given locality? If the party's territorial power matters, we would expect the regime to be more resilient, stronger and more effective in places where the party is most present.

2.2.3 Rethinking Regime Parties as Pillars of the State

The second theory about the contribution of authoritarian parties to regime durability pinpoints their role in patronage distribution, regime parties appearing as the mechanism to buy support from a large network of supporters in a neo-patrimonial fashion (see Subsection 2.1.2). The patronage approach operates both at the local level and at the elite level, complementing arguments about party-based elite cohesion. By subordinating themselves to regime parties, authoritarian leaders are able to credibly commit to providing the ruling coalition with patronage well into the future. Yet states built on corruption alone are not strong states, and regimes built on patronage alone are not resilient regimes. Strong regime parties do more than distribute patronage. From a fiscal perspective, a weak authoritarian party is an organization of costly-to-entertain acolytes, whereas a strong authoritarian party contributes to the material base of the state. A weak party is a fiscal burden, but a strong party is a fiscal asset. The strongest parties help the state with key tasks that the state bureaucracy alone could not implement.

Effective parties help regimes to fulfill core functions of a state, including tax collection and policy implementation. All authoritarian parties distribute material resources as part of their ruling tactics. But *strong* authoritarian parties, apart from costing money, also extract resources and more generally contribute to policy implementation. To draw attention to these largely neglected activities of regime parties, which could more properly be called the parties' contribution to state-building, I extend an argument by Steven Levitsky and Lucan A. Way. The authors argue that beyond patronage, revolutionary struggle has endowed some regime parties with an ideological legacy that helps to sustain their rule.[95] At the center of their argument are nonmaterial sources of power. This book explores the large field of party functions that lie in between nonmaterial functions and patronage provision functions of the regime party. The structure of regime parties continues to provide a tangible base for policy implementation. Four empirical chapters of this book are devoted to an analysis of how the organizational base translates into tangible power at the grassroots level. Strong regime parties empower the state by contributing to policy enforcement. Seeming indispensability of a regime party for the functioning of the state gives that party legitimacy because the aura of indispensability lends credibility to the claim that in the absence of the party, not much would be left of the state either.

Occasionally, parties engage in police functions. In Mali during the early years of postcolonial rule, party committees had their own police detachment controlling the traffic at urban checkpoints.[96] More typically, the party uses civilian tactics, ranging from propaganda to the provision of actionable information that can then be shared with the police forces. Sheena Chestnut Greitens suggests that authoritarian leaders face trade-offs between information-based vs. violence-based organizational structures of their security apparatus.[97] Rather than violent oppression, information collection falls more properly in the ambit of party activities. To the extent that parties do take on policing functions, they tend to be more benign and publicly acceptable. For example, during the SARS epidemic in China, CCP members were manning checkpoints to enforce quarantine rules.

Thanks to their carefully maintained institutional design, strong regime parties have privileged access to information, affording them a distinct, built-in advantage over other state organs. This is an important theoretical point because it suggests a new answer to what Beatriz Magaloni and Ruth Kricheli have termed the "functionalist challenge" to the theory of authoritarian parties.[98] As argued earlier, parties are probably not the most efficient instrument, and certainly not the only possible instrument, through which a regime can dispense patronage to loyalists. By contrast, I argue that parties are a uniquely efficient apparatus to gain access to fine-grained information of the kind needed for regimes to sustain political control and operate an effective government.

Party networks also serve well for extracting resources. At a minimum, almost all parties collect membership fees. In the Chinese case, the revenue from membership fees is a comparatively inconsequential amount of money, used for party training programs and for assisting party members in financial difficulty; it is far from enough to cover the party's operating budget.[99] More importantly, the party supports tax collection, as Chapter 4 demonstrates. The case of China resonates well with Martin Shefter's claim that parties with a legacy of externally mobilizing nonstate resources will continue to have a different relationship to money today.[100] The CCP certainly knew well how to raise resources for its anti-Japanese and revolutionary struggles.[101] The party has not unlearned that experience. Many of the stronger parties have found ways to raise money independently of the state. The Ethiopian People's Revolutionary Democratic Front and its subparties not only spend money on patronage, but also raise money by collecting membership fees and by running their own businesses, including transportation, printing, breweries, and fertilizer companies.[102] Tanzania's ruling party *Chama Cha Mapinduzi* is involved in the everday functioning of the regime, not only distributing campaign gifts during "harvest season," but also engaging in everyday fundraising activities throughout the country, complementing the contribution of wealthy, urban citizens. For example, the party membership card functions as a widely recognized form of identification, and people with business outside the village often find it worthwhile to pay the membership fee, mainly for the sake of having a reputable ID card. Another activity consists of renting out the local party branch offices to government officials on business in the village, as well as to the occasional foreign anthropologist.[103] In short, parties around the world engage in fundraising, which is the neglected mirror image of patronage provision.

Regime parties reinforce state power, picking up where the state bureaucracy has reached its limits. In East Germany, members of the *Socialist Unity Party* lent their practical support to the state for policy implementation, especially when it came to the more unpopular and more ambitious policies. Party members' onerous duties included the task to "rally their colleagues in support of party and state policy."[104] Moreover, because policy implementation was often premised on the illusionary assumption that there would be volunteers from the masses, party members had to stand in. In the Democratic People's Republic of Korea, the *Korean Workers' Party* spearheaded the mobilization of the general population for the successful economic development drives of the 1950s and 1960s. Mass movements, wave after wave, were sustained by life-summary meetings 生活總和.[105] In times of crisis even more depends on the ability of the party to roll up its sleeves and get to work. Shortly after independence, in the absence of a functioning civil service, the *Parti Démocratique de Guinée* and Mali's *Union Soudanaise*, albeit themselves quite limited in their bureaucratic effectiveness, "emerged by default as almost the sole instrument of rule ... responsible for many services normally considered to be within the sphere of administration."[106] In the domestic governance crisis resulting from the Iran–Iraq War (1980–1988) and the Gulf War (1990–1991), Iraq's Ba'ath Party took on "many duties at the battle and at the home fronts to assist the military and state institutions."[107] In light of these diverse activities, one must reconsider the literature's narrow focus on patronage provision.

2.2.4 Information Economics of Authoritarian Parties

To parsimoniously summarize the advantage of party networks over other institutions of the authoritarian state, such as the bureaucracy, the military, or the secret police, one may point to their indispensable function in the information architecture of the authoritarian state. Arguably, regime parties are at the core of authoritarian governance, because they provide their regime with a unique type of information advantage. Leninist-style information processing not only helps to keep the ruling elite in power, but – far from being a pseudodemocratic input mechanism – preserves the authoritarian nature of a regime. The more effectively organized and the more present the party is throughout society, the better the information available to the authoritarian leadership. The party provides information internally on its own members and externally on ordinary citizens.

Information on the Core Constituency: Party as Screening Device
Authoritarian rulers have a lot to gain from knowing who among the population is most committed. Proper management of a regime party creates a group of people that the leadership knows are politically loyal and reliable. However, in authoritarian settings ordinary people have strong incentives to misrepresent their true beliefs. The party functions as a screening device; the process of joining the party resembles a classic screening game.[108] The entrance procedure of many regime parties is designed in such a way that individuals of a loyal type join, whereas individuals of an antagonistic type do not want to join. Depending on the precise arrangement and circumstances, individuals of the loyal type may include both true believers and opportunists, but they do not include those who are less willing to bend. In the German Democratic Republic, it appears that true believers were so hard to find that the party was willing to accept people as long as they were opportunistic enough to support the regime.[109] Reinforcing this potentially very effective screening mechanism, admission procedures usually also include more direct background checks to establish a prospective member's loyalty. Since the screening mechanisms are standardized across the national territory, it allows the central leadership a vision of its territory and an idea of less loyal communities. In Nazi Germany, even when NSDAP party membership was most in demand, some areas apparently had a hard time fulfilling the recruitment target of 10 percent of the population joining the party, as Hitler had stipulated; though this was also the result of a partial recruitment stop.[110] Only parties of a more dysfunctional type would recruit indiscriminately. In Ghana after independence, almost the entire adult population signed up to the Convention People's Party, following the president's motto that one "cannot talk loudly of building a one-party state and yet drive away persons who would want to join the party and help to realize that objective."[111] This did not end well for the president, whose unpopularity led to his overthrow in 1966.

When things are going extremely well for the regime party, it becomes harder to use party recruitment as an effective screening device. In Nazi Germany, the NSDAP's organization department found it challenging to ward off opportunists, meticulously distinguishing between party members who had joined before Hitler's takeover and those who had joined later.[112] Detailed regulations for party membership admission[113] were based on the principle that the party was a giant apparatus for selecting leaders (*Führungsauslese*).[114] As a result, one's membership ID number, indicative of the date of entry, came to serve as a metric of political loyalty. Members with membership numbers below 100,000 were considered the most reliable "old guard" because they had joined the party before the party's ascent to power.[115] A more or less "general" recruitment stop was proclaimed, then partly lifted. But only in November 1944, months before Germany's defeat, did Joseph Goebbels think that it might be possible to fully "open the gates of the party" to new members, because the regime party was then in a situation when "once again the kinds of people we will be able to recruit may have all kinds of reasons to join the party, but not opportunistic ones."[116] Goebbels planned another recruitment stop as soon as Germany had won the war, expecting another onslaught of "knights of opportunity."

Vis-à-vis its members, the party functions as a monitoring device. Members of regime parties submit to "voluntary iron discipline," as China's former president Liu Shaoqi once formulated it in a famous speech on the principles of party organization.[117] Regime parties have a fine-grained arsenal of punishments to maintain party discipline. Party members dread being rebuked by a higher-ranking cadre, knowing that a critical entry in their file will stay with them to the grave. Specialized agencies, such as the Discipline Inspection Commission in China, prosecute party members outside the ordinary legal system, with even fewer procedural protections, as we witness in the current "anti-corruption" campaign. As I will illustrate in greater empirical detail, party members can be deployed to achieve practical state goals, including implementation of vital policies. The membership networks of an authoritarian party provide the regime's leaders with a loyal workforce on the ground that can be quickly mobilized and flexibly deployed, especially in times of crisis. Studying the party as a screening device departs from existing approaches by taking into account the great value for the regime in identifying individuals whose political preferences and personality type render them particularly useful instruments for the authoritarian regime.

Information Acquisition from Society at Large

The party is also the vehicle for reaching beyond the confines of its membership into the broader society, monitoring and mobilizing ordinary citizens. In its most intimate circle, the party disciplines its members and their family members, for whose behavior the party member can be held accountable as well. As mass organizations, parties deeply penetrate society, reaching all across the territory and accessing diverse strata of society – in the Chinese jargon "taking root among the people." During land reform, Chinese cadres learned to collect detailed information on the distribution of power and resources, as well as on personal networks in local communities.[118] The degree of detail known to the revolutionary organizers is remarkable.[119] Today, a key goal of party organization departments is to achieve saturation, which is not omnipresence but a "sufficient" presence throughout society. The recruitment of white-collar intelligentsia by Leninist parties as well as the opening-up of the CCP to capitalists were driven by concerns of legitimacy and participation, but also had the effect of tapping into segments of society with access to important kinds of information. The CCP has developed specialized instructions for cadres leading different types of party cells, fine-tuning organizational practices to the realities of rural communities, urban settings, university campuses, and government agencies.[120] Chinese leaders have arguably turned civil society into an asset serving regime resilience,[121] thanks to being an "attentive authoritarian regime."[122] One important way for the party-state to stay up-to-date when it comes to civil society is to systematically organize party members to join civil society organizations.[123] Another initiative targets migrant workers, making it easier for party members to transfer their personnel file between their home town and temporary workplace. In short, the CCP pursues an explicit strategy of penetrating sectors of society and enhancing access to information.

Thanks to this deep penetration of society, parties often have access to extraordinary information and are the eyes and ears of the regime. In his meticulous study of Saddam Hussein's Ba'ath party, Aaron Faust describes a very well-informed party that kept accurate records on communities and individuals around the country, especially its own members; Faust concludes: "That information about so many aspects of Iraqi state, society, and personal life are included in the Ba'ath Party's archive is just one piece of evidence proving that the party constituted the unifying thread within the totalitarian system that Hussein used to control Iraq."[124] Collecting accurate information poses dilemmas. Relying on denunciation often backfires, sowing discord, proving unreliable and threatening leaders. In Nazi Germany, this led the NSDAP to abandon its erstwhile strategy and declare that "denouncers will be smacked in the face!"[125] From the perspective of the regime, denunciations have to occur quietly and flow straight to the centers of power. China's current party purge, masquerading as an anticorruption drive, can rely on denunciation thanks to a standardized system of public criticism that sidelines government agencies and centralizes the information in the hands of the CCP's Disciplinary Inspection Commission.[126] Similarly, in Communist East Germany, experience with the powerful apparatus of the State Security shows that the party was not safe from investigation by and criticism from the agents. It also shows that a security apparatus could collect a lot of information "like a spider in the web,"[127] yet fail to correctly interpret the massive buildup of popular resentment that led to the fall of the regime. Party structures allow rulers to mobilize communities and implement policies; conversely, by mobilizing communities and implementing policies, otherwise elusive parties develop a tangible presence in local communities throughout the realm. The degree to which ordinary citizens readily participate in party-led campaigns generates information on where citizens stand politically. The mobilization in typical regime parties is top-down; movements are initiated based on instructions from above.

The advantage that the CCP has over the government is not one of creating *more* information in terms of sheer quantity. Instead, the party's advantage lies in its access to a *special kind* of information, one that is both hard to gather and indispensable for maintaining political control. The CCP specializes in soft information about changing popular sentiments and shifting political moods. It puts current events into local context, in terms of both socioeconomic conditions and a comprehensive case history. Local party leaders are trained to conduct comprehensive evaluations, as opposed to the more compartmentalized approach of ordinary bureaucrats. To make this characterization more concrete, take the example of popular protests. I rely here on material from China's Ministry of Public Security, namely an internally published analysis of "mass incidents," which include rural protests, worker strikes, and political demonstrations.[128] After emphasizing the role of information in managing popular protest, the analysis suggests a division of labor between party apparatus and government agencies when collecting information. When the local Office of Public Security first learns about a mass incident, it has to assemble a case file. This file includes hard facts on the time of the mass incident, the number of participants, and the slogans that were shouted, all of which should be collected from the local police department. However, for the softer and less well-defined kinds of evaluative information, the Office of Public Security turns to the party branch closest to the incident to elicit information on "grassroots party strength" 「基層黨組織的力量」 and the local party's "basic attitude toward the incident" 「對事件的基本態度」.[129] No matter how many detailed facts are collected on an incident, it is clear that the strategy for dealing with the incident hinges on the quality of this more evaluative and softer information coming from the party. The local party organization and the information it provides greatly improve the state's ability to deal with turmoil, even when public security organs are also very interested in monitoring the political mood of the citizenry.[130] One reason is that the visit of public security agents is more intimidating and antagonizing than the more cheerful and familiar conversations with a civilian party member. In short, effective regime parties may not have *more* information than the government, but they have the *hardest-to-get* and the *most actionable* kinds of information.

2.3 THE UNIVERSE OF AUTHORITARIAN REGIME PARTIES

This section provides a comprehensive overview of contemporary regime parties around the world. It also gives example of important historical cases. The goal is to illustrate the scope of organizations to which the theory of authoritarian regime parties applies, as per the definition in Section 2.2.1. It is a diverse group of parties. Not all regime parties are equally well equipped to contribute to effective authoritarian governance. Some regime parties have all the characteristics that make them useful to a regime: Through their dense, dedicated, and obedient grassroots networks, such parties allow central leaders to project power across their realm. But others fail to play any major role in policy implementation and are not effective instruments of dictatorial power. The theory predicts that regime strength – defined as effective authoritarian governance – depends on the degree to which the local grassroots of the regime party are a well-organized institution. The case of the CCP is particularly suited to develop the theory of authoritarian regime parties. First, as a relatively strong regime party the CCP affords insight into the micromechanisms of how regime parties can make an authoritarian regime strong. At the same time, the CCP is not equally strong across its territory. Avoiding the problem of holding "everything else" constant in cross-national comparisons, the uneven presence of the CCP allows for a subnational test of the theory, comparing state-building outcomes in the party's strongholds to its weaker spots.

2.3.1 Contemporary Cases

To specify the contemporary universe of authoritarian regime parties, I first identify authoritarian regimes, using the amended polity score (variable code name: "polity2") of the *Polity IV Project*.[131] A score of −6 and below indicates autocracies, and a score of +6 and above indicates democracy. The rest in the middle are hybrid regimes.[132] A narrow definition of very authoritarian regimes would include only autocracies, but a broader definition of authoritarianism also encompasses hybrid regimes. According to my calculation[133], in 2013 some 24 percent of the world's population lived in the twenty remaining plain autocracies, and alltogether 44 percent lived in the seventy-one authoritarian regimes, using the broad definition. The number of people living under plain authoritarianism has declined more markedly than the number of people living under more broadly defined authoritarian regimes (compare Figure 2.1).

By my definition (see Section 2.2.1) every regime can have at most one regime party. With seventy-one countries currently run by authoritarian regimes, there could be at most seventy-one regime parties. In reality the number of regime parties is closer to 50. In some countries, particularly monarchies, one finds no parties at all.[134] In other countries one finds multiple parties, but no regime parties.[135] A clear-cut case is Brunei. The monarchy allows strictly circumscribed activity of the opposition parties, but has never established its own regime party. Both the Brunei National Solidarity Party and the Brunei People's Awareness Party are officially registered opposition parties with few members and with little real significance, in part because the law prevents civil servants from joining any parties.[136] Less clear-cut cases of authoritarian regimes with parties, but without regime parties, occur as well, particularly in the Middle East. In Iran and Morocco, we find parties, but the delimitation of the regime front and the definition of opposition is ambiguous. In Iran, parties compete with each other and are curiously disconnected from the Supreme Leader Ayatollah Khamenei. Yet at the same time, the leading Iranian parties are committed to the constitution and help to cement the authoritarian nature of the system. In Morocco, the main political parties support the constitutional monarchy, but that support is based on an understanding that the monarch continues to carry out his own vision of gradually

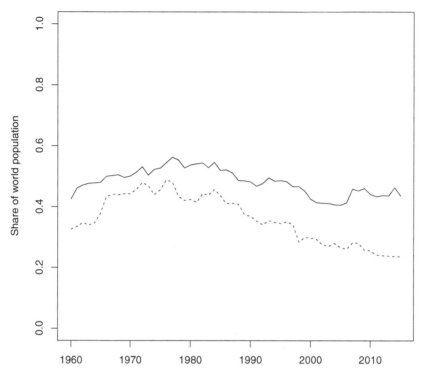

FIGURE 2.1 Share of the world's population living in nondemocracies. Dashed line represents only starkly authoritarian regimes; solid line includes hybrid regimes.

democratizing the country. In the majority of authoritarian countries, there is a competition between a dominant regime party and more or less outspoken opposition parties.

It is clear that regime parties, of which there are at most seventy-one, represent only a tiny subset of the 6,200 or more political parties existing at the present time.[137] Nevertheless, authoritarian regime parties are of great importance, because they are a strong bulwark against political pluralization, affecting 44 percent of the world population. Of these people, again 44 percent live in China. As the number of plain autocracies declines, China becomes a more important case: In 2013, of all people living under these kinds of autocracies, 79 percent were Chinese (compare Figure 2.2). Table 2.1 lists the twenty-five most populous nondemocratic countries, using the Polity IV score for 2013. These countries represent 89 percent of the world's population living under authoritarian regimes, providing a good overview of the contemporary universe of regime

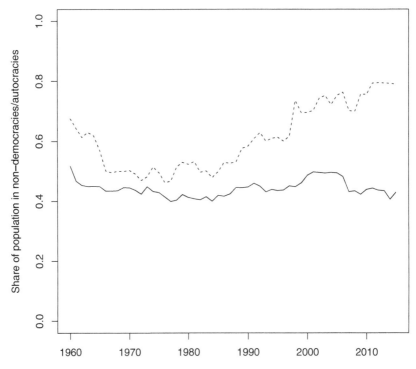

FIGURE 2.2 Chinese citizens as a share of citizens in nondemocracies. Dashed line represents share of starkly authoritarian regimes only; solid line includes hybrid regimes.

parties. Eighteen countries have regime parties; seven countries have no regime parties.

2.3.2 Historical Cases

The scope of the theory covers historical cases of regime parties as well. This book studies the CCP's contemporary functions, as well as the CCP's role during the Mao era. Since regime parties tend to be opaque organizations, historical cases can be more illuminating than contemporary cases, especially when in the meantime the party and its leaders fell from power. While they are in power, much remains hidden from the eye of the observer. After a regime party's fall, depending on historical circumstances, archives are opened and eyewitnesses begin talking. Regime parties usually leave a rich paper trail, even if not all deliberations are put down in writing, possibly in the anticipation of leaks. Sometimes international and domestic criminal courts begin untangling the

TABLE 2.I *Regime parties in the most populous nondemocracies*

Country	Party	Origins
China	Chinese Communist Party	anticolonial, social revolution
Nigeria	People's Democratic Party	established from above
Bangladesh	Bangladesh Awami League	anticolonial*
Russia	United Russia	established from above
Ethiopia	Ethiopian People's Revolutionary Democratic Front	social revolution
Vietnam	Communist Party of Vietnam	anticolonial, social revolution
Egypt	no regime party	
Iran	no regime party	
Congo (Kinshasa)	People's Party for Reconstruction and Democracy	established from above
Myanmar	Union Solidarity and Development Association	established from above
Tanzania	Chama Cha Mapinduzi	anticolonial
Algeria	no regime party	
Sudan	National Congress Party	established from above
Uganda	National Resistance Movement	social revolution
Iraq	no regime party	
Morocco	no regime party	
Venezuela	United Socialist Party of Venezuela	established from above
Uzbekistan	People's Democratic Party of Uzbekistan**	established from above
Saudi Arabia	no parties at all	
Mozambique	Mozambique Liberation Front	anticolonial
North Korea	Korean Workers' Party	anticolonial, social revolution
Yemen	General People's Congress	established from above
Syria	Arab Socialist Ba'ath Party	anticolonial
Madagascar	no regime party	
Cameroon	Cameroon's People's Democratic Movement	established from above

* More accurately: Bengali nationalism, directed against dominance by West Pakistan.

** Communist successor party. In 1996, Uzbekistan's president left that party, making it harder to decide which among the multiple parties of the regime front is the most politically significant.[138]

Note: Entries sorted by population, and taken together cover 89% of all people in nondemocracies. Based on Polity IV and World Bank data for 2013.

mechanisms of the party, meticulously documenting their findings in court files. Studies on the NSDAP in Germany have reconstructed the mechanisms of the regime in unparalleled detail, as a side – product developing the contemporary historian's toolbox and providing much insight into what gaps to expect in the written documentation and in the oral testimonies.[139] As in other cases, the confiscation of documents by the American military played an important role. Even as late as the 1980s, German historians traveled to archives in Washington, DC, to see copies of documents whose originals were not accessible to them at home.[140] In the first decades after World War II, the commanding heights of the party attracted most attention, while research about the party's rank-and-file members began only much later and continues to be a moving research frontier.[141]

Forty years later, the methodological toolbox used for investigating the NSDAP was deployed to study Germany's other authoritarian party, the Sozialistische Einheitspartei Deutschlands (Socialist Unity Party), running the Eastern part of Germany between the end of World War II and the fall of the Berlin Wall.[142] The potential of these sources to illuminate the mechanisms of contemporary regimes is enormous. For example, based on an exceptionally comprehensive study of primary material from a variety of sources, Andrew Port presents a case study to explain the puzzling stability of the German Democratic Republic, also explicating the role of the regime party.[143] Across Eastern Europe, governments allow access to the files of former Communist regime parties, although to varying degrees. Outside Europe, a particularly well-documented case is Saddam Hussein's Ba'ath Party. The Hoover Institution, in an initially controversial move amid the chaos of war, brought large amounts of valuable material from Baghdad to California.[144] Aaron Faust has begun to unlock the potential of these documents, deciphering the inner workings of Saddam Hussein's regime.[145] In Taiwan, the government grants considerable access to information about the Kuomintang (KMT) party during its days as regime party, although access seems to have been better when the opposition party was in power between 2000 and 2008. All in all, around the globe, the third wave of democratization and more recently the jasmine revolutions have lifted the curtain on the inner workings of many regime parties.

2.4 HISTORICAL ORIGINS OF AUTHORITARIAN PARTY STRENGTH

The book goes on to investigate the historical origins of strong party grassroots. Why is the rank and file of authoritarian parties so much more developed in some places than in others? While factors such as socioeconomic structure and electoral institutions determine the size and shape of democratic parties, in the case of authoritarian parties the existing scholarship indicates that the historical circumstances of party creation provide the most promising clues to understanding authoritarian party strength. For better or worse, the foundational moment endows the authoritarian party with an institutional legacy from which it usually cannot break free. This section first provides an overview of existing explanations for authoritarian party strength. It then goes on to suggest how the Chinese case can help to improve extant theories. In China, Japanese occupation during World War II, although not the only factor determining party strength, goes a long way in explaining why even today the CCP remains so much stronger in some areas of the country than others. Combining historical with proximate contemporary reasons for a Chinese state that is strong on the ground, the book argues that the legacy of antiforeign mobilization and the maintenance of an active party network have resulted in regime effectiveness.

2.4.1 War Made the State, and the Party

According to a well-known paradigm of the state-building literature, the emergence of Western European nation states – and probably the emergence of many other states as well – is closely linked to geopolitical competition, summarized by Charles Tilly's pithy dictum: "War made the state, and the state made war."[146] Authoritarian parties have more in common with the violent origins of nation states than with the peaceful origins of ideal-typical democratic parties. Democratic parties tend to arise from peaceful electoral and parliamentary processes,[147] but authoritarian parties are "usually the product of a national or revolutionary struggle:" "[T]he more intense and prolonged the struggle for power and the deeper its ideological commitment, the greater the political stability of the one-party system which is subsequently created."[148] In short, revolutionary and anticolonial wars make strong parties.

The recognition that violent struggles make strong parties has a totalitarian pedigree. In the 1930s, in his insightful study of unitary parties, comparing the Communist Party in the Soviet Union, the Kemalist party in Turkey, the fascist party in Italy, Salazar's party in Portugal, and the National-Socialist party in Germany, the Romanian right-wing intellectual Mihail Manoilescu observed that "too easy a success constitutes a disadvantage for a revolutionary party."[149] This organizational challenge resonated with Social-Darwinist ideology, imagining leadership and membership recruitment as a natural selection of the fittest. At the first party congress after he seized power, Hitler declared: "What has been imposed on us in the past, partly by the strength of our adversary, from now on must be replaced by our own will."[150] Although in reality the adversaries that the Nazi party faced seem minor compared to the enemies faced by other emerging parties, the idea that enemies help to make a regime party strong resonates with other authoritarian rulers as well.

The characterization of Leninist parties as combat parties points to violence as their essential constituent. The Chinese revolutionary leader most concerned with the party as an organization, Liu Shaoqi, saw that the very roughness of the revolutionary drive had toughened the party.[151] Leninist parties are made for struggle, and struggle is their raison d'être.[152] Kenneth Jowitt draws attention to the importance and the difficulty for Leninist parties of sustaining a "combat ethos" during peacetime, long after the violent revolutionary struggles are over.[153] Not only revolutionary Leninist parties, but also "counter-revolutionary" parties, find it vital to maintain a combat ethos. Malaysia's party remains strong as a result of an elite protection pact against the perceived threat from ethnic Chinese citizens.[154]

What is the nature of the foundational confrontation most conducive to a strong party, able to sustain an authoritarian regime even in the 21st century? Besides arguing that single parties are particularly strong if they emerged "in the early and early-to middle phases of modernization," Samuel Huntington also claims that "the strength of a one-party system depends upon the duration and intensity of the struggle to acquire power or to consolidate power after taking over the government."[155] Huntington's idea was vague in that he did not specify what kind of struggle was conducive to strong one-party states. Different authors have taken Huntington's idea in different directions. In the Southeast Asian context, Dan Slater argues that particularly threatening kinds of contentious politics led elites to conclude "protection pacts" fostering elite cohesion. Thanks to elite cohesion, a strong party, a strong state and a strong military emerge. Slater cites Malaysia and Singapore as cases where societal elites faced intractable and threatening forms of contentious politics, so that they stood together and consented to such protection pacts.[156] If Slater is right, party strength, state capacity, and military cohesion are the result of historical experience as well as an ongoing perception of an endemic and unmanageable threat. This path to strong party-states is decidedly counterrevolutionary.

By contrast, other authors have pointed out a revolutionary path to an effective party. Asking why some Communist regimes survived the end of the Cold War, Elizabeth J. Perry observes that all surviving Communist regimes share "a legacy of nationalistic rural revolution."[157] Steven Levitsky and Lucan A. Way offer a well-specified measure for "sustained, violent, and ideationally driven struggle," which is distinct from struggle where participants are "recruited primarily via the distribution of selective material benefits."[158] Although theoretically appealing and empirically convincing in each of the four country cases presented in their paper, the authors themselves recognize that the evidence is not yet conclusive and therefore the case is not yet closed. There are cases that contradict the theory. In the Kenyan case presented in the article, the origins of the regime party were relatively peaceful and as a result, the regime party broke down. By comparison, the case of Tanzania is disconcerting, because the origins of its ruling party were even more peaceful, but against theoretical expectations the regime is even more stable than Kenya's. Moreover, the peacefulness with which the nation's founding father achieved independence and the stability of the country since then are at the core of propaganda messages, which continue to successfully garner support for the regime party during election campaigns today.[159]

2.4.2 Japanese Occupation Kick-Started the CCP

Is it true that a legacy of national rural revolution has made some Communist regimes resilient while others collapsed during the early 1990s? Was it legacies of national rural revolution that have helped Communist regimes survive other challenges to their survival as well? Cross-country analyses, both of the qualitative and of the quantitative type, must necessarily run into difficulty testing this idea. A probably insurmountable problem for quantitative analysis is the small number of surviving Communist regimes.[160] Moreover, the observations are not independent of each other: the CCP and the Korean Workers' Party share a common history of fighting the Japanese alongside each other in Manchukuo, and the Lao People's Revolutionary Party has long been dominated by the Communist Party of Vietnam.

A cross-country, qualitative analysis would run into difficulties as well and would have to wrestle with the fact that under the unifying label of "national rural revolutions" lie drastically different historical pathways. The set of surviving authoritarian regimes (compare Table 2.1) and even the smaller set of surviving Communist regimes is much more heterogenous than one might think at first glance. The idea that Communist regime parties are resilient if they came to power by a nationalist rural revolution fits most comfortably with the case of China, although the CCP's political predominance and its institutional integrity have been overshadowed twice by episodes of Mao Zedong's personalistic leadership.[161] In Cuba, it is already much harder to make the same argument. Historically, the party was not in such a prominent leadership position. Initially propagating ideas of socialist revolution, when push came to shove during the armed revolution between 1953 and 1958, the Communist Party took a backseat. In the first decade after the takeover, Fidel Castro was in charge. Only in the second half of the 1970s, after a new constitution had been adopted following "Castro's Leninist conversion,"[162] did the Communist Party emerge as a force to be reckoned with.[163] Thus in Cuba, it is much harder to trace the regime's durability to its participation in violent, revolutionary struggles. In North Korea, the struggles of the now predominant Korean Workers' Party are not quite in line with the hypothesis either, since much of the rural struggle took place outside the country's national territory in neighboring China, and because the party seems to have deferred to the sultanistic leadership of Kim Il-Sung and his descendants.[164] In the case of Laos, given the unmistakably Vietnamese roots of the Lao People's Revolutionary Party and the enduring domination of the party by Vietnam, the national character of the revolution is very much in doubt. To be sure, none of these cases directly contradicts the idea that a legacy of nationalistic rural revolution bolsters Communist regimes, but this legacy has been transmitted to the present through different channels, taking on different ideological and institutional forms.

The Chinese case has the potential to allow more thorough testing of the hypothesis that national rural revolutions serve to strengthen parties. Moving from a cross-country comparative mode to a subnational comparative mode could be a way to overcome both quantitative and qualitative problems and test the intuition that national rural revolution makes a Communist regime strong. Such a move hinges on the assumption that regime strength is not primarily located at the center of power, since a subnational analysis can only explain party strength at the grassroots level. In addition, the Chinese case allows us to address questions about institutional persistence. If it is true that a legacy of violent, revolutionary struggle is at the origin of strong regime parties, then we must ask whether such legacies will wither away, remain present, or grow even stronger over time. It would appear that some legacies are more persistent than others. In the long run, class-struggle ideology does not serve a regime well, not only because revolutionary parties in power have an interest in domestic stability, but also because successful communists are not supposed to perpetuate class struggle, but to win and thereby end class struggle. By contrast, ideologies based on a foreign enemy or a clearly circumscribed domestic "other," as in the case of the Chinese in Malaysia and white people in Zimbabwe, may serve a regime well. In the case of the CCP, a metaphor from physics best reflects the dynamics by which certain institutional effects of the anti-Japanese legacy disappear: the half-life of history identified in Chapter 6. The anti-Japanese legacy disappears, but at a very slow rate.

Japanese occupation may not be the only factor shaping regional patterns of party membership. After a thorough scholarly debate, today we recognize that the rise of the Communist party had to do with nationalist mobilization against the Japanese, as well as with communist mobilization against landlords.[165] Yet as geographical analysis later in this book shows, the CCP is losing strength in its former base areas, where it once mobilized people more on communist grounds than on nationalist grounds (see Section 6.2.3). This finding highlights the idea that an outside enemy does much more to sustain party strength than a domestic class enemy, because a ruling party interested in stability has good reason to play down and abandon class struggle. Moreover, confrontations at the foundational moment seem to have a much more enduring effect than confrontations later on. The sharp confrontations of the Cultural Revolution, directed against the CCP party apparatus, led to a major effort at institutionalizing elite conflict, but they had a surprisingly modest impact on regional party strength. Although the Cultural Revolution had a much more destructive effect on the party-state, after the end of the turmoil, regional patterns of party strength by and large returned to the status quo ante. The book identifies one additional factor that competes with the history effect and the Japanese occupation, namely conscious and explicit efforts at political engineering, which are carried out by the CCP Organization Department to adjust the party apparatus to the challenges of the time. The following section describes how China's time-honored technique of differentiated governance may guide party-building tactics even today.

2.4.3 Governance Techniques Inherited from the Past

The persistence of regionally uneven patterns of CCP membership raises a puzzle: Why does the Chinese regime, and in particular the powerful Organization Department, not do more to even out party saturation throughout the national territory? Not only is convergence very slow, it is also imperfect, indicating that the government builds up its party unevenly. The fact that the Chinese government is not only tolerating but strategically tailoring the reach of the state to local conditions is due to a technique of "differentiated governance," deeply rooted in Chinese statecraft. When authoritarian state builders set up or reorganize their regime parties, the outcome will be shaped by the collection of governance techniques available to them. Economists routinely take into account the availability of technology to explain a large variety of outcomes, for example in growth models.[166] By contrast, in the political science literature the availability of political techniques, both to the ruler and to the ruled, makes only scattered appearances. Studying the successes and failures of popular protest, some approaches take into account the availability of technologies, more conventionally referred to as protest repertoires,[167] including in the Chinese context.[168] In Thomas Ertman's arguments on European state formation, the changing availability of governance techniques to state-builders at different times in history plays an important role: early state-builders had no choice but to rely on relatively backward governance techniques, leaving them with a "sticky" legacy of patrimonialism.[169] The availability of governance techniques is important to achieve strong authoritarian parties. Herbert Kitschelt argued that internally mobilized parties, which at the time of their formation had access to material resources of the state, are more prone to corruption than externally mobilized parties.[170] Too often, the technical capacity of a party organization is considered as an epiphenomenal side product. The availability of organizational methods mastered by the principals and/or the agents of an organization and often inherited from the past – in short governance techniques – determines party strength.

Chinese leaders have a particularly abundant organizational repertoire at their disposition. Market economic coordination mechanisms coexist alongside the organizational weapon[171] of the Leninist party apparatus, which has survived the "Leninist mass-extinction"[172] of the 1990s. Far from being incompatible with a capitalist market economy, the party organization provided a tool to sustain the market economy, for instance by controlling inflation.[173] The nomenklatura system is one of the clearest indications, since it still remains a key for the regime to exercise political authority.[174] Leninist features are most easily recognizable as a distinct governance technique because in its relentless proselytizing efforts the Comintern codified and standardized Leninism in quasicanonical form. Other governance techniques are less easily recognizable, yet at least as important. At the heart of Chinese politics one also finds governance techniques inherited from a Maoist tradition, such as guerilla-style policy enforcement,[175] or the criticism and self-criticism meetings deployed in Xi Jinping's anticorruption purge.

Governance techniques of the imperial period are also part of the CCP's organizational repertoire. Tellingly, the in-house publisher of the CCP's organization department publishes work on the imperial Board of Personnel.[176] The political scientist Lucian Pye goes as far as to refer to Chinese, North Korean, and Vietnamese political cultures as "Confucian Leninism," in which the revolutionary cadre is more similar to an imperial official than he would like to admit.[177] Elsewhere, the CCP has been called an "organizational emperor."[178] Others have pointed out that Chinese parties, including both the CCP and the KMT, inherited subversive elements of China's secret society culture.[179] The petitioning system and the civil service examination stand for traditions that continued without interruption, or were revived after having been discontinued temporarily.[180] The divide between party and state resembles the divide between Manchu rulers and Han officials; both CCP and the Manchu are conquest organizations; both are founded on principles that are foreign to the "Confucian official."[181] And both then slowly adjusted to the practical habits and necessities of Chinese bureaucracy.

Chinese rulers have always been aware of the great diversity of their empire. Rather than try to standardize their polity at any cost, Chinese governments have treated different areas of their territory differently.[182] Deng Xiaoping's idea of ruling Hong Kong based on the principle of "one country, two systems" has grown out of this tradition, as has the designation of special economic zones, experimental counties and model communities,[183] and selective law enforcement.[184] Aware of the diversity of its realm, the Qing court classified local government positions throughout the country and used different types of procedures to select personnel to different types of counties. One result was that the empire deployed its best talent to places which were both strategically important and home to a difficult-to-handle population. The tradition of classifying local positions was never discontinued for long; it has remained part of the deeply engrained standard operating procedures of the Chinese state.[185] When today the CCP builds up more of a party presence in some places than in others, it follows the same principles.

2.4.4 Governance Techniques of the 21st Century

Strong regime parties not only leverage traditional governance techniques that have served rulers well in the past, but also innovate with a view to potential challenges of the future. Political scientists have drawn attention to one challenge in particular: globalization threatens authoritarian rule. International factors played a preeminent role in regime transitions after the end of the Cold War.[186] Through comparative analysis, Steven Levitsky and Lucan A. Way have isolated two factors in particular, which often determine regime outcome. First, international leverage makes it more unlikely for a regime to remain a stable authoritarian system. Second, and more relevant here, democracy usually will emerge if and only if a country has strong Western linkages, as demonstrated by patterns of democratization in Mexico and Taiwan.[187] If that is so, what measures, if any, does the Chinese regime party take to neutralize the effect of strong Western linkages?

The most innovative and daring party-building initiative of the CCP consists in globalizing its network and setting up party branches abroad. There are many precedents for such initiatives. For instance, the Communist Party of Vietnam entertains a large, underground party network in Tokyo, which is said to coordinate protests against Chinese expansionism in the South-China Sea.[188] Some liberal parties in democratic states also set up fully integrated foreign branches, as the Europe branch of Germany's Freie Demokratische Partei exemplifies.[189] In China's own history, the Tong Meng Hui 同盟會 as the organizational protagonist of the 1911 Revolution, which overthrew China's imperial government, was founded in Japan, mainly by Chinese students studying abroad.[190] Compared to democratic parties, Leninist parties for ideological reasons had a much more fundamentally international outlook, proselytizing through the Comintern and in the case of China through bilateral cooperation, involving organizations such as trade unions. China's government today is reinventing a tradition of building a party organization with global reach.

Maybe the most impressive success of a regime party in creating an organization that allows a group of its citizens to engage in unusually close international linkages, while at the same time greatly reducing much foreign political influences, comes from North Korea. After the turmoil of World War II, a large group of Koreans found themselves in Japan. Some returned to Korea, but 600,000 ethnic Koreans decided to take up residence in Japan, about half of whom registered as North Koreans and the other half as South Koreans. In close collaboration with the North Korean government, the North Koreans founded a General Association of Korean Residents in Japan 朝鮮総連, which today still has 200,000 members. These Korean residents were discriminated against and in some respects excluded from normal Japanese society, even creating their own schools and university, but at the end of the day still lived amid Japanese society, thus necessarily establishing intimate socioeconomic linkages.[191] Despite these linkages, the organization has remained a steadfast supporter of the North Korean regime. The association has remained part of the North Korean regime front and in the 2009 election was assigned six seats on North Korea's Supreme People's Assembly.[192] If a social engineer seeks to understand how to maintain loyalty to an authoritarian regime in the presence of high linkages, there are lessons to be learned from the General Association of Korean Residents in Japan.

In China, the party organization department seeks to put the CCP in a position to counter potential political threats stemming from international linkages. One obstacle to overcome is the widespread perception that party membership might be incompatible with an international career. Many students believe that ambitions to study and work abroad would raise suspicions among party members. Moreover, vaguely familiar with Immigration and Nationality Act INA §212(a)(3)(D), they have the impression that Communist party membership reduces their options should they ever end up wanting to get an immigration visa, marry a U.S. citizen, or get a job in the United States.[193] The fact that party members are advised to deny their party membership to foreign authorities raises additional worries. Yet organization departments also make active efforts to recruit students whose careers seem to have international potential. CCP organizers actively seek out students in foreign language departments, for example. In some universities, the organizers have a hard time fulfilling their recruitment quotas among students aiming for international careers.[194] In other places, party organizers make inroads. This can be seen from recruitment targets at universities.

At present, the CCP is innovating through experimental party cells 學習型黨組織, trying a variety of methods to access groups outside the traditional ambit of the party. The CCP apparatus is seeking to penetrating the Internet, targeting the "instant messaging masses" QQ群, even organizing digital party cells and permitting digital party branch membership 數字支部黨員. A related initiative seeks to access the most internationally linked individuals, in particular exchange students, either operating through primarily virtual party cells,[195] establishing underground party branches,[196] or choosing a mixed form.[197]

"Governance techniques" is a variable that functions similarly to the variable "levels of technology" in the economics literature. In economics, there is the production possibility frontier; in political science there should be a governance possibility frontier. The study of governance techniques takes us to human ingenuity in social engineering. Given the same structural conditions, the cultural availability of governance techniques and the personal inventiveness of party organizers can result in parties of very different effectiveness. It is beyond the scope of this book to develop systematic predictions of how governance techniques affect outcomes. The analysis is agnostic as to whether the cultural availability of governance techniques and the personal inventiveness of party organizers might be explained by deeper structural variables, say, pertaining to party history. Instead, taking a close look at governance techniques gives researchers a sense of the error term: What other factors not usually contained in empirical analyses might explain party strength? Any study of regime parties would miss an important aspect of reality if it were not aware of the organizational toolbox at the disposition of some authoritarian regimes, but not others. A study of the CCP's governance innovation is particularly relevant, because from the perspective of other authoritarian regime parties, the successful Chinese model of organizing and modernizing may appear worthy of emulation.

2.5 CONCLUSION: THE USEFULNESS OF REGIME PARTIES

The case of the CCP does not sit well with the literature on authoritarian parties. Theoretical arguments about parties resonate insufficiently with the empirical reality in China.[198] The CCP is not a democratic concession, nor are its functions limited to mediating elite conflict and distributing political pork. Today almost half the world's population living under dictatorship is Chinese. The neglect of such a large number of people undermines the generalizability of theories on authoritarian regimes. Fundamentally, this book is motivated by the goal to reconcile our theories of authoritarian parties with the case of China. The theoretical interventions presented in this chapter bridge the gap that separates the Chinese case from the literature on authoritarian parties.

The China problem reflects more general flaws in the research on authoritarian parties. Efforts to explain the effectiveness of authoritarian parties have converged around a surprisingly limited number of aspects. There is a tendency to perceive authoritarian parties through a democratic lens, conceptualizing them as liberal concessions. In reality, most regime parties function as an effective instrument of authoritarian control. Moreover, the function of parties is often reduced to patronage dispensing machines. While this characterization might be sufficient to understand the world's weakest regime parties, strong regime parties typically play a more constructive role, assisting the state with collecting taxes and contributing to implementation – in short, empowering the state. Finally, investigations of regime durability focus on the top echelons of the authoritarian leadership, arguing that parties help to mediate elite conflict. One should not lose sight of the difficulty for a regime of achieving territorial reach at the grassroots level. Parties are uniquely well equipped to solve the problem of sustaining control throughout a vast realm. In the case of China, these shortcomings in the literature seem more apparent than in other cases, alerting us to the fact that research has long glossed over similar characteristics of other regimes.

This book unlocks the potential of the China case for studying authoritarian parties. In some regards, the analysis of the CCP refines, but essentially confirms, existing theories about the historical origins of authoritarian party strength. In other regards, the case of the CCP is unsettling. Confronting the CCP, we must rethink existing theories of how authoritarian parties help regime stability. In some countries, parties are best understood as liberal concessions, but in others they are authoritarian instruments of control. In some countries, parties are merely patronage machines, but in others they also fulfill constructive functions. In some countries, the main value of parties consists in fostering elite cohesion, but in others the value of parties lies in penetrating the territory at the grassroots level. With respect to each of these alternatives, most country cases are hybrids. Both for its empirical and theoretical value, the Chinese case promises to change our understanding of authoritarian regime parties and their contribution to effective governance in nondemocratic contexts.

PART II

THE PARTY IN CONTEMPORARY CHINA

3

The CCP as Co-enforcer of the One-Child Policy

China's recently abolished[1] one-child policy was one of the most ambitious, successfully implemented government policies of the twentieth century. The stunning goal of Chinese family planning was to reduce fertility to about one birth per woman, down from five births per woman in the early 1970s. Along with the military draft, family planning stands out as an extremely intrusive manifestation of state power. In China, the one-child policy not only had to deal with strong preferences for multiple children, but also with deeply rooted expectations that every woman must give birth to a male inheritor of the family tradition, a goal that often puts tremendous pressure on couples to reproduce beyond the first, legal child. Exercising biopower[2] over a diverse population of a billion people is a daunting enterprise. For political scientists, family planning is a fascinating phenomenon, where the party state has managed to extract compliance with a policy that – even if ultimately it may be for the common good – clashes with citizens' individual preferences. Whether one approves of family planning or whether one objects to it, it has been a spectacular display of state power.

The case of the one-child policy exemplifies, in one critical policy area, the role of the CCP's local membership for policy enforcement at the grassroots level. Given the high political priority of the one-child policy, it is to be expected that the party state deploys its most powerful tools to ensure smooth implementation – and as this book argues, the party's rank and file are an essential instrument in the state's toolbox. In sync with the following chapter on tax extraction, this chapter provides evidence that the Leninist apparatus empowers the Chinese state throughout its realm. Moreover, the one-child policy provides an opportunity to clarify – analytically and empirically – the separation of party and state. Far from being a formality without substantial implications, the party and the government remain distinct institutions with distinct functions. The boundary separating the two has evolved over time as the result of discrete choices, which have resulted in a relatively efficient design.

By analyzing the party vs. government separation, the chapter directly addresses a central, unresolved puzzle, known in the literature on authoritarian parties as the "functionalist challenge," asking "why autocrats frequently use parties instead of using other institutional structures that could serve similar functions."[3] Why use the CCP's rank and file, instead of deploying the state apparatus or some other alternative arrangement? Game theory, in particular a modified version of the multitask model, provides an excellent tool to formally study this aspect of Chinese Communist statecraft. Whereas the government is best at routine implementation whose success is readily observable, rank-and-file party members contribute to tasks with severe asymmetric information problems. A strong presence of the government is enough to reduce the number of surplus births,[4] but the party is needed to reduce imbalances of sex ratios at birth.

The chapter consists of four parts. The following section develops a theory of the division of labor between party and state, including the results of a formal model[5] to explain why it is useful, for strategic reasons, to deploy two implementing agents instead of one integrated apparatus. The model has implications for the fundamentally different nature of state hierarchies vs. party hierarchies, in terms of their preferences, incentives and behavior. Section 2 introduces the case of China's one-child policy and spells out hypotheses about the party's and the state's effect on policy implementation. Section 3 tests these hypotheses empirically, using one province's census data on the effectiveness of the one-child policy, on the presence of party members and of bureaucrats. The data set in this chapter uses townships as its unit of analysis and thus is one bureaucratic level closer to the ground than most existing scholarship working with Chinese census data.

3.1 WHY EMPLOY LOCAL PARTY ORGANIZATIONS FOR POLICY IMPLEMENTATION?

Rank-and-file party members, the overwhelming majority of whom work outside the government in "ordinary" jobs, help with policy implementation. Scholars have noticed their role in highly visible campaigns, such as the Constructing a New Socialist Countryside movement.[6] This raises a set of puzzling theoretical questions. Why does the party bother with policy implementation, if classic scholarship, such as that of Franz Schurmann, points out that the party/state divide exists precisely to prevent the party from getting bogged down in the nitty-gritty details of governing, instead critically monitoring the decision-making processes?[7] In the context of policy implementation, where does the added value of parties come from? What can party organizations do that government bureaucracies cannot do? When parties engage in administrative tasks, are they even distinguishable from the government? The less competitive a regime is and the more closely it fits a totalitarian model, the more tempting it is to lump together the state, the party, and the government, as if they were functional equivalents. This section lays out the building blocks and intuitions for theorizing about parties that are active in the domain of policy implementation. The analysis draws the boundaries of the party's responsibilities, to identify in which policy areas party presence makes a difference and for which aspects of the one-child policy party presence improves policy implementation.

This institutional puzzle is not unique to China. The historical case of the Soviet Union exhibits close parallels, where the party selectively intervened in the policy implementation phase, especially in the economic domain. Instead of merely hovering over the formal institutions and leaving it to lower-level state bureaucracy to carry out its extremely detailed orders, as one might have expected from the formal statutes, in fact the Communist Party of the Soviet Union routinely took on implementation tasks, through its local organs.[8] This became especially apparent when the Soviet Union experienced times of crisis.[9] In East Asia, Taiwan's Kuomintang (KMT) party was visible as a policy implementer during campaigns, as well as the Korean ruling party under Park Chung-hee during the New Village Movement (Saemaul Movement).[10] Not all political parties are equally effective as policy implementers, however. The Imperial Rule Assistance Association 大政翼賛会 set up in Japan during World War II failed to fulfill its envisioned function as an implementer.[11] The CCP may be a more mature and successful organization than the "average" authoritarian regime party, and in that sense it may not be representative. However, studying the CCP's role in the implementation of the one-child policy does not only illuminate central theoretical questions about the division between party vs. state, and about the mechanisms by which party operations empower the state. The analysis is also important to understand the potential of a regime party, which in a world of institutional diffusion other regimes find inspirational.[12]

3.1.1 The Party/Bureaucracy Divide

The People's Republic of China is a party state. The party dominates the government by means of party committees; in all jurisdictions from the central level down to the village level, the most powerful individual is the party secretary, who is responsible for the entire state apparatus. Nevertheless, the party and the government are separate entities. Most importantly, contrary to common misconceptions, bureaucrats and party members are two distinct groups: Only one third of all bureaucrats are party members,[13] and only 8 percent of all party members are bureaucrats.[14] Ninety-two percent of all rank-and-file party members are working in professions that are not affiliated with the state, and they are motivated differently from bureaucrats. The vast majority of party members form a diverse group easily distinguishable from government bureaucrats.

Even the small minority of party members who work as bureaucrats either in the party apparatus or in the government apparatus are distinguishable from nonparty bureaucrats, with different career paths and motivations. They are transferred more frequently, especially since party work needs to be done outside the government: Party committees are present not only in state agencies, including legislative, executive, and judicial institutions, but also in key nonstate institutions, such as companies and universities. The party and the state have a symbiotic relationship, but the party is by no means indistinguishable from the state. The boundaries of the party are well defined, and its formal organizational chains of command are insulated from governmental authorities. Innumerable volumes of *Material on the Organizational History of the CCP* list in minute detail which agencies and offices are within the ambit of the party. When we find party offices inside the government bureaucracy, it is well understood that these offices are placed within the party hierarchy and function as the eyes and ears of the party inside the government. Both the party and the government are self-contained hierarchies; each adheres to its distinct organizational culture. Analyzing the Chinese state on its own terms also calls for taking seriously the regime's own terminology.

Early scholarship on the People's Republic of China paid great attention to the party and its relation to the government.[15] The secularization of Chinese politics away from Marxist and Maoist ideologies has led analysts to neglect the Leninist aspects of the state and of the party's role in governance, as exemplified by the literature adopting the approach of fragmented authoritarianism, which analyzes China as a secular bureaucracy, albeit with certain distinctly Chinese dynamics.[16] The separation of party and government may not add much analytic gain at the central level of government, but it is key for understanding local governance. While the government functions in ways similar to bureaucracies around the world, the party continues to carry the characteristic imprints of a Leninist apparatus, including a nomenclature system and its accompanying purges, more recently camouflaged as anticorruption campaigns.

In short, the distinction between party and government is far more than a bureaucratic subtlety. It is a fundamental and defining characteristic of local governance in China. Whereas at the centers of power in Beijing the distinction between party and government becomes blurred, it is palpable at local levels of government. The governmental chain of command traditionally ended at the county level, although it has expanded down to the township level. As far as the government is concerned, jurisdictions below the township level are self-governing bodies. By contrast, the party's chain of command reaches down into the majority of villages, thanks to a tightly knit network of party committees. At local levels of government, where both the party and the government are present, the two are easily distinguished. In many counties, the party headquarters and the government headquarters are in separate buildings. In Shandong and Hubei, color-coded door signs indicate whether a department or an office belongs to the party (typically red on white) or to the government (black on white). The precise visual clues may vary, but the responsibilities of the party and the government are always distinct. Invariably, tasks that are considered strategically important for Communist regime survival, including the formulation of propaganda, the selection of leadership personnel and (flattering to the historian), the writing of history, all fall under the purview of the party. In terms of personnel, the size of the party apparatus is only about 5 percent of the government bureaucracy,[17] but this bureaucracy includes the most powerful cadres. Moreover, they lead a hierarchy that directs the tens of millions of rank-and-file party members.

Even though at the local level the distinction between party and government is palpable, there are subtleties that require accurate definitions. Some state agents wear two hats, holding one position in the party apparatus and concurrently another position in the government bureaucracy. Moreover, there is a revolving door separating party organs and government agencies. An ideal-typical career pattern, as envisioned by the CCP Organization Department, involves alternate appointments in the party and in government. Because this vision comes close to the realities on the ground, in addition to the 6 percent of all state agents who work in the party bureaucracy, there would be another 6 percent who temporarily work in the government bureaucracy but are in fact pursuing a party career. Taken together, these 12 percent of all officials are distinct from the rest: Their careers are directed by the CCP Organization Department, they circulate between appointments in different localities and they are locally the most powerful state agents. Possibly, they are also different types of people, more willing to submit to party discipline, more ambitious and more willing to take on the risks that come with the more twisted party careers. The other almost 90 percent of all state agents pursue pure government career paths. Their careers are directed by the Personnel Department, they usually stay in the same locality for a long time – often their hometown – and they are on average less powerful. Arguably, they are also less ambitious and possibly more committed to their local community. Both groups are important and shape local governance. At first glance, the strength of bureaucrats lies in their local knowledge and in their greater numbers, whereas the strength of party cadres is in their more powerful position. In fact, an even greater source of party cadres' strength is their access to the party's rank and file, whose information of local conditions is superior to the one held by bureaucrats.

For terminological clarity, keeping in mind the analytic purposes of this chapter, we disaggregate the state as consisting of the party and the government. The party, in turn, consists of a small bureaucratic apparatus and a large rank and file. Other organizations, such as the judicial system and the military establishment, are also part of the state, but this chapter ignores them, because they are less central to an understanding of local governments and policy enforcement. The conceptual choice of placing the party squarely into the realm of the state is contestable. German authors of the nineteenth century have spilled much ink grappling with the dual nature of political parties, which belong to society as much as they belong to the state.[18] Marxist theory conceptualizes the party as an agent of the proletariat. What continues to make parties such a uniquely powerful institution and such an intriguing object of analysis is precisely their dual nature, bridging state and society. Nevertheless, for the purposes of investigating the division of labor between party and government in the realm of policy implementation, this chapter, and in particular the formal model, works with the useful simplification to analyze the local party apparatus as an agency of the central state.

There is great variation in party-government relations from one county to the next. During my field research, I came to read the physical distance from the party committee to the government as a rough indication for the degree of intimacy between the two organizations, and the size of the party building as an proxy for its power. Even without visiting China's counties, official maps can be interpreted as providing information on party-government relations. In some counties, the two reside in one and the same building and officials of both organizations share their meals in the same canteen. In other places, the two organizations are not even neighbors; their offices are in different corners of the town. The relative fiscal endowment of the two organizations also varies drastically from county to county. In the case of Jinan, an unexceptional provincial capital, the party committee and the government have recently moved together into one huge building complex at the outskirts of the city. Inside this building complex, the distinction between party and government remains tangible, but the move has certainly transformed the everyday interaction and political relationship between the two, especially given difficult traffic in the city, as well as the tendency among Chinese bureaucrats to work out solutions face-to-face.

The competitive yet symbiotic relationship between party and government is an insufficiently understood hallmark of party states. Treating the two as inseparably amalgamated in a unitary state comes at a cost. Scholars concerned with post-Communist transitions in Eastern Europe often think that the two became inseparable during the Communist era and observe how difficult it is to get the party out of the state – that is, to secure continuity in government while undercutting party dominance.[19] This simplification is problematic, since the balancing out of party and government might well be at the origin of party-based regime resilience. Moreover, as Shiping Zheng points out, the distinction between party and government is critical if we want to answer important questions about China's future: Would the fall of the party also mean the collapse of the state? Or has China been successful in state-building to the extent that political order would prevail even under a scenario where the party evaporates?[20] Taking the distinction among party, state, and government seriously, our analysis of the Chinese case will shed new light on a fundamental theoretical problem: Why do single parties penetrate the government apparatus without altogether merging it into the party?

3.1.2 Explaining the Party/Bureaucracy Divide

The following model hinges on the idea that the party is an organization that functions *as if* it had been rationally constructed. In general, it seems unreasonable to assume that all authoritarian regimes shape the responsibilities of the party in such a way as to optimize the reach of the state. Like other institutions, many parties in the world are badly run and imperfectly organized. Yet in certain historic contexts, the rational design assumption seems more justified, as argued later. Even if the role of the party in local governance is *not* a result of any explicit, strategic calculations by the regime, it is important to remember that the CCP developed under historical conditions that made it an exceptionally functional organization. Its struggle for survival, the competition with the Nationalist Party in conjunction with a culture of ambitious, organizational renewal[21] resulted in a highly effective, and in many ways even a highly efficient, institution. Therefore it makes sense to ask what the rationale is for an authoritarian regime to deploy its party for implementing certain policies.

The division of labor between organs of government and organs of the party is a defining characteristic of the Chinese party state, just as the balance of power among the legislative, executive, and judicial branches of government is the defining characteristic of most functioning democracies. But it has yet to be explained. The most authoritative account on the party by Franz Schurmann – written fifty years ago – suggests that the party would not meddle with ordinary policy implementation, because staying aloof gives the party more room to change its course and disclaim responsibility.[22] Yet the party has been present in local-level policy implementation, if only for some select policies and measures. The fragmentalization of authority raises questions about functionality. Is fragmentalization useful or detrimental for the state and for regime resilience, compared to a totalitarian system? Why would authoritarian regimes fragment their authority? Why do authoritarian regimes not try harder to centralize their power, improve coordination, and gain synergies? Why is it useful to have a party?

These questions about the benefits of fragmentation of power in separate hierarchies with different organizational cultures cannot be fully answered by pointing to the benefits of having party members who provide cheap labor (like volunteers) but at the same time are disciplined (like bureaucrats). Divide-and-rule tactics provide one important motive for authoritarian regimes to fragment their authority. Without doubt, the separation of party and government increases the control of higher-level authorities over lower-level authorities. For example, when party and government agencies of a county are closely intertwined, this is bad news for the prefectural-level government, since it will be harder for the prefecture to play the two off against each other and thereby to exercise greater control over county affairs. The keener the competition between the two types of agencies, the more willing they are to denounce each other, thereby improving the information held by higher levels.

Yet the divide-and-rule argument has a number of serious shortcomings. First, divide-and-rule tactics also work upside down, since contrary to the typical divide-and-rule situation, not only low-level authorities but also mid- and high-level authorities are divided in the same way. Low-level authorities can and routinely do engage in venue shopping, seeking out the higher-level authority that is most sympathetic to their cause.[23] Second, government agencies are formally and informally subordinate to the party. By contrast, if the goal is to divide and rule, the divided agents should be made as close to equally powerful as possible. Third, in most places there exist well-established habits of collusion between local party and bureaucrats, which are hard to overcome, say, by appointments. Fourth, and more contestable, higher-level governments have generally good control over lower-level government. Chinese authorities do not usually face defiant, open, and widespread insubordination; what they do face are the kinds of principal-agent problems that we also find in firms. After all, they can easily fire and replace local officials. Fifth, divide-and-rule tactics do not explain why an authoritarian regime would split up tasks between a party and a government, rather than between two separate government agencies. In short, divide and rule is not a sufficient answer to the question of why the CCP is used in the realm of policy implementation.

Instead, the core of this section's theoretical argument is that authoritarian regimes not only create multiple agencies, but create agencies that are fundamentally different from each other. I emphasize different degrees of risk adversity, because it captures the key difference between bureaucratic career strategies and rank-and-file members' incentives. The concept of risk adversity also makes the argument amenable to formal analysis using informational economics. It is not easy for a state to cultivate agencies with different types of agents. Government agencies tend to be isomorphic: They may start out with a different organizational culture, but usually end up looking very similar to each other, because they operate in similar contexts and deal with similar challenges. The party allows the authoritarian ruler to break out of the isomorphic trap. Even at a time when ideological differences play a negligible role, bureaucrats' motivations are different from the motivations of rank-and-file party members and, arguably, even from motivations of bureaucrats in the select party hierarchy. As a result of self-selection, individuals who choose a party career as opposed to a government career also tend to be more ambitious and more willing to take risks. The steep hierarchy of the party promises quick advancement, but also comes with the risk of being purged, including at the lowest levels. Most importantly, the 92 percent of the party membership that are rank and file out of government are so differently motivated and organized that the isomorphic trap of ending up with a party that looks like a bureaucracy in practice is not too hard to avoid. An authoritarian state finds it extremely useful to have such different agencies. The government will be assigned tasks that are best implemented by the most risk-averse individuals: routine tasks with observable outcomes. By contrast, the party will specialize in thorny tasks with only indirectly observable outcomes. In short, authoritarian regimes have good reason to diversify their authority.

If the theory is right and if authoritarian states really do cultivate the differences between their governments and their parties for the sake of more effective policy implementation, this has a number of observable implications. An empirical test proceeds in two steps. First, one distinguishes between policy measures that are better implemented by the risk-averse government bureaucracy, on the one hand, and policy measures that are better implemented by the less risk-averse party members. Based on the underlying assumptions of the model presented in the next section, the key is to identify policies where upper-level authorities receive fuzzy signals about the efforts undertaken by their agents.[24] From the agent's perspective, such policies are the riskiest ones, because there is a likelihood of unjustified punishments as well as unjustified bonuses. As the second step, one compares the relative presence of party members and bureaucrats to the relative success in implementing the two kinds of policies.

3.1.3 The Party State's Institutional Efficacy

To explain party state institutions, this chapter presents a calculus undertaken by a rational leviathan. In other words, I assume that functionality can explain institutional structures. To be sure, there is no law of nature that institutional structures necessarily evolve in a way that is in the best interest of the ruling elites. Yet to explain the organizational setup of the Chinese party state and to understand the puzzling deployment of the CCP for on-the-ground policy implementation, rationality assumptions seem justifiable, partly because the crucible of Chinese history between the party's foundation in 1921 and today has forced CCP leaders to think hard about optimizing the party's institutional configuration.

Historical institutionalists have demonstrated that for historical reasons such as path dependency, irrational and dysfunctional institutions exist.[25] Just as it would be wrong to rule out the possibility of irrational institutions, it would also be wrong to rule out the possibility of rational institutions. Taking historical institutionalism seriously, we must study the historical origins of an institution in order to evaluate whether to expect rational designs.

In the case of the CCP, evolutionary arguments, as well as circumstantial arguments, justify this rationality assumption. According to an evolutionary argument, as a result of natural selection, only the fittest institutions survive. If the party has survived almost one century, its organization cannot be too dysfunctional. To be sure, historically many weak institutions have survived for very long periods of time, because of a lack of competing alternatives. Yet in the case of the CCP, there have been powerful alternatives. Most importantly, before the Communist takeover of 1949, the CCP had been in permanent, direct competition with the Chinese Nationalist Party (KMT) for almost three decades. Ideological differences between the CCP and the KMT might not have been altogether inconsequential, but the competition was first and foremost about smarter organization. The organization of the CCP was smart enough to emerge from an underdog position and displace the entrenched power of the ruling KMT. According to the more circumstantial argument, crises have made the party wise.

The Cultural Revolution (1966–1976) stands out as the most dangerous crisis of the CCP since the foundation of the People's Republic of China in 1949. During the crisis, the distinction between party, army, and government became a vital question of regime survival. Keeping these three pillars of state power was crucial in order to contain the spread of factional conflict across institutional boundaries. In the first few months of the Cultural Revolution, command over People's Liberation Army (PLA) forces and local militia was removed from the local party secretary.[26] Similarly, the political commanding heights were separated from the apparatus for everyday administration. Whereas totalitarian visions of the 1950s and early 1960s mobilized everyone for a small set of tasks and thus did not allow a division of labor, the years of turmoil demonstrated the advantage of having a quasi-government, called Production Headquarters 生產指揮部, in charge of administering the mundane tasks of the state, while political battles paralyzed the quasi-party committee, called the Revolutionary Committee 革命委員會. The crisis prompted earnest reflection about the party's role in the state. Deng Xiaoping's political vision, in particular his vision of the CCP, evolved greatly during his years in banishment.[27] After the end of the crisis, in 1981, the Central Committee passed the influential Resolution on History, deploring Mao's overbearing authority and calling for party reforms.[28] Dengist reforms included a renewed emphasis on a consistent separation of party and government. At the time, some construed this as a move toward liberalization, but in hindsight, the new arrangements served to strengthen the supremacy of the Communist Party. The Cultural Revolution crisis and its aftermath saw Chinese leaders reflecting on party reform as a life-and-death issue.

The Cultural Revolution was not the last crisis to keep the party on its toes. The protest movement on Tian'anmen Square in 1989 spurred multifaceted debates about ways to improve the hold of the CCP.[29] These debates took on even greater urgency when the Chinese leadership watched the spectacular collapse of its erstwhile role model, the Communist Party of the Soviet Union. Jiang Zemin's Three Represents policy and the admission of capitalists as members of the CCP testify to the adaptability of the party.[30] Under the label of *party construction*, teachers at Party Schools and scholars at Schools of Marxism continue to grapple with a broad range of questions pertaining to the institutional development of the party. The extremely powerful Organization Department of the CCP sponsors much of this work, editing the journal *Party Construction Research* 黨建研究 and sponsoring conferences under mottos such as "Promote theoretical and practical innovation in party construction" 推進黨的建設理論創新和實踐創新. The party's nagging self-doubt, which paradoxically is nowhere more palpable than in scientifically argued exhortation that the party can be self-confident,[31] create an alert awareness of the need to innovate in order to counter the "risks" of a "transitional society."[32] Under these circumstances, rationality has a good chance to make itself heard in the party's continual struggle for survival.

Drawing and redrawing the line between party and government has been a central concern for both the state's strategic thinkers and practitioners on the ground. Confronted with constantly evolving tasks, party and government have been readjusting their relationship. As the characterization of the Chinese regime as a form of fragmented authoritarianism highlights, the Chinese state by no means operates as a unitary, top-down hierarchy of the sort characteristic of an ideal-type totalitarian system. Instead, a central characteristic of the Chinese state is that different organizations, levels of government, bureaucratic departments, and localities behave very differently and often seem to work in contradiction to each other.[33] Arguably the most carefully engineered division in the organization of the Chinese state is the division of labor between the party and the state. Therefore, it seems appropriate to analyze party organization not as an accidental by-product of history, but as a rationally designed apparatus.

3.1.4 Formal Model of the Party/Bureaucracy Divide

Game theory provides a good guide as to why and under what circumstances it is advantageous for an authoritarian government to assign local implementation tasks to two distinct agencies, namely a party and a government, rather than setting up one all-encompassing agency. The literature on principal-agent problems provides a wide range of asymmetric information models. Most relevant to the analytic challenge at hand are multitask models, where a principal seeks to incentivize an agent to perform well simultaneously on more than one task. While existing models provide a good starting point, major modifications to the standard models are needed to make them fruitful for the problem at hand. This section describes the intuition of the model, formally developed in Appendix 1, and the major takeaways.

The multitask model is concerned with situations where a principal seeks to incentivize an agent to perform well on several tasks at the same time. The model used here is designed to illuminate the trade-offs involved when a principal chooses whether to rely on one agent or on several distinct agents. Dividing up implementation tasks has costs, because it undermines efficiency. It is a standard result of economics that in a world of perfect information, one agent is better than multiple agents, because one agent would internalize externalities, that is, the agent would take into account side effects that good performance in one task might have on the fulfillment of other tasks. This chapter specifies conditions when it is advantageous to divide up multiple tasks among multiple agents. Thanks to the multitask model, we know the extent to which the principal can incentivize his agents in a context of asymmetric information with interdependent tasks. The original model does not consider multiple agents. With multiple agents, the tasks remain interdependent and the principal continues to internalize the costs of both agents. Yet if information asymmetry and therefore uncertainty is greater with one task than the other, decoupling the tasks and dividing the tasks between one agent, who carries the risk, and another agent, who is not affected by the risk, can alleviate the overall costs of uncertainty. Or in short: Complexity comes at a cost. Whether the principal gives complex incentives to one agent, or whether he gives more simple incentives to two agents, is not always equivalent.

The multitask game captures well the trade-offs that the Chinese central government faces. The model describes why central leaders would assign to the bureaucracy routine enforcement tasks with an outcome that is easily observed. By contrast, the party would be put in charge of more complex tasks, with outcomes that are not well observable. The less complementarity there is between the tasks, the more likely the principal is to use multiple agents. The more agents differ in their risk-taking behavior and the more the tasks differ in the quality of the signal, the more likely the principal is to use multiple agents. Finally, and maybe most importantly, much depends on the type of noise, which makes it hard for the principal to evaluate the task. If mistakes in evaluating enforcement of task 1 are highly correlated to mistakes in evaluating enforcement of task 2, it is advantageous for the principal to separate the tasks. Otherwise the mistakes reinforce each other and the principal has to provide a lump-sum payment to compensate the agent for the uncertainty that comes from faulty bonuses and sanctions.

Arguably, the principal-agent problems in the realm of local government is particularly prone to encounter the kind of asymmetric information problem characterized by noise that is positively correlated across tasks. Take a situation where in a county both tasks have been fulfilled to the full satisfaction of provincial leaders. The greater the positive correlation, the harder it is to tell whether this good result is due to outstanding government performance, or whether it is due to hidden characteristics of the local population. It could well be that the local population is particularly easy to govern, welcoming of government intervention, unlikely to protest, and generally supportive of the authorities. The multitask model with correlated noise will be especially relevant if one thinks that good policy results have much to do with the local population, rather than with the local government alone.

Four crucial takeaways emerge from the formal model. The multitask multiagent model highlights four factors that influence whether the principal will employ only one set of agents, who are given control over both tasks and who are jointly rewarded for their performance on both tasks; or whether the principal will employ two sets of agents, who are each given control over only one task and who are each separately rewarded for their performance on that one task. The principal's choice will depend on the following factors:

(i)   Synergy effects. Is it easy to split the task between two different agents; or are there synergy effects between the two tasks?

(ii) Distinct tasks. Are the tasks very different, with the effort on one task more easily observed than on the other and thus with one task less risky for the implementing agent than the other?

(iii) Distinct agents. Are the two sets of agents similarly risk averse; or is one set of agents risk avoiding and the other set of agents risk accepting?

(iv) Does the observational noise muddle both signals received by the principal in the same direction; or is there a tendency that an overly negative assessment on one task is partly compensated by an overly positive assessment on the other task?

The first factor defines the scope conditions, suggesting that for some tasks, the logistics of setting up and maintaining two partially redundant systems – one run by the party, the other by the government – is prohibitively expensive. If there are two separate agents, there are potential losses, because coordination in the implementation process becomes costly. As we go on to focus on the advantages of separate agencies, we must keep in mind that these advantages only begin to matter if they outweigh lost synergies.

The second factor highlights that tasks must be different, one riskier than the other. If the principal does not receive a good signal as to whether the agent did his best or whether the agent shirked, then he might hand out unjustified rewards, which poses a risk for the agent. The third factor draws our attention to an essential characteristic distinguishing bureaucrats from party members: their different attitude toward risk. The model also indicates that the gains for the principal to employ two separate agencies increases if the two agencies have very different corporate identities and attract different types of personnel. In other words, it is not so helpful to simply employ two largely identical "ministries," one for each task. Instead, it is more promising to work through very different types of institutions, such as a party and a government, whose members react differently to incentives. This is particularly true when the two tasks are different from each other. The model indicates this potential gain from differentiation by distinguishing between an agent who is more risk averse and one who is less so. More broadly, one would expect other agent characteristics to play a similar role. For example, if one organization attracts people with a longer time horizon than the other, the principal would gain from allocating those tasks to the organization, where the signal is more delayed and becomes visible only in the future. The gains from having two separate agencies tend to increase with the differences between the agencies, because these greater differences accentuate each agency's comparative advantage. This is reminiscent of trade theory: There is more potential gain from international trade when the countries involved have very different comparative advantages.

Most importantly, the fourth factor demonstrates that organizational solutions depend on the kind of asymmetric information. This result captures a typical and thorny problem of incentives in local governance. Higher level government agencies receive multiple signals reflecting the performance on multiple tasks. But these multiple signals are treacherous and of little help, because if in one jurisdiction there is a lot of noise in one area of local governance, there will probably be noise in other areas as well. In real life, there are many reasons for this correlation: The local government that cheats on one task is also more likely to cheat on other tasks. The local government that has a particularly easy-to-govern constituency will do well on many tasks, but should not be rewarded for a success that has little to do with its own efforts. The local government may by sheer luck have attracted a foreign investment project, which might be beneficial on many fronts at the same time: creating jobs, reducing pollution compared to indigenous industries, helping local industries to climb the value chain, and improving the skill set of the local citizens.[34] To be explicit: Having two agents does not improve the information that the principal has. But since agents are rewarded only for their own task, they do not have to bear the considerable risk of suffering compound losses across multiple tasks and thus do not have to be compensated for this substantial, additional risk.

3.2 THE CASE OF CHINA'S ONE-CHILD POLICY

The theory on the division of labor between party and government, as laid out above, has observable implications for policy implementation. The one-child policy is an ideal case to test the theory, because the Chinese state could be expected to fully deploy its best resources in well-considered ways for a policy that was so ambitious and was such a high political priority for almost four decades. This section begins with a short overview of the one-child policy, highlighting its twin goals of cutting birth rates while avoiding gender-selective abortion. Descriptive statistics provide a sense that the one-child policy had a formidable impact on the reality of rural life throughout China. After illustrating how the information economy surrounding the one-child policy works with the example of one village, the section concludes with a series of testable hypotheses.

3.2.1 The Twin Goals of Chinese Family Planning

The term "one-child policy" is shorthand to refer to a policy bundle, consisting of legal regulations and administrative measures related to family planning. From its beginnings in the 1970s, the goal of Chinese family planning has been to reduce population growth. To achieve this goal, in 1979 the government decided that henceforth couples could have no more than one child.[35] It quickly became clear that such a policy would have a major unintended consequence. Because Chinese couples are under great pressure to give birth to at least one son, in the 1980s the one-child policy triggered a wave of female infanticide and prenatal sex selection, to make sure that the first and only child would be male. The increasing availability of ultrasound technology continuously aggravated the problem. Family planners had to deal with the side effect by coming up with ways to improve China's gender balance. Partly as a result, in November 2013 the government decided to greatly relax the one-child policy. The one-child policy would now be more appropriately called a two-child policy.

The assertiveness of the one-child policy varied over time and across space. Not all second children were directly in conflict with the official policy, because the Chinese state allowed numerous formally sanctioned exceptions, including for minority populations. The standards of what exactly counted as a surplus baby changed, but throughout the 1990s and the 2000s, typically second-borns were illegal if they were born to urban Han-Chinese mothers or to rural Han-Chinese mothers whose first child was a boy. All births beyond the second child were illegal, except if a non–Han-Chinese mother was involved. This definition approximates the situation in Shandong province around the year 2000. In addition, innumerable informal rules, exceptions, and habits of local implementation led to an extraordinary variety of outcomes, puzzling to the observer.

The unevenness of policy implementation has been the subject of previous scholarly inquiry.[36] This variation does not come as a surprise considering the variety of local challenges to implementation, even in a single, relatively homogenous province like Shandong: different cultural and ethnic traditions, different degrees of urbanization and modernization, and different tensions between the local government and its citizens.[37] These exceptions are compromises to accommodate societal pressure and reflect that the Chinese government chooses to retrench in the face of potential popular opposition to its policy. For instance, most women in Tibet can legally give birth to more than one child: For political stability, the government sacrificed its local one-child policy. In that sense, the prevalence of non–first-born children indicates that the state is weaker in some places than in others. From a pragmatic point of view, if the main goal is to reduce overall population growth, it is irrelevant whether birth rates are evenly cut, as long as this is not perceived by the population as being overly unfair. This flexibility of the Chinese state reflects a traditional permissiveness toward uneven implementation, also called "differentiated governance."[38] It is precisely the ability to enforce differentially that makes China's governance highly effective, presumably going a long way in bolstering regime resilience.

For the following analysis, it is important to emphasize that the goal to reduce fertility competes with the goal to even out the gender balance. This tension is obvious not only to people who study macro-level statistics, who see that low fertility in most cases is accompanied by uneven sex ratios. It is also clear to local administrators. In an ideal world, modernization promotes both goals simultaneously, by changing people's preferences, so that they want fewer children and become more indifferent between raising a boy or a girl. In Shanghai, fertility preferences have declined and son preferences have weakened so much that low birth rates and balanced sex ratios go hand in hand. In the short run, for most of China, the goals conflict. If a family can have only one child, they want to make sure that the one child is a son. The more flexible the government is in allowing multiple sons, the less incentive for sex-selective abortions (or hidden daughters). Conversely, the more effective the prohibition on gender-selective abortions, the greater the incentive to give birth to more children.

3.2.2 The Twin Implementation Challenges in Numbers

The one-child policy succeeded in its primary purpose of reducing population growth. China managed to reduce the country's fertility rate (births per woman) from the pre–Cultural Revolution high of 6.2 births in 1965 to a low of 1.51 births in 2000 and 1.7 births in 2012.[39] In order to understand variation of state strength across territory, one approach would be to calculate the fertility rate of lower-level jurisdictions. Unfortunately, the kind of data necessary to calculate fertility rates are only available at aggregated levels.[40] Instead, as a measure of success, the paper will use data on the number of non–first-born children. As the name suggests, the one-child policy pursued the ideal of having each woman give birth to only one single child. Deviations from this policy ideal can hence be interpreted as relative weakness of the state in some places compared to other places. Of the 1.2 million children born in 2010, almost 38% were non–first-borns.[41]

The existence of certain formally sanctioned and far-reaching exemptions should not obscure the fact that nevertheless the majority of non–first-borns are illegal. To assess the prevalence of illegal births, let us take a look at data from the 2006 edition of the *China Health and Nutrition Survey*.[42] In that year, the survey was administered to a nationally representative sample of 9,788 adults in nine provinces. All in all, the married women under age 52 among the respondents had given birth to a total of 3,830 children throughout their lives.[43] Out of these, 36% were non–first-borns. Taking into account that ethnic minorities are exempt from family planning policies and that rural residents are allowed to have a second child if the first was a daughter, I find that 754 children, that is, 55% of all non–first-borns, were illegal. For all of China, this would imply about 250.000 surplus births per year. The number of non–first-borns not only reflects that the government is deviating from its ideal point, but also can serve as a proxy to identify jurisdictions that have an enforcement problem.

The second goal, to avoid too drastic a deviation from the natural sex ratio at birth, has turned out to be even more challenging. Missing baby girls are bound to create social problems, in the form of leftover men on the marriage market. Authors point to a variety of social problems resulting from unbalanced sex ratios, including higher crime rates and collective violence.[44] Some authors go as far as to suggest that at aggregate levels, "[t]he security logic of high-sex-ratio cultures predisposes nations to see some utility in interstate conflict," predicting that China's "bare branches" increase the likelihood of war.[45] Historically, bandits and rebels could be understood as "frustrated bachelors."[46] Certainly, uneven sex ratios at birth have been of great concern to the Chinese leadership.

The sex ratio at birth in China had been an unremarkable 95 girls for every 100 boys until the late 1970s. According to conventional wisdom, the sex ratio then deteriorated dramatically, until reaching an alarming level of 87.9 girls born for every 100 boys born in 1989.[47] This was the time when Amartya Sen deplored 50 million missing women in China alone[48] The census conducted in the year 2000 showed a sex ratio at birth of 85.6 girls for every 100 boys.[49] If instead of the information from the full census, we prefer the answers by women in a 10 percent sample of the population, who in conjunction with the census were subjected to more detailed questioning, the sex ratio might have been even be lower, namely 83.4 percent. In the most recent census of 2010, sex ratios at birth hit a new record of 84.8 percent, or 82.5 percent according to the 10 percent sample. Apparently the availability of ever more advanced technology to identify an embryo's gender – most recently the option of sending a blood sample to Hong Kong early in the pregnancy[50] – prevailed over the effects of education and urbanization. A worsening gender imbalance goes a long way to explain why leaders at the Eighteenth Party Congress in 2013 found it so urgent to liberalize family planning.

This mainstream view has repeatedly been questioned by census analysis as well as field research:[51] Since many children, especially female ones, are not reported to the authorities – not even to the census takers – there is large underreporting. Many of the missing women may not be missing, they may just be concealed from the state. A recent article provides new evidence, based both on the census and on field research, pointing to a severe underreporting of children, with implications for China's gender imbalance.[52] While the findings from the grassroots provide a vivid image of how children are concealed from the government, a comparison of some cohorts in the census indicate that this sort of concealment translates into a significant undercount at the aggregate level.

Without denying the problem of unbalanced sex ratios, it is important to note that the established scholarship probably exaggerates the extent of the problem. Carrying out systematic intercensus comparisons of various cohorts, I find that many young cohorts grow from one census to the next – a phenomenon that may be explained as a result of undercounting.[53] In 2010 alone, 23 million individuals appeared out of nowhere; since more women than men belatedly enter the statistics, this has implications for China's sex ratio at birth. Taking into account these new adjustments, it appears that sex ratios were almost normal until 1995 and that Amartya Sen's classic missing women problem in the case of China had much to do with elder generations. Sex ratios only began to diverge from the normal ratio in 1995, but these intercensus comparisons have little to contribute to our understanding of more recent developments. Since 2000, with the increasing availability of technologies to determine the embryo's gender, many families opt for sex-selective abortions instead of hiding their children.[54] While this is a moving research frontier, for the purposes of this chapter it is enough to notice that, even in the light of the new data, China faces a gender imbalance, although its proportions are under debate.

3.2.3 The Informational Foundation of Family Planning

Informational constraints are at the core of the difficulties that central authorities face when implementing the one-child policy. Now that the one-child policy has been abandoned, social scientists have begun to realize just how badly the government was informed. In order to explain the division of labor between party and government, my argument begins with the essential discovery that for the two aspects of the one-child policy, the informational constraints are of a very different nature. It is less informationally demanding, and therefore easier to enforce, a policy that every woman would only have one child. It is more informationally demanding, and therefore harder to enforce, a policy prohibiting the manipulation of the natural sex ratio.

In the case of Chinese grassroots implementation, the role of information is by no means just an analytic construct by theory builders. The struggles around information are tangible to the observer in the field, both in cities and in the countryside, thanks to a variety of public billboards 公開欄 (Figure 3.1). In villages, one usually finds such billboards close to the seat of the village committee, making transparent village finances 財務公開, minimum wage guarantee recipients 低保人員, disbursements of food subsidies 糧食直補發放, and the state of family planning 計劃生育. One primary function of the billboard is to empower citizens by making them aware of their entitlements. In the case of the one-child policy, however, the publication of information empowers the state. It also invites denunciations, if villagers find incomplete or faulty information.

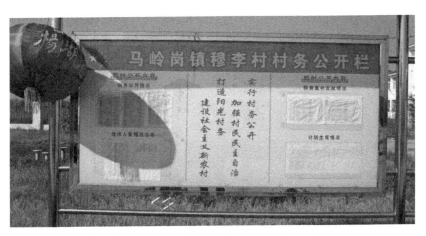

FIGURE 3.1 Information economics in plain sight at the grassroots

The origin of the information posted epitomizes the role of grassroots party members. Superficially, it is not the party branch, but the village committee that prints out the documents posted on the billboard. The village committee is a self-governing body, belonging neither to the state bureaucracy nor to the party hierarchy. As in the context of other countries, one would not expect these village organs to exhibit much discipline. In fact, it is the party that instills the discipline. Local party members take the lead in collecting the information. While ordinary villagers are also encouraged to denounce illegal pregnancy, typically it is party members who transform the rumor into administratively useful information. It is also the party members who are held responsible for suppressing information in this critically important policy era.

Regarding the one illegal pregnancy posted on the billboard in Figure 3.1 and partly translated in Table 3.1, what is striking is the missing and inconsistent information concerning the length of pregnancy before

TABLE 3.1 *A village billboard: information economics at the grassroots*

女方 姓名 Woman's name	出生年月 Birthday	男方 姓名 Man's name	出生年月 Birthday	結婚登 記日期 Date of marriage	計劃生育服務 手冊發放日期 Date of handing over family planning booklet
XXX	1987- 12-14	XXX	1986- 01-07	2008- 07-22	
XXX	1986- 07-23	XXX	1983- 08-16	2010- 05-27	2010- 8-28

懷孕日期 Beginning of pregnancy	流引產日期 Day of abortion	孕產結果 Pregnancy result	日期 Date	生育情況 Birth Data		合法 是否 Legal/ illegal
				性別 Gender	孩次 Birth order	
	2011- 04-25	< 12 周引產 induced birth < 12 weeks	2011- 04-09	女 female	2	外 outside (illegal)
2010- 06-20		剖宮產 Cesarean	2011- 03-23	男 male	1	內 inside (legal)

Note: This table transcribes part of the billboard shown in Figure 3.1. Not included are columns with no data for the two individuals. The two are not statistically representative of the entries on the billboard; for instance, almost all pregnancies reported on the billboard were legal.

abortion. The billboard notes that the pregnancy lasted less than 12 weeks, but there is no date provided for the beginning of pregnancy. Moreover, the advertised abortion date is 16 days later than the "birth date," which might hint at an attempt to cover up for an abortion in the 14th week of pregnancy, which is later than desirable for the family planners.

For the parents involved, the costs of hiding a child are greater than the costs of hiding a sex-selective abortion. To hide a surplus birth from the authorities, citizens need to cover up not only the full nine-month duration of pregnancy, but also the birth itself and the existence of the unregistered child. Even when village and possibly township authorities collude with citizens in such a scheme, families with invisible children bear tremendous costs, not to speak of the ethical burden. Part of the problem is underregistration. When families have two baby girls and plan to try a third time for a boy, they may choose not to report the second baby girl. On a ferry from Shandong to Japan, I encountered such an unregistered second girl, who had lived a transient life on the run to escape the state's attention, until at age 14 she finally decided to take the offer of a human trafficker and join a group of other women emigrating to Japan for presumably illegal work in a factory or some other workplace in Shikoku. Abortion, exclusion, infanticide, and neglect of girls all contribute to China's greatly imbalanced sex ratio. If my in-depth interviews with one invisible child can be any guidance, parents decide to hide away their child while not fully realizing the future implications and costs of this decision. Schemes to recruit child slave laborers, including for work in mines in central China, function because despairing parents break down under the burden of surplus children and then decide to sell their child, trying to believe false promises of human traffickers.[55] Even if some parents decide to hide births, this is an enormously expensive strategy. By comparison, sex-selective abortions are easier to hide. The most widely used ultrasound technology allows one to identify the gender of the embryo just before the 20th week of pregnancy. Slightly more advanced technologies allow identification up to a month before that date. Even in the context of China's closely knit village communities, it is possible to hide an early pregnancy. In this context, at least in the case of Shandong, seasons seem to play an important role, as later empirical analysis will confirm.

Even more important than the costs of concealing a child is the different kind of information needed to sanction surplus births vs. gender selection. At the aggregate level, the ratio of male births to female births makes it perfectly obvious that gender selection is occurring on a large scale. But at the individual and at the village level, it is much harder to tell who is practicing gender selection and who is naturally giving birth to sons rather than daughters: Is it suspicious if in a given year a village reports the birth of eight girls and ten boys? Is it suspicious if a county reports the births of 8,500 girls and 10,000 boys? The closer to the ground, the less clear it is whether gender selection is occurring. This is very different from surplus births. As long as local authorities do not overlook children, they can and do determine for each birth whether is "inside" or "outside" the rules. In short, the signal that authorities receive about surplus births is deterministic and unambiguous, whereas the signal that the authorities receive about gender selection is only probabilistic and noisy by nature.

This fundamental point can be illustrated with the example of Village No. 371702108200, located near Heze, a prefectural city in the less developed Southwestern corner of Shandong province. Returning to the village's notice board outside the party office (see Figure 3.1), we find details on the village's family planning situation, as is customary throughout rural China. The existence of this board shows that the one-child policy is not carried out in the dark by discreet bureaucrats, but invites the participation of ordinary citizens. The notice board includes intimate information about all local couples. For each birth, this list reports whether the child is legal or illegal, *inside* 内 the regulations or *outside* 外 of them. Like all of Shandong province, the village seems to be in line with government policies when it comes to preventing surplus births. The only noteworthy incident was the abortion of one illegal embryo before the 12th week of pregnancy.

Even with all this detailed information, it is hard to know whether the village is doing well in terms of preventing gender selection. Are there missing women? Out of 14 live births reported on the notice board, only five are girls. The sex ratio of 56 girls for 100 boys is far below the natural sex ratio at birth of 94 girls for every 100 boys. Should higher level authorities sanction this village for not preventing gender selection? The problem is that there is a good chance that the ostensibly artificial sex ratio is actually a natural outcome. If the likelihood for a girl is approximately 48.5%, according to the combinatorics of binomial processes, the likelihood that among 14 children there are five or fewer girls is 25%.[56] Even in this village, where the birth ratio is particularly skewed, there is a 1/4 chance that in fact the outcome was natural and any punishment therefore unjustified. Assume that over a long period of time, the villagers regularly perform sex-selective abortions, so that the resulting birth ratio on average is 85 girls for every 100 boys. Assume further that higher-level authorities choose to punish villages only if they can be 95% sure that the sex ratio at birth systematically deviates from the natural sex ratio at birth. Then it would take 14 years of reporting until upper-level authorities could mete out a punishment. By contrast, surplus births can be confidently sanctioned immediately, down to the village and even down to the couple that gave birth to the child. The law of large numbers allows to discover missing children in the aggregate, but not in specific cases and small communities.

3.2.4 Hypotheses on the Role of the Party in the Domain of Family Planning

According to the theory just presented, China's one-child policy should be implemented with a division of labor between different agencies, because there are competing goals in the context of imperfect information. With perfect information, task separation would not make a difference, because the principal decides the trade-off and gives instruction to his agents accordingly. Yet the asymmetric information problem creates a trade-off. On the one hand, if a single agent is put in charge of both tasks, this one agent internalizes the trade-offs involved and reaches his own ideal point. Because of asymmetric information, the ideal point of the agent could be very different from the ideal point of the principal. On the other hand, having two agents work in parallel, while forgoing the synergies of collaboration, can lead to better results. Each agent would make efforts to achieve his own goal, without taking into account that his own efforts make it harder for the other agent to achieve his goals. In certain contexts, it could even be efficacious to assign one task to halfhearted, foot-dragging bureaucrats. The multitask multiagent model developed in the preceding section is designed to answer such questions and is thus appropriate for analyzing the case of China's one-child policy. It illuminates why China's leaders employ two distinct agencies with different organizational cultures and different types of employees to implement the one-child policy.

The hierarchy of the state bureaucracy officially ends at the township level, and generally there are no bureaucrats permanently stationed in the villages. Most villages have enough party members to form a party cell.[57] These form the most powerful link of the state into the village. The village committee, on the other hand, is a self-governing body that has a somewhat more democratic quality to it, in the sense that it is more bottom-up, in theory representing the interests of farmers. In village governance, managing the conflict-prone relationship between party cell and village committee is a major concern of party organizers.[58] In recent years, issues related to land use rights have been the most divisive issues, with the one-child policy being another important point of contention between party cell and village committee, to the extent that they consist of different individuals. In any event, the village committee is by no means an extension of the state.

The multitask multiagent model suggests that division of labor is a particularly promising strategy, if the tasks are very different and if the agents are also very different. In the case of China's one-child policy and the Chinese party state, both conditions prevail. The informational structure of the enforcement problem is such that the principal finds it much easier to monitor whether lower-level agents were able to prevent surplus births than to monitor whether lower-level agents were able to prevent sex-selective abortions and absconded children. The individuals in the two agencies – party members vs. government bureaucrats – are of a very different type. Individuals who self-select into the party are going after the greater payoffs, since the party hierarchy is much steeper, but at the same time they are the type of individuals who are prepared to take higher risks. Government bureaucrats have predictable careers and will only very rarely be able to serve in positions outside their original posting.

First, we will test the big, structural-functionalist assumption underlying the model. According to this structural-functionalist assumption, the separation of tasks between party and government, at the end of the day, works out very well. Or to put it in more exact language, the institutional structures are successfully designed so as to optimize implementation, from the leviathan's perspective. The government makes rational choices, which all in all improve the effectiveness of policy enforcement. It does not follow that implementation works perfectly, but it does follow that the presence of the state apparatus improves implementation. Thus, the presence of state agents will reduce the number of surplus children as well as the number of sex-selective abortions.[59]

Hypothesis 1a: Not distinguishing between the party members and government bureaucrats, taken together, a greater presence of the party state makes enforcement more effective in terms of preventing surplus children.

Hypothesis 1b: Similarly, taken together, a greater presence of the party state makes enforcement more effective, in terms of preventing prenatal sex selection.

According to the model, the riskier task would be assigned to the less risk-averse agency. This implies that the informationally less demanding task of preventing surplus births is assigned to the government and the informationally more demanding task of preventing prenatal sex selection is assigned to the party. Higher-level bureaucracies would evaluate government officials based on the prevalence of surplus births in their district. By contrast, they would evaluate party members and local cadres based on their ability to prevent gender selection before birth.

Hypothesis 2a: A greater presence of the party is associated with less pre-natal sex selection.

Hypothesis 2b: A greater presence of bureaucrats is associated with fewer surplus children.

Because the two tasks are interdependent, each group is tempted to undermine the success of the other group. It becomes easier for bureaucrats to prevent citizens from having multiple children, if the last legal baby is a boy. Once a couple has a boy, the incentive to have additional children diminishes. As a result, local bureaucrats have an interest in tolerating or even encouraging the use of medical devices to identify the embryo's gender. Conversely, it becomes easier for party members to prevent sex selection if couples can have multiple children. If couples know that they can try again for a boy, they will be less eager to force their luck with the first or second child. Party members thus have an interest in being more tolerant when it comes to sanctioning surplus children. This leads to

Hypothesis 3a (strong version): A greater presence of the party is associated with more surplus births.

Hypothesis 3b (strong version): A greater presence of government bureaucrats is associated with more prenatal sex selection.

These hypotheses are extremely stark. They ignore interactive effects between party and government. In particular, it is the task of party agencies to supervise the government. As a result, the presence of party members not only has the direct effect of increasing surplus births, but also indirectly affects the effectiveness of bureaucrats in reducing surplus births. Conversely, so the presence of bureaucrats will also influence the effectiveness of party members. If the model is a good guide to reality, the interactive effects should not invalidate the result, but they do call for a more moderate version of hypotheses 3a and 3b. Instead of absolute effect of party members and bureaucrats, the moderate version of the hypotheses emphasizes the relative importance of the party and the government in each of the two family planning tasks.

Hypothesis 3a (moderate version): The presence of bureaucrats has a greater effect on reducing surplus births than the presence of the party.

Hypothesis 3b (moderate version): The presence of the party has a greater effect on reducing prenatal gender selection than the presence of bureaucrats.

3.3 EMPIRICAL EVIDENCE FROM CHINA'S ONE-CHILD POLICY

Thanks to newly available, exceptionally fine-grained data, quantitative analysis can dissect the party state, detecting the division of labor between party and bureaucracy. The presence of party members and the presence of bureaucrats each have a distinct effect on policy implementation. Manifestly, the party machine and the government apparatus are engaged in very different activities. The dissection of the party state becomes complex, especially taking into account the differential effect of male vs. female party members and bureaucrats. This complexity should not obscure a simple yet critically important takeaway: The presence of party members makes a big difference for the implementation of China's one-child policy.

3.3.1 Specification

In order to test the eight hypotheses just formulated, two distinct empirical models are needed, corresponding to the two distinct implementation tasks. The first model predicts the number of non–first-born children. This number directly reflects the success of the government in achieving its ultimate goal of reducing birth rates. In addition, the number is a close proxy for the existence of surplus children. The prevention of non–first-born children is a relatively easy-to-monitor routine task, assigned to the government. The second model predicts the number of female children as a close proxy of gender-selective abortion. The prevention of gender selection is a difficult task that is hard to monitor. It is a paradigmatic example of the party stepping in to alleviate the unintended consequences of a highly intrusive policy.

The specification of the first model includes demographic variables that could be associated with the likelihood of having surplus children, as well as with the presence of state agents. For example, there are size effects, since in more populous jurisdictions, there will be more births as well as more state agents. Unlike cities such as Shanghai, urban areas in Shandong typically have not passed the population transition. If urban citizens want multiple children, they are more likely in a position to afford potential sanctions. Moreover, the definition of what counts as "illegal" is stricter in urban areas than in rural areas, so that we will find more surplus births in urban areas. The specification also controls for the presence of ethnic minorities, migrants, female migrants, health care workers and female health care workers. Finally, since the number of births varies by season, the specification also includes monthly fixed effects.

The second model explains the number of female births, controlling for the number of male births born in the same jurisdiction during the same time period. If it was all about biology, there should be about 1.05 female births for every male baby. More importantly, the two variables should be closely correlated, almost perfectly colinear. The residual should be perfectly random. Yet in China, as we will see, socioeconomic variables greatly influence the number of baby girls born, even when comparing localities with the same number of baby boys. To make the results between the two implementation tasks as comparable as possible, the second specification uses precisely the same control variables as the first specification.

3.3.2 Data and Results

China's populations census provides extraordinary insight into the effectiveness of the one-child policy. For a long time, the Chinese census was considered to be of relatively high quality, although scholars noticed the problem of counting migrants and the political stakes involved in the counting process.[60] Although there have been voices warning against a significant undercount of young children, especially female ones,[61] the mainstream view has not considered the problem important enough to adjust for this undercount.[62] Recent analyses reveal that a large number of children had been thoroughly concealed from the state, including from the census, as discussed in Section 3.2.2. In line with the argument of the book, we might expect that concealment and fake compliance was more of a problem in "pink" areas with few party members, so that the effects shown in the following analysis are underestimating the real effect of party membership.[63] However, it is beyond the scope of this chapter to evaluate and work out the implications of this recent result. Going forward, the result may well change the established consensus, in which case much of the literature on the effects of the one-child policy would need to be revisited.

Data from the most recent census in 2010 are only released selectively and at more aggregate levels. Instead, all the data used in this analysis come from the 2000 census.[64] Initially it was precisely the information related to fertility and sex ratios that was off-limits, but accessibility is no longer a serious problem. The data are available at an unusually fine-grained level, namely the township. Some observations are collected for the full census; other observations are collected only for a 10 percent sample.[65] For the analysis of non–first-born children, we can work with Shandong's 2,482 township observations of the 10-percent subsample (representing almost 100 million people). To study gender imbalance, we even have the luxury of monthly data from the full census. For every township for every month between November 1999 and October 2000, we know the number and sex of newborn children, so that we can work with 12 monthly observations of 2,482 townships – that is, a total of 29,784 observations. For the variables used in the present analysis, there are no missing data.

The 10-percent sample counts the number of officials and party cadres. It does not count the number of party members, but the size of the cadre corps stands in as a proxy for the number of party members and the presence of the party on the ground. Of China's 14 million state agents, 94 percent are bureaucrats and only 6 percent party cadres. Based on the census, it is not possible to ascertain how many of these state agents work at the township level, as opposed to higher levels of government. Dividing the number of state agents by the number of townships, there are nineteen party cadres per township. Since many party cadres work at higher levels of government, the number of party cadres, which are actually posted in a typical township would be much smaller than nineteen. The point here is that at the heart of local power, there is a small elite, consisting of a handful of party officials. The data also indicate an extremely unbalanced sex ratio at birth, already discussed. According to the census, for every 100 boys born between November 1st, 1999 and October 31st, 2000, there were only 85.6 girls.

Table 3.2 presents important factors that explain performance on the most basic task of the one-child policy, namely to avoid non–first-born children. In the unitary state model (first column of results), which does not distinguish between cadres and bureaucrats, we see that more state agents mean fewer non–first-born children. Each additional state agent on average is associated with a decrease in the number of non–first-born children by 8.3, controlling for a number of demographic control variables and also controlling for seasonal effects. Overall, confirming hypothesis 1a, the party state is an effective implementer.

The second specification separates out the effect of party members and state officials, revealing fundamental differences between the two groups. Whereas the presence of bureaucrats continues to be associated with

TABLE 3.2 *Party effect versus bureaucracy effect on surplus births*

	Unitary state model	Model separating party versus government	Party government interaction model
All officials	−8.3***		
Party cadres		54.5***	−51.4***
State bureaucrats		−10.4***	−16.0***
Party * state officials			508***
All births	0.06***	0.06***	0.06***
Total population	−0.36***	−0.36***	−0.38***
Urban population	0.63***	0.71***	0.79***
Ethnic minorities	2.49***	2.7***	2.8***
Migrants	11.0***	11.0***	10.8***
Female migrants	−9.6***	−9.8***	−9.5***
Health care workers	32.3***	31.8**	27.6**
Female health workers	11.3	4.9	8.1

*** Significant at 0.001, ** significant at 0.01, * significant at 0.05, . significant at 0.1
Note: OLS estimators. 29,785 observations. Dependent variable: Surplus births. The number of party cadres serves as a proxy for the size of the party. All specifications include intercepts and monthly fixed effects. The township-level data come from the Shandong Province portion of the 2000 census and the accompanying survey among a 10% population sample.

fewer non-first births, a greater presence of party members is associated with an increase in the number of surplus births, a clear confirmation that party and government make very distinct contributions in implementing the one-child policy (hypothesis 2b and hypothesis 3a, strong version).

The third specification further refines the results by including interactive effects. A simulation is needed to interpret what the highly significant, yet differently signed coefficients mean on balance, when all variables take on realistic values. Table 3.3 demonstrates how the number of surplus

TABLE 3.3 *Party effect versus bureaucracy effect on surplus births, simulation*

Number of non-first births	Small-sized party	Middle-sized party	Large-sized party
Small-sized government	+86%	+63%	+39%
Middle-sized government	+10%	ZERO	−10%
Large-sized government	−66%	−63%	−59%

Note: Simulation calculating the number of surplus births in various "typical" contexts based on the coefficients of 3.2. Middle-sized refers to the sample mean, small-sized to the sample mean minus one standard deviation, large-sized to the sample mean plus one standard deviation.

births changes under different scenarios, compared to the baseline scenario of a township where all variables take on their mean value.[66] To the right of the value "zero," is a scenario of a jurisdiction with more party members; specifically, their number is increased by one standard deviation. In other words, the scenario is well within the range of "normally" sized party machines. This decreases the number of non–first-born children by 10 percent. Increasing the size of government has a much more sizable effect. An increase in the number of bureaucrats by one standard deviation cuts the number of non–first-born children by more than half. This confirms hypothesis 2b, but would support only the weak version of hypothesis 3a: Presence of party members does not lead to more surplus children, but it does not help nearly as much as the presence of bureaucrats.

As it turns out, success in the prevention of sex selection is the mirror image of the success in the prevention of non–first-born children. Each additional state agent on average is associated with three additional female children, confirming hypothesis 1b (Table 3.4). Disaggregating the state, party members are the ones who prevent sex selection, whereas government officials are associated with more sex selection, confirming hypothesis 2a and 3b (strong version). This drastic assessment, as before, is put into perspective once we take into account interaction effects. Table 3.5, which is constructed in the same way as Table 3.3, shows that this time, it is the party that for practically relevant values of the dependent variables makes a more important difference and reduces the imbalance of the gender ratio by increasing the number of baby girls, confirming hypothesis 2a, but advocating for the weak version of hypothesis 3b.

3.3.3 The Gendered Division of Labor in Family Planning

In the domain of family planning, issues of gender introduce an additional level of complexity, a thorough treatment of which is beyond the scope of this chapter. While academics and officials in China largely ignore the fact that party and government focus on different aspects of the one-child policy, they emphasize the division of labor between male and female officials, with females supposedly spearheading family planning. Indeed, as Gail Hershatter discovers, in the 1980s female survivors of the Great Leap Famine were most eager activists promoting the one-child policy.[67] Yet as Great Leap Famine memories are fading and as women today have different concerns from women of the 1980s, is family policy implementation

TABLE 3.4 *Party effect versus bureaucracy effect on female births*

	Unitary state model	Model separating party versus government	Party government interaction model
State agents	3.6***		
Party		48.9***	76.8***
Bureaucrats		1.9**	3.5***
Party*bureaucrats			−134***
Male births	0.55***	0.55***	0.55***
Total population	1.8***	1.8***	1.8***
Urban population	0.26***	0.32***	0.31***
Ethnic minorities	−1.43***	−1.26**	−1.3**
Male migrants	−0.96*	−0.95*	−0.91.
Female migrants	−0.06	−0.18	−0.22
Health care workers	11.2	10.8	11.9.
Female health care worker	−39.8***	−44.4***	−45.2***

*** Significant at 0.001, ** significant at 0.01, * significant at 0.05, . significant at 0.1
Note: OLS estimators, with intercepts and monthly fixed effects. 29,785 observations. Dependent variable: Female births. The number of party cadres serves as a proxy for the size of the party. All specifications include intercepts and monthly fixed effects. The township-level data come from the Shandong Province portion of the 2000 census and the accompanying survey among a 10% population sample.

still female? Instead of faithfully carrying out the tasks assigned to them, women leaders might also feel sympathetic vis-à-vis women citizens, who want to rear multiple children or who are under pressure to live up to traditional family expectations to give birth to a son. Fundamentally, Hershatter may be right that women leaders are particularly sympathetic to the interests of women citizens. In the 1980s, the best way to promote women meant to actively support the one-child policy, but in the context

TABLE 3.5 *Party effect versus bureaucracy effect on female births, simulation*

Number of female births	Small-sized party	Middle-sized party	Large-sized party
Small-sized government	−4.5%	−1.5%	+1.4%
Middle-sized government	−2.5%	ZERO	+2.5%
Large-sized government	−0.5%	+1.5%	+3.6%

Note: Simulation calculating the number of surplus births in various "typical" contexts based on the coefficients of 3.4. Middle-sized refers to the sample mean, small-sized to the sample mean minus one standard deviation, large-sized to the sample mean plus one standard deviation.

of contemporary China, the best way to promote women might well be to quietly tone down the one-child policy. Precisely because they remain in charge today, female state agents might be in an excellent position to soften the policy.

While the size of the effects are not large enough to fundamentally change the preceding results – partly because female party members are still a minority – the data provide evidence that female party members are indeed undermining the one-child policy, rather than promoting it. Holding the overall number of party members constant, the more female party members there are, the more non–first-born children are born and the more sex selection takes place, as shown in Table 3.6. For government officials, the evidence is mixed. Depending on the specification, the sign of the coefficient changes. Whether or not female government officials appear to be helpful for the one-child policy or whether they are resistant to the policy depends on whether one isolates the interactive effects. It could be that female government officials just do not have much leeway in undermining the policy, given that they are officially put in charge and given that non–first-born children are relatively easy to discover. In the context of a task that is less easy to monitor, female government officials – just like female party officials – create more space for female citizens to carry out sex-selective abortions.

These results, to the extent that they question the conventional wisdom that women are the best promoters of the one-child policy, invite further research on how gendered enforcement works partly against the purpose of the state. The greatest caveat concerns the interpretation of the female party cadre variable: Is the result due to the fact that there are more females in positions of power within the party? Or should the result be interpreted as a proxy for the presence of women among the rank and file of the party, similar to the interpretation of the preceding results? The evidence presented here does not provide conclusive answers. With this uncertainty about the interpretation in mind, for understanding the role of the party in the domain of family planning, there still are three important takeaways. First, if it were not for the presence of women in the party, against conventional wisdom, the party might be an even better tool for implementing the one-child policy, maybe even in its main mission to reduce non–first-born children. Second, given that female party cadres are in a small minority, and given the size of the effects, overall each additional party member helps enforcement. Moreover, when controlling for the effect of female party members, the presence of the party still helps policy enforcement.

TABLE 3.6 *Party and gender: are female officials "properly" enforcing?*

	Non-first children party vs gov	Non-first children with interaction	Female births party vs gov	Female births, with interaction
Party cadres	8.9	−81.4***	66.1***	86.6***
Female party cadres	226***	140*	−135**	−115**
Bureaucrats	12.5***	7.1*	25.7***	27.0***
Female bureaucrats	−80***	−80.4***	−82.7***	−82.5***
Party * bureaucrats		506***		−115***
All births	0.06***	0.06***		
Male births			0.55***	0.55***
Total population	−0.37***	−0.39***	1.7***	1.7***
Urban population	0.74***	0.81***	0.36***	0.34***
Ethnic minorities	3.2***	3.53***	−0.52	−0.56
Male migrants	11.2***	11.8***	−0.41	−0.39
Female migrants	−10.5	0.72*	−0.88.	−0.91.
Health care workers	28.8**	22.9*	0.31	1.5
Female health care worker	6.4	12.2	−31.4**	−0.31**

*** Significance at 0.001, ** significance at 0.01, * significance at 0.05, . significance at 0.1

Note: OLS estimators, with intercepts and monthly fixed effects. 29,785 observations. The number of party cadres serves as a proxy for the size of the party. All specifications include intercepts and monthly fixed effects. The township-level data come from the Shandong Province portion of the 2000 census and the accompanying survey among a 10% population sample.

3.3.4 Seasonal Variation in State Strength

There are striking seasonal patterns in the frequency of female children compared to male children (compare Figure 3.2). All specifications include monthly fixed effects; the month of January serves as comparison line. Compared to January, in all the other months, fewer female children are born. Most female children arrive in winter, between December and March. The fewest female children arrive in summer, between June and October. These findings already control for seasonal fluctuations in the overall number of births, which results from things like happy family reunions over the spring festival, as well as the other control variables. In other words, more girls are missing in the summer months than in the winter months. The differences are enormous, as a simulation based on the fitted interaction model 6 shows. Letting all variables take on their

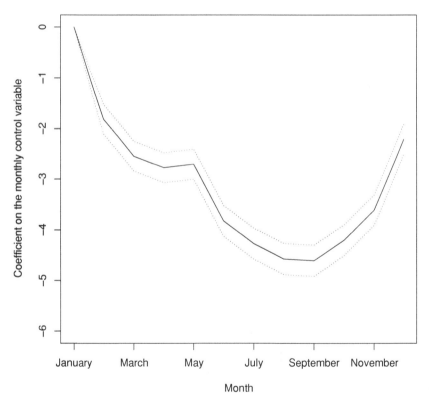

FIGURE 3.2 Seasonal variation in state capacity. Coefficient of the monthly fixed effect in the baseline regression of Table 3.2, January being the reference point.

average value, the model suggests that there are 33 percent fewer girls in September compared to January. If it were always January, there would be 419,000 baby girls born in Shandong every year – by contrast, if it were always September, there would be 281,000 baby girls. What explains this enormous seasonal variation in the number of female births?

To interpret these seasonal regularities, we combine scholarly findings with facts about how people take advantage of the four seasons in the climatic context of Shandong. Missing baby girls can be explained either as the result of underreporting or as the result of sex-selective abortions. If at least recently sex-selective abortions have become the primary cause for missing girls,[68] they also provide a plausible explanation for seasonal birth patterns. Abortions are carried out after an ultrasound B scan about five months before the due date. Only rarely do more sophisticated prenatal diagnostics allow earlier abortion. The girls missing between June and October have been aborted between January and May. A woman during her early pregnancy has the choice to hide her pregnancy from her family and from the authorities. It is easier to hide a pregnancy during winter months, because women find it more natural to stay at home during the agricultural slack season, to justify extended periods of absence for family visits over the spring festival, and to wear more clothing to cover up a pregnancy. In combination, these factors make it easier for women to have an abortion during the winter months. It has even been suggested that women plan their pregnancy for the winter, so as to keep it secret.[69] Ostensibly, the state is stronger between December and March, because there are more female births during winter. Yet in reality, we must take into account the time lag of abortion. The state is more likely to overlook sex-selective abortions during winter. "Seeing like a state" in this case means having a blurrier vision in winter, resulting in seasonal variation of state strength with surprisingly few baby girls born during the summer.

3.4 CONCLUSION: THE CCP'S ROLE IN POLICY IMPLEMENTATION

The rank and file of the party plays a prominent role in policy implementation, distinct from the bureaucracy. To describe the separate domains of party activity and bureaucratic activity, and to explain why it makes sense for state builders to maintain such separate domains, this chapter analyzes the case of the one-child policy. Based on a game-theoretical argument involving asymmetric information, the chapter finds that the party apparatus, consisting of agents who are less risk-averse, is used selectively for the state's most difficult and most vital tasks. Whereas information might play an important role, one additional reason for the different capabilities of party and government is the different characteristics of party members vs. government officials. More risk-averse people would self-select into government positions and therefore be more appropriate agents for implementing routine tasks with little asymmetric information. In the case of the one-child policy, the theory implies that the government takes care of the first-order problem of preventing non-first births, whereas the party takes care of the second-order problem of preventing sex selection, which is the most serious unintended side effect of the one-child policy. The party apparatus is a great source of strength of the Chinese state, precisely because it is used sparingly.

The one-child policy, because it is such an important and challenging policy to implement, reveals much about the bases of Chinese state strength. The government focuses on preventing surplus births and its agents are rewarded for performance on that routine task, which is relatively straightforward to observe. On the other hand, an unintended side effect of the one-child policy is the unbalanced gender ratio at birth. This problem has taken on great urgency and proves much harder to solve. The party is put in charge of solving this problem, including through "thought work." The smaller risk aversion of CCP members, compared to bureaucrats, has consequences, both positive ones and negative ones, beyond the realm of one-child policy implementation. On the downside, the less risk-averse party members may be more tempted by corruption than the more risk-averse government officials. On the bright side, the less risk-averse party cadres might be more enterprising, thereby fueling economic dynamism.

The next chapter will reinforce and complement the findings from this chapter, by showing that the party is not only deployed to extract compliance, but also to extract resources in an information-poor environment. We find that governance is differentiated not only across space, but also across agencies. At the core of Chinese statecraft lies the government's ability to distinguish between routine tasks on the one hand and priority tasks on the other. The leadership knows its priorities and dispatches its most powerful agency, the party apparatus, to take care of the most difficult priority tasks. Moreover, the party-government tension that occurs while implementing the one-child policy is more desirable from the viewpoint of the government than it might seem at first glance. The fact that party members and bureaucrats are working somewhat against each other reflects the fact that they have been assigned different tasks in a rational way.

If the analysis in this chapter is correct, the CCP plays an indispensable role in allowing the state difficult interventions into local communities, such as with the one-child policy. Concerning China's future if the CCP were displaced from power, this finding raises concerns: Would the Chinese state be sustainable if one day the CCP evaporated, leaving behind only the bureaucratic government structure? Much of the state-building that has taken place over the past seventy years was centered on the party. It is not clear whether China's bureaucracy could continue to function the way it does today independently of the party. Consciously or unconsciously, the party has made itself indispensable for the operations of the Chinese state.[70] Comparing localities with differently sized local party apparatuses and differently sized government bureaucracies, this chapter demonstrates that the success of China's one-child policy depends on the party. Success of the one-child policy in its primary task, namely the reduction of birth rates, can be attributed to government officials. But progress on the secondary task of alleviating the unintended and potentially regime-destabilizing effect of uneven sex ratios at birth can be attributed primarily to party members. There has been state-building beyond the party, yet the party has made itself indispensable for managing the severe side effects of a highly intrusive policy. For the most difficult tasks, the capacity of the Chinese state rests on the Leninist party. In that sense the Chinese state is not a secular bureaucracy, which could easily be transformed into a postparty apparatus, at least not while maintaining a firm reach across its territory.

4

The CCP's Support in Generating the State's Material Base

Rank-and-file party members serve not only to implement distinctively Chinese policies, such as the one-child policy. They are also involved in fulfilling universal state-building tasks, such as tax collection. To maintain the material base of their polity, state-builders everywhere need to find ways to raise fiscal resources. In transition economies like China, tax extraction runs into problems of asymmetric information coupled with administrative transaction costs that are high compared to the tax potential: In the rural economy, small sums are extracted from numerous individuals engaging in increasingly diverse economic activities. In the urban economy a large part of the economic activity occurs in the informal sector, where small and medium-sized companies come and go. The argument of this chapter applies to both sectors: Party networks help the state to extract resources, either by convincing and coercing citizens to contribute to common projects, or more generally by solving severe asymmetric information problems between the lowest level of the state hierarchy and grassroots society, at low cost. As a result, the state is better at extracting fiscal resources in places with dense party member networks, both in rural and in urban areas. In short, local party organizations help to maintain the material foundation of the People's Republic.

This chapter contrasts with – but by no means contradicts – conventional views of authoritarian regime parties as networks for patronage distribution. One exemplary model, which incorporates leading research on the functions of parties in authoritarian polities, analyzes the dictator's commitment problem vis-à-vis his followers and describes regime parties as tools serving to effectively share the benefits of power.[1] In a nutshell, the patronage approach to regime parties holds that party members are politically loyal in exchange for material benefits. This approach implies that in time of crisis, when the state has fewer benefits to distribute, the loyalty base of the party quickly dissipates, so that parties would be of limited use to authoritarian regimes. Based on this observation, researchers have questioned whether the patronage approach can fully explain the usefulness of parties for authoritarian regimes, pointing to the importance of understanding the nonmaterial sources, such as legitimacy based on historical achievements[2] and the way in which regimes mobilize the resources on which they rely in the first place.[3] Concentrating on the material aspects of the arrangement, the contribution of this chapter is to point out that a strong regime party not only distributes resources, but also collects them. Findings from rural China suggest that the revenues created by the CCP outweigh the benefits granted to party members in terms of informal rules amounting to tax breaks. Strong parties are not merely acolytes consuming costly state privileges; they also generate resources for state projects.

The first half of this chapter develops hypotheses about the role of the party for taxation in rural areas (Section 4.1) and in the cities (Section 4.2). The second half of this chapter presents quantitative evidence, again beginning with the countryside (Section 4.3) and then continuing to the cities (Section 4.4). While knowledge about the recruitment process allows ruling out the possibility that fiscal revenues are directly affecting membership recruitment targets and local party size, a more serious empirical difficulty consists of ruling out the possibility that both taxation rate and the size of the party are driven by other community characteristics, including hard-to-measure factors such as ideologically motivated political interest, trust into hierarchies, or traditional tendencies to be discontented. To address this issue, this chapter uses a double-pronged approach. First, analyzing rural China, it builds on prior research to take into account a host of other determinants of subnational variation in rural tax extraction.[4] Fine-grained household-level data reflect the privileges enjoyed by households with a link to the party, as well as the contribution party members make by increasing tax revenues in their surroundings. Second, turning to the taxation of the urban economy, which by now is the pillar of China's government finances, the analysis deals with endogeneity issues by taking advantage of an unusual data set that shows politically sensitive, regionally disaggregated information on the amount of resources transferred to the center by each provincial unit. The empirical identification strategy for the urban data employs a difference-in-differences design, to rule out possibilities that unobserved community characteristics drive the relationship between the size of the party and the degree of taxation.

The process by which resources are taken from peasants to fund state activities goes straight to the heart of how government authority functions in the countryside.[5] Rural revenues in China, while representing only a minuscule proportion of all national revenues, provide excellent insights into the governance of rural areas, where despite migration about half of the country's population is based. If our primary purpose were to study central government revenues, we might choose to neglect the tiny contribution from the countryside, since urban revenues are the fiscal backbone of the Chinese state. Central planners are concerned about rural finances only to the extent that the meager contributions add up to significant funds for local projects, whose costs might otherwise burden the national budget. But since our purpose is to analyze governance techniques of the party state, tax extraction in the countryside promises to shed light on how the state functions at the grassroots level across the vast Chinese territory. In urban areas, tax collection largely eludes ordinary citizens, but in the countryside citizens more consciously experience tax-collecting operations, personally negotiating the various demands put on them. The origins of the Chinese tax system lie in the countryside, and during Deng's reform era impulses for fiscal reform first came from rural areas. It may therefore be unsurprising that the argument of this section, namely that party members play a central role in rural tax collection, also applies to the cities, as the next section shows.

4.1.1 The Party's Involvement in Rural Finance

For a regime that is known as an ambitious state-builder seeking rigorous control in many areas of life, the formal institutional setup of rural governance is remarkably *laissez-faire*. Villages are self-governed, the state hierarchy generally does not have officials permanently stationed in the villages, and upper-level governments do not impose a budget. This arrangement receives widespread support in China, with prominent experts arguing for further widening the political space created through decentralization at the grassroots level.[6] Since popular discontent in rural area is a major concern to the government, it is welcome that electoral processes as part of village self-government promote trust in the government – even if they are severely flawed from a democratic point of view.[7] In the absence of a formal state hierarchy reaching into villages, the rank and file of the CCP becomes the primary organizational linkage through which the state exercises power across its vast territory. County and township governments vitally depend on support from party members to exercise control and effectively govern their jurisdictions.

Party members are advocates and supporters of the state in the field, not a hierarchical extension of the bureaucratic apparatus into the villages. CCP members are not government employees, but usually pursue full-time occupations unrelated to government. Even village leaders do not receive regular government salaries, but meager and unstable remunerations tied to project budgets, which usually amount to a small share of their income from their civilian profession.[8] Rank-and-file party members are not implementing through the kind of routines that bureaucrats would employ: Instead of detailed instructions shaping their daily schedule, CCP members receive generic orders and political guidelines. Instead of administering budgets and dealing with paperwork, they talk to villagers, among themselves, to township officials and party cadres. Formally, they are not subordinate to the government bureaucracy, but only to the Leninist party apparatus, which at the local level is clearly distinct from the bureaucratic hierarchy. For instance, in most of the several dozen counties I visited, the party headquarters are not in the same building as the government headquarters. The lowest echelons of the party, namely its rank and file, are present in the places where the government does not have a permanent presence.

As a result of village self-government, most resources collected by village authorities, legally speaking, are not taxes, and are not formally administered by the state. But they are also not the community funds to finance projects that are collectively decided and jointly administered, as which they are sometimes described. Legal definitions aside, these resources provide the material base for state activity in the countryside. While possessing much autonomy, village authorities are still imbued with statelike authority, acting under the long shadow of a state that stands ready to back them up if challenged. Villagers have little choice but to pay. Moreover, the projects funded by village fees are usually the result of initiatives from higher-level authorities, connected to state-building agendas set by the top leadership. Village authorities must be loyal to higher-level authorities despite village elections, because party and state heavily influence the appointment of village officials, issue instructions, exercise control, and distribute privileges. Even if the revenue streams to village authorities do not show up on any budget, for the villagers concerned they are like taxes, and they are effectively under state control. Therefore, revenue flows to village authorities constitute state extractive capacity.

The indispensability of the party for the smooth functioning of the state in the countryside is reflected in the tax and fee collection process. Village finances are not embedded in the government's accounting system. Instead, party members are involved in the fiscal affairs of their villages, from the time of revenue collection to the time of spending the money. Well aware that their superiors face the conflicting goals of completing numerous projects and providing an increasing number of public services, while at the same time reducing the fiscal burden on rural citizens, party members are involved in negotiating the trade-offs. Although this is rarely discussed openly, more internal documents explicitly reveal the function of party members in rural fiscal affairs. Village finances are delicate enough that party members are routinely involved, but they take on a particular role in times of crisis or at times of important reforms.

The transmission of information during ordinary times is of great value to the state, but the role of party members is particularly critical at times of political change. For instance, the tax-for-fee reform in the early 2000s aimed at decreasing the fiscal burden on villagers, by abolishing a range of financing schemes prevailing in the countryside to pay for government activity. Predictably, to the extent that it was carried out according to plan, the policy crippled fiscal revenues and undermined the village governance as it had existed up to that point. In an internal guidance, the organization department saw that "the tax-for-fee reform created new tasks for grassroots party building" which had to manage the resulting instabilities: making sure that the new division of labor between township and village worked, that cadres would not get demotivated by the lack of resources to fulfill their tasks, and that the new financing method of publicly agreed-upon projects 一事一議 takes off. In their characteristic concern about laxity and indulgence, the organization department suggested that these tasks were an opportunity for party building and a reinvigorating challenge to battle 挑戰,[9] keeping party members on their toes.

The essence of party members' diversified roles in the domain of tax collection could, for the sake of parsimony, be understood as one of information transmission. The rank and file feeds into the system the kind of information that directly helps in the assessment of taxes, the monitoring of payments, and the disciplining of citizens with overdue taxes.

Rural tax collection systems in countries throughout the world suffer from often insurmountable asymmetric information problems; governments have great difficulties in accurately monitoring income and tax payments. In the countryside, most of the time, it is prohibitively costly to collect information and enforce payment, compared to the modest rural tax potential. In China, rural populations have historically resisted information collection efforts by the state, posing a formidable problem to state-builders.[10] However, these days village communities make very significant contributions to local projects. Party members in the village are the critical link, since they are both well-connected in the village and also willing to take instructions from the township government. In this role, village party members are more than tax collectors; they serve as mediators between the government and the village. Each party member keeps eyes and ears open, and critical information needed in the tax and fee extraction process is compared and centralized in village party committee meetings. The more party members there are in a village, the greater the extractive capacity of the local government.

Party presence matters for tax collection in a less mechanical, but maybe even more important way as well. The top leaders of China's county and township governments dread protests. If a protest escalates and reaches a significant size, it becomes an ugly blot on the resumes of the officials under whose watch it occurred. The prevention of protest is a key criterion in the cadre promotion procedure, since the occurrence of a protest has "veto power" and can invalidate outstanding performance on all other dimensions. When implementing ambitious projects and collecting the corresponding fees, the county and township leaders need local leaders who communicate the goal of these projects well, so that they are better understood and hopefully endorsed by local citizens. They need an early warning system when the project creates discontent and when therefore it also becomes riskier to ask citizens to pay for it. And if tax protests do erupt, they need channels to mediate the conflict before it escalates to a level that would be noted by the media and upper-level government. It is the subgovernmental party system that provides these tools. Formal and informal contacts, party meetings and consultation across hierarchical levels – meetings may include up to three hierarchical levels at a time, seldom more – provide a regular, steady flow of information. The more reliable this flow of information is, the more confidently county and township governments can carry out projects without great risk of protest. The goal is not simply for the government to squeeze out the maximum amount of money, but also to understand better what kinds of projects would be genuinely welcome. In that sense, rank-and-file party members make the state strong, promoting both enforcement and better policy.

4.1.2 Collecting Revenues without Taxation

In the context of Chinese rural finances, the collection of resources in the countryside can be thought of as a form of state strength, but only with caveats. First, the state's rural revenues pale in comparison to its urban revenues. Second, the central government laments its limited ability to reduce the "peasant burden," so that high levels of revenue might appear as a weakness rather than a strength. Third, local communities have much autonomy in the administration of their finances, so that one may be tempted to question to what extent fiscal affairs in the countryside are state activity. Finally, if local governments embezzle money or waste it on projects, it appears that having collected the resources is not always conducive to strength. The following paragraphs clarify concepts, arguing that ultimately the collection of resources in the countryside is an integral part of the state's schemes to secure its material base.

Because nowadays wealth is created overwhelmingly in urban areas, Beijing's fiscal policy toward rural areas is characterized by a lack of interest in agricultural activities as a source of revenue. Direct taxes related to agricultural activities, including the farm land occupancy tax, the deed tax, and the tobacco leaf tax, only account for 3 percent of total tax revenues.[11] Nontax revenues – the ones that are most controversial among peasants and will be the focus of the empirical analysis – are either considered local affairs, not to be reported in the government budget, or they occupy a negligable proportion of the national budget. For the Ministry of Finance, the question is how to limit fiscal transfers to rural areas. In combination with the overall priority to maintain stability in the countryside with the help of ambitious socioeconomic programs, the result is a quick proliferation of "unfunded mandates," despite voluminous transfers.[12] To fulfill the many ambitious programmatic expectations of higher-level government, local officials are under pressure to raise income on their own.

Contrary to official government messages, the countryside, including the agricultural sector, continues to be taxed. When in 2006 the government abolished the presumably 2,600-year-old agricultural tax, the accompanying propaganda fanfare hailed the end of a long history of peasant exploitation, as if the agricultural tax were the only resources collected from rural citizens. For one thing, in the year after the much-advertised abolition, the disappearance of the agricultural tax was more than offset by the increase in closely related taxes: The amount of direct taxes related to agricultural activities (of which the agricultural tax had been a part until that year) increased by 33 percent, a year later in 2008 reaching an all-time high.[13] For another, the state extracts resources among its rural population through levies, fees, and other payments for public projects, as well as in-kind and labor contribution. Despite the labels, these transfers are compulsory and best understood as taxes in disguise.[14]

Because of the informal rules and ad-hoc nature of some revenue categories, and the large discretion left to local officials in other revenue categories, the Chinese state taxes very unevenly. Holding those factors constant that legitimately determine a household's tax burden, such as cultivated land, family composition, and overall household revenue, there still is great variation in the amount of taxes paid by households, even within local jurisdictions. Beijing promulgates uniform regulations, but these regulations leave much room for interpretation by local cadres. Variation in levels of taxation provide valuable clues about state–society relations, as reflected in the fruitfulness of cross-national comparisons.[15] For a variety of reasons, most importantly the impossibility of distinguishing between the ability to tax and the willingness to tax, this variation can be interpreted as indicating a strong state only with a broad definition of "strength."[16]

In China this interpretation is further complicated by the fact that the center has declared its commitment to reduce the "peasant burden," publicly and adamantly urging local officials to reduce the taxes borne by peasants.[17] Given these central policy declarations, is it a sign of strength if CCP members help tax extraction? In light of widespread protest in the countryside, these admonitions are more than mere rhetoric. The tax-for-fee reform in 2002, which commuted a variety of fees into a unified tax to stop abuse, as well as the abolition of the agricultural tax in 2006 indicate commitment to lighten the peasant burden.[18] Different policy preferences may induce central leaders to be genuinely more benevolent toward citizens than local cadres. Their different place in the hierarchy of the state shapes their outlook on policy, in terms of their self-identification as individuals with a national mission, as well as in terms of instrumental reasons. The literature contrasts the long time horizon of national leaders, who often remain influential long after the expiration of their terms, with the short time horizon of local cadres, the most influential of whom rotate to new positions in different localities every four years or so.[19] Different time horizons also have implications in the realm of fiscal activities. To enhance their chances for promotion, leading local cadres stealthily seek to extract revenues to fund highly visible projects welcomed by upper-level cadres.[20] To the extent that peasant discontent builds up over time and is easier to suppress in the short run, such behavior undermines long-term stability in the countryside, with today's local leaders free riding at the expense of tomorrow's local leaders. Central leaders, by contrast, have little to win from taxing peasants and much to lose from systemic insta-bility, so that they forego revenue maximization in the interest of equality, fairness, and sustainability.

Clearly, the image of a benevolent central leadership entirely commit-ted to reducing the peasant burden is not accurate. After what may well have been an effective policy intervention in 2006, the central government has shown less interest in policies to reduce the peasant burden, as if it were relatively content with the current state of fiscal affairs in the coun-tryside. Moreover, if despite the rhetoric the peasant burden has remained high for two decades, it was probably not only the central government's lack of ability, but also its lack of will to enforce lower taxation.[21] After all, central leaders incentivize local cadres to carry out projects that the central leadership knows to be costly. Central leaders know that local cadres have little choice but turn to their citizens, because many local gov-ernments financially stand with their backs against the wall.[22] Thus, when central authorities deplore that they exercise only limited control over rural finance, thereby comfortably disclaiming responsibility for local aberrations, their rhetoric is at least in part an "evasive strategy."[23]

To complicate things even further, local finances resemble a leaky bucket. Some villages have relatively transparent finances, but not oth-ers. Visiting a village, it is enough to check the bulletin or ask for the account book to find out how transparent village finances are. While the former agricultural tax and the continuing taxes related to the agricul-tural tax find their ways into normal government accounting, most levies and a large portion of the fees do not find their way into aggregate statis-tics. An unknown sum of revenues flows into illegal schemes, some well intentioned, others fraudulent. The resources collected from citizens in the name of the state and in the long shadow of the state do not equal the amount brought under state control and spent for projects in line with government intentions.[24] The money is lost halfway on its way from society to the purposes intended by the state. This analysis of extraction strictly focuses on extraction, including any resources collected by state agents, no matter how the money is used in the end. Contributions from society do not always translate into revenue of the state.

If CCP members help to create the material base of the state, this should count as a state-building success with two caveats: First, according to the central authorities' political message, their goal is to reduce resource extraction in the countryside, so that high levels of resource extraction could indicate a lack of central control over local agents – a well-known feature of the Chinese state.[25] Yet the difficulty of deciding whether resource extraction represents a success or a failure ultimately points to the analytical limits of the unitary-state concept:[26] One agency's success can be the other's failure. From the point of view of rural tax payers, not Beijing but the tens of thousands of fiscally autonomous county and township governments are the most relevant fiscal agents, who are revenue maximizers under the constraint of avoiding protest. Second, the degree to which resource collection can count as state-building success also depends on the fairness of collection, the level of conflict in the collection process, and ultimately how wisely the money is spent. If similar households in different localities give up different shares of their income to the government, thereby providing local agents of the state with more money to spend, this could be because the coercive infrastructure works more effectively in some areas than in others. But it could also be that citizens in some areas have stronger preferences to be served by the government, for instance when local authorities have a track record of delivering valuable services.

4.1.3 Hypotheses: The Quid-pro-Quo in Tax Extraction

Let us now move to the motivations of the party members to fulfill the mandates assigned to them by higher authorities. In one essential respect, their position is comparable to the leaders of Maoist production teams:[27] It is characterized by a dual loyalty mediating between village interests and state instructions. On the one hand, as villagers, they seek good relations with a local community, whose continuing goodwill is central to the well-being of the entire family. On the other hand, as party members, they take orders from an organization that provides their families with a higher status and privileges. Because other villagers recognize the benefits to the village, if the party member maintains good relationships to his superiors, he acts as negotiator between the village and the state. There is great potential for conflict in the relationship between the village and the authorities, even if the latter claim to have only the best interest of the former at heart. However, one should also note that to yield tax revenues, it is crucial first and foremost that the system be able even to collect the "low-hanging fruits": gaining information about households who are generally willing to pay taxes, in local contexts with little conflict goes a long way in collecting significant resources.

Without ignoring the fundamental conflicts of interests, one should by no means imagine the local party member as an untouchable villain betraying his village – after all, his success in the information economy depends on remaining a trusted member of the village community. At the time of the Great Leap Forward, when the state strong-armed poor villagers into badly conceived communization projects resulting in famine, the stakes for local party members were high, because their choices could make the difference between life and death. Today the stakes are lower, the state is less ambitious, and local authorities prefer party members to use as little coercion as possible. In the face of rural discontent,[28] the party has a considerable interest in avoiding conflict between its local members and society at large. In this context, one should think of information transmission as part of routine procedures, only occasionally taking the form of soft denunciations, and often involving persuasion of the villagers concerned. After all, local leaders find that the large majority of peasants are pliable to the demands of the state, so that ultimately the need for severe enforcement procedure is rare.[29] In the realm of taxation, where at the end of the day it matters how much money could be accumulated, it is crucial to ensure a generally smooth information transmission; it is not important to extract information from the most resistant peasants, so that open conflict and ugly denunciation can be avoided.

To summarize the relationship between the state, party members, and rural citizens, the following paragraphs formulate three hypotheses about taxation in the countryside, highlighting that the party is an important variable in explaining the variation in how much a given household must pay. Rural incomes typically consist of revenues from agriculture, migrant labor, and, to a lesser extent, small businesses. By design, taxes increase with the area and quality of land that a household uses for agricultural activities, as well as with the size of a household and overall household income, including from nonfarm revenues. Topography also affects how much taxes a household has to pay, with remote places being outside the full reach of the state, and places close to government receiving preferential treatment.[30] But the microvariation of state power in rural China also depends on the presence of party members in the village, and on whether the household is connected to the party. Leaving aside the agricultural tax, which was abolished in 2006, the analysis will focus on other levies, imposed for projects that are carried out either by higher-level authorities, such as infrastructural projects more or less benefiting the village, or within the village, such as health projects. Contributions can either be monetary or come in the form of labor contributions. The informal nature of revenue collection in rural China turns taxation levels into a negotiated outcome, reflecting state–society relations and the local strength of the state.

On the one hand, party networks alleviate asymmetric information problems, thereby providing local governments with an organizational infrastructure to access even peripheral communities. They empower the state. On the other hand, party networks are sustained by patronage and as a result jeopardize tax collection. To do justice to this ambiguous role of party members, as facilitators of and as compromisers of state action, the theory must illuminate the quid pro quo of authoritarian parties at the grassroots level. For the grassroots organizations of authoritarian parties to function well, citizens need incentives to be loyal to the party, and the party needs to have good reasons to maintain local-level grassroots organizations. To be sure, reasons for the state to have the party are diverse, as are the motivations of party members to join the organization. Inertia and apolitical, personal loyalties certainly play a role. Authoritarian parties reap political loyalty from their members, although the depth of loyalty only becomes fully observable in times of political crisis and although there is debate as to whether the CCP has moved into a postideological age or whether the current president, Xi Jinping, is resuscitating ideology.[31] Conversely, some party members certainly gain immaterial satisfaction from being part of a larger cause.

A parsimonious description of the relationship between the party and its members might focus on the material exchange between them, as in Table 4.1. This approach contrasts with two alternative approaches: The conventional approaches hold that the party provides material benefits in return for intangible political loyalty, while another approach points to the nonmaterial side of a historically grown relationship.[32] This chapter

TABLE 4.1 *The political give-and-take at the grassroots*

	Supporters reap material benefit	Supporters reap intangible benefits
Regime reaps material benefits	Patronage in exchange for support with extraction	Support with extraction historically motivated
Regime reaps intangible benefits	Patronage in exchanges for political loyalty	Political loyalty historically motivated

suggests a third way: Not only do party members receive material benefits, but also the party receives material benefits thanks to its members. This chapter tests the hypothesis in the area of fiscal policies. It shows that the effectiveness of local party organization can be understood in a parsimonious way as a two-way exchange of material benefits: Party members gain privileges, and the party gains access to local resources. Overall, the party state gains tangible and even material benefits from having a grassroots organization. The central argument of this chapter is that there is an implicit quid pro quo: Party members serve as a crucial link allowing the state to tap into rural resources, but in return they are more lightly treated.

On the one hand, the CCP has been designed as a power-wielding device, for the top-down transmittance of instructions, for the bottom-up transmission of critical information, and more generally as a guarantor of political order. On the other hand, the party exhibits characteristics that have emerged as unintended yet unavoidable consequences. Ever since the party evolved from the pre-1949 conquest organization to the post-1949 government constituency, party members have been demanding privileges. This trend has intensified as the ideological basis of party membership has given way to transactional motives. Upper-level cadres prefer to grant material benefits rather than political influence to the rank and file, in the interest of predictability and control.

Hypothesis H_1: Party networks alleviate severe asymmetric information problems inherent to any rural taxation system. Communities with greater party presence carry a heavier tax burden than communities where party members are few and far between.

Local governments pay a price for the indispensable services they receive from the party members in their jurisdictions. There is a principle-agent problem, because party members in the village can collude and treat each other lightly in the process of tax collection. This works as long as none of them is defecting in order to ingratiate himself with township officials and thus improve his own power position. Party members also have more interaction and easier access to township and often even county-level authorities. They will be better able to present their case if they plead for exemptions from taxes and levies under particular circumstances. Most importantly, the government has an overwhelming political interest in maintaining good relations with its party constituency, on which the local government's power rests. Spoiling the relationship with the party members in its constituency would pose a vital threat to the local government, cut the local government off from the rural population, and make projects impossible. As a result, ordinary citizens suspect that most people nowadays join the party for some kind of material benefits ("haochu"), a view that is amply confirmed by empirical evidence.[33]

Hypothesis H$_2$: The party also functions as a patronage network; party members expect and receive tax rebates.

On balance, does the party strengthen or weaken the state in terms of extractive capacity? According to a structural-functionalist argument, the party could not weaken the state, for if it were not an effective instrument of power, the state would dispense with it. One may or may not find this line of argument convincing. After all, many institutions have survived even when they were severely dysfunctional and had outlived any usefulness. But even conceding the problems with structural-functionalist arguments, it seems reasonable to expect that on balance, the CCP's rank and file help tax collection. About one fourth of all rural households are party households (defined as having at least one party member in the household). Therefore, as long as the patronage distributed to each party household is not four times the amount of additional taxes extracted from all village households as a result of the party presence, overall the party improves extractive capacity. Thus the conjecture is that the party strengthens the state even in purely monetary terms.[34]

Hypothesis H$_3$: Taking into account both the contribution by party members to tax-collecting efforts and the privileges that party members enjoy, overall the CCP's presence in the countryside strengthens the material base of the state.

4.2 HYPOTHESES ON EXTRACTION IN THE URBAN SECTOR

The fiscal resources collected in the countryside pale in comparison to those collected in the cities. The preceding analysis of the rural sector provides an intuition about the role of the CCP in urban tax collection, and about the mechanism through which the party contributes to tax collection. Such an intuition is essential, because the interaction between government agencies and the party's rank and file is much more opaque in the cities. This section proceeds in three steps. It first demonstrates that negotiation is a central feature of China's tax system, so that there is room to determine taxes on a case-by-case basis. Provided that tax agencies are sufficiently well-informed, negotiation can help to increase extractive capacity, similar to negotiated prices helping to increase the profits of a price-discriminating monopolist. Second, the section describes the persisting presence of party cells in the industrial sector, being well embedded in many firms, despite the transformation to a (state-dominated) market economy. Third and finally, the section shows that party cells have a mandate to enforce legal rules, at least up to a point, and have the means to play a pivotal role in administrating local taxes. As before, without denying that party members are also self-serving, the central hypothesis is that a greater presence of the CCP will lead to higher taxation rates. A quantitative test of this hypothesis is deferred to Section 4.4, which shows that the amounts of resource extraction facilitated by the CCP make a substantial difference to the fiscal base of the People's Republic.

4.2.1 Discretion in Industrial Tax Collection

If tax agencies in China were perfectly informed and applied fully standardized procedures, the CCP would have little room in tax collection. Yet in fact, tax collection is fraught with irregularities, across all sources of revenue. Even the value-added tax (VAT), which for a long time has been the most important source of revenue, accounting for 25 percent of all revenues in 2014, is known for its inconsistent collection techniques[35] and loopholes. One dissertation studying VAT losses points to their gigantic scale and lays out common ways that allow for tax avoidance and tax evasion, especially the widespread use of manipulated invoices. Such practices are to be expected in a context where tax regulations require invoices that do not occur as a "natural" by-product of actual business transactions. Apart from asymmetric information problems between tax agency and tax payer, the dissertation discovers that asymmetric information between different government agencies also cause tax irregularities. While mainly focusing on institutional imperfections, including rent-seeking by tax authorities, in one section the author suspects that the system also faces a cultural problem: Citing Laozi and Confucius along with attitudes toward invoices, he argues that justice and equal treatment are not a core concern in the domain of taxation, expected neither by taxpayers nor by tax agencies.[36]

As a result, negotiation is the hallmark of taxation. Unsurprisingly, as in many other countries, the central government negotiates with provincial governments over the division of fiscal revenues. More unusual, lower-level agencies also haggle among themselves – within the same hierarchical level and across hierarchical levels – to determine who retains what share of local fiscal revenues. These negotiations cover all major sources of tax revenues and a number of minor taxes. For instance, during research in China I have come across an overview of the various fiscal arrangements, compiled by the budget office of one provincial-level Department of Finance. The division of revenues between prefectures and their subordinate counties varies across – and to some extent within – prefectures, as well as across different revenue types.[37] Over the past few years, some counties even have achieved a preferential status as a "directly governed county," which implies that they no longer have to share their revenues with the prefecture.[38] Apart from taxes, other fiscal revenues, related to state-owned companies and public investment projects, provide additional room for bargaining between different levels and different sectors of government: A state-owned company might belong to the provincial government, but the county and even township government where the company is placed are usually important stakeholders who expect parts of the company's revenues.

Accustomed to the idea that tax collection is a negotiation process vis-à-vis *state-owned* companies, tax departments do not use a radically different approach vis-à-vis *privately owned* companies. As accountants know well from their everyday experience, the broad discretion that tax official have is related to tax reporting rules that are completely inconsistent with accounting rules – the "tax versus accounting gap" 税會差異. This definitional gap creates ambiguity, blurring the line between tax avoidance and tax evasion. To make sure that this gap is not interpreted to the disadvantage of the state, local government sometimes send in teams to investigate the accounts and make "special tax adjustments." Only a small percentage of firms receive such teams, often resulting in major tax payments.[39] Given how widespread the practice of tax avoidance is, the decision to pick some company and send in an investigation team thus gives tax departments very substantive room for making their own decisions about whom to single out for additional extraction.

Much more could have been done to further develop taxation rules and reduce ambiguities. From a perspective of fairness, one might wish for a tax system whose rules can never be bent. But an inflexible system also has disadvantages, especially when tax legislation cannot keep up with a quickly evolving and diverse economic system. A developmental state with its focus on economic growth may wish to modify tax rules on a case-by-case basis in such a way as to encourage fresh investments and prevent bankruptcies. Similarly, when the state seeks to increase company taxes in the long-run, a most promising approach would be to tax profits only to the extent that they are not reinvested, requiring in-depth company analyses and even negotiations with company owners.

Developmental concerns certainly are high on the agenda of tax offices throughout China.

Decades of economic growth have alleviated the pressure on the government to reform the tax system. Government revenues have been abundant, growing even faster than the economy. To be sure, tax regulations are evolving from year to year. Yet taking a historical perspective and comparing the changes of recent years to the radical transformations of the early Deng era (after 1978), or even the revamping of the system in the first half of the 1990s, more recent reforms are less comprehensive.[40] To keep up with the rapidly diversifying economy and with businesses eager to avoid taxes wherever they can, much more would be needed to institutionalize the rules.

4.2.2 The Presence of the CCP in Companies

Three decades after Deng Xiaoping's economic reforms that dismantled the Socialist planned economy and with it the work unit system, the CCP maintains its prominent place in the industrial workplace. Not only has the party defended its position in state-owned companies; it has successfully established itself in private companies as well. To be sure, Socialist work units have long lost their erstwhile power, which used to place them along with their associated party cell at the center of social service provision and also allowed them to regulate people's lives.[41] Yet party cells have adjusted to a new context and remain powerful agents under *Socialism with Chinese Characteristics*. Their time-honored sources of power – instrumental and personal ties cultivated by disciplined party organizations – tap into modes of exercising authority that predate the Maoist era[42] and that have survived it as well.

It is hard to understate the intensity of the party's involvement in factories for a long period of time. The CCP is certainly well acquainted with politics in industrial companies. Decades before the Communist takeover of 1949, party organizers mobilized followers in the factories of agglomerations like Shanghai,[43] and in the mining industry or among railway workers in more remote localities.[44] After the takeover, factories remained challenging to the new regime, as workers now laid claim to the fruits of their revolution.[45] The prerevolutionary cadre was best acquainted with the factory floor, but the postrevolutionary party learned to deal with the managerial side of administering the industry. In the leadup to nationalizing private industry, party cadres investigated the management and gained deep insight into business operations, including through a major anticorruption campaign in the early 1950s.[46] The CCP needed to be alert to worker demands and economic imperatives, as they mediated distributive conflicts and designed welfare policies that invariably created winners and losers.[47]

After the capitalist turn, marked by the Reform and Opening policies of 1978, the party has by no means disappeared from the firms. According to detailed party statistics of the year 2008 from one large province, comprising some of the most advanced industries along the coastline as well as more traditional industries in its hinterland, party cells are well represented throughout large parts of the industry. In the state sector, which employs more people than the private sector, 95 percent of firms have at least a party cell, if not a general cell or a full-fledged party committee; 18.1 percent of employees are party members. In firms where there is no party cell, more often than not the CCP's organization department already has found an entry point for establishing a presence in the future – for example, by organizing party cells with responsibilities for more than one firm, or by recruiting party members reporting to a nonindustry party cell.[48]

In the private sector, the party is not as omnipresent. Statistics for the same province show that 31 precent of private-sector firms have at least a party cell; 5 percent of the employees are party members. Disconcertingly for party organizers, over half of the firms do not employ even a single party member.[49] For all of China, at the end of 2014 roughly half of all 30 million private companies were covered by a party organization.[50] On the one hand, we have to keep in mind that the party probably is better represented at larger companies, which also matter most. But on the other hand, these estimates overestimate the reach of the CCP – potentially severely, since they do not count firms in the informal sector, which are below the radar of the party state. In the villages, the situation is not much better. Party organizers are working hard to further improve the CCP's presence in the private sector. Aware that party members who migrate from the countryside to urban factories, and between factories, tend to lose touch with the organization, Gansu province started a "double search" movement. Relying on social media such as QQ and Weibo, but also on personal contacts, "the organization was to search for its members, and the members were to search for their organization."[51]

Apart from showing the zeal with which the party seeks to enter firms, this latter campaign also raises questions about the effectiveness of party organizations: A larger number of party cells do not necessarily indicate a stronger state presence. Presumably, most of the lost party members targeted by Gansu's double search policy are migrant workers who have left their rural village and come to work in urban factories. At the bottom of the urban pecking order, these individuals may be in a privileged position to keep the party-state connected to the more afflicted strata of society.[52] But migrants would have limited insights into managerial matters. As far as one can tell from statistics, in both public and private companies, roughly half of all party members are on the factory floor and the other half in administration, indicating that overall the presence of party members is well balanced.[53] To evaluate the effectiveness of the CCP inside private firms, more detailed investigations are necessary. Chinese researchers, often belonging to one of the many Institutes for Marxist Studies, have engaged in such studies through surveys. The message of such studies is mixed and in sync with the data presented earlier. The CCP has made significant inroads into private firms, but the party's presence is highly uneven, with some party cells being much more actively engaged than others.[54]

4.2.3 The Functions of the CCP in the Industrial Sector

Party cells embedded in public and private companies fulfill a number of responsibilities. Managing labor relations is high on their agenda, as one would expect from a party with historical roots in a labor movement.[55] While the labor unions are to defuse conflict before it turns disruptive, the party is in charge of crisis management once strikes occur.[56] But the responsibilities of the party are defined much more comprehensively. Reference material for cadres, edited under the watch of the CCP's powerful Central Organization Department, begins its enumeration of tasks to be carried out by the party inside private companies as follows:

(i) 宣傳貫徹黨和國家的路線方針政策，引導和監督企業遵守國家的法律、法規，依法經營，照章納稅。
Propagate the implementation of the party's and the state's principal policies, guide and supervise companies' compliance with government laws and regulations, the legality of the companies' operations and payment of taxes according to the rules.

(ii) 關心企業生產經營的重大問題，提出意見和建議，支持和促進企業發展。
Take care of important problems of production and management, make comments and proposals, support and advance companies' development.

...

(ix) 完成上級黨組織交辦的任務。
Carry out tasks assigned by higher-level party authorities.[57]

The party's role in tax collection is the most specific task at the very top of its agenda. The other responsibilities further down in the list of tasks also include managing labor relations and maintaining a vibrant and disciplined party organization.

The definition of tasks is also notable for setting conflicting goals. This is obvious, for instance, when it comes to environmental standards: Under the first task, party cells are supposed to watch over their implementation, but given their high costs to the firm the party cell should show flexibility, in the name of promoting company growth under its second task. With tax extraction, the party cell faces similarly competing goals. Should the party cell emphasize stricter interpretation of tax legislation, or should it lobby for lighter treatment? With firms in a period of quick expansion, it can be in the best interest not only of the firm, but also of the state, to be lenient on taxes in the short run, in order to achieve growth and receive more tax revenues in the long run. Whereas government agents do not have enough information to understand the situation of the firm, party cells are uniquely well placed to make an informed judgment, emphasizing more stringent compliance with tax regulations at times when the company is flush with cash and pleading for lenience from the tax department at times when liquidity is needed to avoid bankruptcy or to promote a growth strategy.

Party meetings in various formats ensure that information circulates within the party apparatus. In principle, all party cells should meet once a week. Party members participate in training activities, ranging from formal workshops to informal tourist excursions, where much information is exchanged across different firms and institutions. The higher one's position in the hierarchy, the more one will be invited to fora outside one's firm. Sometimes the party establishes work committees 工作委員會 to facilitate contacts between party cells in different government agencies on the one hand and in private firms on the other. Looking through the list of 280 people invited to a training session organized by a work committee, one finds representatives from Siemens and other big companies, from party cells formed jointly across smaller companies based on their location in the same building, and from party cells inside local government agencies.[58] Significantly, not only party secretaries but also other selected party members participate in such meetings. In addition, the meeting encompasses only companies from the communication sector, bringing together firms that are in competition on the market. By relying on parallel communication channels in a Leninist fashion, the CCP prevents lower-level cadres from keeping secrets from their superiors.

Organizational arrangements and multiple meeting formats help information find its way, directly or indirectly, from party cells in companies to party cells in the fiscal bureaucracy.

At the receiving end of the information, party cells in the tax offices also do not hold narrowly bureaucratic views of enforcing tax payments. Under instructions from the local party secretary, they are at least as concerned about economic growth as they are about tax regulations. Take the example of a member of a party cell in the National Tax Office in one remote prefecture of Shandong province. In an interview, before going through the formal regulations, he describes the context of the tax office's work in broad geostrategic terms, pointing to the country's 一带一路 One Belt One Road policy: the development of a "silk road economic belt" and of a "21st-century maritime silk road." The key task of the tax office, from the perspective of this official, is to support local economic growth in the context of this major national policy, for example by opening up a 綠色通道 "green channel" to facilitate trade with Korea through easy tax rebates.[59] Tax offices use their discretion, which can be considerable, to promote economic growth. To do this successfully, they need precisely the information that party cells in companies can provide.

To summarize, a close observation of party cells inside companies lead one to expect that taxes are higher for firms where the party is more present. Party cells are specifically tasked with enforcing tax regulations. Party cells are omnipresent in the still very large state-run sector, and also very present at least in the bigger companies of the nonstate sector. They are well embedded and well connected, creating quasi-ideal conditions for information to travel from companies to the government, alleviating asymmetric information problems. Section 4.4 not only tests whether the party contributes to extraction, but also estimates the size of the party effect. Before that numerical study of the urban sector, the next section returns to the countryside to carry out an empirical test there.

4.3 THE WORM'S EYE VIEW: EXTRACTION IN THE COUNTRYSIDE

To test the hypotheses about the CCP's role in taxation, this section uses household-level data and analyzes the variation of taxation rates in rural China. While tax collection in the countryside is of secondary importance for the state coffers, it affects the livelihood of about half the country's population. Thanks to the availability of the rural data set at the household level, this section can evaluate the dual role of rank-and-file party members: While letting the households of its members enjoy tax privileges, overall the presence of party members in a village increases the state's tax extractive capacity.

4.3.1 Empirical Data and Specification

Under the umbrella of the Chinese Household Income Project (CHIP), a joint international research effort led by Li Shih from Beijing Normal University, the Chinese Academy of Social Sciences has carried out a series of surveys among Chinese rural and urban households at regular intervals since 1988.[60] The primary goal of the project is to estimate household income, and the survey is recognized by economists for its accuracy – especially the high standards in the sampling process, which make this survey representative at the national level and at lower levels as well, depending on the edition.[61] The project consists of a household survey, which is complemented by focus group interviews of village leaders to respond to questions about the village. The questionnaires include a changing set of variables related to the political economy, whose potential has barely been explored for political science. For the purposes here, the 2002 edition of the survey contains all the necessary information (Table 4.2).

The CHIP data provide robust information on the microvariation of state extractive capacity. Because questions about taxes, levies, and fees are highly politically sensitive at a time when the peasant burden is one of

TABLE 4.2 *Descriptive statistics of the CHIP survey, 2002 edition*

	Mean	Std. Dev.	Minimum	Maximum
Main Variables of Interest				
Levy Paid in 2002	143	264	0	2,990
Village Party Strength [%]	8.9	3.4	0	23
Household Party Membership [dummy]	0.21			
Control Variables (not including dummies)				
Distance to County Seat [km]	24	20	0.5	160
Distance to Township Seat [km]	5	5	0	33
Household Income [Yuan]	10,873	8,401	0	139,807
Household Cultivated Land [Mu]	6.2	6.1	0	78
Household Size	4	1	1	11
Village Population	1,852	1,192	186	8,815

All statistics exclude Xinjiang and other outliers, as described in the text.

the most salient issues on the political agenda, there are clear limits to the information enumerators could possibly elicit on such a large scale, from more than 38,000 individuals. But the survey has the merit of investigating the whole picture of household finances. Taxes, levies, and fees are just several lines among literally hundreds of questions on other aspects of household finances. Moreover, survey designers try to match income and expenditures, just like a balance sheet, further increasing the likelihood that both income and expenditures are quite fully recorded. Since the survey has been regularly fielded since the 1980s, it routinely includes questions about the nonmonetary and the informal-sector economy of rural China; it is one of the most sophisticated surveys used in any non-OECD country. The richness of the data must be emphasized, because as this chapter now moves from concepts to measurement, it is not so much problems with the data, but challenges in defining what is meant by concepts such as "extraction" and "state," which require attention.

From the household survey, levies are calculated in three steps. First, the calculation adds up the following categories of household expenditures:[62] payments to the village 村提留, payments to the village and town 鄉鎮統籌, other fees for collective contracts and educational fees. Each category comprises cash payments as well as in-kind contributions, which have been turned into monetary values by the National Bureau of Statistics survey team. Second, the calculation multiplies the days of unpaid labor, as reported by the household, with the daily wage for labor reported by village officials.[63] Third, the calculation adds any payments a household has made to buy its members out of labor contributions.[64] The calculation does not include penalties, because of doubts about the reliability of the data and because they would amount only to a minor share of the peasant burden in 2002, namely 1.2 percent.

The data include observations from Xinjiang, which risks confounding the coefficient estimates. The ethnic conflict between Han Chinese and Uighur citizens does not allow the party to function in the ordinary way, and very unusual arrangements in the domain of fiscal affairs do not sit well with the argument presented earlier. Therefore the 400 household-level observations from Xinjiang are excluded. Furthermore, two counties were rolling out the tax-for-fee reform right at the time when the questionnaire was fielded. This creates problems for interpretation, and there is concern that the questionnaire in the minds of respondents was an integral part of the tax-for-fee reform, prompting strategic answers. Thus, another 170 households from these counties are excluded. After these two adjustments, the data set contains observations for 8,630 households in

436 villages in 112 counties in 21 provinces. Finally, there are drastic out-liers in the ratio of party member households in the population. To pre-vent these outliers from unduly influencing the results, the analysis sets to "missing" the twenty observations that are more than four standard deviations above the sample mean (two villages). Taking into account the various problems of missing data in the original data set, the analysis ulti-mately can still work with 7,390 observations.

The empirical specification for testing hypotheses H_1 and H_2 predicts that the amount of levies to be paid by a household (in logarithmic form) increases as a linear function of the number of party members in a village, and decreases if at least one household member belongs to the CCP. In other word, the empirical specification is designed to capture the dual effect of the party.

$$Ln(Levy) = a * party - presence + b * party - membership$$
$$+ \overset{*}{,} distance_{county} + d * distance^2_{county} + e * distance_{township}$$
$$+ f * distance^2_{township} + g * household + h * village + county$$
$$(4.1)$$

Household Control Variables. The regression includes three control variables for household characteristics. First, all specifications control for the area of the land cultivated by the household, since village leaders use cultivated land as a proxy for household revenues and as a base for their tax assessments. Richer households – singled out as those using more land – are expected to contribute more to common projects than poorer households. Second, the assessment of levies sometimes also depends on household size, which is controlled for. Finally, the regression controls for household income, although the income of a household does not play an important role in the assessment of taxes in rural China.

Other Controls. The baseline specification controls for county fixed effects. Apart from village population size, the regression includes the fol-lowing dummy control variables

- Physical Geography: Is the village located in a mountainous area? In a hilly area?
- Village Finances: Does the village have income from collective enter-prises? Is it in debt? Did the village have any industries during the Mao period? Did the village experience any kind of calamity during the last year (very broadly defined in China to include bad weather)?

- Official Designations: Is the village located in a county nationally recognized as poor? Is it located in a county recognized as poor by the province? Is it located in a township recognized as poor by the province? Has the village been designated as an experimental spot to carry out a pilot project?
- Connections: Is there any official working at the county level or above who originates from this village? – A surprising 52 percent report that they do have such connections.
- Political Interest: Are people checking the documents and village fiscal statistics published on the village blackboard?

Estimate coefficients for two alternative specifications are consistent with the findings. Including county fixed effects greatly reduces the variation of some variables and thus is a particularly hard test to pass. An alternative specification leaves out fixed effects. Because the regression still contains a large set of meaningful control variables, one can be confident that the result does not suffer from omitted variable bias. Without the county fixed effect, the specification also adds two variables that indicate whether a village is part of a nationally or provincially designated poor county with the accompanying political and media attention. It also moves from the logarithmic baseline model to a simple linear model, so that the coefficients can be interpreted in absolute terms instead of percentages.

4.3.2 Results and Illustration

As the regression coefficients and their high statistical significance shows, there is a systematic relationship between taxation rates and party presence. The first substantive column of Table 4.3 lists the coefficient estimates in the logarithmic baseline specification, controlling for a large number of household and village characteristics, and including county fixed effects. The two coefficients related to the party point in the predicted direction and are significant. The role of the CCP in the process of levy extraction – and by implication the role of the party in the exercise of power by Chinese local governments – is characterized by an implicit quid pro quo. Households containing at least one party member on average contribute 15 percent less in levies. But on the other hand, the existence of party networks facilitates levy extraction: An increase in party membership by one percentage point is associated with a 1.8 percent increase of levies from all villagers. Within normal parameters[65] this certainly is a

TABLE 4.3 *Party presence and rural households' fiscal burden*

	Preferred specification	W/o fixed effects w/o logarithm
Party Presence		
Number of party members in the village	1.80*	543***
Does household include party member?	−0.15**	−20**
Legitimate Factors: Household Characteristics		
Household Cultivated Land	0.05***	6.24***
Household Income [1000 Yuan]	0.08.	16**
Household Size	0.06**	4.0
Physical distance from power		
Distance to county seat	0.01**	1.16**
Distance to county seat, squared	−0.00***	−0.01***
Distance to township seat	0.05***	14***
Distance to township seat, squared	−0.00*	−0.43***
Village Characteristics		
Mountainous area	−0.67***	−80***
Hilly area	−0.13	−35***
Village has collective revenue	−0.04	16*
Village has debts	0.05	10.
Village with industrial history	−0.22***	−13*
Village experienced calamity	0.13*	.09
Village located in national poor county	−0.57***	−38***
Village located in provincial poor county	0.24*	65***
Village located in officially poor township	0.42***	−3.4
Village designated as pilot case	−0.28***	−14*
Village population [1,000 people]	−0.00.	−0.01**
Village with good connections	−0.11*	−27***
Village level of political interest	−0.02	12*
Constant	−0.14	−110*

*** Significance at 0.001, ** significance at 0.01, * significance at 0.05, . at 0.1
Notes: OLS estimators. 7,390 household observations. Dependent variable: Tax-like expenditures in the year 2002. *Source:* CHIP survey, available from ICPSR, University of Michigan.

good deal for the government. The bridges that party organizations build into village communities improves extractive capacity, albeit at a price.

To illustrate the findings and the magnitudes of the effect, Yanggu County may serve as an example. Yanggu county is an unexceptional county in the western part of Shandong, whose level of economic development is close to the national average: The average household income in 2002 was 2,265 yuan, as compared to a national average of 2,454 yuan.

TABLE 4.4 *Rural tax extraction as a prisoner's dilemma*

		Household A	
		Joins party	Does not join party
Household B	Joins party	Both pay "normally"	A pays very high taxes B pays very low taxes
	Does not join party	A pays very low taxes B pays very high taxes	Equilibrium: both pay high taxes

Table 4.4 presents predicted values of how much a household has to pay in terms of levies, depending on whether there is at least one party member in the household, and whether the household lives in the sample village with most party members (17%) or in the village with fewest party members (7%). We know that it is advantageous for a household to join the party. However, there is a collective action problem. It would be better for a household to be a nonparty member and live in a village with few other party members, rather than be a party member in a village with many other party members. If the majority of party members in the village with 17 percent party members (upper-right cell) would collectively decide to leave the party, this group of defecting party members would lose their 14 percent membership privilege. But since this collective action would remove the village somewhat from party control, on balance the defecting party members would gain 3 percent (lower-left cell). Admittedly, this slight improvement would not motivate people to defect from the party. From the point of the party that seeks to motivate members by material advantages, however, the fact that the exit option is profitable could potentially be a weakness (Table 4.5).

This illustration suggests that one could describe the function of the party as turning the taxation "game" into a prisoner's dilemma, profitable to the state, and profitable to whoever gains from the state's fiscal activity in the countryside. The point is not that citizens are necessarily opposed to taxation – after all, they may appreciate the public goods they receive in return. But naturally citizens would usually prefer someone else to pay

TABLE 4.5 *Levy extraction through the CCP*

	Village with 7% membership	Village with 17% membership
Party member	443	528
Non–party member	512	610

the bill. Narrowly evaluating the added value of the party in fiscal terms, relying on the party for rural tax extraction, despite the costs of providing privileges to its members, is a good deal for the state. Even in villages with many party members, they are a minority, so that the taxes collected thanks to the presence of additional party members can be expected, in light of the empirical analysis, to outweigh the fiscal losses from taxing party members lightly.

4.4 THE BIRD'S-EYE VIEW: EXTRACTION IN THE CITIES

Moving from the micro to the macro level, this section tests whether some provinces extract more revenues than others thanks to a greater number of party members. Mimicking an experimental design, a difference-in-differences approach isolates the association between party member recruitment and increases in tax revenues. Complementing the evidence of the preceding section, this section moves from the traditional rural-agricultural sector to the modern urban-industrial sector. As mentioned earlier, the traditional sector has long lost its significance for overall government revenues and is of interest mainly because it still reveals the operating principles of Chinese fiscal affairs. Nowadays, it is the modern sector that provides the state with its material bases and is of utmost salience to state-builders. Moreover, the following analysis comprehensively investigates overall tax revenues and compares provinces instead of households, thereby testing whether the micro-level mechanisms add up to important effects at the macro level. The substantively very important effects found here clearly warrant the distinction between pink and red provinces.

4.4.1 Causal Identification Strategy

To estimate the effect that CCP members have on tax collection efforts, the analysis deploys a difference-in-differences approach with a continuous treatment variable. This design mimics an experiment that assigns different numbers of party members to different jurisdictions and observes the effect on tax collection: Over the period from 1997 to 2007, between two CCP party congresses, additional party members are assigned to each Chinese province through recruitment. If party members help with tax collection, these additional party members should result in an increase in taxation levels during the period of the Tenth Five-Year Plan (2001–2005).[66] The difference-in-differences approach controls for the fact that the number of new recruits is *not* random by studying change over time.

What makes the difference-in-differences approach so valuable in the context of analyzing the party effect is that it significantly reduces concerns about path-dependent effects confounding the result. If the main argument of this book is right, historical legacies that are related to party member recruitment before the Communist takeover of 1949 still influence outcomes today. By analyzing the rate of change in party membership, the analysis controls for some effects of history. As Chapter 6 shows, the preexisting number of party members is a main determinant for party membership. In other words, the growth rate of party membership is not independent of the initial stock of party members, though this applies somewhat less since the early 1990s. This is a problem for the analysis, because at the same time, the initial stock of party members should also affect fiscal revenues. To address this problem, the number of CCP members prior to the quasi-experiment is included in the specification. In addition, population serves as a control variable for size effects. Finally, distance from Beijing is often cited in conversations as influencing any number of local outcomes. Although not entirely plausible in an era where transportation costs vary little, thanks to air transportation, the specification controls for distance from Beijing.

$$Revenue_{i,t} = \alpha + \beta * T_{i,t} + \gamma * R_i + \delta * T_{i,t} * R_i + \epsilon * C_i + u_{i,t} \quad (4.2)$$

Revenues are observed for every province i at two points in time t. T is a dummy indicating whether an observation is pretreatment (beginning of five-year plan, 2001) or posttreatment (end of five-year plan, 2005). R counts the number of recruits between the Fifteenth Party Congress in 1997 and the Seventeenth Party Congresses in 2007. C is a vector of five province-level control variables: Population in 2002, Gross Regional Product in 2002, distance from Beijing, the same distance squared, and number of party members in 1997. u is the error term. The average treatment effect is equal to δ.

Although the specification by design controls for community-level characteristic that could bias the effect of party membership on fiscal revenues, this does not rule out the theoretical possibility that additional fiscal revenues generate additional party members. The substantive context suggests that such reverse causation is unlikely. First, there certainly is not an explicit mechanism that connects fiscal revenues to recruitment, because fiscal revenues do not appear as a relevant concern in the planning documents. Second, unlike when hiring an additional official, there is no apparent cost to admitting an additional party member. Although the membership fee may not cover the costs for administering a party member and providing him with training, especially at a time of quick fiscal expansion, these costs are negligible compared to political considerations. These assumptions seem much safer than the assumptions one would typically need for design-based inference, say, by constructing a natural experiment.[67]

The same specification is tested for other outcome variables as well, to test the robustness of the findings and to identify what areas of the fiscal administration are most dependent on party members. Apart from overall revenues, eight alternative outcome variables are used. Two specifications juxtapose the role of the party members for revenues that go to the central government and those that go to the province. Next, four specifications analyze the major kinds of taxes – excluding customs duties – separately: VAT, business tax, corporate income tax, and personal income tax. Finally, the role of the CCP in generating tax revenues is compared to its role in generating no-tax revenues.

4.4.2 Newly Available Data

Thanks to material from the budget office of the Chinese Finance Ministry,[68] the following analysis stands on an unusually firm empirical basis. The key improvement over more widely available statistics is the inclusion of taxes that provincial governments remit to the central government. Widely available statistics report local revenues 地方收入 but mention neither overall revenues 總收入 nor remittances 上劃中央, explaining that this latter category of resources – though collected in the province – belongs to the center. Remittances are sensitive information, since they reveal the redistribution of resources among Chinese provinces. It is easily justifiable why Beijing remits 61 percent of revenues collected in its jurisdictions to the central government, which also spends a lot of resources in the capital. However, it might be contentious that Yunnan retains only 42 percent compared to the 62 percent retained by Inner Mongolia. Thus, it is no surprise that national-level aggregate data are well known, but that it is hard to come by provincially disaggregated information on remittances from the provinces to the center. Because on average about half of the revenues collected in a province belong to the central government, inclusion of remittances avoids a severe measurement error.[69] Getting this information from one unusually well-placed data source, instead of culling it from diverse sources, further improves reliability as uniform definitions apply.

TABLE 4.6 *Party member effect on urban fiscal capacity (diff-in-diff)*

Dependent Variable	All Revenues	Central Revenues	Local Revenues	VAT	Business Tax	Business Income Tax	Individual Income Tax	Tax Revenue	Non-tax Revenue
Year = 2005	30 (0.2)	8.8 (0.1)	17 (0.3)	-0.2 (-0.0)	-0.8 (-0.0)	9.2 (0.9)	-1.2 (-0.2)	8.4 (0.1)	7.2 (0.8)
Recruitment	-10 (-0.3)	-0.4 (-0.0)	-9.7 (-0.5)	-2.5 (-0.8)	-0.7 (-0.1)	10.7** (3.2)	1.4 (0.7)	10 (0.6)	-21*** (-7.1)
Year * Recruitment	121*** (4.3)	69*** (4.1)	53*** (4.4)	11*** (5.4)	17*** (3.5)	-1.3 (-0.6)	1.1 (0.9)	40** (3.4)	13*** (7.1)
Population	-0.08 (-1.2)	-0.04 (-1.2)	-0.03 (-1.2)	-0.01* (-2.1)	-0.01 (-1.1)	-0.01** (-2.8)	-0.00 (-0.9)	-0.06* (-2.0)	0.02*** (5.2)
Gross Regional Product	0.24*** (9.5)	0.11*** (7.7)	0.12*** (11.4)	0.02*** (12.0)	0.04*** (8.3)	0.02*** (11.0)	0.01*** (9.9)	0.11*** (10.1)	0.01*** (7.4)
Distance Beijing	-0.17 (-0.8)	-0.15 (-1.1)	-0.00 (-0.0)	0.02 (1.0)	0.03 (0.6)	0.01 (0.6)	-0.00 (-0.3)	0.03 (0.3)	-0.03. (-2.0)
Distance Beijing Squared	54 (0.6)	48 (0.9)	-6.1 (-0.2)	-6.4 (-1.1)	-11.1 (-0.8)	-5.8 (-0.9)	0.10 (0.0)	-18 (-0.5)	12* 2.3
Party Members in 1997	-17 (-1.3)	-10 (-1.3)	-7.1 (-1.3)	-0.2 (-0.2)	-3.8 (-1.7)	-1.3 (-1.3)	-1.4* (-2.6)	-115 (-1.0)	-1.4 (-1.6)

*** Significance at 0.001, ** significance at 0.01, * significance at 0.05, . significance at 0.1
Difference-in-differences approach. OLS estimators. 60 observations. Data sources: Party member recruitment from CCP Organization Department, 2011, 中國共產黨內統計資料彙編, fiscal data from Chinese Finance Ministry, Budget Office, 2006, 中國省以下財政體制, population data from National Bureau of Statistics, various years, 中國統計年鑑.

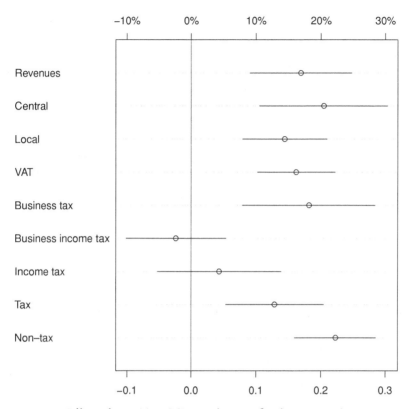

FIGURE 4.1 Effect of recruiting CCP members on fiscal revenues. Average treatment effect associated with the recruitment of 100,000 new CCP members on fiscal capacity. Calculation based on Table 4.6

4.4.3 Results

As shown in Table 4.6, the average treatment effect is highly significant and substantially important for most of the outcome variables under consideration. Recruitment of an additional 100,000 party members between the two party congresses is associated with an increase in provincial revenues by 12 trillion yuan (USD 2 trillion) during the tenth five-year plan, controlling for associations between recruitment and taxation levels that are unrelated to the treatment period. Variation in the number of recruits by 100,000 party members is very normal; it corresponds to just one fourth of a standard deviation. Figure 4.1 shows how substantively important the treatment effect is compared to the average volume of the various taxes involved. The treatment effect amounts to a 17 percent increase in overall tax extraction and is somewhat higher for taxes submitted to the central government (20%) compared to taxes kept in the province (14%). The average treatment effect is much larger for nontax revenues (22%) than for narrowly defined taxes (13%). For the two types of taxes where the party makes a difference, recruitment of 100,000 additional party members leads to a 16 percent (18%) increase.

For the Corporate as well as the Individual Income Tax, an increased presence of the party has no significant effect. Although both taxes have existed since 1980, they have become more relevant only in the past decade in the context of experimentation with modernized tax collection procedures. The procedures for collecting income taxes differ from the more traditional taxes, and in the case of the personal income tax, having informers in the taxpayer's work unit is unlikely to create better information than information about revenues provided to the government by its banks.

4.5 CONCLUSION: EXTRACTION IN PINK VS. RED PROVINCES

Because more CCP members lead to better policy implementation and more effective tax collection, it makes sense for the party to expand its membership base. This does not mean, however, that more party members are always better. One cannot extrapolate to as-yet-untested levels of party penetration, which lie outside the current experiential horizon.[70] Beyond a certain "optimal" point, membership growth might be counterproductive. Most importantly, the more people are recruited, the less stringent the selection criteria, and the less reliable the resulting pool of party members. The party publicly addresses concerns over the quality of party members, as in one official announcement that "the composition of the CCP membership ranks has advanced toward an optimal development and the quality of party members is incessantly increasing."[71] Since 2006 membership growth has slowed down,[72] and by 2014 the party had grown more reluctant to accept new members,[73] with the result of a marked 15 percent fewer individuals designated as recruitment targets 發展黨員.[74] In addition to the quality of new members, the provision of privileges to new party members also comes at a cost. In the context of revenue collection, in addition to the direct fiscal costs of granting informal tax exemptions, one might have to add the hard-to-quantify costs in terms of regime legitimacy. These costs of the privileges enjoyed by party members might be one important reason why the CCP's Organization Department has limited the growth of the party's membership base, despite the apparent contributions by the party's rank and file.

Party members are likely to remain involved in tax collection well into the future. To be sure, tax authorities pursue an agenda of institutionalizing tax collection, to reduce opportunities for corruption and to live up to their own sense of professionalism. But in light of the empirical results in this chapter, this process of formalization seems to be much more effective in some areas of taxation than in others. It certainly is not a coincidence that the two taxes for whose collection the CCP is relevant are also the ones that have been the predominant sources of government revenues for decades. By contrast, the business income tax and the personal income tax have become salient only in recent times and are modeled on taxation strategies in the developed countries. Given the nature of the party state, where the party is seen as legitimately dominating all branches of government, the party in the domain of tax collection may also not automatically appear as an illegitimate interloper. In fact, one should keep in mind that the party, including the lawmakers at the top and the party members on the ground, have no reason to take themselves out of the picture of tax collection, thereby making themselves indispensable. The more the party stays involved in everyday tasks such as tax collection, the less superfluous it makes itself. Collecting taxes is a quintessentially routine task of any government in the world, where the CCP's rank and file prove their value to the state on an everyday basis. Another question is what role the party might play in terms of crisis, when state-builders seek to maintain order. The next chapter addresses this question by turning from routine governance to governance in times of crisis.

PART III

THE PARTY'S ORIGINS

5

War Contingencies at the Origin of the CCP's Power Base

沒有你們皇軍侵略大半個中國，中國人民就不能團結起來對付你們，中國共產黨就奪取不了政權. If it wasn't for your Imperial Army invading most of China, the Chinese people could not have united to deal with you and the CCP would not have been able to seize power.

Mao Zedong[1]

Having demonstrated in the previous two chapters that the party's penetration of local communities is extremely consequential, this chapter turns to history in order to explore why the party is so much more present in some localities than in others to begin with. Founded in 1921, the CCP was on the run for the first decade and a half of its existence. After the party's near-defeat in Southern China and the Long March, the survivors took refuge in a remote mountain area known as the Yan'an base area, with few prospects of future success. Yet the fate of the party was to change dramatically, because the outbreak of the Sino-Japanese War in 1937 granted the CCP a second chance. The enemy not only shielded the party from persecution by the incumbent government, which under the circumstances had little choice but to agree to a united front. In addition, the foreign aggression facilitated recruitment among civilians most affected by the war. Behind Japanese enemy lines, Communists set up local party branches and even full-fledged governments. Many of these institutions would be kept intact until the foundation of the People's Republic. This chapter explains how the geographic patterns of Japanese occupation shaped the party's rank-and-file power base until the eve of the Communist takeover in 1949. That these early membership patterns persisted even after 1949 and are still reflected in the party's power base today is demonstrated by the following Chapter 6.

As reflected in the epigraph, Mao Zedong recognized that the Japanese invasion provided the CCP with a golden opportunity for mobilizing the masses and for reviving the Communist movement. The blunt realism of Mao's assessment – even cynicism, considering the human toll of the war – invites the question to what extent the CCP's commitment to fighting the Japanese was propaganda to recruit citizens in the fight against the CCP's primary enemy, namely the incumbent Kuomintang (KMT). Did the CCP contribute as much as it could to the war effort? It could have been a smart strategy to save strength for the coming conflict with the KMT, which might have been a more potent challenger than usually claimed.[2] Without disputing the human sacrifices made by both parties, as well as unaffiliated citizens, both CCP and KMT propaganda barely credit the outside actor who was indispensible for the eventual defeat of Japan, namely the United States.[3] Seventy years after the war the legitimacy of the CCP, at least in part, feeds on its widely propagated merits of saving the nation from Japanese colonization. In that sense the Japanese invasion continues to provide the CCP with opportunities.

The patriotic cause was serving the CCP, so that one should not ascribe unadulterated patriotism to the Communist organizers. Similarly, one must question the importance of popular patriotism against Japan for facilitating recruitment. An idealistic interpretation holds that ordinary Chinese developed a sense of patriotism that inspired them to fight alongside the CCP as the only party to keep the nation's flag flying. This assessment was widely expressed by leaders at the time (see Section 5.1.2). The political scientist Chalmers Johnson argues that the CCP did in fact hold great patriotic appeal to peasants, who were disappointed by the incompetence of the incumbent KMT party in dealing with Japan's gradual encroachment and eventual invasion.[4] While aggression may indeed have engendered active patriotism among ordinariy Chinese,[5] the link between Japanese occupation and Communist build-up is not only about patriotism:[6] For one thing, peasants displaced by violence had little to lose and were easier recruitment targets for the CCP, compared to peasants who led poor but settled lives. Most important of all, CCP could grow behind Japanese enemy lines, because they were safe from persecution by the KMT, which had little choice but to agree to a united front policy.

The argument in this chapter deviates from the debates surrounding Johnson's initial hypothesis, because the goal is not to explain the root causes of Communist success, but regional patterns of party strength in the wake of World War II. The root causes of Communist success in China are found in a combination of factors, including socioeconomic conditions, landholding patterns, illegitimate local elites, and traditions of peasant uprising, but these have not been linked to the geographical patterns of Communist success. In fact, the existing literature draws attention to regional variation in the CCP's mobilization strategies, but does not explain this regional variation. The analysis here begins with the observation that the timing of events matters greatly for regional patterns of Communist success. The CCP was driven out of the places of its greatest initial success, but the party was lastingly successful in the places where it established a presence after the arrival of the Japanese, behind enemy lines. Although not a root cause for Communist success, Japanese occupation trumps other potential factors as an explanation for the party's regional patterns of success. In other words, this chapter is different from Johnson's initial argument in one fundamental respect. While Johnson considers Japanese occupation as the ultimate cause for overall Communist success, this chapter sees it as the predominant factor to explain subnational variation in the strength of Communist party buildup. While Japanese occupation is by no means the only determinant for the strength of local party organization, it goes a long way in explaining the uneven presence of the party. To explicate the link between the Japanese presence and organization-building outcomes, this chapter surveys existing scholarship and primary material before moving to a quantitative analysis, which takes into account that Japanese occupation in the statistical sense was not a random treatment.

The contemporary political map of China carries the imprint of the past. The state is most effective in red areas, thanks to the presence of many more party members, than in pink areas. The preceding two chapters have shown that this differential presence has far-reaching consequences for local government outcomes today. Similarly, the two chapters of Part IV will demonstrate that the presence of party members shaped outcomes during the Mao era. Moving back the causal chain, this chapter asks why some parts of China ended up being red, whereas others remained pink with less of a party presence. Exploring the origins of the party's power base, this chapter finds that war contingencies stand out as the paramount determinant for geographic patterns of party membership in 1949. The effect of war contingencies overrides other potential determinants of Communist party growth, such as landholding patterns or center/periphery divides. This chapter unpacks the notion of "war contingencies," conducting qualitative as well as a quantitative analyses. A key result is that patterns of Japanese occupation go a long way toward explaining the membership patterns at the foundation of the People's Republic.

The Republican era (1911–1949) was the CCP's formative period and laid the foundation for the party's future evolution. Most crucially, the Sino-Japanese War from 1937 to 1945 shaped the party's organization and ideology. Historical legacies of Japanese occupation are omnipresent in contemporary China. Innumerable TV series as well as museums around the country – big and small, sophisticated and dull, dovish and hawkish – not only keep this historical memory alive, but draft it for legitimizing CCP rule.[7] The party state is so anxious to control the historical discourse about this era that the relevant archives, namely the Second Historical Archives in Nanjing, have been practically off limits for research, at least until mid-2017. Based on preciously detailed overviews of the archives' content in one official publication – easier to find[8] in the United States than in China – one can only speculate what evidence must be hidden so carefully: Popular sympathies to the KMT, including among some workers? Sacrifices made by the KMT to resist Japanese colonization? The extent of friendly collaboration with the Japanese? The hesitation to open this history to debate is understandable: As waves of anti-Japanese protests[9] remind us, the CCP holds legitimacy as a successful defender of the nation, a reputation it first earned during the Sino-Japanese War.

This section follows the CCP's development from its founding in 1921 to its victory in 1949, distinguishing among three distinct phases of popular mobilization and membership recruitment. The initial phase, which lasted until the onset of the Sino-Japanese War in 1937, ended in near-defeat and arguably left few historical traces. From then on until the end of World War II the party made its breakthrough. The years 1937–1945 were decisive for the CCP's development and continue to shape the geographical patterns of party membership. While the following Civil War saw a further rapid expansion of the party's membership base, the war fronts during that era were shaped by the preceding Japanese occupation. Even in the places where despite the Japanese occupation the party at first was less successful – notably Manchuria, under Japanese control for decades prior to the war – the Japanese departure left a political void that the Communist party filled more quickly and effectively than their Nationalist competitor.

5.1.1 Short-Lived Successes in the Early Base Areas

Prior to the outbreak of the Sino-Japanese War, the CCP's presence throughout China was widespread but short-lived. Local histories, carefully recording instances that could be suitable to prove a revolutionary pedigree, document recruitment activities of the CCP in almost any corner of the country. Areas where the party was most successful are referred to as base areas and often served as experimental spots for radical reform. In the ten years following the Communists' expulsion from the cities in 1927, base areas sprang up in many parts of China, the most notable exception being provinces such as Hebei, Shandong, and Shanxi in Northern China.[10] Even in localities where party organizers were less successful and that are not recognized as base areas, Communists could still have a notable presence. Gaoyou, at the time a rural county in Jiangsu, is emblematic for developments in areas that are not part of any officially recognized base area: The party started activities and set up a branch in 1927, then expanded its membership from student circles to a wider population, until in 1933 the government abruptly cracked down on the movement. The official local history describes the complete inactivity of the party between 1933 and 1939 as a situation where "the revolutionary tinder was already deeply stuck in the hearts of the people," but in fact there is no indication whatsoever that the first round of mobilization helped mobilization later on.[11] Having experienced the suppression and punishment of Communists presumably made people more hesitant to accept the risks and join the movement. Similarly in base areas: once extinguished by the incumbent government, typically there was hardly any party activity at all.

At the national level, fluctuating membership with a peak at 120,000 members in 1930–1931 (see Figure 5.1) reflects the unstable power base of the party during this early period. Until settling down in the famous Yan'an base area in 1935, the CCP was on the run. The First Party Congress of 1921 began in a Shanghai back alley, but after French police intervention had to abscond to a lake outside the city, so that the foundation of the party was declared while floating on a boat. As pressure from the secret police mounted, the CCP soon had to abandon the cities and the workers, turning to the countryside and the peasants instead. Soviets were established and subsequently crushed in the provinces of Anhui, Jiangxi, and Zhejiang. Before long, increasingly intense military operations sent the CCP on the Long March, passing through most provinces in Southern China and coming into touch with minorities in Western China. At each

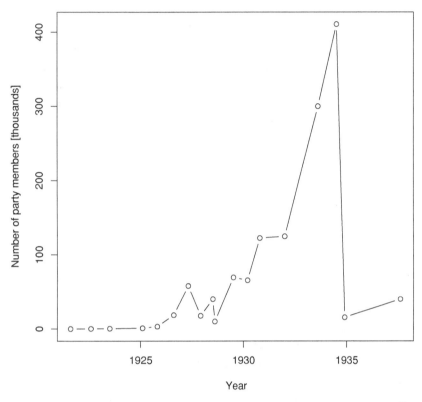

FIGURE 5.1 Fluctuating party membership prior to the war. Official sources.[12]

stop, the CCP left behind its agents for underground work and for setting up depots with weapons and provisions. Memories from this early period of revolutionary struggle were revived after the Communist takeover.

Amidst the ostensibly amorphous geography of armed struggles and warfare between the foundation of the CCP in 1921 and the party's victory in 1949, the Communist base areas stand out as relatively well-delineated places where the party first gained a foothold. One might think that the Communist base areas of the past would exhibit the strongest grassroots party organizations today. Yet in fact, there is no such simple relationship. The important revolutionary site of Anyuan is emblematic of base areas away from Japanese-occupied Northern China: The Communist movement could recover after being shattered for the first time in 1925, but because of persecution under Nationalist control, the CCP's local organization all but disappeared from the early 1930s until the Communist victory in 1949, when it had to be built from scratch.[13] In many base areas forceful military persecution by the Nationalists sharply discontinued erstwhile party organizational strength, and ideological legacies were of little help in advancing local party strength.

Militarily, base areas were transient phenomena. Although the KMT eventually lost the war, its early counterinsurgency campaigns were thorough and effective. In the first decade of the CCP's existence, KMT government forces annihilated many important base areas, so that the CCP had little choice but to abandon them, disappointing the loyalty of a population that had thrown its own fate in with the party. In such places, the party left little in the way of a local legacy. In the context of historical peasant uprisings, especially the Boxer rebellion, historians have observed that once the imperial army defeated a movement in a particular location, the movement could reappear in other locations, but rarely returned to a place of defeat.[14] An analysis of name lists comprising Communist "martyrs" from Xianning, a locality in Southern Hubei, shows that mobilization in that area was very swift early on, but stopped when the party fled the area during the Long March and only resumed during the Civil War beginning in 1945 after a lapse of 10 years.[15] In short, the destruction of base areas in Southern China was effective.

During this early stage of its struggle, the party left only a limited impact on its numerous but temporary host communities. Membership gains during that early period turned out to be elusive. Another peak in membership occurred in 1933, no longer reported in the official statistics today, when the party for a short period of time had 300,000 members.[16] In any case, five years later it had been decimated to just 15,000 members, recovering only slightly to 40,000 members once settled in Yan'an. The CCP was struggling for survival, not building a lasting organizational network. To be sure, discontinuities in formal institutions may not automatically imply that there were no legacies whatsoever, including subterranean popular sympathies, a point to be addressed in Section 6.2.3. For now it is sufficient to note that early recruitment was short-lived and inconsequential for subsequent party strength, at least as reflected in the number of party members.

5.1.2 Party Growth behind Japanese Enemy Lines

The Sino-Japanese War provided the party with the historical opportunity to break out of its remote base area in Yan'an to establish a lasting organizational network across Northern China. Similarly, in the occupied cities, "[t]he Japanese invasion afforded the Communists a second chance at mobilizing a revolutionary labor movement."[17] In the relatively short time span of eight years, the CCP's membership exploded from just over 40,000 members to 1.2 million.[18] Chalmers Johnson famously argued that Japanese occupation was crucial for Communist success, because it became a rallying cause allowing the party to mobilize peasants on nationalist grounds, for the first time letting them play an active role in modern political life.[19] Subsequent scholarship fully bears out Johnson's close linkage between Japanese invasion and Communist success.[20] However, the literature barely discusses the geographic aspects of this correspondence that tie Japanese occupation to CCP recruitment and subsequent party membership patterns.

Although few authors doubt the close connection between Japanese occupation and Communist success in China, the notion that the Communist success was mainly based on peasant nationalism is contestable. According to Johnson's original hypothesis, the Sino-Japanese War instilled a sense of nationalism among peasants, thereby mobilizing them into modern politics and faciliating the rise of the CCP. The war not only brought political modernity to China, but also secured the party's place in the emerging political community. Extrapolating from Johnson's argument, the war did more than determine numerical membership patterns across space, which would survive the Communist takeover of 1949. The war would also create privileged relationships of loyalty and trust, which the party could develop in some areas of the country in the crucible of war. Anticipating the argument in the following chapter, to explain the persistence of uneven party membership patterns even until today, in the spirit of Johnson's argument one would emphasize the ideological committment between these communities and the CCP's status as the standard bearer of national resistence against Japan. But did peasant nationalism actually exist? Peasant nationalism might in fact be a popular sentiment reminiscent of primordial xenophobia as during the Boxer Rebellion.[21] Without revisiting the controversy around Johnson's peasant nationalism hypothesis,[22] we may not know whether or not a Chinese peasant whose house was destroyed as a consequence of Japanese invasion (more likely by Chinese troops collaborating with Japan than by the main Japanese army itself) felt anything resembling nationalism. We do know that a person whose livelihood had been destroyed would have little to lose from joining the Communists, and that therefore the Japanese presence surely helped Communist recruitment.

In addition, and probably the most important factor, Japanese occupation served as a shield from persecution by the nationalist KMT government. Beleaguered by the foreign enemy, the government decided to temporarily stop its campaigns against the Communists, partly in the hope that they could be deployed against the common enemy, and partly because the CCP no longer appeared as a serious threat. Faced with the military challenge from Japan, the Nationalist government had little choice but to give the Communists some breathing space and enlist them in the war effort, resulting in a united front policy. This policy explains the remarkable geographical correspondence between Japanese-occupied territory and Communist strongholds, expecially at the macro level, since the united-front policy only allowed the CCP to be active in certain parts of the country.[23] The CCP grew most rapidly behind enemy lines in Japanese-occupied territory. At more fine-grained levels, within Japanese-occupied territory, more nuanced distinctions can be made to identify as accurately as possible the geographic relationship connecting the presence of Japanese troops to Communist mobilization. While on the one hand Japanese destructiveness facilitated Communist Party growth, on the other hand a permanent and fully fledged Japanese presence posed an obstacle to recruitment. If it is true that the regional patterns were mainly a result of strategic united-front policies and tactical advantages in recruiting among victims of occupation, then this has implications for the type of historical transmission that one would expect: Instead of ideological traditions being inherited from one generation to the next, organizational reasons might make membership patterns sticky and lead to their transmission over time.

Let us have a closer look at the degrees of Japanese occupation and Communist success: Neither did Japan occupy all of China, nor was the CCP evenly successful in its recruitment efforts. As Chen Yung-fa's definite study of the party's mobilization strategies demonstrates, experiences during the 1930s and 1940s varied vastly across China.[24] Chen's analysis calls for multiple fine-grained distinctions. Instead, I suggest that a parsimonious analysis can go a long way in capturing subnational differences, by paying attention to one particularly salient distinction: The CCP's own party historiography suggests that the party thrived behind Japanese enemy lines, but had little success in areas that were not under foreign occupation. This two-way distinction accounts for very different dynamics of party development in the 1930s and 1940s, as reflected in the chapters on the Sino-Japanese War of the various local editions of the party's *Organizational History*. They summarize the overall events during this period very differently, depending on their geographic location. In Yunnan party development followed a policy of "lying low for a long time, saving up strength, awaiting a good opportunity," whereas in Shandong the party "had a free hand to mobilize the masses."[25] The case of Yunnan represents places that saw little Japanese occupation and were thus part of Nationalist-controlled territory 國民黨統治區, to which the lying low policy applied. By contrast, Shandong stands for places with a strong Japanese presence, where the Nationalist Party had all but disappeared.

The CCP was quick to adjust to the new strategic environment of the Sino-Japanese War. One day after the Marco Polo Bridge Incident, which marked the beginning of the war, the Central Committee gave out new strategic directions along with a set of slogans fit for the occasion:[26]

武將保衛平津，保衛華北! 不讓日本帝國主義佔領中國寸土! 為保衛國土流最后一滴血! 全中國同胞，政府與軍隊團結起來，筑成民族統一戰線的堅固長城，抵抗日寇的侵掠! 國共兩黨親密合作抵抗日寇的新進攻! 驅逐日寇出中國!

Militarily defend Pinjin, defend North China! Don't let the Japanese imperialists occupy even one inch of China! Defend China to the last drop of blood! All Chinese compatriots, government and army stand up together, build a strong Great Wall of a nationally united front, resist the invasion of the Japanese bandits! Nationalists and Communists work intimately together to resist the new attack by the Japanese bandits! Expel the Japanese bandits from China!

To be sure, the CCP had occasionally resorted to patriotic slogans before the outbreak of the Sino-Japanese War. Yet the new set of slogans, which are symptomatic for the Communist agenda throughout the 1937–1945 period, put a markedly different emphasis on a nationalist agenda. Momentarily eschewing land reform and class struggle, the Communist leadership found it more expedient to adopt a patriotic rhetoric, which shielded them from the Nationalist government and at the same time gained them popular sympathies.

One of the provinces where this process unfolded in a typical way was Shandong. The Japanese army invaded the province at the end of 1937, shortly after the outbreak of the Sino-Japanese War. Protection of civilian lives and property was not a priority. In fact, the first victims after Japanese units crossed into the province were a group of peasants who had been drafted to reinforce the ditches and who were so removed from the military command structures that they were informed neither of the impending arrival of Japanese units, nor of the retreat of the Nationalist army, which obviated the need for ditches. The peasants were put to death on the spot. The iron fist of the Japanese occupiers did not win them hearts and minds. In areas invaded beginning in 1937, Tokyo did not plan to establish Japanese settlements, so that rural popular acquiescence seemed dispensable. The Japanese presence almost immediately brought instability. As people's livelihoods were threatened, peasants transformed into floating bandits, as so often was the case in Shandong's history. A downward spiral of widespread violence and economic downturn had begun.

In Shandong as in other provinces, the Nationalist government had lost its credibility as a defender against Japanese invasion. The powerful governor of Shandong, Han Fuju, had brought some prosperity to the province, even if he was feared for his brutal methods. The life of farmers throughout the province improved greatly as a result of the governor's successful efforts to suppress bandits and establish civilian order, often with the help of locally organized militias. As streets were repaired, Shandong was also economically recovering from decades of instability. In the early Republican period, large numbers of immigrants left the province and settled in China's Northeastern territories. When Han Fuju took over Shandong, the stream of migration was reversed. But the governor was powerless in the face of Japanese encroachment. Ordinary people would hardly have been able to appreciate Han's strategic efforts to ward off the dangers of Japanese occupation. What counted was that, at the end, Han Fuju's forces left without even putting up a fight, making the way free for the Japanese. The Nationalist government reinforced this impression by labeling the governor a traitor and executing him – a decision that had to do with Han Fuju's decade-long defiance of government policies. All in all, the message transpiring in the countryside was: the Nationalist government, as represented by Han Fuju, was dysfunctional and unable to protect the prosperous province from the destructive Japanese presence.

The Communists gradually became an important element in people's strategies of survival. Villages did not turn Communist overnight. At first, they may have offered food or shelter to Communist fighters as a way of hedging their bets and taking out insurance against yet another armed group. Support for the Communists was not an exclusive strategy; villages could try to seek some kind of arrangement with the Communists, the Japanese, the Nationalists and other bandits all at the same time.[27] When the Japanese army focused on controlling some broad territorial corridors along the railways, it might not have been apparent to local community leaders in more remote places that sheltering Communist fighters could be an extremely risky strategy. When confrontation with the Japanese became unavoidable, throwing in their lot with the Communists might have promised a way out. Signing up with the Red Army was not necessarily about sacrificing oneself for a higher cause.

The Communists' higher cause was, nonetheless, an additional factor. What made the Communist appeal distinctly modern and fundamentally different from the classic appeal of local militias or bandit armies was that for the first time, the CCP mobilized ordinary peasants on political grounds as well. The modern version of a peasant army needed a cause, and as it turned out, Communism and patriotism against the Japanese provided an effective ground for peasant mobilization. Beyond simply serving the interests of poor farmers through land reform and security interests of Communists, patriotic Communism appealed to peasants as agents of a modern political arena in unprecedented ways.

Areas in southwestern China, far away from Japanese imperial expansion, were the mirror image of developments in the North. To be sure, Japanese occupation did have a systemic effect on the southern economy as well. But there was no tangible presence: Japanese occupation occurred beyond the experiential horizon of the peasants and was thus not effective as a rallying call. Party organization could not prosper in the same way. Interestingly, the places in the South where the Japanese were present, namely industrially developed port cities such as Shanghai, did have a large and flourishing underground Communist movement, despite intense persecution in an urban environment. Official Shanghai party history describes the ten years prior to Japanese occupation as an era where the party experienced "big ups and downs,"[28] but the period of Japanese occupation as one of "steady growth."[29] Having been reduced to fewer than 200 members on the eve of the Sino-Japanese War, in the first two years of Japanese occupation party membership in Shanghai grew tenfold.[30] This suggests that Japanese occupation worked as a catalyst for mobilization not only with peasants in the countryside, but also with intellectuals and workers in the cities.

In 1938, one of Deng Xiaoping's first well-known speeches analyzed the mobilization success of the CCP. In a methodological spirit reminiscent of comparative politics, he calls on his comrades to look closely at localities where the party had most success in recruiting followers, to see what was done right. Deng's first concern was with particularly effective propaganda techniques that could be deployed to other areas, including theater, songs, and mass meetings. But the grand scheme that he saw underlying all recruitment success was to mobilize preexisting anti-Japanese sentiments as a result of Japanese occupation. His speech is in full agreement with the observation that areas with Japanese occupation showed stronger recruitment. However, Deng Xiaoping also raises an important exception, to be pursued as a refinement of the theory later in this chapter: Recruitment is hard in places where the Japanese had a long-established presence and where the war appears far away. Apparently, Deng is referring to places like Manchuria, where Chinese lived in relative prosperity, at times alongside peasant immigrants from Japan, and possibly to the best-protected core areas of Japanese occupation, as discussed in a refinement of the argument later on in this chapter.[31]

Ideologically, recruitment in base areas was primarily based on pro-peasant redistributive policies, such as radical land reform.[32] Base areas epitomize the argument that, besides peasant nationalism against Japan, the other side of the Communist revolution was pro-poor policy and a modern version of traditional peasant rebellion.[33] To the extent that few scholars had doubts that the revolution was won in the countryside,[34] academic debates in the 1960s and 1970s revolved around the question of whether the CCP attracted rural support primarily thanks to its patriotic appeal or thanks to its Communist appeal. Today scholars recognize that both factors played a crucial role, so that the bitterness of prior debates appears as a reflection of American political polemics.[35] Chen Yung-fa expresses a new scholarly consensus when he identifies a need to "differentiate peasant support by place, time, and kind" in order to discern the underlying peasant motivations and the CCP's mobilization strategies.[36] My analysis subscribes to Chen's nuanced view about the origins of the CCP's rural success during the revolutionary wars. In some places the party's anti-Japanese credentials motivated people to join the CCP; in other places the party's pro-peasant policies were essential to attract new party members.

5.1.3 Recruitment during the Civil War, 1945–1949

The following years of the Civil War between Communists and Nationalists did little to fundamentally alter this regional pattern. Party membership at the time of the Communist takeover had much more to do with the time of Japanese occupation than with the Civil War. First, Japanese occupation lasted twice as long; thus membership networks had more time to grow. Second, during the Japanese occupation, party membership grew thirty fold, from an initial 40,000 in 1937 to 1.2 million in April 1945, whereas during the Civil War it expanded only threefold.[37] Third, and most importantly, even as the frontline during the Civil War was changing, the Communists generally remained strongest in places that they had already taken over by 1945 and could only advance in the Nationalists' heartland in the South during the last few months of the war. In short, when we talk about pre-1949 legacies of party strength, for the most part the geography of party expansion followed the geography of Japanese domination.

After the Japanese defeat in 1945, the Communists consolidated their grip on formerly Japanese territories. The CCP quickly stepped into the power vacuum left behind by the retreating Japanese before Nationalist troops could arrive from the South. Now the party took over the railroads and connected base areas that had been isolated from one another, precariously linked via secret transportation channels. All of Northern China, with the exception of some major cities like Beijing and Tianjin, became the power base from which the CCP was able to wage and win the Civil War. The only Japanese-occupied territories where the CCP remained unsuccessful were those in Southern China. These territories were small compared to the Japanese-occupied territories in Northern China and presented a logistical challenge to the CCP, since the areas were disconnected patches of land, with Nationalist-controlled areas in-between. At the end of World War II, the geographic overlap between Japanese occupation and party strength was almost perfect.

For Manchuria the bottom line is the same as for the rest of the country: Japanese occupation allowed the Communists to establish a strong local party organization long before their victory in 1949. However, there are notable differences in how this effect worked. Japan's influence in Manchuria dated back to the Russo-Japanese War of 1904–1905 and culminated in the foundation of the Japanese puppet state of Manchukoku in 1932. By the time the CCP had made a close escape from annihilation in the South thanks to its Long March in 1935, Manchuria was not only firmly under Japanese control but was also doing relatively well economically, making it extremely difficult for Communist agents to attract followers to their cause.

The sudden breakdown of Japanese authority at the end of World War II provided the Communists with an opportunity to make inroads into Manchuria. Japanese occupation had kept the KMT out of Manchuria, and the hasty departure of the Japanese occupiers created a void, which the Communists knew how to exploit. To be sure, the KMT was competing to fill the void, airlifting troops into major cities of previously Japanese-controlled territory.[38] Fierce battles between CCP and KMT forces in Manchuria led to large numbers of civilian casualties, such as during the Communist siege of Changchun in 1948. While Communist superiority in Manchuria was not a foregone conclusion, the fact that KMT forces were also just arriving in the theater was a decisive strategic advantage for the Communist forces, compared to the consolidated KMT presence in Southern China. At the end of the day, Communist tactics of encircling the cities from the countryside, now well-rehearsed, worked well in Manchuria, not least because of open support from Soviet troops who had crossed the border at the time of Japanese defeat. Shortly after the Japanese surrender, the CCP established a strong presence in Manchuria's countryside. Japanese occupation accounts for a strong presence of the Communist party in Manchuria in 1949, both because occupation had kept the KMT out and because the end of occupation had created a political vacuum in 1945.

Also outside Manchuria, Communist recruitment occasionally faced counties with a strong Japanese presence that preceded the Sino-Japanese War. In Shandong in particular, there were places that resembled a "Manchuria away from Manchuria." As a result of migration from Shandong to Manchuria and back, there were strong personal ties to the Japanese puppet state. The Manchurian Railway Company, which was at the heart of Japanese colonization efforts, was actively recruiting workers in certain counties in Shandong. In the year before the outbreak of the Sino-Japanese War, more than 200,000 people from Shandong had joined the workforce in Manchuria, so that in some counties a substantial proportion of the rural population had close connections to the Japanese. Table 5.1 displays the percentage of households with at least one member working in Manchuria.[39] Even without the Manchuria connection, in Zaozhuang in Southern Shandong, thanks to a coal mine, locals had encountered Japanese first as employers and only later as soldiers of an invading army.

Based on such cases, one may conjecture that Manchuria's historical pathway could also be discovered in other places where the Japanese presence had longer-standing ties predating the war. In such places, the CCP buildup during the Sino-Japanese War tended to be slow, because the Japanese invasion was less disruptive and did not provide a powerful enough rallying call. Nevertheless, the Japanese presence kept the KMT government out and created a political vacuum after Japan's defeat in World War II. In the areas most tightly under Japanese control, the CCP profited from being able to fill in this political vacuum more quickly, thanks to a small but effective presence on the ground. This is true not only for Manchuria, but also for many county seats, which in contrast

TABLE 5.1 *A "Manchuria-style" Japanese presence in parts of Shandong (1936)*

County	Number of people working in Manchuria	Number of people working in Manchuria divided by the number of households in the county
Ye Xian (today: Laizhou)	20,375	55%
Huang Xian (today: Longkou)	15,752	30%
Muping	15,660	20%
Penglai	11,857	47%
Wendeng	11,100	16%

Source: A document available at the Academy of Social Science in Tianjin contains a table called "県別入満労働者の比較" [County-level comparison of people joining the Manchuria workforce] (see CASS 183, p. 248).

to their rural surroundings were under tight Japanese control. In areas where the Japanese were present, but where there was still room for the CCP to operate, such as much of the Shandong countryside, both effects came into play, creating optimal conditions for the party to thrive. Conversely, most difficult for the CCP were territories that the Japanese had never reached.

5.2 THE JAPANESE OCCUPATION EFFECT

To the question why at the moment of the Communist takeover in 1949 some places ended up with so many more party members than others, an exhaustive answer would include a detailed description of military contingencies and the CCP's geostrategy. The goal of this section is more modest, in the interest of parsimony, limiting itself to one aspect of these war contingencies: the degree of Japanese occupation. While some areas of China were fully under Japanese control, other areas were barely touched by the military operations of the Imperial Army. This one variable stands out as a good predictor and goes a long way to explain geographic patterns of party membership after the foundation of the People's Republic. This section first provides a province-by-province overview, putting the account of the previous section on a map and thereby demonstrating the close linkage between occupation patterns and membership patterns. The next section takes the first step to investigate the persistence and mediation of the occupation effect. It turns out that the effect of Japanese occupation is almost entirely mediated by the initial membership patterns in the early years of the People's Republic. Historical transmission occurs through the mechanical inertia of the Leninist organization structure.

5.2.1 War Contingencies, Province by Province

The description of the war contingencies suggests three reasons why the Communist party was able to build up a strong organizational base in areas under Japanese occupation. Japanese occupation functioned as a shield from persecution of the revolutionaries by the incumbent government, with Japanese persecution being not nearly as dangerous to the party as persecution by the Nationalist Party. Second, Japanese occupation allowed the CCP to mobilize rural citizens who had been dislocated by the war on nationalistic or xenophobic grounds. Third, in places that were firmly under Japanese control, especially Manchuria, recruitment efforts by the party during the time of Japanese occupation were limited. But as soon as Japan retreated at the end of World War II, the Communists were able to step into the political vacuum left by the Japanese.

To compare the degree of occupation and party presence, Table 5.2 presents, for each province, the estimated percentage of territory under Japanese control. Comparing maps, both by scholars in Chinese history[40] who base their research on Communist maps and by scholars in Japanese history[41] who base their research on Japanese military maps, it appears that there is a widely shared consensus as to the reach of the Imperial Army's presence. Party membership statistics for the early years of the People's Republic are more problematic. In order to assemble the best available data for the year 1949, I gleaned information from various sources. While the results are essentially the same as the ones presented here, the problem with this approach is that definitional standards were not fixed at that transitional stage, creating problems in particular with the month of reference. At a time of quick party growth, this creates important distortions. Instead, a more reliable approach is to use data from 1956. For the purposes of determining the size of seats allotted to each province, membership statistics are collected at times of party congresses. The Seventh Party Congress, held briefly before the Communist takeover in 1949, was a chaotic event that did not allow the compilation of good membership statistics. The Eighth Party Congress, held in 1956, provides the earliest reliable data.

Using data from 1956 not only increases the accuracy of party statistics. It is also a much harder test as to whether Japanese occupation really had an effect. Between 1949 and 1956, membership of the CCP tripled,

TABLE 5.2 *Japanese occupation and party presence in 1956*

Province	Party members per 10,000 citizens	Percentage of territory under Japanese control	Beginning of Japanese occupation
Beijing	436	complete	1937
Hebei	328	complete	1937
Shanxi	308	67%	1937–1938
Shanghai	305	complete	1937
Tianjin	284	complete	1937
Heilongjiang	266	Manchuria	1931
Liaoning	252	Manchuria	1931
Shandong	225	complete	1937–1938
Inner Mongolia	222	67%	1933
Gansu	218	none	n/a
Qinghai	208	none	n/a
Jilin	196	Manchuria	1931
Xinjiang	175	none	n/a
Jiangsu	172	complete	1938
Shaanxi	170	none	n/a
Jiangxi	167	9%	1939
Henan	151	77%	1944
Anhui	142	46%	1938
Fujian	140	none	1938–1941
Guangdong	137	58%	1944–1945
Hubei	132	50%	1938
Yunnan	129	none	1942
Guangxi	120	8%	n/a
Sichuan	119	none	n/a
Zhejiang	118	28%	gradually
Guizhou	116	none	1944
Hunan	109	43%	1944
Tibet	18	none	n/a

Sources: CCP members from internal party statistics; missing data for Tibet supplemented from a local source but not included in subsequent analyses.[42] Population data from *China Data Online*. Percentage of territory under occupation derived from an authoritative map collection using GIS technology.[43] The beginning of Japanese occupation follows generic historiography and in some cases is contestable.

so that some regional convergence in party strength could occur, blurring initial differences. Nevertheless, as it turns out, party statistics from 1956 continued to closely reflect the patterns of Japanese occupation. Despite the impact of the Civil War and despite post-1949 efforts to boost membership in areas where the hold of the party had been more tenuous, membership patterns clearly reflected legacies of Japanese occupation.

Table 5.2 ranks all provinces according to party membership density in 1956. Column three indicates the extent of Japanese occupation. The ten provinces with lowest party penetration are all situated in Southern China and did not come in close contact with Japanese occupation; if they did have contact, then only late in the war. By contrast, the three provinces forming the Japanese puppet state of Manchuria all have a very high membership density of 2% or more. Most of the ten provinces with highest party penetration had been fully under Japanese control. Most strikingly, the ranking of provinces closely reflects the progression of Japanese occupation over time.

The greatest outliers are Gansu, Qinghai, and Xinjiang, whose relatively strong party presence is not related to Japanese occupation, but to geostrategic interests of the USSR. These areas would have been the bridgehead for Moscow to secure influence in China in case the Chinese Communist Party lost to the Nationalist Party. The other unusual case is the province of Sha'anxi, where the famous and large Yan'an base area was located. While it confirms the theory that the absence of Japanese occupation made mobilization difficult, it seems counterintuitive that the party would be so weak in its former base area. This receives further investigation in Section 5.2.3. Overall, the findings do more than confirm what historians already knew, namely that Japanese occupation gave the party an opportunity to escape from extinction and make a strong comeback. They also refine this understanding by demonstrating that the link between Japanese occupation and party strength was also of a geographical nature: Places that experienced occupation had a stronger party presence than places without occupation.

5.2.2 Mediating the Japanese Occupation Effect

The close relationship between Japanese occupation and early geographic patterns of party membership, apparent in Table 5.2, remains strong even today. With a view on isolating a causal connection, the following regression analysis controls for the three most likely confounding factors that may have influenced Japanese occupation patterns and which may shape party membership patterns today: the presence of minorities, the degree of urbanization, and the size of a province's territory. Controlling for these three factors, the specification predicts the number of CCP members in a province in 2010, based on the percentage of its territory that was occupied by the Japanese army. The effect is both significant and substantively important. As the coefficient displayed in Table 5.3 indicates, a province

TABLE 5.3 *Party members as mediators transmitting the occupation effect*

	Direct Effect	With Mediator
Occupation [% of provincial territory]	1,626,347**	359,500
Party members in 1956 [persons]		3.085***
Territory [area]	7,920	–907
Minority presence [%]	–42,860**	–12,010
Urbanization [%]	–78,018***	–24,300

*** Significance at 0.001, ** significance at 0.01

Note: OLS estimators (with unreported intersects). 31 provincial observations. Party membership and extent of occupation as in Table 5.2. "Minority presence" signifies the proportion of non–Han Chinese, "urbanization" the proportion of nonrural citizens in the population. Ideally, one would use data prior to the onset of Japanese occupation in 1931, but in the face of shifting provincial boundaries (the latest being the creation of Chongqing as a provincial unit), these variables are proxied by using the 2010 census (China Data Center, University of Michigan). Territorial areas derived from maps accompanying this census.

that experienced full occupation by the Imperial Army is associated with 1,626,347 additional CCP members, compared with a province that did not experience occupation. Since the average province has 2.4 million party members, Japanese occupation makes a big difference indeed. This overarching result foreshadows the more detailed analysis of Chapter 6, which demonstrates that membership patterns persist over long periods of time. The first substantive column of Table 5.3 is consistent with the idea that occupation in the late 1930s and early 1940s partly explains which provinces today are red with a strong party presence, and which are merely pink with fewer party members.

The causal channel is that Japanese occupation has shaped initial membership patterns, and that in turn initial membership patterns shape contemporary membership patterns. But it could also be that instead of or in addition to this mechanism, war contingencies are affecting membership density today through other causal ways, as sketched out in Figure 5.2. For example, the experience of wartime cruelty, recounted by grandparents to their grandchildren, could give citizens more nationalistic preferences and as a result they might be more amenable to the nationalistic aspects of the CCP's ideology today. Given the role of national memory transmitted in schools and propaganda overriding locally experienced memory, however, one may regard such a hypothesis with skepticism. My experience in the field has been that citizens usually know very little about wartime events in their communities, but a lot more about wartime events recounted in national propaganda. Methodologically, the

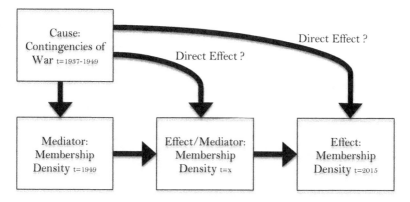

FIGURE 5.2 Direct and indirect effects of war contingencies

question is whether the effect of Japanese occupation on contemporary membership patterns is a direct effect[44] or an indirect effect mediated by another variable, in this case initial membership patterns.

Table 5.3 presents a simple test whether Japanese occupation effect was indeed transmitted over time through sticky party membership patterns. To analyze causal pathways, one widely used empirical test consists of including the hypothesized mediating posttreatment variable in the regression and seeing whether the effect disappears. If the initial cause affects the contemporary outcome mainly through the mediating variable, then controlling for the mediating variable should leave no explanatory power to the initial cause, so that the coefficient on the initial variable disappears. The approach can result in biased estimates,[45] yet it is nevertheless widely used, partly because it is intuitive and partly because the estimation of controlled direct effects requires hard choices based on assumptions about potential controls, as well as causal ordering. The result is clear-cut, comparing the two substantive columns of Table 5.3. The effect of Japanese occupation is almost entirely mediated by the initial geographic patterns of party membership. After controlling for initial membership patterns, the Japanese occupation effect is statistically insignificant; it is substantively much smaller than the previously identified effect. By contrast, the relationship between party membership in 1956 and 2010 is strikingly strong, as noted before. The coefficient indicates that after controlling for minorities, urbanization, and territorial size, an additional party member in 1956 is associated with three additional party members today, and in a statistically highly significant way. This suggests that the party apparatus is at the heart of the

TABLE 5.4 *The occupation effect on one-child policy outcomes*

Japanese Occupation [% of prefectural territory]	−0.058***
Minority population (2000)	0.226***
Gross Regional Product (2000)	−0.104***
Government employees (2000)	0.036**

*** Significance at 0.005, ** significance at 0.01, * significance at 0.05,
. significance at 0.1
Note: OLS estimators. 344 prefecture-level observations. Japanese occupation by overlaying a digitized version of the authoritative map Wu Yuexing, 1999, 中國現代史地圖集, p. 162, with the maps that accompany the 2000 census data.

transmission mechanism. The historical legacies of Japanese occupation shape outcomes today through the formal institution of the Leninist party apparatus rather than through informal socialization or other mediating pathways.

5.2.3 Tying war contingencies to one-child policy outcomes

The empirical strategy of this book is to proceed in three steps, as outlined in the introduction: explain contemporary outcomes based on contemporary party membership patterns, then explain contemporary party membership patterns as a result of early party membership patterns, and finally explain early party membership patterns with war contingencies (see Figure 1.1). If the main argument of this book is correct, it seems inherently difficult – albeit not impossible – to directly tie present outcomes to a historical cause, for two reasons: First, the effect of history on the outcomes under consideration here tends to decline, as the reach of the party evens out over time. Second, and most importantly, party membership patterns affect many different outcomes, each of which will also affect the other outcomes. Japanese occupation is an important variable, precisely because it stands at the beginning of several causal chains with downstream effects later on.

As a robustness check of the argument, it is useful to analyze the correlations between Japanese occupation and the main outcome of the one-child policy. The goal is not to test the effect of party presence, which has been demonstrated in Chapters 3 and 4. In other words, Japanese occupation does not merely serve as an instrumental variable,[46] but is itself the substantial variable of interest. Using the same maps as in previous regressions, the empirical specification tests whether Japanese presence in 1937–1938 is associated with more effective enforcement of the one-child policy, as measured by the percentage of surplus births among all births in the year 2000. The unit of analysis are China's 333 prefectures. The regression includes the number of government employees in the prefecture to control for size effects, the presence of minority population who are exempt from the one-child policy, and the Gross Regional Product to control for levels of economic development. Table 5.4 indicates that a prefecture in 1937–1938 occupied by Japan in the year 1999–2000 experienced 5.8 percent fewer surplus births than an unoccupied prefecture, controlling for the presence of minority population, economic wealth, and size effects.

5.3 REFINEMENTS OF THE JAPANESE OCCUPATION HYPOTHESIS

Japanese occupation gave the CCP an opportunity for a formidable comeback. In addition, by comparing Chinese provinces, we found that geographical macropatterns of party membership reflect macropatterns of Japanese occupation. This view of history resembles the proverbial "looking at flowers from horseback" 走馬觀花. A local perspective of Japanese occupation and party development significantly complicates the picture. Zooming in to county-level historical developments, the following section suggests that at the local level there is a U-shaped relationship between Japanese presence and party development. In places firmly under Japanese control, such as many county seats in Shandong, party recruiters had little maneuvering space. In places unaffected by the Japanese invasion, the party also had difficulty mobilizing people. The places where party recruitment was at its best were localities out of reach of well-established Japanese authority, but where people had been displaced by the turmoil of war. This refinement draws attention to the fact that the scale of geographical analysis is essential. Macrofindings at low levels of spatial resolution do not simply translate one-to-one to a more fine-grained microscale.

5.3.1 Local Centers of Power, Local Peripheries

The most important primary evidence on the geographic patterns of party development are maps found in Japanese archives and in Chinese archives. The Imperial Army not only knew where its own forces were deployed, but was also carefully tracing the development of Chinese enemy forces, including the CCP. Impressionistic evidence from archives at the Japanese Defense Ministry and at the Yasukuni Shrine suggests that early on in the war the Imperial Army was much better informed about

CCP movements than later on, when Japan was approaching defeat. On these early maps, compiled by researchers at the Japanese Defense Agency after the war, the party had most of its members at the fringes of Japan-occupied territory.[47]

One might object that Communists further away from the frontline were invisible to Japanese intellegence services. Yet Communist sources, recording information about the local evolution of party cells as well as the presence of its enemies, by and large confirm the insights gained from Japanese sources. The definitive book series on this issue is the "Material on the Organizational History of the CCP in county X (province Y)" 中國共產黨某某省某某縣組織史資料, compiled by all counties as well as other administrative units. The series contains near-complete information on the establishment of local party organizations, most of the time including detailed maps, such as the ones used in Figure 5.3, which reflect the situation in Linyi County in 1944 and in Chiping County (both in Shandong) in the early 1940s, respectively.[48] The battles fought in and around Linyi were among the fiercest battles of the Sino-Japanese War, because Chinese forces had exceptional and transient successes, holding the county seat of Linyi against repeated attacks, destroying 30,000 troops fifty miles Southwest of Linyi in Taierzhuang and finally resulting in military stalemate.[49] Even after a Japanese campaign to wipe out Communists in October 1941 had reduced party membership in Linyi from more than 1,500 members to no more than 338 members, the party ultimately had great recruitment success, with almost 2,000 party members in 1945 and almost 5,000 party members in 1949.[50]

In counties with a strong Japanese presence, such as in Chiping (compare left map in Figure 5.3), typically we find a pattern where the CCP settled in the periphery, but stayed away from the county seat. On the map, the county seat is where an important east–west highway crosses with a less important south–west road.[51] The CCP set up its operational base along the borders of the county (hatched areas). Mao's tactical doctrine to surround the cities from the countryside played out between rural county seats and their surrounding villages. Party development and membership recruitment occurred not at the heart of Japanese occupation, but at its fringes.

As for Linyi, the case does not only confirm that the Japanese invasion kick-started the party. In conjunction with the dates when village-level party cells were established, all recorded in the Organizational History, the map on the right of Figure 5.3 also suggests that the CCP was not primarily active in the areas fully under Japanese control. In the map,

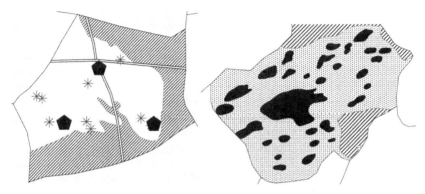

FIGURE 5.3 The confrontation behind Japanese frontlines. Communist-held areas are shaded, Japanese-held areas black with pentagons symbolizing strongholds and stars outposts. Contested areas are dotted. Based on maps in the Organizational History of Chiping (left) and Linyi (right) counties.[52]

the large black area represents the Japanese-occupied county seat; the smaller black areas show Japanese outposts. The large shaded area in the North is a Communist base area. It shows KMT-government forces, although they are barely visible on the map, apparently because the editor thought that they were irrelevant for local party development. The map highlights areas targeted by guerrilla warfare (dotted area). Throughout the map, there are ten red flags planted, the majority of which are in the contested area. Guerrilla warfare was concentrated on areas in proximity of Japanese occupation, but was not intruding into the occupied areas themselves.

5.3.2 Opportunities in a "Close Distance" to the Imperial Army

The CCP grew fastest in intermediate distances to the Imperial Army. On the one hand, as an influential study of the Sino-Japanese War in Shandong points out, "[i]n the vast area not directly impacted by the Japanese army the initial reaction of the peasantry was apathy," at least in the early years of the war.[53] On the other hand, at times and places where the Japanese military presence was firmly entrenched, Communist recruitment was slow. Both Japanese and Communist observers at the time paid close attention to the geography of occupation and the effectiveness of the party's anti-Japanese propaganda. One detailed account on the microgeography of Japanese occupation and Communist recruitment comes from two Japanese investigators, whom the North China Liaison

Office of the Asian Co-Prosperity Institute sent in 1939 to report on the situation along a large section of the Grand Canal, including on "ordinary people's ideological state of mind."[54] As the investigators traveled by boat along the Grand Canal, at the time no longer central for transportation and thus penetrating peripheral areas, they found people who had made their peace with the occupiers and others who called for violent opposition to them. When the investigators disembarked from the boat, in some places they experienced a friendly welcome and in others encountered things like graffiti next to the landing dock calling for "opposition to Japan, rescue for the country."[55] The observers provide a rich account, involving a local who graduated from a Japanese university, refugees who destabilized the situation, "devastating" rumors of Japanese defeat, and hosts of Communist propaganda teams urging people to rise against Japan.[56] Their summary suggests that a strong Japanese presence preempted anti-Japanese "agitation" and that the key was stability 安定.[57] The occupier had nothing to fear as long as citizens had enough to eat and as long as they could live in safety, but a half-hearted presence could be a recipe for disaster.

This point is reinforced by another Japanese investigation team, painting a grim picture of the security in one county, where the Imperial Army was able to defend itself and secure key strategic points in the county seat, but was too thinly spread to prevent bandit attacks against ordinary people. In the village under investigation, the investigators experienced regular bandit incursions[58] and even the county seat was not safe from occasional bandit incursions.[59] In the light of this report, joining either the Japanese "Railway-Loving Youth Team" 愛路青年團 or the Communist forces were survival strategies employed by ordinary people to defend their livelihood from ordinary bandits. To the extent that ordinary people joined military forces as a survival strategy, it may be conjectured that they turned to whomever looked like the stronger player at a certain point in time. At the same time, it could be that investigations by the colonizers were biased, tending to exaggerate material motivations and downplaying the potential for patriotic mobilization.

Communist accounts confirm that mobilization based on peasant nationalism was most straightforward in areas which were directly affected by the Japanese invasion, but not fully under Japanese control. The first systematic mobilizers were sent to Shandong's countryside as soon as the Japanese army had moved into the province. Some were released from Nationalist prison as the Imperial Army approached, others returned from big cities and other provinces. Some underground party members had stayed at Yan'an, where they participated in the University of Japanese Resistance and then returned to build up the local party organization. Others had attended or taught in schools and returned to the hinterland.[60] But the success of these organizers varied substantially from one locality to the next. According to one such account, most peasants were indifferent toward the Japanese occupation and found it a "matter for secret rejoicing" that the Imperial Army brought instability and misery to the lives of local landlords. By contrast, "the peasants who lived near the cities and along the highways" held different attitudes, because they had "seen Japanese soldiers plundering their property, raping their sisters, slaughtering their brothers, and burning down their villages."[61] It was these peasants whom organizers of the CCP first mobilized.

In Shandong, land reform was inadequate for mobilizing locals. The slogans reported in Japanese sources[62] usually do not refer to land reform. Communist accounts have a hard time explaining the class composition of their anti-Japanese alliance in Shandong, especially the greater enthusiasm of better-off peasants compared to poor peasants in joining the anti-Japanese front.[63] Given the original anti-Japanese battle cry, establishing a Communist order involving land distribution created much irregularity.[64] The people who had valiantly fought against the Japanese in Shandong and who therefore ended up in powerful positions were oftentimes not the landless and therefore organized land reform in ways that deviated from the ideal of taking from the rich and giving to the poor. Communists oftentimes discovered that local landholding patterns did not allow proper land reform to be carried out: one county on the Shandong peninsula, for example, not only lacked landlords in the conventional sense, but "middle peasants actually rented out more land than the landlords."[65] One study on Shandong finds that land reform was counterproductive in Shandong, because it alienated all but the poorest peasants, whose practical grievances were better addressed by groups such as the Red Spears.[66]

Competing with other local groups set up for self-defense, the Communists' competitive advantage was of an ideological kind, because they were the most credible and effective force against the Japanese invader. The anti-Japanese appeal helped Communist organizers to overcome the great challenge to insert themselves into existing local self-defense organizations, such as the Red Spear Society, organized out of secret societies. In Shandong secret societies could be so strong that instead of the CCP taking control of secret societies, occasionally the Daoist organizations co-opted grassroots cadres during the Cultural Revolution.[67] Liangshan County, known in Chinese fiction as a gathering site of Robin-Hood type bandit-rebels, in reality also was home to protective bandit groups. Yet the CCP had a hard time mobilizing these groups to its cause, possibly because the Japanese threat seemed remote. The low number of "notable martyrs"[68] from this county is a telling indicator: While on average counties in Heze Prefecture produced thirty-two martyrs, Liangshan brought forth only eight, two of whom had joined after the Communist victory and died in the Korean and the Vietnam War respectively.

5.4 TRACING BACK THE CAUSAL CHAIN EVEN FURTHER

This section argues that Japanese occupation was a historical watershed and as such a very good starting point for historical explanations of local party strength and local governance outcomes. To be sure, the Imperial Army did not randomly occupy China, as would be the ideal treatment to isolate an independent effect of Japanese occupation on later governance outcomes. But at the same time, war contingencies were so complex that the geographic patterns of occupation cannot easily be reduced to preexisting geographic patterns. Neither economic potential nor traditional administrative priorities provide satisfying proxies of Japanese occupation. The railway may be the best available proxy for patterns of Japanese occupation, but its linkage with colonization is so intimate that going back along the causal chain from Japanese occupation to railway lines may not be a great conceptual gain. There does not seem to be a parsimonious way to push much further back up the causal channel. In short, war contingencies created a new political landscape.

5.4.1 Japan's Lack of Economic Priorities

The prospect of economic gain did not provide Japanese colonizers with any clear sense of geographic priorities. There is no apparent economic logic behind Japanese occupation patterns in Shandong. At the time, investigators compiled volume after volume assessing China's economic potential, and they found abundant riches almost everywhere. Raw materials, for instance, were on the minds of Japanese industrialists who could potentially have influenced decisions made by the government and the military; yet the investigators showed that raw materials were spread throughout Shandong province, not concentrated in any particular geographical zone.[69] Making the case for an expansion of Japan's activities in China, synopses of Shandong's economic potential, compiled by think tanks close to the government, such as the Co-Prosperity Institute,

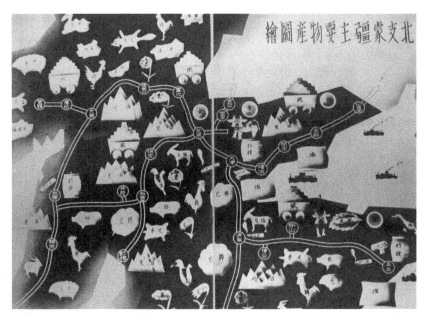

FIGURE 5.4 Riches everywhere! Popular views on Japanese "strategy." Illustration from a magazine by the North China Transportation Company, which dissolved at the end of World War II.[70]

would praise the widespread presence of raw materials, industrial potential, trading opportunities, investment opportunities in agriculture and the
raising of livestock, as well as the transportation sector, all at the same
time.[71]

Japan's interest in agricultural development complicated the formulation of geographic priorities based on economic potential. Historically,
as a result of the scarcity of arable land, the strategic thinking of Japan's
state-builders revolved around arable land as being fundamental to power.
Controlling arable land was equivalent to amassing power.[72] Early on in
the colonization process, Japan had gathered county-by-county data on
arable land,[73] but in terms of land, most of Shandong would be desirable –
except for the mountainous areas, which were attractive for the sake of
raw material exploitation. In addition, the Asia Co-Prosperity Institute
had high-flying ambitions to encourage investment into new land development projects, which would use capital-intensive technology to turn
wasteland into arable land.[74] Wherever in North China the Japanese colonizers looked, they saw economic potential. This outlook, bereft of geographic priorities, was well summarized by an illustration in a popular
magazine (Figure 5.4).[75] The lack of priorities were part of Japan's "myth

of empire" that pushed the army to expand further and further in ways that in hindsight seem hard to rationalize.[76]

Japan did not follow in the footsteps of the Chinese government, and it did not prioritize the same places that Chinese governments had traditionally prioritized. This is particularly apparent in the Northwest of Shandong province, where the imperial government had traditionally maintained a strong presence despite the area's decline in importance during the twentieth century.[77] The Japanese marched through that area at the end of 1937 without stationing any substantial military forces. Instead, the Japanese established a strong presence in Dezhou.

5.4.2 Following the Railroad

In Shandong, Japanese occupation patterns closely followed the railroad. Troops were deployed to secure a corridor along the Shandong section of the busy Beijing–Shandong line, as well as the branch line from the provincial capital to the major port city of Qingdao. There were three or four other minor branch lines, also under firm control. The width of corridor varied substantially, from just a dozen miles to almost 100 miles in the area around Jining, and the density of military protection was also uneven, with more troops covering the North than the South.[78] Some branch lines were built after the occupation, complicating things further. Yet unlike other provinces, in Shandong the railroad is a very good approximation of occupation patterns. If one were to go further back in the causal chain, one could establish a link that begins with railroads affecting occupation patterns, which in turn led to a strong party and predictable governance outcomes.

Because railroad geography and Japanese occupation in Shandong are highly colinear, based on county-level statistics, it is hard to disentangle in a quantitative way the causal effect of each. The railroad passed through a very diverse set of counties. It passed through plains as well as mountainous terrain, touched on some economically backward localities, and left out some of the more prosperous local economic centers. At the time when the two railroad lines were constructed, the goal was to connect important end points in an economic fashion, from a railroad engineering perspective: Beijing to Shanghai and Qingdao to the Beijing-Shanghai trunk line.[79] While falling short of a "random treatment" in the statistical sense, it would be hard to identify county-level characteristics that could predict the construction of the railway.

Being left with a choice between the colonial railroad of the 1910s vs. Japanese occupation of the late 1930s and early 1940s, this book has chosen the latter as the starting point. Arguably, Japanese occupation was a more important watershed event than the construction of the railway three decades earlier. Although the railway fundamentally changed the established travel routes and brought modernity to Shandong, the railway line in and of itself had a limited impact on the province's political map. Only because the railroad later on became the backbone of the Japanese invasion could it become such a consequential infrastructure, determining the geographic patterns of party membership and China's political geography even today.

5.5 CONCLUSION

An irony of history, an ostensibly anti-Communist Japanese invasion gave rise to anti-Japanese Communism in China. This legacy is reflected in the geography of the party's power base, shaped by the Sino-Japanese War. Foreign occupation protected the CCP from government persecution and allowed the CCP to mobilize members for a patriotic cause. In the aftermath of World War II, the CCP was better placed to move into the power vacuum left behind by the retreating Japanese Imperial Army. When the People's Republic was founded four years after Japan's departure, the CCP enjoyed its strongest organizational base in the very provinces that had been under tightest Japanese control. The channel through which the Japanese occupation affects present-day outcomes has little to do with local mentalities or memories, but with party organization. Organizational inertia strongly links the present to the past.

In contrast to the persistence of the occupation effect, the base area effect is largely ephemeral. In the first half of the 1930s, in the Long March operation, the CCP abandoned its early base areas in South China, leaving behind no significant underground organizations, and presumably no pro-CCP sympathies. But even in the later base areas in North China, much of the party's organizational presence was transient, moving to the new centers of power or strategically more important – and more liveable – localities after the Communist takeover of 1949. Therefore, transmission through organizational inertia did not occur in base areas. To the extent that the base-area ethos has survived, it appears to be turning against the party itself. This may help explain why today the party has a smaller presence in its former base areas.

While the results seem robust for macrogeographical spaces such as provinces and prefectures, the relationship between Japanese occupation and party development becomes more complex at the level of micro-geographical spaces. It seems that the CCP could develop fastest in localities at an intermediate distance to the Japanese strongholds. In areas that were very close to the Imperial Army, locals would not risk supporting the party; their best survival strategy was to accommodate the occupation. In areas unaffected by the invasion, people continued their habitual life and their habitual survival strategies and had little reason to get involved in the fight against Japan. Yet in contested areas, directly affected by the violence and where the violence destabilized people's everyday lives, supporting the CCP was more likely to be a good survival strategy, and attacking the Japanese was more likely to be a desirable option.

This chapter contributes to arguments about the origins of strong authoritarian regime parties. It has been observed that the handful of surviving Communist parties all have in common "a legacy of nationalistic, rural revolution."[80] Based on a comparison of four countries, researchers have suggested that strong parties may be the result of a "sustained, violent, and ideologically-driven conflict."[81] This chapter in conjunction with the following chapter confirms these arguments at a subnational level: The CCP today remains stronger in localities where it fought against the Japanese army during the Sino-Japanese War. The legacy of nationalistic violent revolution continues to invigorate regime parties.

6

The Shifting Geography of the CCP's Power Base (1949–2016)

After the foundation of the People's Republic in 1949, instead of contending themselves with geographic patterns of control inherited from the war, party leaders were keen on penetrating areas where up to that point Communists had little of a presence. In the 1950s and 1960s, policy planners were well aware that later acquired territories posed distinct governance challenges to the Communist regime. For instance, by 1949 land reform had already been completed in one third of the country's territory, but not in the two thirds classified as newly liberated areas – indicating not only different ownership structures, but the persistence of traditional systems of local authority.[1] Along with a quick expansion of the CCP's membership, strategies to grasp firm control of grassroots society throughout the realm were, by and large, successful. However, this success does not imply that the CCP controls its territory uniformly, or that historically inherited patterns of control vanished without a trace.

In the seven decades after the foundation of the People's Republic, the geographic power base of the CCP has shifted remarkably little, despite great political upheaval. Comparing party penetration, that is party members per citizens across provinces in 1956 and 2010, a correlation coefficient of 0.78 indicates that membership patterns drifted, but did not change dramatically.[2] Membership patterns in the early years of the People's Republic go a long way predicting membership patterns today: 61 percent of the variation in membership patterns in 2010 can be explained as a result of membership patterns in 1956.[3] Is China's political geography "under the thumb of history"?[4] Clearly, China's political geography, as reflected in party membership patterns, proved very persistent over time – the question is why. Are recruitment priorities targeting the same geographic areas? Or are membership patterns sticky, following historical precedence and adjusting only slowly to new priorities?

The first section of this chapter argues that the party's recruitment procedures result in path-dependent outcomes. The strategic priorities, formulated by Organization Departments at all levels of the hierarchy in membership recruitment plans 發展黨員計劃 in the 1950s, aimed to cover the territory with a more uniform party member network. Today, these plans have other priorities, notably related to countering challenges that come with urbanization. These priorities tend to override preexisting geographic membership patterns, but only in part. It is still easier to recruit party members in places where the CCP already has a strong presence, because it is better informed about potential candidates and because smaller party cells are reluctant to accept new members – the smaller the party cell, the larger each additional member's influence. In short, recruitment is a strong institutional transmission mechanism connecting the past to the present.

Section 6.2 addresses alternative explanations for the similarity between membership patterns in the 1950s and today. First, for purely demographic reasons, aggregate membership patterns have a tendency to persist, because CCP members usually do not leave the party until their death. But as the data show, such an effect of simple hysteresis does not add up to the observed high degree of persistence, especially because the quick growth of the party gives ample room to move away from earlier patterns. Second, an empirical analysis shows that recruitment priorities today focus on the cities, but cannot explain the larger number of party members in traditional party strongholds. Finally, another alternative transmission mechanism moves away from institutions and draws attention to local political cultures: Does an experience of revolutionary struggle form political attitudes that strengthen the party? Given that the political identity of the party has fundamentally changed since the times of the revolution, ideational factors turn out to be irrelevant at best.

Section 6.3 develops a party growth model that allows describing and testing dynamic characteristics of the party's membership base. Based on an economic growth model, the model is applicable to membership-based organizations, where under certain conditions entries and exits are expected to create a more even penetration of the organization across space. Estimating the model coefficients not only allows for testing the null hypothesis that there is no convergence; it also allows estimating the speed of convergence. Returning back to the case of China, section 6.4 applies the model to China and revisits the history of the People's

Republic to explain why convergence was so much faster during some historical eras than others. The central finding of this chapter is that the effect of Japanese occupation on membership remains central to understanding the CCP's power base, because the Leninist organization preserves membership patterns inherited from the past.

Even after the Communists had settled in power for decades, regions with thinly spread party networks had a hard time catching up, in terms of recruitment, with regions where the party had been present from 1937 onward. Leninist recruitment procedures and inner-party power politics gave jurisdictions who had more party members in 1949 a first-mover advantage, affecting the CCP's power base to the present. The historical legacy of recruitment behind Japanese enemy lines persists over generations, so that those areas still have more party members today, with the implications described in Parts II and IV of this book. The persistence of the CCP's membership base provides an institutional transmission mechanism through which events of the past shape outcomes in the present. This chapter inscribes itself into the effort to place politics in time, to better take into account the timing and duration of events.[5] In the course of this chapter, we touch on the CCP's institutional history, recruitment strategies, and contemporary challenges. While the substantive question is limited to the CCP, the methodologies developed in Section 6.3 can be used to analyze historical dynamics of any membership-based organization.

6.1 THE CCP AS A TRANSMITTER OF HISTORICAL LEGACIES

The recruitment procedures by which the party incorporates new members create path-dependent membership patterns. Although at times party leaders proactively moved to expand their membership base in places where the party was least secure, they have also learned to cope with the unevenness of their power base, making the best of the inherited membership patterns. As the following section describes, recruitment in the early People's Republic clearly sought to reduce unevenness, but thereafter took more complex patterns. Since the 1990s, strategic planning of membership recruitment is notable for targeting urban areas. In principle, such planning works against the persistence of historical patterns that are not in the party's contemporary best strategic interest. But in practice deliberate planning runs into obstacles. Recruitment procedures have institutional characteristics that make it easier to recruit in places where there are already many party members.

6.1.1 Recruitment since 1949: the Very Big Picture

After the defeated Japanese Imperial Army fled from China in 1945, the Communists engaged in another four years of warfare to wrest power from the incumbent Republican government. Contrary to what one might expect, during this period the party's geographic membership patterns did not change fundamentally. This was a result of military developments. During the first two years of the Civil War, the People's Liberation Army (PLA) barely expanded its power base, and even the third year saw only gradual extensions to link up core areas of control. Only during the fourth and final year of the Civil War, when the military balance tipped decisively in favor of the CCP, did the PLA swiftly expand its territorial reach. By late 1949, the Communists had gained military superiority over almost all of mainland China, having taken over roughly one half of China's territory within a single year. The military victory was so rapid that civilian party organizations lagged behind and were underdeveloped in the territories gained during this last one-year stretch of the Civil War.

In the immediate aftermath of the Communist victory, establishing an authoritative presence through the entire territory became a high political priority of the new government. At once, the CCP took deliberate measures to gain a civilian foothold in the more recently conquered areas of the South. As early as 1948, a year before the Communist victory, the party selected tens of thousands of its more capable and experienced cadres and trained them to take over and administer cities of the South.[6] But their mission was difficult. For one thing, after the military balance had tipped in favor of the Communists, telling opportunists from true believers was hard. For another, without overstating the lingering tension between North and South, there must have been resentment in the South against a group of people from far away dominating their local governments.[7] While rotating cadres between different regions had been a long-standing practice in Chinese governance, the one-way street of Northerners going to govern the South was unusual. In short, even the many well-trained Southbound cadres could not unmake history. The difference between areas that were dominated by the CCP early on and other areas that turned Communist only in the last months of the Civil War defined the 1950s and 1960s.

The following instructions, promulgated by the Central Committee in 1958, provide internal guidelines for recruiting party members and are explicit about balancing out the reach of the party. These instructions represent similar documents regularly appearing in the period between 1949 and the beginning of the Cultural Revolution in 1966.

Provinces and regions where the proportion of party members in the rural population has not yet reached 2% can, in the coming years, recruit until 2% are reached. Provinces and regions where the proportion of rural party members already reaches or exceeds 2% can also recruit moderately, but must not exceed 2.5%; in provinces and regions with extraordinarily many party members [i.e. Hebei and Shanxi] the number must not exceed 3%. But it is absolutely forbidden to abruptly develop too large numbers, it is imperative to pay attention to quality.[8]

The instructions not only reflect that the party's uneven presence was of concern to central leaders and that they sought to achieve a balanced penetration throughout the realm. They also reflect countervailing reasons militating against too inflexible an approach. The Central Committee highlights that fast recruitment comes at the expense of quality. In addition, the Organization Department's original opinion, forwarded by the Central Committee along with its instructions, emphasizes the need to "infuse fresh blood into the party," so that one cannot simply stop recruiting in localities with too many members. In short, the leadership was well aware that a strict enforcement of the 2 percent penetration rate throughout China would have been too costly compared to the benefits.

When Mao unleashed the Cultural Revolution, the CCP entered an era of upheaval where the Organization Department focused on the survival of the institution. Party hierarchies broke down and organizational rules were cast aside in the name of revolution, supposedly held back by a bureaucratic spirit prevailing in the party. To secure their own political position, rebel leaders in tenuous positions of power recruited allies and relatives to the CCP, without regard for orderly procedures. Entry into the party was so much in disarray that it was no longer clear who was a real party member, and that only a few localities could report party membership statistics for the period between 1966 and 1971. When the party took back control of the country, the exclusion of many hastily recruited party members was an important element of party leaders' tactics. While other newly recruited party members were allowed to remain in the party, the overall tendency was a return to the status quo as it had existed prior to the Cultural Revolution. Thus, if anything, the Cultural Revolution accentuated preexisting party membership patterns. Afterwards in the 1980s, often considered the most liberal decade of the People's

Republic, state-builders focused their attention not on Leninist party building, but on reform experiments. Compared to the first fifteen years of the People's Repbulic, the period between the mid-1960s and the mid-1980s was marekd by an absence of deliberate recruitment strategies, so that membership patterns floated without particular direction.

This changed markedly in the late 1980s and early 1990s, an era marked by a resurgence of interest in Leninist-style party building. The Tian'anmen crisis of 1989 along with the extinction of Communism in other parts of the world suggested to leaders that in order for the regime to survive, they had to do more than they had done in the 1980s and they had to do more than the Soviet Union had done. Rather than casting aside Leninism, leaders embraced its organizational principles, refining them to counter the challenges of China in the 21st century. The creation of two new magazines by the Organization Department, namely *Party Building* 黨建研究 in March 1989 and *Party Building – Internal Reference* 黨建研究内参 in 1991, marks this Neo-Leninist turn. The latter publication was classified until recently, but enough articles from the first ten years have been leaked[9] to provide rare glimpses into the explicit and self-aware approach to strengthening the party in a way that improves its effectiveness in the 21st century. Since the early 1990s, recruitment plans have reshaped the power base of the party in new ways.

After more than sixty years of Communist rule, the number of party members exceeds the population of a country like Germany: 7 percent of all Chinese citizens are members. Yet the party's penetration of society is far from complete. While it could be in the party's strategic interests to have more party members in some places than in others, it is not in the interest of party organizers to have places that lack a party grassroots structure. In the mid-1980s, at a time when the administrative village approximated the natural village community, one third of China's almost 1 million villages did not have a village committee.[10] Even in Shandong, where the party has always been exceptionally present, at that time about 16 percent of villages did not have a party committee.[11] Nominally, the problem was solved by merging natural villages into larger administrative villages, so that today only 131 out of 593,966 administrative villages lack a party organization.[12] In practice, rural-urban migration has further reduced the party's presence in rural areas. It is common to find villages that seem to lack a party presence, since they are run as part of a larger administrative village, or because the CCP members have more or less temporarily moved away.

6.1.2 Strategic Recruitment under Constraints

Party-building 黨建 is a technical term referring to all activities that serve to expand, maintain and reform the effectivness of the CCP's organizational structure, especially at the grassroots level. In practice, party-building focuses on persons – party secretaries and party members – and their beliefs; less on procedures and finances; and least of all on organizational charts and standardized administration. Strategies concerning new party members find their most concrete formulation in recruitment plans, which are designed as a strategic response to the party's most pressing challenges. The admission of capitalists into the party is a definite sign that the CCP is prepared to pragmatically shift its social base, accommodating and co-opting new strata into the system, depending on strategic needs.[13]

Recruitment plans are derivatives of more abstract strategic blueprints. Full of jargon, abstract concepts, and coded meanings, at first glance many documents on party-building appear devoid of content. For instance, coming across the word "democratic" in a party document, Western readers may shrug it off as no more than a cynical label, as in *Democratic People's Republic of Korea*. In fact, in the context of party-building it has very specific meanings and can signify, for instance, a requirement to let non–party members participate in certain meetings. To be sure, this kind of participation is not a democratic one in the Western sense. But it is an authoritarian top-down tool to increase the pressure on party cells and could signal the beginning of a purge, say, in the form of an anticorruption drive.[14]

Masterminding party construction policies are the powerful Organization Department and a top-level steering committee called *Small Coordinating Group for Country-Wide Grassroots Organization Building* 全國基層組織建設協調小組. The group has considerable political weight: Although the exact composition of the group remains undisclosed, the group's importance is reflected by the fact that its secretariat is headed by Wu Yuliang, a Vice Director of the Central Discipline Inspection Commission who has been intimately involved in Xi Jinping's formidable Anti-Corruption Campaign. At lower levels we also find much strategic thinking on strengthening party organization, both inside the party and in academia.

As is characteristic of state-led central planning procedures, recruitment quotas are at the heart of these documents. For example, the Organization Department of a county typically sets targets for how many party members each party committee within its jurisdiction should recruit; in addition it may stipulate that, say, at least 75 percent of all incoming party members have a senior high school degree, at least 70 percent be under 35 years old, and at least 30 percent be women.[15] Although the recruitment plans include additional, detailed political guidance, local party leaders tend to ignore these aspects and see only the quotas,[16] interpreting them as a minimum requirement. This is comprehensible, since higher-level authorities observe recruitment statistics as the only readily observable signal about local party-building performance. When quotas are not met, higher-level authorities will ask for explanations.[17] Even if central recruitment policies are only imperfectly implemented – with overperformance creating more imbalance than underperformance – they allow central planners to discourage organization building in some places and accelerate it in others.

A central theme running through the thinking about party organization work is innovation in the face of various challenges of socioeconomic modernization, including globalization.[18] The more specific the authors are in describing the concrete challenges, the clearer it is that they are almost exclusively concerned about challenges in the cities.[19] As became clear under Jiang Zemin's leadership in the 1990s, the party is prepared to embrace modernization. The party is ready to work with "the newly productive forces in society" and accept their representatives into the party. To penetrate the newly productive force, party recruitment in the past decade has been fixated on the cities, reducing the CCP's presence in less developed rural areas and increasing it in highly developed urban areas. Section 6.2.2 provides more detail on the urban turn and provides some numerical material to assess the importance of this priority.

The case of Tibet illustrates the difficulties of forcing organizational growth of the party. The CCP arrived late in that province. Not counting party organizations deployed from outside, the first homegrown party cell and the CCP's first full-grown organizational presence at the grassroots of Tibet came with the establishment of a party cell in a remote village after the uprising of 1959.[20] Mindful of the geostrategic stakes involved, party leaders for once decided to make vigorous efforts to overcome their historical weakness and to organizationally penetrate the province. The promise of having party members on the ground in areas dominated by ethnic minorities is described as follows:

Maintain most direct, most frequent and most intimate relations with minority people, to directly hear the voices of all minority people, to directly understand their emotions, to accurately perceive the ideological pulse of the ethnic masses, to reflect the wishes of all minority populations, really serving as a bridging bond between the party and the people.[21]

For the first time in the 1970s and then consistently since the 1990s, the CCP made extraordinary recruitment efforts in Tibet. In 2002 party penetration was still below the national average, but in 2010 Tibet had 23 percent more party members than the average Chinese province. But it is highly questionable whether the fulfillment of this numerical quota was effective. Presumably, to achieve effective penetration, it would be desirable to mingle with the ethnic communities. But in this respect, penetration continues to be fundamentally flawed, since 62 percent of the party members are ethnic Han Chinese, in a social context where over 90 percent of the population are ethnic Tibetans.[22] If deemed to be a strategic necessity, party membership certainly can be grown at will, but compromises along the way result in an organization that is in fact not well rooted in society. An organically grown membership is more useful than one that is the result of bureaucrats energetically fulfilling recruitment quotas.

Demand for party membership has also certain limits. Surely, in almost any jurisdiction at least 10 percent of the population will be opportunistic enough to seek CCP membership – numerically more than enough to make that jurisdiction a well-penetrated one. But the Organization Department does not seek to recruit just anyone, preferring well-educated individuals in influential positions, with true commitment to the CCP, and ready to actively engage in time-consuming party activities. This can be a problem. For instance, long-established Shanghai residents are not the most zealous in pursuing party membership. By contrast, newly arrived migrants have a great interest in joining the party, since they lack other venues of social advancement. However, accepting too many "immigrants" creates discontent among the "old Shanghainese," who are weary of sharing the privileges of their urban wealth. Currently a central contention in Shanghai revolves around the ratio of long-established Shanghai residents to new Shanghai residents. While it is unclear whether the presence of outsiders in the party would lead to a more migrant-friendly policy, the individual opportunities that the party provides to its members in the long run will leave more migrants in powerful and profitable positions, creating envy among old Shanghainese. Even more importantly, a major concern of Shanghai party leaders is to make their city appear politically loyal, since the center might have many reasons to distrust the metropolis for its capitalist traditions and foreign connections.[23]

The Organization Department is extraordinarily powerful, but its recruitment strategies are formulated under constraints. In order to be successful, recruitment strategies must take into account the local setting. Too much ambition can backfire. For instance, it turned out that the recruitment drives of the 1950s were hasty. Many new members turned out to be politically unreliable, so that quick expansion was followed by a period of purges.

6.1.3 Path-Dependent Recruitment

An important organizational principle of the CCP holds that 黨要管黨 "the party must run the party." This rule, first formulated in the wake of Mao's devastating Great Leap Forward Famine, enshrines the supremacy of the party over all other institutions of government in the People's Republic. It is consistent with the rule that prosecutors cannot investigate party members – the party's own discipline inspection system has to expel the party members first. The principle also implies that recruitment must be fully carried out through party institutions alone. The CCP cannot cooperate with other state agencies to set up its grassroots network. As a result, the principle poses a fundamental obstacle to recruitment in places with inadequate party networks.

Recruitment experiments in Hubei, a province of Central China, illustrate how this principle works in practice. In the late 1990s, the Organization Department internally noted that screening procedures of incoming party members were lacking and that local party organizations often failed miserably in gathering accurate information about these individuals. Other authoritarian regimes would involve government agencies, such as the police, to improve the informational base on which membership decisions are made. In Communist Germany, the state security apparatus even observed party members' ideological uprightness after they joined the party. However, such a solution is unthinkable in China. Hubei's Organization Department instead implemented a "public announcement system:" Through public announcement boards and occasionally even through radio and TV, ordinary citizens were provided with the names and personal details of recruitment targets, along with a telephone number for denunciations. Of course, local party leaders could make their recruitment decision without being bound by public opinion.[24] But the mass line helped to check information on potential party members. The case illustrates that the party is open to many solutions, but does not allow government agencies to provide help in recruitment. Being on its own, it is more challenging for the party to recruit in places where it has less of a presence.

The highly formalized procedures for admitting new party members make it easier to recruit in localities where there are already many party members. For example, the party requires each new party member to garner recommendations from two existing party members, who will guarantee politically loyal behavior of the new party member for the rest of his/her life. Not only are existing party members reluctant to give such guarantees, there also appear to be rules – at least informal rules – that each member can recommend only a limited number of people throughout his/her party career. In places with few existing party members, it can be hard to find a guarantor. More generally, upper-level party organizations expect party cells to provide detailed and personal information on membership applicants. As with other kinds of information, so also with recruitment-related information: The greater the presence of the party within a given locality, the easier it is for party administrators to collect and verify the information needed during the admission process of new party members. Thus, places with few party members find it hard to catch up.

In work units or villages where there are no existing CCP members, it will be exceedingly difficult to recruit the first member. The risk is great that the party will not pick the right person and that empowering such a person will create new tensions in the village or in the work unit. In the past, the solution would have been to dispatch work teams to investigate carefully and to carry out recruitment. Especially before the Communist takeover, the materials collected by such work teams were impressively detailed.[25] We do not see such work teams, because the organization department seems satisfied with rural recruitment and, as described later, because more innovative solutions exist for urban settings. Nevertheless, enormous efforts are needed to carry out proper recruitment in places where there is little in terms of grassroots party organization.

Besides organizational dynamics, there are also political obstacles to convergence. To the extent that local party leaders are concerned about power arithmetics, small party cells recruit fewer new members than large party cells. Consider the marginal effect of admitting a new party member on the power of the incumbents. If a party cell is large, an additional member would have only a negligible effect on the power games within the party cell. However, if the party cell is small, the new party member might well shift the power balance among the members. Here it is important to note that according to the party regulations a party cell must consist of at least three members, and that many party cells are actually very small organizational units of three or four members. Clearly, power dynamics in such a setting are easily swayed by an additional party member, who eventually will take a side in party-cell internal disagreements. The incumbents of small party cells and large party cells alike are wary of new recruits, who may displace them from their position of influence. However, incumbent members of large party cells have less to fear from new recruits than incumbent members of small party cells. The same power arithmetics also apply to larger aggregates of party organizations, such as party committees at the various hierarchical levels. Since new recruits have a larger marginal influence in small party organizations, small organizations tend to grow more slowly than bigger party organizations.

The problem of incumbent party members protecting their turf is also related to the question of how many migrants to admit into the party in places with large numbers of domestic immigrants. The established party elite tends to be wary of new recruits, especially if they have a different socioeconomic background or a greater education or superior wealth. After all, once admitted into the party, new members may displace the old members from their positions of power and influence. In case of a political campaign, it is important for the old members to recruit new members who will be loyal. This gives incentives to recruit among family or at least among citizens with a similar life path. A side effect of the current anticorruption campaign is to remind party members of the importance of personal loyalty, since that is the only hope for surviving the erratic political winds of a cleanup campaign that leaves much room for discretion in choosing its victims. It is believed that membership in one of the People's Republic's old ruling families is the best guarantee for one's safety, unless your family was connected to Bo Xilai's clan.[26]

In sum, party organizers steer recruitment in response to strategic challenges, but they do not make an all-out efforts to defy historically grown patterns. The unusual case of Tibet shows how counterproductive a more strong-armed approach would be. Usually, party organizers try softer approaches to level the playing field and recruit more party members in places where so far the party is underrepresented. In addition, the recent focus on urban areas is bound to result in a new unevenness, over time leading to a drastic underrepresentation of the party in rural areas. The party has long worked toward a more uniform presence throughout its territory. These efforts at evening out the power base are best described as patient yet consistent: When there is a chance, the party grows in places where it had henceforth been less present. Yet the party has a very long time horizon and will not compromise the quality of its networks and the reliability of its members. Determining the success in evening out and the speed of convergence is an empirical question.

6.2 CCP RECRUITMENT PATTERNS OVER TIME

This section turns to statistical data to illuminate the causal path through which the past influences the present. First, descriptive statistics refute the idea that party demography alone can explain persistence: The fact that people join the CCP for a lifetime only explains a small fraction of the observed persistence. Second, contemporary strategic priorities of recruitment fail to explain contemporary patterns. Even after taking into account known recruitment criteria, history looms large as a decisive determinant of degrees of party penetration. Finally, the analysis of former base areas suggests that institutional mechanics and not Communist identities provide the link to the past.

6.2.1 Continuity as Demographic Hysteresis?

Demography contributes to the stickiness of membership patterns. When leaders of an organization change the focus of recruitment, membership patterns will not fall into place instantaneously. For a while, members recruited according to the new priorities will remain a minority compared to the bulk of incumbent members. Therefore, steering an organization takes foresight. This phenomenon of hysteresis is particularly relevant in an organization like the CCP, which typically individuals join at a young age and do not leave until their death. Demographic hysteresis creates geographic stickiness, since for many decades rank-and-file party members were fixed in their places and could not be strategically deployed like party cadres. Demographics are one reason why geographic patterns of membership change only gradually. But as the following paragraphs demonstrate, demographic hysteresis makes only a very minor contribution to the stickiness of geographic membership patterns.

The phenomenon of demographic hysteresis is the most elementary form of an accumulation effect and should be distinguished from path dependence. Let P_{t-1} be the stock of party members at the end of year $t-1$. R_t is the inflow of new recruits and D_t is the outflow of dropouts, both during year t. Then the stock of party members at the end of the following year is $P_t = P_{t-1} + R_t - D_t$. As long as not all party members drop out, that is, $D_t < P_t$, we will observe demographic hysteresis, because

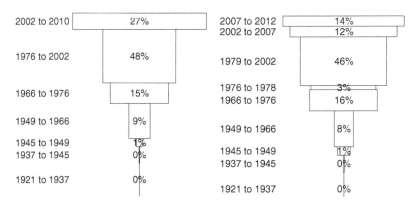

FIGURE 6.1 Party membership as accumulated stock. Left: China 2010, based on internal party statistics.[27] Right: Shandong 2012, based on party yearbook.[28]

the stock of members in year t carries over to year $t + 1$. Truly path-dependent accumulation effects work through a different channel. If R_t is independent of P_t, that is if recruitment is not affected by the number of preexisting party members, there is no path dependence. Yet if it is easier to recruit people in places where there are already many party members to begin with, recruitment is a positive function of preexisting membership $R_t(P_t) > 0$, so that there is path dependence. Even in the absence of path dependence, membership patterns would still be linked to history, because the number of current members would always depend on the stock of party members in the preceding year.

In case of the CCP, the phenomenon of demographic hysteresis does little to explain the high degree of persistence, as inspection of the party's demography shows. Figure 6.1 illustrates the practical irrelevance of demographic hysteresis. The left-hand side looks at all party members at the end of 2012 and divides them into groups, depending on the time of their recruitment.[29] One fourth of all party members were recruited since 2002, coinciding with the Hu Jintao era. Another half were recruited after Deng Xiaoping took over in 1979. Even if we consider a province like Shandong, with a particularly strong presence of party members at the eve of the Communist takeover in 1949, the demography of party members exhibits almost identical traits, as reflected in the right-hand side of Figure 6.1.[30] If there were no path dependence, recruitment patterns preceding the Cultural Revolution – and certainly those preceding the Communist takeover in 1949 – would be irrelevant to explain membership patterns in 2012.

These results are unsurprising for two reasons. First, demography cannot explain transmission of membership patterns across three generations. When the People's Republic was founded in 1949, party members above age 25 constituted 75 percent of all party members.[31] By 2015 the survivors from this cohort would be over 91 years old. In practice, already by 2010 there was little of a demographic carryover from the era of the Sino-Japanese War and the Civil War. Second, proactive expansion of the membership base meant that the pool of party members recruited prior to the foundation of the People's Republic was quickly diluted by newcomers. As early as 1955, persons recruited after 1949 constituted a majority of the CCP membership. At the eve of the Cultural Revolution, 82 percent of party members had joined after 1949.[32]

Under such circumstances, demographic hysteresis could not have prevented party organizers from arriving at a geographically perfectly balanced membership base very early on. For instance, declaring a complete recruitment stop in localities with many party members would have gone a long way in evening out penetration across space. To be sure, party organizers have recruited significantly more party members in places where the party is underrepresented. But they have not privileged these places enough for the unevenness of the party's power base to disappear – even after 70 years. This suggests that path-dependence was at work.

6.2.2 Continuities of Recruitment Strategies?

To establish that there was path dependence in the true sense of the word, resulting from recruitment dynamics as laid out in Section 6.1.3, we must rule out another, alternative explanation: Theoretically speaking, geographic persistence of membership patterns could be the result of contemporary recruitment strategies resembling the occupation strategies of the Japanese Imperial Army. In practice, there is little overlap, as the following pages show. By far the most likely confounding variable could be socioeconomic prosperity, and in particular urbanization. As mentioned before, the Japanese may to some degree have targeted well-off areas, and Jiang Zemin's redirecting the party to the society's most productive forces may give the party a similar focus, at least to the extent that formerly well-off areas coincide with current well-off areas. Under such a scenario, it is not the case that a strong party presence facilitates strong growth, but rather that the Japanese Imperial Army and the Organization Department target similar geographic areas. If the localities with most active recruitment prior to the Communist victory of 1949 remain a political priority today, for reasons other than the ease of recruiting in localities with a strong preexisting party infrastructure, there would be persistence without path dependence. As Chapter 5 showed, there are no easy predictors for the areas invaded by Japan. Moreover, previous sections demonstrate that the CCP's recruitment strategies in the 1950s and 1960s sought to balance out party membership, self-consciously working against persistence. Finally, the organizational focus on urban areas is likely to even out membership patterns, almost as a side effect.

This section introduces empirical evidence from Shandong, a province for which I have obtained particularly fine-grained data. The following regressions shed light on contemporary recruitment strategies. The focus of recruitment is on the cities, where socioeconomic development creates the need for bolstering government control. In addition, a secondary concern is to balance out membership patterns, though this balancing out proceeds at such a slow rate that membership patterns do not shift much.

Urbanization as driver of contemporary recruitment

Jiang Zemin's slogan of the "Three Represents," elevated to party dogma at the Sixteenth Party Congress in 2002, calls for the party to represent the most advanced productive forces in society. The most well-known implication of Jiang Zemin's instruction was that the CCP could henceforth recruit entrepreneurs, that is precisely the capitalist class it once had vowed to overthrow. In practice, the recruitment of capitalists has not yet changed the face of the party. In 2012 out of all party members in Shandong only 1.5 percent belonged to the "new classes" 新的社會基層; of these, 77 percent were self-employed 個體勞動者 and therefore do not fit the ideal type of a capitalist.[33] The "Three Represents" had other types of practical implications for local party organizers. To party organizers in Qingdao, Jiang Zemin's injunction was disconcerting, because their local party branches represented mostly the least productive forces in society. As a result, they engaged in recruiting not capitalists, but workers in the more successful sectors for the economy.

The urban challenge begins with the incumbent party members themselves. Marxist theory reserves a prominent place to the urban proletariat, so that workers in large, state-owned factories for many decades used to be the privileged class of the Chinese Socialist state. This group formed the core constituency of urban party organizations. Yet with Deng Xiaoping's policy of Reform and Opening, the privileges of this group dissipated. The urban proletariat turned from the winners of revolution to the losers of reform. Instead of the erstwhile complacency among its rank-and-file members, the CCP had to face disgruntlement from within. To be sure, having some unemployed workers in its own ranks might help the party to keep connected to and informed about sentiments in this group. But in many cities the number of unemployed people and retired workers among CCP members far exceeds what could by any stretch of the imagination be a politically useful level. The city of Qingdao epitomizes this problem. It may entail one of the major port cities that prospered under the socialist market economy, yet many of the party members lost their privileges and were forced into early retirement or unemployment. Statistics from the Northern district of the city reflect the alarming dimensions of the problem: "Altogether 26,610 party members, of whom 17,378 are either retired or unemployed . This is 65.3% of the total membership."[34] Since mass exclusion of party members for socioeconomic reasons is not a legitimate option, the organization department resorted to diluting the incumbent membership by recruiting large numbers of new party members.[35]

Part of the urbanization challenge comes with migration. After the Communist victory, party organization was designed for citizens who remain in the same locality and in the same work unit for their entire lives. Two decades of large-scale migration have destabilized grassroots party organization. When villagers leave to work in the cities, their relationship to the village party committee becomes attenuated. Many of them turn into members who "pocket the party" 口袋黨員 or turn into "hidden members" 隱形黨員. It is too much bureaucratic hassle for migrant party members to transfer their file and join a party cell in their new community, especially if they frequently switch workplaces. In addition, local party cells tend not to welcome outsiders. From the perspective of higher-level party organizers this is regrettable, because migrant party members would provide a much-needed link into migrant communities.

Several initiatives are designed for the party to penetrate China's floating population: One is to offer practical support to migrant party members in their new environment, thereby providing them with incentives to identify themselves with the party organizers in the cities. Another consists in strengthening party branches in residential communities with many migrant workers.[36] In addition, the Organization Department raises awareness that party members are responsible for maintaining their relationship to the organization 組織關係, reviving the use of letters to transfer party membership from one unit to another.[37] In order to put pressure on the party member to quickly register in the city, the document contains an expiration date. One example that the author came across gives the member no more than ten days to get in touch with a new party cell.[38]

The urban factory floor has remained a critical frontline for the CCP's organization work. Economic reform has made the task of organizing the proletariat harder than during Maoist times. Although party organizers are at ease[39] in state-owned enterprises,[40] the emergence of new economic actors presents difficulties. Partly because in the absence of strictly enforced labor regulations the potential for labor conflict is enormous, the CCP is concerned about penetrating the quickly evolving nonstate sector:

作為佔非公企業總數90％以上的小微企業，由於黨員數量少，業態分類廣，人員流動快，存在週期短等原因，一直是黨組織覆蓋和黨建工作開展的難點。In micro-companies, which make up more than 90% of all companies in the private sector, as a result of few party members in the firms, their diversity, the quick turnover of personnel and the short life-span of these firms, it has been a great difficulty to organizationally cover that ground and carry out party-building.[41]

Local party organizations employ innovative strategies to improve their reach. A party-building project in Shandong that was highlighted as exemplary tried to work around the principle that the factory floor is observed by party cells established within each factory. Instead, observing that in their jurisdiction migrant workers switch factories more often than they switch homes, local party organizers recruited the workers in their living communities, thereby hoping to establish a lasting link into several factories through just one party cell.

Especially in urban settings, the party has been warily watching the rise of "new societal organizations" 新社會組織, roughly corresponding to nongovernmental organizations (NGOs) in a broad sense and including anything from community associations to employers' associations. Their existence comes to party organizers' attention through the registries of the Civil Affairs Office and through the security apparatus.[42] Once aware of an organization's existence, party organizers may decide to penetrate it by setting up a party branch. To get a foot in the door, the organization department can either encourage existing CCP members to join the NGOs in question or try to recruit NGO members. At the very least, potential new party members could not be turned down just because they are also active in the NGO sector.[43] Success quotas in penetrating new societal organizations may be part of local CCP organizers' yearly reports on their achievements.[44] Because new societal organizations are predominantly an urban phenomenon, attempts to be present in NGOs further accelerates the tendency for urban recruitment.[45]

Contrasting with the party's endorsement of all *productive forces in society* is its opposition to any societal force perceived as backward. Most notably, the CCP disapproves of religious movements, deriding them as superstitious. Its aversion to Falun Gong is visceral. According to an internal analysis of the organization's activities in Anhui, in the late 1990s the organization department was appalled to find that thousands of party members had joined the sect, representing no fewer than 11 percent of all Falun Gong followers in that province. Two political rallies, each assembling 700 to 800 individuals in front of the provincial government seat in late 1999, certainly raised alarm. But even more importantly, the systematic approach of the sect to recruiting followers, reminiscent of party member recruitment itself, made the party leaders uneasy.[46]

The attitude to other religious organizations is similarly intolerant. In a 1957 case that was widely noted case at the time, a party member had to choose between party membership and his Muslim affiliation, which he had taken for the sake of marriage.[47] Nowadays, while religious party members are tolerated under certain conditions in certain places, generally speaking the party is not much more tolerant. The following quote from an important instruction concerning the party's dealings with religion is the only section that shows a minimalist approach to accommodating religion. The party is not ready to compromise very much:

In ethnic minority areas where religion is widespread..., in order not to break away from the masses, to respect and comply with customary practices, participation in some traditional marriage ceremonies and mass festivals should not be considered as expressing religious belief or participating in a religious event.[48]

Private markets, which lack a centralized organization and follow the dogma of making money, are no match to the party, but religious movements pose a real challenge, because they involve deep personal commitments tying persons to organizations outside the party's reach. As a result, the party is making few compromises when it comes to religion. Challenges from ethnic communities and religious movements are dealt with by a strategy of containment rather than penetration.

Data and Results

The available quantitative evidence supports the argument presented above. Since the beginning of the 21st century, CCP organizers have focused on recruiting in urban areas more than in rural areas. Despite formidable obstacles inherent to a Leninist apparatus, party organizers sought to achieve as uniform a party presence as possible. The following

TABLE 6.1 *Provincial data on party recruitment in the 21st century*

	Mean	Median	S.D.	S.D. (w/o outliers)
Population	669,060	622,000	287,909	289,130
Members	32,216	30,244	14,371	14,311
Members 2001	29,966	28,957	14,384	14,387
Membership percentage	5.0%	4.7%	1.5%	1.5%
Yearly membership change	563	446	2,214	718
Yearly membership change percentage	2.4%	1.6%	10%	2.7%
Urbanites	245,325	201,866	16,085	16,017
Urbanization [urbanites per population]	41%	32%	28%	28%
Minority population	4,514	2,582	5,418	5,347
Minority presence [minority per population]	0.7%	0.4%	0.8%	0.9%
Big religious organizations	3	1	9	9
Religious presence [organizations per 10,000 people]	0.05%	0.01%	0.1%	0.1%
Economic development [million yuan]	39,308	23,963	44,910	43,780

Source: Party statistics from various additions of provincial party yearbook.[49] Census data available at Harvard Geospatial Library. Distribution of registered religious organizations derived from China Geo-explorer II, China Data Center.

quantitative test of these hypotheses is possible thanks to uniquely complete and fine-grained time series data of party member statistics. The data set contains county-year observations and covers all 140 counties of Shandong between 2001 and 2012 – that is the Hu Jintao era plus one year.[50] Since only five observations are missing, the data set contains the number of party members for 1,673 county-year observations.[51]

To put a spotlight on recruitment trends, the dependent variable is defined as the increase in party membership.[52] Party member recruitment statistics exhibit remarkable characteristics. Between 2002 and 2012, counties on average recruited about 500 new party members a year. While most counties carried out recruitment close to that average, numerous counties carried out reorganization campaigns that resulted in recruitment – and very rarely in exclusion – of party members at different orders of magnitude, reflected in a large standard deviation. Therefore the outliers at the tail-end of the distribution should not be brushed aside as reporting errors.[53] As a robustness check, one estimation of the baseline model excludes outliers, defined as yearly membership percentage change below the 1 percent quantile and above the 99 percent quantile, and arrives at essentially similar results.

Data from the 2000 census provide the number of urbanites and the number of people belonging to minority populations. The number of officially registered religious organizations can be inferred from data available at the China Data Center.[54] I measure the degree of a county's urbanization by dividing the number of residents with an urban hukou by the number of all residents. Similarly, the presence of minorities and the religious presence divides the absolute numbers by population size. The alternative specification in the fourth column of Table 6.2, as a robustness check, uses a different strategy to control for size effects. Instead of membership change, the outcome variable is membership change divided by total membership in the previous year. The independent variables also are transformed from absolute numbers to percentages as indicated in the table.

The results of the baseline model indicate that for each 10,000 additional urbanites, there tend to be 9.2 additional party recruits every year, controlling for population size among other things. The effect is not only significant at the 5 percent level, but also substantively important. Comparing an entirely urban jurisdiction to an entirely rural jurisdiction, one

TABLE 6.2 *Party recruitment in the 21st century: results*

	Baseline Model	W/o outliers	Alternative Model
CCP members in 2002 [10,000]	−260***	−77**	−0.01**
Urbanites [10,000]	9.2*	11.3***	
Urbanization [urbanites per population]			0.062***
Minority population [10,000]	−34	54	
Minority presence [minority per population]			0.12
Big religious organizations	−4.7	−2.7	
Religious presence [organizations per population]			−91
Economic development [log GRP, 10,000 Yuan]	157**	72***	0.000
Population [10,000]	13	1.6	0.000
Population square	−0.032	0	−0.000

*** Significance at 0.001, ** significance at 0.01, * significance at 0.05, . significance at 0.1
Notes: OLS estimators. 1,377 county-year observations. Dependent variable: number of party members. *Sources:* See Table 6.1.

would expect 615 additional recruits in the urban area, which is twice the average yearly recruitment. Moreover, party organizers successfully work toward convergence, recruiting fewer party members in places that had already many party members at the beginning of the Hu era. Each 10,000 additional initial party members in 2002 are associated with 260 fewer recruits in each of the following years. There is convergence.

As it turns out, growth trends in party membership do indeed reflect the organization builders' twin goals of urbanization and evening out their reach. Importantly, the fact that the party tends to recruit more members in places where it is underrepresented says nothing about the speed at which this evening out takes place. In other words, the results should by no means obscure the high importance of history to explain spatial variation in party membership patterns. In fact, looking at the bigger picture, current recruitment patterns are only the last layer in a series of sediment layers accumulated over time. The data speak clearly. Because 25 percent of all party members were recruited during the Hu era (2002–2012), one might think that recruitment during this time goes a long way in explaining variation in local party presence. If evening out party membership patterns had been the top priority, much could have been done to level the number of party members. From a historical perspective, however, recruitment activities in the past ten years have had only a comparatively small effect on membership patterns. A bivariate regression that models the number of CCP members in 2012 as a linear function of party members in 2001 can explain 90 percent of the variation. To control for size effects, a regression that models the proportion of party members in the population in 2012 as a function of the proportion in 2001 can still explain 74 percent of the variation. Despite the fact that party organizers have been seeking to even out the reach of the party, the presence of the party in local communities is still strongly shaped by the past.

During the Hu Jintao era, recruitment strategically targeted the cities and sought to even out membership patterns. Controlling for the rapid increase in urban population, the CCP has been disproportionately recruiting members in urban areas. Besides the striking retreat from the countryside, there are notable attempts to achieve a regionally more balanced membership base. Nevertheless, these contemporary determinants of recruitment patterns should not obscure that history remains the key. Counties with many party members in 2002 still have more party members in 2011; the correlation is 95 percent. Accounting for population size, counties with many party members per capita in 2002 continue to display a high party penetration rate in 2012; the correlation is 85 percent. These continuities occur despite the fact that ostensibly party organizers had ample of room to shape geographic patterns of CCP membership according to their contemporary strategic needs, since 26 percent of Shandong's party members in 2011 had been recruited since 2002.

To see how much flexibility organizers had, numerically speaking, to reshape membership patterns, consider the following thought experiment. Assume that the goal was to even out membership patterns as much as possible, constrained by the overall number of recruits prescribed from higher-level authorities. Assume further that party organizers sought to achieve this goal by proclaiming a recruitment stop in counties with party penetration above the 2011 average penetration of 4.8 percent, and instead recruiting members in such a way as to minimize the standard deviation of party penetration. Since the hold of the party was very uneven in 2002, reflected in a standard deviation of 1.4 percent, despite a recruitment stop, still 20 percent of the counties would have more party members than the average in 2011. Given that 1 percent of the party membership exits each year[55] and that party membership grew by 14 percent over the nine years under consideration, party organizers could still have reduced the standard deviation of penetration to less than 0.8 percent by 2011.[56] In 2011 the actual standard deviation of party penetration was 1.5 percent, even slightly higher than in 2002.

Contemporary determinants of local party presence pale in comparison to historical determinants. There is no lack in strategic thinking and efforts to readjust the CCP's power base, undertaken in particular by the party's powerful organization department. Recruitment plans are designed to counter challenges that come with modernization, such as socioeconomic differentiation that tends to obstruct the reach of the state. Because many of these challenges are most severe in urban areas, party organizers are paying most attention to the cities. Empirically, geographic recruitment trends of the Hu Jintao era (2002–2012) reflected this focus on the cities. The party also recruits more new people in places where it is least present. Yet at the same time the data indicate that these attempts at evening out the membership base are half-hearted at best and have a limited impact on geographic patterns. Therefore it is necessary to adopt a longer time horizon and study how historical contingencies shape contemporary outcomes. The regression analysis is helpful to isolate contemporary determinants of party membership, but in doing so can be misleading and obscure how closely the present is tied to the past. Later on in this chapter, Section 6.3.2 suggests a methodology to analyze these complex temporal dynamics.

6.2.3 A Base Area Effect?

Former revolutionary base areas play a central role in CCP mythology. In textbooks as well as TV series, they serve as the stage for legendary stories of loyalty and betrayal, of heroism and cowardice. Yet the actual places have by and large fallen into oblivion, except for the comparatively small number of more accessible sites that have turned into popular destinations for Red Tourism. Just as in imperial and Republican times, the quintessentially remote and impoverished base areas once again do not have much strategic importance for the country as a whole, and by now they have returned to their erstwhile marginality. Former party leader Bo Yibo begins his memoirs describing the post-1949 challenge of transplanting party organizations from the countryside into the cities, just as they had been transplanted from the cities into the countryside a couple of decades earlier.[57] Base areas were not the cradle of Chinese Communism, but a stepping stone to power, which could lightheartedly be abandoned once the party had achieved political predominance. As the CCP transformed itself from a conquest into a ruling organization, the former base areas ceased to be the power base from which the party drew its strength.

Given this radical transformation of the CCP, has the party at least sought to retain a special relationship with residents of former base areas, whether for sentimental reasons, to shore up its own legitimacy, or in order to prevent them from becoming the base areas for another revolution? Alternatively, if party leaders' attention has been absorbed by other pressing tasks, do people in the former base areas have a more deeply rooted and more loyal commitment to the party than in other places? The following section suggests that the contrary is the case. Historical revolutionary base-area legacies no longer translate into intimate party–society relations.

If local communities are true to their own convictions, people whose parents knew the enthusiastically committed revolutionaries of the pre-1949 period may be all the more critical of cadres in market-oriented post-Mao China. The most faithful supporters of the CCP by now may have turned into its most ardent critics. And former power bases have turned into a liability. People in the former base areas are growing up listening to stories told by their parents and grandparents, about enthusiastic revolutionaries emerging from the Long March, with promises for a better future. They also hear about the disappointments when land newly acquired during land reform was taken away again in the name of collectivization, when hunger struck the liberated peasants and turmoil tore apart village communities. Most of all, they see that the Communists have turned into technocrats ruling from far away in Beijing. They might have realized that since Jiang Zemin's *Three Represents* principle, they and the workers are no longer the indisputable core constituency of the party; instead, the party represents the most productive forces of society. In short, the CCP is not what it used to be. Precisely because of the firsthand experience of their grandparents, embellished by creative peasant narration, people in the base areas may not like real existing socialism. Therefore one might argue that some time during the last thirty years of reform, base areas turned from the party's power base to the party's weak spots.

The party's relationship to its oldest members gives the CCP leadership reason to pause. An internal assessment, circulated among leaders of the organization department and eventually leaked to the public, points out a host of problems.[58] The report carries special weight, because it is written by a leading cadre from the Organization Department of Shanxi, a province with large and historically important base areas.[59] Noting that most rural party members who joined the CCP before 1949 now live in destitution, the official also point out their aloofness to party affairs, along with the negative attitude of local cadres toward them: "Some even think that old party members are a burden, creating a lot of trouble: If you care about them, they are a pain; if you care less it's less of a pain; if you don't care at all that's even better." Beyond its emphasis on the material aspects of the relationship to its old party members, the analysis makes it clear that old party members must still receive proper ideological training and must be included in local activities, because they represent the historical roots of the party.

Few eyewitnesses of the revolution survive, and these citizens in their eighties are unlikely to pose an immediate threat to the regime. However, even after the disappearance of these eyewitnesses of the revolution, their families and communities may inherit some of their legacy. The following analysis suggests that former base areas have turned from strongholds into weak spots of the CCP. As before, party membership serves as an indicator of party strength. The analysis proceeds in two steps. First, I analyze the determinants of individual party membership, using 2002 data. Living in former base areas makes it significantly less likely for a person to be a party member, holding other socioeconomic factors constant. Second, to identify the tipping point in time when base areas ceased to be CCP strongholds, I calculate the proportion of party members in the population, comparing membership in base areas to membership in ordinary rural areas. T-tests indicate that base areas turned from strongholds into weak spots in the early 1990s.

The data come from the China Household Income Project (CHIP), as described in Section 4.3.1 Designed primarily to estimate household income and income inequality, the project has generated a series of datasets that – as a valuable by-product – contain essential information on historical legacies and the presence of the CCP. Specifically, the survey asks focus groups whether their survey village is part of a former base area. The survey also asks individuals in these villages whether there are any party members living in their household. Data are available for three waves of surveys, namely 1988, 1995, and 2002. Recording household income inequality is particularly challenging and requires extraordinarily careful sample selection. Among economists, the CHIP surveys are considered the methodological gold standard for studying China's grassroots economy. Thus, we can confidently make inferences.

One caveat concerns perceptions of history. The dataset reveals that local history, as recounted by village representatives, is a shifting target. To be sure, even historians would be hard pressed to pin down on a map precisely which areas should count as a former base area. There is considerable room for interpretation. Nevertheless, it is remarkable that an important question of local history, namely whether a village had been an old revolutionary base area or not, is answered differently over time. According to well-informed village focus groups, in 1988 almost 15 percent of all rural households lived in former base areas. Less than ten years later in 1995, that number had dramatically increased to almost 24 percent. According to the 2002 edition, that number has declined, indicating that 20 percent of rural households lived in former base areas. Neither demographic trends nor migration patterns could explain such discrepancies. Instead, the discrepancies reflect the volatility of historical accounts, depending on whether it is fashionable and lucrative for a village to pass as a former base area. In the 1990s, village representatives tended to interpret the meaning of a base area more broadly, eagerly portraying their village as an active participant in a revolutionary past. Even if former base areas have long lost their special relationship to the CCP, red legacies serve former base areas well as a rhetorical and marketing tool. There are both idealistic and opportunistic reasons for claiming revolutionary legacies. The inconsistency is unlikely to be a problem with the data, but reflects the reality of shifting historical priorities and perceptions.

The first step tests whether living in a former base area affects the likelihood of being a party member. If a local legacy of pro-peasant Communist

TABLE 6.3 *Determinants of party membership in rural China*

	Linear model, no controls	Probit, no controls	Linear model with controls	Probit with controls
Former base areas [binary]	−0.008**	−0.076**	−0.031***	−0.169***
Income [logarithmic]			0.016***	0.088***
Education [years]			0.013***	0.074***
Minority [binary]			−0.014	−0.072
Member of PLA [binary]			0.374***	1.236***
Constant	0.058***	−1.568***	−0.091***	−2.388***
N	37969	37969	10511	10511

*** Significance at 0.001, ** significance at 0.01, * significance at 0.05, . significance at 0.1

revolution today has turned into a liability for local party construction, we would expect it to be less likely for people in former base areas to be party members. The outcome variable of the specification, individual party membership, is a binary variable. I therefore estimate both a linear and a probit model. Control variables include income, education, minority status, and whether a person has served in the PLA. Citizens in the generally remote and poor former base areas will be different from the average Chinese citizens in all of these socioeconomic factors, which are also likely to affect party membership. Table 6.3 displays a series of coefficient estimates.

As the results indicate, the base area effect on the likelihood of contemporary CCP membership is negative, controlling for other important socioeconomic determinants of party membership. The preferred probit specification with all control variables (Table 6.3, last column) indicates that the fact of living in former revolutionary base areas is associated with a decrease in the likelihood of party membership by 17 percentage points. This is a very substantial effect, since the overall likelihood of being a party member is only 5.8 percent. As of 2002, people who live in a former revolutionary base area are much less likely to be party members. The result is statistically highly significant at the 99.9 percent level.

The results also reflect the party's new focus on recruiting what Jiang Zemin calls the "most productive forces of society," that is, the wealthy and the well-educated. On average, a 1 percent higher income level is associated with a 9 percentage point greater likelihood of being a party member. Similarly, an additional year of schooling is associated with a 7 percentage point greater likelihood of being a party member. Only the ethnicity variable is insignificant – but this result must be taken with a grain of salt, because the survey could not be fielded in Tibet as well

TABLE 6.4 *Party presence in China's rural areas*

	1988	1995	2002
Party strenth in all rural areas	3.4%	3.9%	5.7%
Party strength in former base areas	3.8%	3.3%	5.0%
Party strength in ordinary places only	3.3%	4.1%	5.8%
Difference compared to former base areas	−0.48%	+0.77%	+0.84%
Statistical significance	0.0173	0.0007	0.0022

as some other places known for ethnic tensions. Unsurprisingly, another well-known determinant of party membership, whether or not a person has served in the PLA, has a strong effect on the likelihood of party membership.

The next step identifies the tipping point, when the base areas became alienated from the CCP. Table 6.4 shows the results of simple t tests. Between 1988 and 2002, party membership has rapidly expanded, in rural areas from 3.4 percent to 5.7 percent of the population. The expansion has been much slower in former base areas. In 1988, the party was still significantly more present in former base areas, but by 1995 the situation had reversed. In 2002, it was almost 20 percent more likely for a rural citizen to be a party member if the person did not live in a former base area. In 1988, the party still had a particularly good presence in its former base areas, but no longer today.

In part, these findings are the result of a secular trend of convergence, since local memories of the base area history fade, just like memories of the Sino-Japanese War. As fewer and fewer people with good memories of the pre-1949 period survive, and as older generations fail to transmit their historical experience to their descendants, the base areas' exceptional historical experience becomes less salient for present-day outcomes. But there must be other factors at play, because party strength in former base areas does not simply converge to the national average of 5.7 percent in 2002, but is noticeable for falling behind the rest of China. This loss of influence could be the result of official neglect, with party organization departments not investing organizational capital in the ever-marginal base areas. Having seen other communist parties collapse in the early 1990s, CCP organizers concentrate their energy on building the party in strategically important places, not in the poor backwaters that former base areas typically are.

Even official neglect may not be a satisfying explanation. As Table 6.3 suggests, conventional measures of marginalization such as income and education levels do not fully account for the weakness of the party in former base areas. An alternative explanation for the party's reduced influence in former base areas might be that older generations do instill in their children a revolutionary tradition, but that this tradition does not translate into CCP partisanship and, starting in the 1990s, began to turn against the CCP itself. This indicates historical reversal. Those who best remember the party's Communist ideals and who benefited little from Opening and Reform are no longer the power base of the party.[60] Since only 20 percent of China's shrinking rural population lives in former base areas, and since base areas tend to be far away from the centers of power, this trend may not be too dangerous for the party. However, the trend in the party's former base areas also reflect broader trends of the CCP losing its legitimacy as a party known for pro-peasant, pro-poor redistributive policies.

To the extent that ideological legacies have survived until today, they reinforce patterns of party strength. While both peasant nationalism and redistributive appeals were crucial in the wars preceding the Communist takeover of 1949, the anti–Japanese War legacy may be an asset, whereas the Communist-revolutionary base area legacy may be a liability. Distinguishing between base areas and areas suffering most sustained and direct confrontation with the Japanese occupiers, the assumption is that peasant nationalism was most important in the latter areas. The distinction between non–Japanese-occupied areas, occupied areas and Communist base areas is reminiscent of the three-way classification used by the CCP itself in the 1950s, distinguishing between "later liberated areas," "early liberated areas" and "old revolutionary bases."[61] This distinction plays an important role in Chapter 7, because in the wake of China's Great Leap Forward, local party networks in formerly occupied areas were stronger and resisted the most devastating central policies, resulting in fewer famine deaths.

In short, legacies of patriotic mobilization trump legacies of redistribution as sources of contemporary party strength. This is by no means to deny the hardships that Communists suffered in their base areas, nor the commitment of those Communists who suffered the deprivation and dangers of the Long March. However, locals who joined the party inside the base areas arguably had more opportunistic motivations compared to those who joined the party in territory in immediate proximity to the enemy. Joining the party outside the base areas behind Japanese enemy lines carried greater risks and promised fewer rewards. This resonates with the conjecture by Steven Levitsky and Lucan A. Way that authoritarian parties are strongest when they are built on a legacy of violent struggle rather than on material incentives.[62] Nonmaterial motivations have a much longer half-life than material motivations. The effectiveness of material gains wears off quickly, once the erstwhile material benefit disappears.

6.3 A TOOL TO ANALYZE THE DYNAMICS OF MEMBERSHIP

Initially shaped by war fronts during World War II, the geography of local party membership networks shifted at a remarkably slow speed, thereby transmitting the war legacy to the present. Functioning as an institutional nexus, persisting membership patterns bridge the seventy politically tumultuous years that separate the relatively short-lived event of Japanese occupation from outcomes in the present. So far, the quantitative approach has consisted of paired comparisons of cross-sectional time slices. This section addresses the core of the transmission phenomenon, developing a tool to analyze the dynamics of membership patterns, to test dynamic characteristics of membership networks, and to quantify the speed of their transformation over time. While referring to and arguing with illustrations from the Chinese example, the analysis is not country-specific, but generally applicable to political parties and other membership-based organizations. The next section applies this tool to the case of China and the CCP.

Economists have developed methods to analyze dynamic growth processes. To assess the persistence of membership patterns, this chapter presents a party growth model. Noting that accumulation effects and path dependence also occur in economic growth processes, I translate the recruitment dynamics of the CCP into a simple formal model inspired by a standard economic growth model. Estimating the parameters of the model, I show that the Japanese legacy disappears over time, but only at a very slow rate. Using a model instead of a regression design has important advantages. While regression analyses that compare current party membership to past party membership are extremely robust, they say nothing about dynamics: Are differences disappearing over time, or are they aggravating? The modeling approach is also more satisfying than standard time series analyses, because of the ad-hoc assumptions needed for the latter.[63] Instead, the modeling approach uses the known structure of membership accumulation and estimates the parameters of the dynamic process.

6.3.1 Competing Hypotheses on Persistence

Making an argument for a slow disappearance of the historical traces left by the Sino-Japanese War, this book primarily argues against presentist approaches, which largely dismiss the relevance of history to explain contemporary outcomes. However, the book does not support the idea that the Sino-Japanese War created strong path dependence in the sense that the initial event sets localities on such distinct paths that they will look increasingly different from each other over time. The empirical model expects persistence of historical legacies, but also their disappearance at a slow pace. Regression models comparing paired time slices to prove an effect of the past on the present would not allow this level of nuance, but the modeling approach here, in combination with time series data, does.

To distinguish between the different possible ways in which history shapes the present, it is useful to employ a terminology of convergence. Let us assume that prior to a certain "big" event, all localities look the same in terms of a variable of interest. The occurrence of the event disturbs this even distribution, so that now localities look very different. Convergence means that over time, localities will revert to the erstwhile situation and look indistinguishable again. This would be a case of absolute convergence, but the definition of convergence can also be relative when relaxed in the following way. Convergence means that for a while units of analysis carry the imprint of a historical event, but that this imprint disappears over time, so that the units of analysis tend toward a distribution as if the erstwhile event had never taken place. This distribution does not have to be the same as the one prior to the historical event. Employing this terminology, the following four hypotheses are competing views of the impact of a historical event on contemporary outcomes. The possibilities range from historical events that are simply inconsequential (hypothesis 1) to those that set a jurisdiction on an altogether different historical path (hypothesis 4).

Hypothesis 1 (Irrelevance of History): The event, once it is past, does not matter. Past events are forgotten and contemporary determinants shape the organization. As a result, there is rapid convergence: For example, revolutionary base areas today are just as loyal to the CCP as any other area. Places that served as the CCP's power bases in the early People's Republic today are just as supportive as any other places, controlling for other variables.

In a presentist interpretation, historical causes leave no trace, because their effect vanishes quickly; there is speedy convergence. While it lasted, Japanese occupation of the East Asian mainland was extraordinarily consequential for Chinese politics and for the lives of ordinary Chinese. Yet the moment the United States defeated Japan, the occupation turned into history. In the blink of an eye, China found itself in a different political-strategic universe. The rupture can be timed with unusual accuracy to an announcement by the Japanese Emperor at noon on August 15. Up to that point, the common enemy of the Communists and the Republicans was the foreign aggressor, a struggle superseding the two parties' own enmity. Afterward, the two parties began to focus on defeating each other. Their two armies raced to occupy the vacuum left by the departing Japanese army. Despite a futile American mediation attempt, sporadic fighting turned into another war lasting four years and killing millions. In such an eventful era of deadly confrontation, certainly to the political actors involved, Japanese occupation quickly turned into a more or less distant memory. Under such conditions, one needs to question how consequential the Japanese occupation was, and for what kind of outcomes it still mattered.

If one were to believe in the omnipotence of party organizers, the Japanese occupation could seem to have become irrelevant as soon as the Japanese army left. As soon as the initial determinant for membership patterns ceases to exist, present factors alone would predict absolute convergence, expecting the disappearance of any kind of variation across China. For example, party membership in the base areas as well as in the CCP's power bases of the 1950s will converge to the national average. In the spirit of modernization theory, the convergence process could be thought of as approximating a growth trajectory, which in the long run tends toward a steady state. By contrast, the moderate version of this hypothesis predicts not absolute but relative convergence. A set of structural characteristics, such as the geographic setting or the level of economic wealth, prevents absolute convergence. Nevertheless, places with identical structural characteristics will tend to have the same number of party members per capita, whether or not they had been base areas and whether or not they had served as the CCP's power base in the 1950s. People who believe in absolute or relative convergence also disagree on how long it takes for the dust to settle and for history to become irrelevant.

Hypothesis 2 (Puff Theory): The historical legacies do not survive great upheaval. Disruptions such as the Great Leap Forward and the Cultural Revolution, as well as the political reorientation of Reform and Opening, change the political geography of the party's membership base beyond recognition.

The continuities in membership patterns bridge moments of great upheavals that took place between 1949 and today. Mao's personal leadership turned the party upside down, almost entirely paralyzing it at the height of the Cultural Revolution. Transformations resulting from Reform and Opening make one wonder whether under such tumultuous conditions, historical transmission would be possible. Some would suspect that the shocks of these great disruptions hit places independently of their historical past. Once the Cultural Revolution had struck, the pre-1949 revolutionary past would be no more than a remote echo, drowned out by more recent uproars. A place that did not have much revolutionary merit before 1949 might have earned it in a later movement. And rural communities that had stood out for revolutionary achievement pre-1949 may have lost their good relationship to the party later on.[64] With every wave of history, legacies should increasingly average out, until there is convergence and the party is similarly strong throughout the country. However, places with good revolutionary credentials and governed by old revolutionaries did not have to prove their loyalty and could afford to defy or at least modify orders from Beijing. Even nowadays, local leaders are eager to claim their jurisdiction's revolutionary legacy, trying to "own" the revolution.

Hypothesis 3 (Erosion of History): Historical legacies do not easily go away just because of great political upheaval. Only time slowly erodes the party's uneven historical legacies.

If neither deliberate policies nor great disruptions erase historical legacies, then the investigation of institutional change must shift focus to slow-moving processes. The complex interplay between forces of sturdy inertia and the forces of dynamic change will determine whether an institution drifts away from historical legacies and at what speed. It might even be that dynamic change itself amplifies historical legacies and contributes rather than diminishes the history effect. An important feature of dynamically changing systems is whether there is convergence or divergence. Economists have developed sharp methodological tools to analyze slow-moving processes of accumulation. Section 6.3.2 formally conceptualizes the steady flow in and out of the pool of party members in any given jurisdiction. The interplay of these forces can potentially result in the following macropolitical outcomes.

Legacies endure, even across great societal transformations. Historical continuities are transmitted (1) through people, for instance from parents to children through upbringing; (2) through formal institutions; and (3) through less tangible informal institutions. As for people, parents heavily influence their offspring's politics in many political contexts. The American case is particularly well researched. Party identification is inherited from generation to generation, even if it has lately become more responsive to policy preferences as well.[65] Interestingly, party identification is more easily transmitted than political preferences.[66] If this result provides any guidance for the nondemocratic Chinese context, it implies that old revolutionary families would remain loyal even if the CCP has radically changed its program. As for informal institutions, the Chinese one-party systems may exhibit complementary transmission mechanisms, which are less relevant in a democratic system. Leaders of the CCP trust some communities more than others, because they had occasion to show their loyalty to the party's cause. Trust can work like a self-fulfilling prophecy: Given their privileged place in the system, there is a lot at stake for these communities, if they disappoint the party's trust. In contrast, some places may never overcome the self-reinforcing spiral of suspicion and disloyalty.

Hypothesis 4 (Strong Path – Dependencies): The historical watershed event sets different jurisdictions on distinct historical trajectories, so that there is a great divergence. In other words, the initial effect not only persists, but escalates over time.

Hypotheses 3 and 4 express that linkages exist between the present and the past. These linkages could be continuities, but they could also take the form of historical reversals: For instance, transforming themselves from revolutionary conquest networks to ruling status-quo organizations, political parties might experience a metamorphosis of their membership patterns into a near mirror image. In the case of the CCP, geographic membership patterns are characterized by continuities rather than reversal, with the caveat introduced in Section 6.2.3: The party has disproportionately few members in the particular subset of rural areas that self-identify as former base areas. Hypotheses 3 and 4 must be open-ended in that way, because whether something counts as reversal or not is a matter of perspective. The reversal in revolutionary base areas means that people have remained faithful to themselves: revolutionaries then and regime critics now. To avoid such ambiguity of definition, the hypotheses claim that history matters, though it could matter in unexpected ways.

6.3.2 A Membership Growth Model

The first goal is to test empirically whether party membership in different provinces is converging over time. If there is convergence, the second goal is to numerically estimate the speed of convergence. The approach builds on well-established theoretical and empirical work in the field of economics, especially the seminal approach by Robert Barro and Xavier Sala-i-Martin,[67] which has become a standard methodological tool for economists working on capital accumulation, economic growth, and economic convergence. After presenting a model of party membership growth, I will transform the model into an empirical model, the coefficients of which can be estimated using nonlinear least squares.[68] With these estimated coefficients, the speed of convergence can be described, finally leading to the half-life of history indicator.

The growth model approach is an alternative to more conventional approaches to studying historical legacies. The latter involve the comparison of two or more time slices, to see whether an event in the past is associated with an outcome down the line in a later era. The growth model is primarily interested in the dynamics itself, the changes in a variable over time, tracing the intermediate variable that links the present to the past. While the comparison of time slices uses generic tools of regression analysis, the growth model incorporates prior knowledge about the structure of the time series. As this section argues, the membership base of an organization is likely to follow certain growth patterns, under fairly generic conditions.

The mathematical formulation of the party growth model is laid out in Appendix 2. In essence, the model follows the intuition that certain dynamics of growing *political* capital can fruitfully be analyzed with the same tools as the dynamics of growing *economic* capital. After all, accumulation processes share almost universal dynamic characteristics: growth is conditioned on the previously accumulated stock, and there is attrition along the way. In the social sciences, economists have developed the most formally rigorous growth models. Similar dynamics are also encountered in the natural sciences. When it comes to convergence, ordinary regression analysis runs into "Galton's fallacy:" Contrary to the simple intuition, the coefficients found when regressing average growth rates on initial levels imply little about convergence.[69] Explicitly modeling the dynamics of party growth also takes advantage of substantive prior knowledge about the underlying process. The model is not only valid for the CCP; it could be applied more broadly to study growth of membership-based organizations, including for instance churches, NGOs, and the mafia.

The model begins with assumptions about annual changes in membership. In any given location, the number of new recruits[70] depends on the number of incumbents, although the model imposes only a very generic functional form. Moreover, the model factors in that there is population growth and that members exit the party, either because they are expelled or because they die. Mathematical transformations demonstrate that this conceptualization of annual membership changes implies a very specific organizational growth path: The logarithm of party membership at any point in time is a weighted average between initial party membership and party membership at some future steady state. The speed at which the influence of initial party membership recedes depends on the parameters of the model.

The model assumes that the proportion of members exiting the party is constant. This assumption holds in the post-Mao era, when we observe only slight fluctuations as a result of demographic trends. The assumption is problematic for the Mao era. From the foundation of the PRC to the Cultural Revolution, each year there were more expulsions than natural deaths leading to party exits. The rate of expulsions varied greatly depending on the political winds and the occurrence of purges (see Figure 6.2).

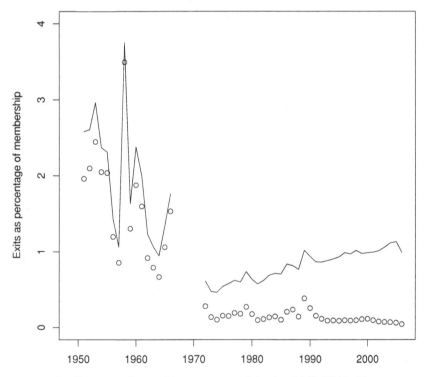

FIGURE 6.2 Party members exiting: purges and deaths, 1951–2010. Lines represent exits, dots are expulsions. *Source:* CCP Organization Department.[71]

As another useful simplification, the model assumes constant population growth. In the early years of the People's Republic, annual population growth accelerated to a 2.8 percent peak in 1966 and subsequently slowed down to about 0.5 percent since 2007.[72] While the simplifying assumptions serve the interest of parsimony, the following empirical section estimates separate model coefficients for different historical eras, to account for changing dynamics over time.

The model has some noteworthy characteristics. First, within the practically relevant range of parameters, convergence proceeds along with a growth trend. In other words, places where the party is strong do not experience membership decrease. Membership grows everywhere. Convergence can still occur if the party grows more slowly in places where it is already strong. Second, the convergence process ends in a steady state. The percentage of party members in society does not cross a fixed upper bound, although the model is silent about where the upper bound lies. Third, there is no "systematic overshooting." In other words, the model rules out cases where convergence occurs as with a pendulum, swinging from one extreme to the other, until places reach the steady state. This characteristic makes the convergence test more demanding. With the possibility of "systematic overshooting," temporary divergence could still be interpreted as a complex adjustment mechanism. Fourth, the specification itself predicts absolute convergence: In the steady state all places have exactly the same membership penetration. To test relative convergence – that, say, only places with similar income level have the same membership density – one must include additional control variables. Finally, the two model coefficients are substantively meaningful and readily interpretable: Taken together, the speed-of-convergence coefficient and the steady-state coefficient provide a clear characterization of the dynamic growth process of party membership.

6.3.3 Empirical Estimation of the Model

The empirical task consists of estimating the two coefficients in Equation A.21 (see appendix), namely the steady state m^* and the speed of convergence λ. After determining these two variables, the model is fully determined and can be used to predict party growth dynamics. Depending on initial party strength, which varies from province to province, the model predicts the growth trajectory into the future, again different for every province. The first empirical approach consists of using the two endpoints of our time series – that is, initial party strength in 1954 and final party strength in 2010 – for every province, and finding the best possible fit for the steady state and the speed of convergence coefficients, using nonlinear least squares. Based on Equation A.21, the baseline specification becomes

$$m_{2010,i} = e^{-\lambda 54} m_{1956,i} + (1 - e^{-\lambda 54}) m^* + \epsilon_i \qquad (6.1)$$

Only including membership statistics at the start date and at the end date of the panel data is not an efficient use of the information. The approach loses membership statistics along the way, which provide further information on membership dynamics. For every province, we possess eleven data points along the growth curve. In order to make use of every time slice, each observation starting in 1965 is linked to the previous observation, so that there are ten time periods that can be analyzed. This procedure increases the number of observations from just under 30 to almost 300 observations.

$$m_{t_2,i} = e^{-\lambda(t_2-1956)} m_{1956,i} + (1 - e^{-\lambda(t_2-1956)}) m^* + \epsilon_i \qquad (6.2)$$

The two preceding specifications test absolute convergence. Predicting conditional convergence is a more modest claim to make, but it is probably more realistic. By introducing control variables, the model can be transformed from a model of absolute convergence to a model of relative convergence. In keeping with the earlier analysis, the specification includes controls for the level of wealth, degree of urbanization, and presence of minorities. Each of these factors is often said to determine the strength of the party.

$$m_{t_2,i} = e^{-\lambda(t_2-1956)} m_{1956,i} + (1 - e^{-\lambda(t_2-1956)}) m^* + \beta controls + \epsilon_i \quad (6.3)$$

6.4 APPLYING THE MODEL TO THE CCP

We now apply the party growth model to the case of the CCP's membership growth between 1956 and 2010. Party membership statistics come from the recent compilation by the CCP Organization Department (see Section 1.4.1). Data on the Gross Regional Product of various provinces, which is a control variable, are found in the 2009 edition of the *China Statistical Yearbook*. The division of the national territory into Coastal, Middle, and West follows a widely used Chinese convention.

6.4.1 Estimating the Growth Model Coefficients

As Table 6.5 shows, the rate of convergence is positive and highly significant at the 0.001 level in all three specifications. In addition, the

TABLE 6.5 *Nonlinear estimates of party growth model coefficients*

	Baseline growth model (Equation 6.1)	With controls (Equation 6.2)	Using all years (Equation 6.3)
Rate of convergence λ	0.02***	0.027***	0.04***
Steady state indicator (log) $m*$	−2.24***	−2.54***	−3.12***
GRP (log)			−0.99***
Share of rural population (log)			−0.06***
Share of minorities (log)			0.00
Party strength at steady state	10.6%	7.9%	
Half-life of historical disparities	109 years	66 years	
Year when half-life is reached	2065	2022	

*** Significance at 0.001

Notes: Nonlinear least-squares estimators. First model has 27 province-level observations, second and third model have 293 province-year observations. Sources: CCP members from internal party statistics.[73] Population and Gross Regional Product from *China Data Online*. Proportion of rural/minority population in 2000 from census data available at *Harvard Geospatial Library*.

baseline model of absolute convergence predicts that, extrapolating from the trend over the last fifty-four years, around 10 percent of the population will belong to the party in the long-run steady state. In the conditional convergence model with controls, a province located in the Eastern party of China and with an average per-capita income party strength would eventually reach a party strength of 7.9 percent, with richer provinces hosting significantly more party members than less affluent places, even in the long run.

To illustrate the results, compare Hebei province and Guangxi province (see Figure 6.3). The Northern province of Hebei, fully occupied by the Japanese at the very outset of the Sino-Japanese War, was the province where the party was strongest throughout the 1950s. By contrast, the Southern province of Guangxi province, located in the South, had barely been touched by Japanese occupation and subsequently was the province where the party was weakest in the 1950s. Both provinces belong to the Eastern region, but Hebei is wealthier. In 1956, the difference in party strength between the two provinces was 371 party members per 10,000 people in Hebei vs. 109 members per 10,000 – that is, Hebei was a "red province" with a party strength more than three times greater than the "pink" province of Guangxi. The baseline growth model predicts absolute convergence moving toward 1.060 party members per 10,000 people. The half-life of the historical disparities between the two provinces is 109 years: It would take Hebei and Guangxi until 2065 to bridge about half

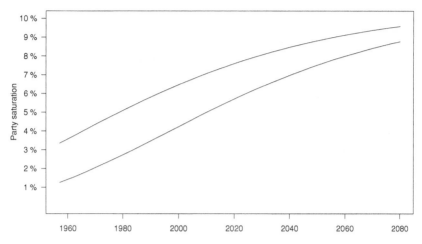

FIGURE 6.3 Slow convergence between a red and a pink province (simulation): The changing degrees of party penetration in Hebei and Guangxi were calculated based on the the baseline growth model (Equation 6.1) with fitted values (Table 6.5) and initial party penetration in 1956 (internal party statistics as above).

of their initial difference. The historical legacy of Japanese occupation on the party organizational network does disappear, albeit at a rather slow pace.

The takeaway from the model of conditional convergence is similar. Again comparing Hebei and Guangxi, this version of the model predicts that there would be a lasting disparity in party strength of sixty-one party members per 10,000 people, due to underlying economic disparities, which are significant but not great.[74] This time, the half-life of historical disparities would be defined as the number of years until the initial difference has shrunk half-way to the persisting disparity in party membership.[75] In the case of Hebei and Guangxi, the half-life is reached in 2013, that is, fifty-seven years after the departure point in 1956. In order to explain the CCP's regional power base, historical legacies are a key factor.

As an alternative to the nonlinear model above, one could also envision a simple convergence test. For convergence to occur, in provinces with an initially lower party presence, party membership must expand more rapidly later on. The simplicity of such a test comes at a cost. A negative relationship between initial party presence and later expansion can count as an indicator of convergence, but mathematically speaking it is possible for the variance of party presence across space to decrease

TABLE 6.6 *Alternative convergence test using linear model*

	Baseline specification	Recruitment in 1965	Recruitment in 2010
Initial party penetration	−0.41**	−2.20***	−0.56*
Minority population	0.02*	0.06**	0.00
Rural population	−0.02	−0.02	0.03
Gross regional product (per capita)	14.29	−1875	39.37
City jurisdiction	0.01	0.06*	0.01

*** Significance at 0.001, ** significance at 0.01, * significance at 0.05
Note: OLS estimators. Dependent variable party growth defined as compound annual growth rate.[76] All specifications include intercepts, baseline specification include year fixed effects. Sources: Internal party statistics CCP Organization Department, 2011, 中國共產黨黨內統計資料彙編, population census data from *Harvard Geospatial Library* – minority and rural population for the year 2000, GRP data from *China Data Online*. The number of observations used in the estimation is, respectively, 268, 27, and 26.

even if, on average, we do not observe the negative relationship. Moreover, a linear specification is of limited use for describing the dynamics of membership development. Note for instance that, extrapolating into the future, converging lines will necessarily cross, ostensibly indicating a divergence that reverses the strongholds of the party.

Table 6.6 presents estimation results regressing average annual party growth rates against initial party penetration, defined as the number of party members per population in 1956. A one percentage point higher membership density in 1956 is on average associated with a 0.41 percentage point slower party growth rate between 1956 and 2010, controlling for the presence of minorities, degrees of urbanization, wealth, and whether the province-level jurisdiction is a city (Beijing, Tianjin, Shanghai, Chongqing). This result is statistically significant and substantively large, given that the annual growth rate is 3.5 percent and that the difference in growth rates quickly compounds over time. For example, in Guangxi only 1.2 percent of the population had been party members in 1956. The growth rate of 3.8 percent was 0.25 percentage points greater than the national average. The province is still a pink province with 22 percent fewer party members than the average province. At the same time, from the perspective of party organizers there has been great progress, since in 1956 the province used to have 61 percent fewer party members than the average province. Providing less information about party membership dynamics than the party growth model, a linear convergence test indicates that the CCP evens out its reach, although the substantive effect is not enough to overcome the initial patterns.

6.4.2 Six Decades of Convergence and Persistence

The speed of convergence fluctuated over time. As the very short history of recruitment since 1949 (see Section 6.1.1) indicated, the party leadership has not always been equally concerned about achieving a regionally balanced membership base. Averaging out membership growth over fifty-four years simplifies the growth path, as if it had been a continuous process essentially exhibiting similar characteristics over time. The panel data allow to quantify the speed of convergence from one party congress to the next. The resulting estimates of party membership convergence and persistence reflect political developments and their effect on membership recruitment.

Before the Eleventh Party Congress in 1977, marking the end of the Mao era, legislative periods were irregular; thereafter, the legislative period was five years. When was convergence unusually fast, and when unusually slow? Table 6.7 estimates the speed of convergence for every legislative period, using the baseline non-linear growth model with controls (Equation A.21). As it turns out, in four of ten periods, there was no statistically significant convergence. During the early period of the Great Leap Forward and Famine (1956–1965), during the transition into the post-Mao era (1977–1982), during the years of political repression (1992–1997), as well as in most recent times, a very strong trend of convergence prevailed. Interestingly, during the Cultural Revolution, convergence was only mildly significant; this defies conventional wisdom, according to which the Cultural Revolution was a sharp break with the

TABLE 6.7 *Speed of convergence, by party congress legislative period*

Characteristic event	Period	Annual party growth	Rate of convergence
Great Leap Forward/Famine	1956–1965	4.6%	0.06***
Proletarian Cultural Revolution	1965–1973	6.0%	0.041
Final years of the Mao era	1973–1977	5.4%	0.01
Transition into Post-Mao era	1977–1982	2.8%	0.09***
Years of political liberalization	1982–1987	3.7%	0.00
Tian'anmen crisis	1987–1992	2.0%	0.01
Years of political repression	1992–1997	2.8%	0.03**
Turn to nationalism	1997–2002	1.8%	0.01
CCP opens up to capitalists	2002–2007	2.2%	0.03*
Harmonious society era	2007–2010	2.7%	0.04**

*** Significance at 0.001, ** significance at 0.01, * significance at 0.05

past. Instead, party rectification campaigns and party construction drives following the Ninth Party Congress had the intended effect of revitalizing the old party organization and reversing the impact of the Cultural Revolution. Convergence comes in spurts, but it never ceases for long. The privileged relationship that some areas have traditionally entertained with the party as a legacy from the Sino-Japanese War is a slowly dissipating legacy.

6.4.3 Simulation of the Disappearing War Legacy

The absolute size of the convergence rate indicates – in a rather abstract way – how long it will take for the war legacy to disappear and no longer be reflected in party membership patterns. To be sure, according to the model, the degree of party penetration becomes increasingly similar across provinces over time, but the effect of history will never vanish completely. The differences will become harder to perceive, but the better the observational tools, the longer the history effect will be visible. Therefore, to interpret the convergence rate in practical terms, we need an observational yardstick. In this section, the observational yardstick is a province-level bivariate linear model regressing party membership in the present on initial party membership in 1956, both logarithmic. We can then answer how long it will take for the war effect to become imperceptible to an observer employing a bivariate linear model.

A simulation approach[77] allows a specific and intuitive interpretation of the convergence rate and its numerical value. If the party growth model along with its coefficient estimates is correct, how long would it take for the history effect to become imperceptible, given the previously mentioned observational yardstick? After how many years of history fading into oblivion would observers make a type I error of mistakenly rejecting the null hypothesis that historical legacies continue to influence the present? Because the model is stochastic and includes an error term, each simulation of history leads to different outcomes. The following simulation analyzes fifty realizations of history and proceeds in two steps:

(i) The first step is to calculate fifty panel data sets of party membership with province-year observations from 1957 to 2056. Each panel data set represents one realization of history and consists of one time series per province. The simulated party membership statistics are calculated based on the party growth model (Equation 6.1), including the stochastic term ϵ, using the coefficient estimates found in Table 6.5 (column 2) and initial values for 1956.[78]

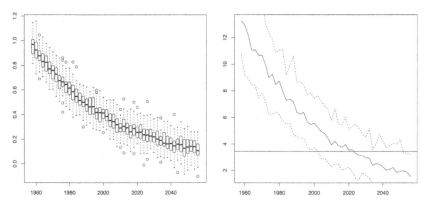

FIGURE 6.4 Illustrating the slowly fading historical legacy: The history effect (coefficient, left) and its statistical significance (*t*-value, right) when correlating simulated membership patterns at different points in time to the initial membership patterns. Sources: as in Table 6.5.

(ii) The second step consists of judging whether the historical legacy is still "perceptible." It applies the observational yardstick of the simple regression model described above to each realization of history for all even-numbered years. The further away from the initial party membership patterns we find ourselves, the more likely it is that the bivariate regression yields statistically insignificant coefficients. The history effect is indistinguishable from zero.

Figure 6.4 summarizes the findings of the simulation. The history effect in the left panel is equal to the coefficient estimate when regressing party penetration in the present on party penetration in 1956. The earliest coefficients are close to 1, since party membership patterns are very close to the initial patterns in 1956. Coefficient estimates in the mid-21st century are getting closer to zero. For every year, the tiny box close to the trend line indicates where 90 percent of all estimated coefficients fall. By 2042 the history effect is so small that regressions begin to disagree on the sign of the coefficient: In that year, for the first time more than 5 percent of regressions give the history effect a negative sign.

To judge perceptibility, the thick, downward-sloping line in the right panel depicts the median *t* value when regressing party membership in different years to party membership in 1956. Given the sample size, all *t* values above the horizontal line indicate statistical significance at the 99.9 percent level. Historical significance of the history effect becomes tenuous as early as 2000, though a majority of regressions still find a

highly significant result until 2020. Historical patterns of party membership patterns in 1956 cease to affect outcomes in a statistically significant
way in the mid-2030s. This leads to the practical interpretation of the convergence rate: Given the initial membership patterns and the choice of an
empirical yardstick, the rate of 0.02 implies that the history effect will be
perceptible for about 80 years. The model implies that with better data,
for instance county-level party statistics, history would be perceptible for
an even longer time.

To compare the simulation with the party membership patterns actually observed, let us return to the comparison at the beginning of this
chapter. The simulations on average find a history effect of 0.28, with
90 percent of the regressions in the [0.15; 0.37] range. The actual realization of history yields a history effect of 0.35, within the range of typical results. The simulations yields results with t-values averaging 3.5, in
the [1.6; 4.9] range. With a t-value of 5.5, actual party membership patterns are even more closely related to the past than the simulation would
suggest.

All in all, the simulation portrays the implications of the convergence
rate, essentially indicating that war legacies disappear, but at a very slow
speed. The statistical afterlife of the war effect disappears only over several generations.

6.5 CONCLUSION

This chapter has provided a differentiated picture of party membership
recruitment and its implications for long-term trends in party membership patterns. There are three major takeaways: Most importantly, early
patterns of party membership, which emerged during the Sino-Japanese
War, continue to shape contemporary patterns. Moreover, the degree to
which CCP leaders balance out the geographic reach of the party varies
over time. Finally, party recruitment in the last ten years targets the cities.
Yet as in earlier periods, recruitment strategies result only in slow drifts
away from the historically inherited geographic patterns.

The establishment of Communist base areas, if anything, had a reverse
effect on the evolution of grassroots party organizations down the line.
Today the party is *not* more present in the former base areas. As one would
expect in light of the previous chapter, the transmission of the Japanese
occupation effect is mediated primarily through the Leninist party organization. The war was inscribed in the foundation of the party apparatus, which reproduced geographically similar membership patterns from

generation to generation, thereby creating a strong link between contemporary outcomes and past events.

The path dependent effect is subtle in the sense that it does not reinforce and escalate spatial differences, which would lead to divergent patterns. It is powerful in the sense that it delays convergence of the party base by almost a century. The geography of party membership is a slowly shifting target. It is not frozen in time, nor is it moving swiftly enough to be analyzed as a result of contemporary factors alone. To arrive at a satisfying theory of party membership patterns, one must consider both present and past influences. As the previous chapter showed, when Communist recruitment picked up speed in the late 1930s and early 1940s, the CCP was most successful establishing its presence behind Japanese enemy lines, shaping its presence at the end of World War II and its takeover in 1949. As this chapter demonstrates, initial party membership patterns go a long way toward explaining why the CCP today is so much more present in some parts of its realm than in other parts. The central finding of this chapter is that the uneven patterns of the immediate post-war era continue to shape the CCP's territorial presence today, despite great political upheaval and despite the party-state's attempts at penetrating society more evenly. The party still has most members in areas that Japan occupied during wartime.

Local party strength is the result of a combination of anti-Japanese war legacies and strategic considerations in the present. Contemporary party organizers are focusing on urban areas, because that is where the party state faces the most governing challenges. If the legacy of Japanese occupation, as reflected in the membership patterns during the first years of the People's Republic of China, remains the single most important *historical* factor shaping China's political landscape today, the degree of urbanization stands out as the most important *contemporary* factor shaping the CCP's membership base today: The CCP is becoming more present in urban areas and retreating from the countryside. Whereas the dynamic analysis is built on an absolute convergence model, if current trends are any guide, a relative convergence model would indicate a lasting imbalance between CCP presence in the cities and in the countryside.

To analyze the dynamics of change, I formulate a party growth model and use previously highly classified statistics to estimate its parameters. The half-life of history, defined as the time it takes for the effect of Japanese occupation to be cut in half, is about sixty to ninety years. In physics, the half-life period measures the speed of decay. Here it reflects the slowly declining influence of historical legacies, which are more context-specific than in physics. There is a slow-moving process of convergence away from historically conditioned patterns. These dynamics are reminiscent of Kathleen Thelen's proposition that slow institutional change in "normal" times may be more consequential than change in times of crisis.[79] The dynamic model simplifies a complex process, because historical legacies do not decay in a linear fashion, being manipulated in myriad ways.[80] It is also clear that not all legacies decay over time. For example, Eastern Europe has experienced the swift comeback of pre-Communist legacies, which had been temporarily swept under the the table during the time of Soviet dominance.[81] Going forward, we might see slower decay of the anti-Japanese war legacy. Since 1991, the government has promoted a Patriotic Education Campaign to kindle anti-Japanese sentiment and prop up CCP legitimacy.[82] However, the campaign is nationwide and affects places indiscriminately, whether they had actually experienced Japanese violence or not. Therefore, the local effect of actual anti-Japanese war experience – as opposed to the effect of textbook indoctrination – will likely continue to decay.

This chapter contributes to research on the origins of effective parties, showing that anticolonial struggle can be a long-lasting source of party strength. Are Communist regimes more durable in countries where they have mobilized peasant masses on patriotic grounds, during their party's ascent to power? Does anticolonial struggle produce strong parties? It is hard to generalize from the small number of surviving Communist regimes. But my subnational analysis of the Chinese case suggests that the legacy of peasant mobilization on patriotic, anti-Japanese grounds does contribute to effective authoritarian governance even today. Legacies from the anti-Japanese war continue to loom large in Chinese politics and continue to shape the Chinese party-state. Regional patterns of the CCP's membership base carry the imprint of the past. Since rank-and-file party members are vital for the functioning of the party-state, we can say that China's regime strength still flows from successful patriotic peasant mobilization before 1949. Even as the patterns of party membership remained relatively stable, as the following chapter will show, the functions and effect of the party's grassroots changed over time. Gradual evolution from a revolutionary party to a party in power implies changes in the nature of the party's effect, to be considered in the next chapter.

PART IV

THE PARTY IN THE MAO ERA

7

Can the CCP Disobey? The Great Leap Famine
(1958–1961)

To achieve effective authoritarian governance, the best regime party is
not one that slavishly implements policies, but one that functions as a
self-corrective device, where disobedience limits the devastation brought
about by bad policies that delegitimize the regime. Generally speaking, as
the result of Leninist discipline, the CCP is *not* such a party. However, this
chapter suggests that China's Great Leap Forward (1958–1961), along
with its horrific famine, is a partial exception where the strongest local
party cells slowed down implementation. Such party cells were disobedi-
ent, because the catastrophic movement occurred less than a decade after
the Communist takeover, for which some cadres had risked their lives.
Only because at that point in time the CCP's local leadership had not
yet fully transformed itself from a party-of-revolutionaries to a party-in-
power could we observe foot-dragging. In order for party members to
push back, it took policies that were not just bad, but deadly. The push-
back against the policy was the exception rather than the rule and had a
statistically significant yet substantively small effect. All of this does not
bode well for the party: The CCP is closer to an unquestioning implementer than an effective self-corrective device. This sobering result points
to the institutional limits inherent to authoritarian regime parties.

Chapters 3 and 4 have shown that strong party grassroots help with
implementation. Chapter 8 shows how the party grassroots contributed
to regime survival in the midst of the Cultural Revolution turmoil, because
party members acted on their own initiative in the interest of political stability. This chapter suggests that in at least one historical instance, some
members dragged their feet on self-destructive central policies, thereby
(marginally) dampening their catastrophic impact. Only because local

experiences of the revolution were still fresh, its legacy influenced the behavior of local cadres, rank-and-file party members, and – possibly to a lesser extent – ordinary citizens. The following Section 7.1 discusses the Great Leap policies. Section 7.2 describes local variation in policy implementation and proposes a nuanced hypothesis about this variation, to be tested in Section 7.3.

7.1 ENFORCING GREAT LEAP POLICIES

The Great Leap Forward refers to a bundle of radical policies adopted by the People's Republic of China to leap from the capitalist stage of development straight into a communist utopia, while skipping the socialist transition stage embraced by other communist parties. Bold policy proclamations at the 8th Party Congress in 1956 foreshadowed the official launch of the Great Leap Forward two years later. Rural collectivization was the centerpiece of Great Leap Forward policies. Another devastating idea was to boost steel production by constructing backyard furnaces in the countryside; instead of reaching the goal of surpassing Britain's steel production, this turned into a tremendous waste of resources. Other policies were even more surreal – for example urging people to systematically kill and extinguish mosquitoes and sparrows. Turning a Marxist materialist worldview on its head, Mao Zedong believed that by sheer willpower the Chinese people could overcome almost any difficulty. The Great Leap Forward ended in 1960 with the realization that people were starving to death. The movement resulted in a famine that killed tens of millions of people.[1] Maybe more accurately than the statistics, fiction writers capture the unspeakable suffering of ordinary people throughout China during this era.[2] After Mao Zedong's perceived success in the Korean War, the famine disaster put Mao so much on the defensive that for several years he had to relinquish some of his powers, before he could recover them in the late 1960s.

7.1.1 Activism of Provincial Leaders

The radical communization policies of the late 1950s were highly controversial among party leaders from the beginning of the campaign, but even more so after the campaign's disastrous consequences became increasingly obvious.[3] Among ordinary people the policies were, to say the least, unpopular: In order to create communal property, the CCP essentially took back from the tillers the land which it had distributed to them during land reform a decade[4] earlier. The more localized famines of the early twentieth century, such as the infamous Henan famine in the 1940s, pale in comparison to the countrywide famine caused by the Great Leap Forward – since the Taiping Rebellion in the mid-nineteenth century, China had not seen comparable mass starvation. For a party that had come to lift up the peasants, the famine was an acute threat to its legitimacy, undermining the remains of revolutionary idealism. The extreme misery disappointed rank-and-file party members as well as many cadres, as we read in autobiographies, because they had fought for the Chinese peasants. Moreover, expectations that party policies aligned with popular preferences turned out to be mistaken, so that the party had to deploy fear to implement its policies against resistance. Instead of moving the peasants out of the traditional subsistence economy, the party pushed them over the cliff. Despite doubts from the beginning and despite the human price that quickly became obvious, by and large local cadres not only complied with the policies, but were zealous implementers.

In an effort to explain compliance, comparative political scientists have analyzed regional variation in Great Leap outcomes, focusing on the provincial top leadership. At the pinnacle of the hierarchy, Mao Zedong was able to prevail over more moderate leaders, because his power had reached a climax after the perceived success of the People's Republic in the Korea War. At the provincial level, the degree of activism varied, although overall compliance was very high. Existing studies show that career incentives help to explain the degree of activism, with aspiring alternate members of the Central Committee being the most eager implementers.[5] A dissenting view suggests instead that in the context of the Maoist polity, loyalty to Mao and inner convictions were far more important than rational career incentives.[6] Both hypotheses focus on the characteristics of individual leaders to explain famine outcomes. In part this is because of the literature's focus on the provincial level, which is partly a result of the limited availability of subprovincial data.

Institutional variables, such as ones measuring the organizational strength of the party, have received scant attention. Dali Yang pointed out that a stronger party – measured in terms of membership – might have alleviated the pressure for local cadres to be activist implementers. By contrast, those areas with few party members had to show their loyalty and be "more Catholic than the pope."[7] Dali Yang did not elaborate his theory and only provided preliminary tests – at the time he did not have access to the kind of provincial membership statistics presented in this book, let alone to famine data below the provincial level.

7.1.2 The Great Leap Forward and Party State Formation

The Great Leap Forward was a momentous event in the twisted process of transforming the CCP from a revolutionary party to a ruling party. For one thing, the movement was accompanied by a formidable expansion of the party's membership and its authority over the bureaucracy.[8] For another, incumbent cadres lost power to central authorities and to zealous newcomers. This was part of a longer process by which China's top leadership disciplined independently acting revolutionaries to blend into a smoothly functioning, hierarchically organized cadre corps. Whereas a party struggling to attain power needs independently thinking individuals who take bold decisions on their own initiative, a party in power values obedient foot soldiers. This transformation took time. In the first years after their takeover, the new leaders consolidated their power and targeted perceived enemies outside the party state apparatus. Most importantly, triggered by the Korean War, the ferocious Campaign to Suppress Counterrevolutionaries in the early 1950s killed tens of thousands, creating an atmosphere of fear among people who were distant from the regime,[9] in Shandong notably among religious organizations.[10] In the second half of the 1950s, the top leadership used increasingly coercive methods to instill Leninist discipline within its cadre corps,[11] justifying its harsh measures by pointing to foreign agents supposedly trying to destabilize China from within during the Korean War.

Evoking the Yan'an Rectification Movement of the 1940s, in preparation for the Great Leap Mao decried "subjectivism, bureaucratism and factionalism" and in two related campaigns – the Party Rectification Movement and the Anti-Rightist Movement – launched purges inside the organizations of the party state.[12] In 1958, in Shanghai alone 3.6 percent of the incumbent party members were purged;[13] nationwide the quota was 3.5 percent, which is more than in any other year of the PRC's existence.[14] The fear that these purges instilled among cadres and bureaucrats allowed Mao Zedong to enforce his radical collectivization policies of the Great Leap Forward with generally good compliance among the lower ranks.

7.1.3 Implementation Procedures

A primary bureaucratic channel for transmitting the policies of the Eighth Party Congress from the center to the country at large was through party meetings at various levels of the hierarchy, all the way down to the local party branches. After the Eighth Party Congress in 1956 had decided to fulfill the targets of the second five-year-plan in merely four years, local party leaders felt the need to display their own loyalty by making additional commitments. They did so by formal decisions to overfulfill the already inflated production targets. Some local party committees went further than others.

Cadres were made more pliable by shrewd organizational measures. One set of organizational measures brought local politics more firmly under central control by increasing the social distance between the rulers and the ruled. For instance, the Organization Department deployed new cadres unfamiliar with a particular place to replace long-serving cadres, who had attained their position before the Communist victory. Such outside cadres tended to be more willing to enforce unrealistic grain procurement targets.[15] Reposting new cadres to an unfamiliar environment made them dependent and obedient to their superiors. Redrawing jurisdictional boundaries helped to break local resistance in a similar way. Successful implementation depended on undermining the common sense of local cadres familiar with local conditions, and on reducing their empathy for the plight of their policies' victims.

The other set of organizational measures was designed to strengthen bureaucratic discipline by inspiring fear of severe punishment. For bureaucrats the most imminent threat was to be demoted from their office desk into production. The Great Leap Forward drastically reduced the number of jurisdictions at all levels, for instance reducing the number of counties in Shandong from 139 to just eighty-five counties in 1960. The Organization Department sent the redundant cadres to the urban-industrial or rural-agricultural "production frontline," where living conditions were life-threatening. This was called the Initiative to Streamline Administration and Send Cadres to the Countryside 整編機構下放幹部工作. The prefecture of Jinan in 1958 sent 52 percent of its cadre corps to the countryside, that is a total of 17,000 cadres.[16] Another typical prefecture in Shandong in mid-1957 decided to reduce the number of bureaucrats by 15 to 20 percent; and in the course of 1958 they realized this goal, making 11,000 cadres redundant and deploying them to take care of more arduous tasks.[17]

7.2 UNEVEN IMPLEMENTATION, UNEVEN FAMINE

Overall the central leadership was remarkably successful in achieving compliance with Great Leap Forward policies. Yet amid widespread compliance, there was also resistance.[18] In the two years leading up to the official launch of the Great Leap Forward, examples of resistance are plentiful. In the second half of 1957 and especially in 1958, resistance became increasingly dangerous. Different degrees of enthusiasm are more easily discovered, but resistance never fully disappeared.

7.2.1 Life-and-Death Choices by Local Leaders

Foot-dragging was dangerous in Maoist China. Being sent down to the poor countryside as a cadre who had been made redundant at the height of the famine was almost tantamount to a death sentence. Starvation was not only a concern of farmers in rural areas. Bureaucrats, even at the top of the provincial administration, found themselves in a precarious situation facing starvation, as the following description from the Finance Department of Shandong Province shows:

Current situation of Jinan staff with edema symptoms (according to phone call from Shandong Production Headquarters, November 12, 1960): The provincial Finance Department now consists of 54 people, of whom 19 (35% of total) have edema symptoms. Reason for falling sick: lack of nutrition, work overload. The Finance Department used to have 191 officials, of whom 106 were dispatched to the first frontline of production and 31 went to support the third harvest, so there are only 54 people left. They must shoulder all the work, plus supplemental production (cultivating more than 70 mu of land), the department is busy with many extra shifts and extra hours. Cadres' food rations are low, they also have to let their children eat some of it; there are some people who suffer from other diseases. Similar edema outbreaks are occurring in other departments. Reasons: food rations too small, wrong nutritional balance, undernourishment. Measures being taken: (1) The sick eat canteen food at their workplace, stop working and receive some supplemental medicine. (2) The severely sick with edema developing above the abdomen are treated in hospital.[19]

The lives of the thirty-one officials who were sent to help with the third harvest production were at greatest risk. By late 1960, people throughout Shandong's countryside were starving to death, and there was not much of a harvest. Arriving in the countryside as outsiders, the officials would have very little chance to find support from people who were struggling for their own survival. The lot of the 106 people on the production frontline was similarly uncertain, although chances of survival were better as long as they could stay in urban areas. Staying at the provincial Finance Department and avoiding being sent to the countryside was a question of life and death, although the report shows how extremely precarious conditions were even there.

Measured by the risks local leaders were taking, foot-dragging was a form of courageous resistance. Local leaders who actively implemented policies despite the harm to the population might be called opportunists – if you can term as opportunists the kinds of people who were not out for riches, but who sought to preserve the lives of their families. Locally powerful people, including party members and cadres, were under extreme pressure to go "all out" in implementing the Great Leap policies. They had minimal discretion of their own, at a time when the slightest form of foot-dragging could lead to one's dismissal.

7.2.2 Resistance to Implementation

Zibo prefecture was one of the places in Shandong where local cadres complied with policies, but displayed a lack of enthusiasm that borders on resistance. Foot-dragging started as soon as the 8th Party Committee in 1956 set the tone for the Great Leap Forward. Contrasting with the ambitions of the central leadership, local leaders in Zibo decided to exceed production targets by merely 7 percent.[20] Later on, when large meetings were to transmit the spirit of increasingly radical central government directives, local leaders failed to convene the expected meetings altogether. Half a year after calling for large-scale meetings of grassroots-level party organizations, prefectural leaders ran out of patience with their intractable subordinates and tasked the Organization Department to carry out an investigation. From the point of view of eager prefectural leaders, the progress report was sobering indeed. Not even half the party committees and general party branches had convened the required meeting. Worse, 20 percent of all grassroots organizations in Zibo self-responded that they were not preparing for any such meeting.[21] Although it was clear that the promulgation of directions from a party congress had utmost priority, certain leaders at the party grassroots were defying orders and slowed down the mobilization effort.

Throughout the Great Leap Forward, the party identified local cadres who failed to follow radical communization policies. Not using generic labels such as "rightist" and "counterrevolutionary," the party would refer to such cadres as "right-leaning conservatives," "wave the white flag" over them, and "temporarily relieve them from their posts for self-examination."[22] To be sure, resistance from local cadres and party members was not necessarily a result of their own inner convictions, but also reflected pressures from ordinary citizens. Ordinary citizens also stood up to increasing state intrusion. In Heze prefecture, local authorities found it most difficult to deal with local secret societies of the Daoist creed. In Cao County, when the government refused to provide emergency provisions, local citizens made a point of burning incense in a Daoist manner. The cadre in charge of collectivization felt threatened enough to call in security forces. After an attempt to crush the movement, the government ended up giving in to their demands.[23] In Zibo prefecture, local leaders had to beware of another religious network, namely the ethnic Hui Muslims. When in the early phase of Great Leap Forward mobilization, tensions arose in one township, it spread quickly throughout the whole prefecture, and even beyond, thanks to informal networks among the Hui Muslim minority.[24] When collectivization policies created too much popular discontent, local leaders had reason to drag their feet because disturbances would be held against them.

In the atmosphere of the Great Leap Forward, few cadres dared to report resistance and failures. In Linyi grassroots cadres had a remarkable tolerance for local protest, and local leaders informed the center about the unrevolutionary realities on the ground. As far as we can tell from currently available archival material, Linyi's leaders did not go through official channels. But they found other channels. For instance, early on in the crisis amid an atmosphere of quickly rising pressure, they let Xinhua news agency report as follows:

Xinhua New Agency, Linyi, 8th [of April, 1957]. In Linyi Prefecture (Shandong) there are still many rural communes where due to protest from its members the spring/summer harvest is severely affected.... Currently nearly 15,000 trouble-making households demanding to retreat from the commune.... They gang up and collectively loot food, firewood, drag off livestock and retreat from the commune. If commune cadres resisted in any way, there would be fighting.... At the communal spring sowing, generally about 30% to 50% commune members attended, production activities were slacking, about 40% of the fields for spring sowing have not been sown, fertilization is in bad shape.... The prefectural committee's analysis: There are multiple reasons for the disturbances, such as production shortfalls, poor management, undemocratic cadres, fiscal disorder and cadre corruption, and 90% of the problem has to do with contradictions among the people.[25]

What is remarkable is not that locals were resistant to communization policies and that communization policies failed – Mao's radical Great Leap Forward policies failed in most places, as the disastrous famine revealed. What is remarkable is how permissive grassroots party leaders were toward discontent, how local leaders let the center know about their problems, how they spelled out the consequence of these problems for production output and even pointed out the fundamental difficulty of implementing the Great Leap Forward policies. The official analysis by the Prefectural Committee, while referencing "cadre corruption" in the conventional way, by mentioning production shortfalls, "undemocratic cadres," and "contradictions among the people" in an unusually frank way pointed out that people were fundamentally opposed to communization, years before the central government began to acknowledge the problems with the Great Leap Forward. Even today, official historiography denies the realities pointed out by leaders in Linyi at the time. The provincial government responded strongly by replacing leaders and sending in trusted officials from the provincial government such as Mu Lin.[26]

Two months after Mu Lin's arrival on his post in Linyi, in August 1958 Linyi County became known throughout North China as the main experimental spot for establishing People's Communes.[27] Locals had to pay for their leaders' activism. Mortality rose to a catastrophic 49 per thousand, whereas the provincial average at the height of the famine was 24 per thousand.[28] Mu Lin was confronted with locals who did not believe in the utopian promises of the Great Leap Forward, as one can infer from a close reading of the following quote. The quote describes a visit by leaders from Linyi to Shouzhang, the other county in Shandong known for "success" in carrying out the Great Leap Forward. Shouzhang was a "production satellite" that had been extolled by People's Daily for supposedly having achieved a bumper harvest yielding 10,546 jin per mu of land.[29]

對「大躍進」和公社化異乎尋常地發展中暴露出的問題，我們當時就有所察覺、產生疑問，並通過適當方式表示了意見。壽張現場會後，我和縣委副書記包培智帶領20多名鄉、社幹部前去參觀，面對任意虛報產量，感到驚訝。雇工出身的包培智對此更獨居看法，他說：臨沂那樣好的生產條件，畝產也不過三、四百觔，壽張那麼超過臨沂？回到濟南，我專門向省委負責人談了對壽張產量的看法。

Concerning the problems encountered during the extraordinary developments of the "Great Leap Forward" and communization, we at the time had a certain awareness, we had doubts and we did express our opinions in appropriate ways. After the on-the-spot-meeting in Shouzhang, I and county vice-party secretary Bao Peizhi took more than 20 local township and commune cadres on a tour in the field, confronting them with random misreporting of output numbers, to their astonishment. Bao Peizhi, who himself used to be a farm laborer, could see what others could not, saying: 'Linyi with its good agricultural production conditions cannot yield more than 300 or 400 Jin, how could Shouzhang surpass Linyi?' Back in Jinan I talked to people in charge at the Provincial Party Committee, telling them my opinion on the output numbers of Shouzhang.[30]

It is not possible to evaluate Mu Lin's complicated role in the Great Leap Forward based on his own autobiography. He had worked as the top provincial cadre in charge of agriculture and was demoted to a position in Linyi county, apparently as a result of his hesitation to radically implement the Great Leap Forward. Yet once posted in Linyi county, it is hard to see him as siding with moderates like Bao Peizhi, as the pronoun "we" in the autobiography suggests. In private conversations with friends at the party committee Mu may have voiced doubts, but it was under Mu Lin's lead that Linyi turned into the province's example of rapid communization. The important information in this quote concerns Bao Peizhi. He had joined the CCP in late 1940 and stood at the dangerous frontline of resistance against Japan in his native Linyi. Since 1951 Bao had been among the three top leaders in Linyi. He was present in 1957 when difficulties in communization were communicated from Linyi to the central leadership. Given his biography, it is plausible that Bao Peizhi had the courage to openly challenge Great Leap Forward policies at the very site that was presented as Shandong's first production satellite. A local gazetteer, apart from listing Bao's official positions between 1940 and 1975, in coded language highlights his "being present at the grassroots" 經常深入基層 and "sharing weal and woe" 同甘共苦 with the people during the Great Leap disaster.[31] A speech of his, delivered in early 1960 at the height of the Great Leap, ostensibly agrees with the party line and dutifully refers to yields of 1,000 jin per mu, but only to go on and deplore not only "rightist," but also "leftist mistakes."[32] Although his maneuvers were careful enough to allow him to remain in power, Bao's behavior represents subversive foot-dragging of local cadres.

In other places, resistance to Great Leap Forward policies was more successful in averting the famine disaster. At the height of the movement, Guan County in the Western part of Shandong experienced a veritable uprising, which at the time alerted even leaders in Beijing. When serious food shortages occurred in the winter of 1958–1959, social order broke down, accompanied by massive outflows of people.[33] It is hard to establish how much of this turmoil was due to restive citizens and how much to recalcitrant local cadres. It is significant, however, that the part of Guan county where the uprising occurred had been an independent county until December 1958, when higher-level government decided to abolish that county and incorporate it into Guan County, indicating dissatisfaction with an insubordinate leadership of that earlier county. The discredited leaders may have done less than expected to stop their people from emigrating. Other counties in the area routinely deployed agents at train stations and river crossings to stop emigration.[34]

The party grassroots were indispensable for alerting higher government to the deteriorating situation. During the Great Leap Forward, numerous investigation teams traveled the country, only to let themselves be deceived by local cadres. By contrast, when in early 1959 a provincial investigation team came to Guan County a significant number of basic-level cadres filed their complaints. For instance, the managers of 82 out of 1,195 mess halls self-reported that they had altogether stopped giving out food; many more reported that they had "half-stopped" giving out food.[35] Other cadres reported cases of food theft, human trafficking, numerous suicides, and famine deaths.[36] The eighty-two mess hall managers, as well as the other cadres, must be judged as extraordinarily courageous because at the time their reports came close to self-indictments. Although they were in the minority, they were numerous and outspoken enough that food requisitioning was cut and emergency supplies shipped in. Without being able to pin down exactly how much of the resistance originated with the people and how much of it originated with the party grassroots, apparently the resistance saved the county much distress. Guan County is extremely peripheral and thus prone to famine, but the mortality rate in the wake of the Great Leap Forward increased only slightly to 13 per thousand, whereas for all of Shandong mortality doubled to 24 per thousand.[37]

7.2.3 Previously Embattled Areas as Most Resistant

Why was there so much more resistance in some places than in others? To understand where resistance against the Great Leap Policies was most likely, this chapter suggests local party history as a highly relevant variable. Since the Sino-Japanese War and the Civil War had ended only one decade earlier, local experiences of violence still shaped the behavior of rank-and-file party members and local cadres. Arguably, in places that experienced the sharpest confrontation, a spirit of resistance had survived the Communist revolution and helped to reduce the devastating impact of the Great Leap Forward. Beyond the politically salient distinction between party members recruited before the Communist takeover and those recruited thereafter,[38] not all early recruits took the same risk. It was much more dangerous to join the CCP in some areas than in others.

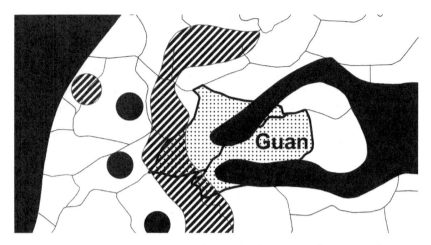

FIGURE 7.1 Guan county as an exemplary embattled area: Reflecting war fronts in 1941, this map illustrates that Guan County (dotted area) was contested territory, where Japanese troops (black area) faced Communist resistance (shaded area). Sources: War fronts according to Japanese military maps.[39] County boundaries from 1964 census material at Harvard Geospatial Library.

The case of Guan County is a good example, because both its resistance against Great Leap Policies and its exposure as a battleground during the Sino-Japanese War were striking. The area of Guan County was at the fringes of Japanese-occupied territory and not far away from a Communist base area. As a result, the area epitomizes an "embattled area" where both parties clashed, as shown on Japanese military maps[40] (compare map in Figure 7.1). In such a place, the party could mobilize successfully.[41] Some of the individuals in power during the Great Leap Forward, although not always from the county itself, were battle-experienced and presumably particularly committed party members, like the county party secretary Chen Guanghan 陳光漢, who had spent time in a Japanese prison. There existed a personal link between local resistance and revolutionary history.

Guan County continued to defy the politics of centrally prescribed mass mobilization during the Cultural Revolution. A local coalition for stability, built around incumbent party cadres, held onto power and kept radicals down until the spring of 1969, when provincial rebel leaders decided to take down the conservatives. The local coalition was so strong that rebel leaders had to recruit large numbers of outsiders. In the end 10,000 violent rebels from eight counties, half of them armed, descended on the county.[42] Locals refer to this troop as the "Eight Nations Alliance," evoking the memory of the eight nations who came to Shandong to quell the Boxer uprising in 1900, and put the death toll at more than sixty people.[43] Guan County is the mirror image of the observation that the famine disaster had prepared the ground for anarchical violence:[44] Cadres shielded the county from the Great Leap Famine and later on were relatively safe from local attack during the Cultural Revolution, until the combined force of eight counties in the neighborhood conducted a veritable invasion. The origin of party strength in Guan lies in its encounter with the Japanese Imperial Army.

More systematically, one can distinguish among three different historical pathways according to how much violence a locality had experienced and under how much risk locals had joined the party: base areas, embattled areas and Japanese strongholds. Base areas were firmly under Communist control and were typically located in the province's periphery, so the Japanese threat there seemed remote. To be sure, punitive expeditions occasionally reached into peripheral areas, but people did not join under the same kind of permanent threat as people in immediate proximity to the Japanese. In these embattled areas, chances were that people had been displaced as a direct result of Japanese violence. Calling people who joined the Communists in the base areas "opportunists" and people who joined in the embattled areas "idealists" might go too far. But in fact the risks people took depended greatly on the locality where they joined the party. And so did the violence that people experienced during the wars before the Communist takeover.

This three-way distinction, rather than a dichotomous base-area dummy variable, has been a conventional geographical distinction made by decision makers and academics alike. Party documents at the time of the Sino-Japanese War routinely classified territory into three groups: liberated, contested, and occupied areas.[45] Chinese analyses as well as Western scholarship, to the extent that they take subnational variation seriously, employ similar categories: base areas, early-liberated, and late-liberated areas;[46] or base areas, guerrilla zones, and areas outside the party's reach.[47] Decision makers at the time found this three-way distinction practically useful, and scholars later on found it to have analytic value as well.

Prior to the Communist takeover in 1949, the party's base areas in rural areas of China's periphery were the geographic center of the revolution. Communists took refuge there, experimented with government, and then started their expansion, which finally encompassed the whole country. Once in power, the CCP lost much of its interest in the base areas. As was to be expected, the national capital was not established at the seat of the CCP's leadership during the war in the remote mountains of Shaanxi, but rather in the geopolitically and symbolically vital city of Beijing. Like the party's top leaders, who left the periphery to rule the country from the center, low-ranking cadres and rank-and-file members were needed in less marginal places, which were also more comfortable for living. In other words, the wartime base areas, which had always been understood as a transient way-station of the revolution, saw an exodus of the party.

Hypothesis: Those areas most embattled during the Sino-Japanese War saw most resistance to collectivization policies and as a result had lower mortality rates. By contrast, areas firmly under Japanese control, where the party gained a foothold very late in the war, as well as safe havens far away from Japanese occupation both were home to more obedient cadres.

7.3 QUANTITATIVE EVIDENCE

7.3.1 Famine Data

This chapter uses data on the severity of the famine, which the author discovered in newly acquired materials at the Harvard-Yenching Library.[48] Population statistics, collected by the Chinese security apparatus, provide the most reliable data on the severity of the Great Leap Famine. On a yearly basis, public security bureaus collect population data, including birth and mortality rates. For Shandong province, the most fine-grained data available, as of today, are disaggregated to the county level. The relative autonomy of the public security apparatus from the local party secretary to a certain extent insulates these statistics from pressures to downplay the devastating effect of the famine. Yet the mortality statistics should nevertheless be considered as a lower bound. An additional bias might occur when the public security bureau decides whether to explain the missing population as having outmigrated or as having died. Yet it is not clear in which direction the bureau would be biased: On the one hand, deaths represent a severe failure of the local government, but on the other hand, outmigration represents a failure of the public security office, which is supposed to keep people in place.

7.3.2 Mapping Contested Territory

In the mind of historians, Communist base areas are geographically well defined. Primary material pertaining to local history, such as the detailed maps in the well-known series *Material on the Organizational History*, reveals that in reality the borders were more ambiguous than simplified historiographies suggest. Chapter 5 shows that among locals on the ground there is considerable confusion as to where exactly the base areas were. To identify base areas, I rely on a map by Rana Mitter showing "areas under Communist control in Northern China" in August 1945,[49] which reflects well the scholarly consensus among historians of China. Ultimately, Mitter's various borderlines sit well with the cartographic material published by CCP historians. After geo-referencing, I assign a dummy variable to each of the counties in the 1960 borders, defining counties as having been a base area – as opposed to an embattled area – if the entirety of their territory falls within one of the areas designated by Rana Mitter's map as "under Communist control."

The areas most firmly under Japanese control can be identified from Japan's military maps. The range of Japanese control varied over time, but in Shandong two corridors were securely under control: one along the railroad from Beijing to Shanghai, and the other along the railroad from the provincial capital, Jinan, to the most important provincial port of Qingdao. To be sure, the army could not always ward off all surprise attacks by guerrilla forces, but it could prevent an open presence of Communist troops. Because the thickness of the corridor was highly uneven, I use an authoritative map, which the historical research office of the Japanese Ministry of Defense compiled based on its own maps from the time.[50] After georeferencing the map, I assign a dummy variable to each of the counties in the 1960 borders, defining counties as having been fully under the control of the Imperial Army if the entirety of their territory falls within the area designated as being "under Japanese control."

7.3.3 Units of Analysis

Until the Communist takeover, counties had been stable administrative units, persisting over hundreds of years with only minor adjustments.[51] In the early years of Communist rule, the number of counties proliferated to around 140 in Shandong and has remained at that level until today, with one exceptional time period: The Great Leap Forward was accompanied by radical restructuring of the administrative apparatus, reducing the number of counties in Shandong by over one third to eighty-five in 1960. The motivation was partly ideological, seeking to scale up every imaginable aspect of administration. But as described earlier, uniting counties also had the political effect of keeping lower-level cadres in line and on their toes, because the likelihood that their workplace would be made redundant was high. Administrative restructuring poses an analytic problem, because at different points in time data are reported in different units of analysis. Using counties as units of analysis poses difficulties, because jurisdictional boundaries changed quickly and drastically during the Great Leap era.

The solution for the present analysis is to use counties of 1964 as the reference point and then develop a concordance to map the 1953 counties and the 1960 counties on the map for 1964. This requires a close analysis of various volumes of *Material on the Organizational History*, local gazetteers, and party histories and chronologies. For the 1960 to 1964 concordance, in many cases the 1960 county is split into two "new" jurisdictions, so that I assign the 1960 statistics from one county to two or (rarely) more new counties. In other cases "new" counties were made out of parts of several "old" counties, usually by reassigning entire townships. In this case, I calculate what percentage of townships from the "old" county were assigned to the "new" county and weigh the 1960 statistics accordingly. In both cases, the methodology is an approximation because it is based on the assumption that the famine was evenly severe throughout each county. It could well be that the most severely affected parts of a county were purposefully joined with townships from a less affected county. These are well-known problems of working with historical data and using data pertaining to historical jurisdictions. The 1953 to 1964 concordance is less problematic, because in many cases the former administrative units of 1953 had been restored by 1964. Using historical GIS data on Communist base areas and occupied areas avoids difficulties with the units of analysis, since geodata do not depend on county boundaries in the first place.

7.3.4 Specification and Results

To control for confounding factors related to overall levels of development, the specifications control for mortality in a "normal" year prior to the Great Leap era. I use mortality data for the year 1952, which is the midpoint between the Communist takeover in 1949 and the beginning of collectivization in 1956. The data come from the same source as the famine data, and GIS techniques allow me to map the 1952 data to the jurisdictions of 1960. The second most important confounder might be

TABLE 7.1   *History effect on famine mortality in 1960*

	Specification 1	Specification 2
Mortality 1953	1.034*	1.032*
Rural	0.242*	0.234*
Embattled area	−7.558**	
Communist base area		7.905*
Japanese stronghold		6.988*

** Significance at 0.01, * significance at 0.05
Notes: OLS estimator. 112 county-level observations from Shandong Province. Sources: Famine mortality from police statistics.[52] Extent of Japanese occupation from a map that was compiled based on Japanese military maps.[53] Degree of urbanization from census data at *Harvard Geospatial Library.*

urbanization, because Japanese occupation focused on urban centers and the famine hit rural areas the hardest.[54]

Table 7.1 shows the result. Having been an embattled area decreases mortality by 7.6 per thousand, compared to all other areas. Reversely, choosing the embattled areas as comparison point, places that used to be Japanese strongholds and base areas on average experience 7.0 and 7.9 more deaths per thousand, respectively. The results are not only statistically significant, but also substantively very important. As a point of comparison, note that in Shandong mortality doubled from 12 per thousand in 1953 to 24 per thousand in 1960 (county averages), the difference being 12 per thousand. If on average the fact of having been an embattled area reduces mortality by 7.6 per thousand, this is a large effect indeed: It means that the impact of the famine was cut in half.

The results are statistically significant at the 95 percent and 99 percent level, respectively. The main reason why one could not expect higher significance levels is related to the inaccuracies that are unavoidable when working with shifting jurisdictional boundaries. For example, one might have expected that mortality in 1953 is very closely correlated to mortality in 1960, at least if one assumes that the famine tended to strike initially poor places harder; but this is not the case, as the first line of Table 7.1 shows. Apparently the main problem is that the unit of analysis was not stable. Apart from the fact that the mergers of jurisdictions left only eighty-five county-level units as opposed to 140 before these mergers, inaccuracy is a result of projecting mortality from counties in the 1953 borders onto counties in the 1960 borders.

7.4 CONCLUSION

In the case of the Great Leap Forward, the strongest party grassroots functioned as a self-corrective device. This historical instance of disobedience in the interest of the common good occurred a mere ten years after the Communist takeover. As the party state was still in the process of institutionalizing its bureaucratic routines, local party members still retained their fresh revolutionary memory. It is questionable, however, whether such local traditions of disobedience, supported by revolutionary identity and the success with earlier episodes of disobedience, have been transmitted to the present.

To be sure, there are examples suggesting that traditions of bottom-up party-based disobedience to certain destructive policies can persist. As described in this chapter, Guan County in Liaocheng Prefecture stood out not only for resisting the Great Leap Forward, but also for resisting the disruptive schemes of the Cultural Revolution. More recently, when Shandong's leaders rolled out a movement to construct a socialist countryside accompanied by rhetoric reminiscent of the Great Leap, Liaocheng Prefecture was slow to implement the policy, citing worries that this top-down policy involving public appropriation of land might not be in the best interest of local farmers. While higher-level authorities deplore the failure of local officials to implement what they praise as constructive policies, local-level authorities are convinced that before long their deviation from central policy will be recognized as people-friendly behavior.[55] But on the whole, as the previous chapters have demonstrated, by now the rank-and-file members of the CCP function as reliable implementers of central policy.

In principle Leninist party doctrine acknowledges that internal dissent can be in the best interest of the party. The top social engineer of the CCP, Liu Shaoqi, in the 1940s highlighted that the new party constitution for good reasons guaranteed the right of party members with minority views to express themselves without fear. After the Cultural Revolution, Deng Xiaoping and the "Resolution on CCP History" emphasized that the turmoil had much to do with one man's arrogant leadership and that it was essential for the party to return to the founding principle of inner-party democracy.[56] This democratic lesson from the political disasters of the past has been lost on the post-Tian'anmen leadership. The historical legacy of anti-Japanese resistance, while fresh on the minds of people who themselves risked their lives, in the aftermath of the war could in some localities still turn the party into a self-corrective device. Tens of millions of famine deaths in China as a result of ill-guided party policy are the context against which some local cadres managed to avert the worst. As the following chapter shows, during the Cultural Revolution the party once again functioned as a self-corrective device – this time as a result not of localized revolutionary idealism but of personal interests.

8

The CCP and Regime Survival in Times of Crisis (1967–1969)

Under ordinary circumstances, local party members empower the regime by assisting in policy implementation, as Chapters 3 and 4 have demonstrated. But what if in a moment of crisis the party's ordinary chain of command breaks down, leaving local party cells with no instructions? Are local party organizations of any help in the hours of the regime's greatest need? To address these questions, this chapter focuses on the Cultural Revolution (1966–1976), an era when Mao Zedong, for fear of revisionism inside the CCP, called on people to "attack the headquarters" by overturning local party leadership. The movement brought China to the brink of anarchy. As a moment of existential crisis, the Cultural Revolution reveals how the party functions in emergency mode and brings to light the forces of order that ultimately prevailed. Whereas the previous chapters explain how an authoritarian party empowers the regime on an every-day basis, this chapter gives clues as to what to expect from the party when the regime is in crisis. Based on a large variety of documentary evidence, the analysis reveals the central role of the party for regime survival and identifies multiple mechanisms at work. Without the continued presence of the party at the local level, the People's Republic would have been unlikely to survive the turmoil.

To understand the durability of a party-based authoritarian regime, it is not enough to investigate its operations under favorable conditions. In the case of the Chinese party state, during the past three decades conditions have been very favorable indeed. Since 1983, in seventeen years out of thirty-two, China experienced double-digit economic growth rates. Furthermore, since 1997 state budgets have grown faster than the economy. The annual growth rate of fiscal revenues was 51 percent higher than the growth rate of the economy.[1] The resilience of the Chinese party state has drawn much scholarly attention,[2] but few political scientists study contemporary regime resilience with attention to the era when it was under greatest threat, namely at the height of the Cultural Revolution in 1967–1968.[3] Although the party state lost its monopoly on violence and could not guarantee the physical safety of its citizens, it maintained authority in key areas of governance, such as in the socialist state economy. What were the forces of order, which in the absence of normally functioning formal institutions prevented China from falling into an anarchical abyss? And how could the state make such a formidable comeback after the Ninth Party Congress in 1969? Conventional answers, pointing out that in 1966 Mao unleashed the masses, suggest that later on Mao put the masses back on the leash with the help of military force. Much better answers are needed and possible, because Mao's whims alone can hardly explain how political order was feasible after such extreme political turmoil.

To understand the resilience of a system, ideally one would want a stress test. A political stress test is a kind of natural experiment comparable to doctors assessing the physical robustness of astronauts, elite soldiers, and sportsmen by measuring their vital signs while the patients are exerting themselves under extreme conditions. Stress tests are conducted on banking systems, computer systems, and other complex engineering systems, such as nuclear power plants. An alternative to stress tests is crash tests, which effectively destroy the system – in China the fall of the Qing Dynasty and the flight of the Republican government to Taiwan provide such crash tests, but they are relevant for understanding the institutions of the People's Republic only to the extent that the present regime continues certain governance strategies. A natural stress test of a political regime brings that regime as close as possible to its demise, but lets it survive. Political scientists have recognized the value of studying times of crisis. Peter Gourevitch argues that moments of great economic crisis expose societal cleavages and their impact on a state's decision making.[4] Similarly, in her analysis of authoritarian regime breakdown, Barbara Geddes devotes attention to theorizing the behavior of regimes when they "run into unexpected problems."[5] Influential models of regime transition predict that "democratizations are more likely to arise in a situation of economic or political crisis."[6]

The Cultural Revolution was the most severe stress test of the People's Republic. In 1966 Mao Zedong unleashed the Cultural Revolution by calling on the masses to "bombard the headquarters," using his personal authority to attack the authority of a party state of his own creation.[7]

After China's mass famine resulting from Mao Zedong's Great Leap Forward policies in the late 1950s, party leaders had pressured Mao to abandon radical politics and even forced him to temporarily relinquish some of
his powers by "retiring to the second front." With de-Stalinization having
occurred in the Soviet Union, de-Maoization in China seemed a possibility.[8] The Cultural Revolution was Mao's recipe for combating moderate
forces and training the younger generation to wage revolution, maintain
the movement's combat ethos, and thereby secure Mao's own legacy. Current President Xi Jinping is a product of the movement, having experienced the downfall of his powerful father and having actively participated
in the movement as a Red Guard. The first targets of the Cultural Revolution were the government bureaucracy along with the CCP's cadres,
who had become bulwarks of the status quo. Mao Zedong's personal-
ist authority prevailed over the party's authority, especially at the commanding heights of the state.[9] Party cadres came under physical attack.
Red Guards and worker rebels toppled local governments. The party
hierarchy stopped functioning. Yet at the end, the CCP made a narrow
escape. Despite the violent onslaught, the party survived. To be sure, Mao
might have hesitated to give the party its final death blow. Nevertheless,
in most other countries it does not take a Cultural Revolution to throw
the polity into permanent disorder. In China, as this chapter shows, the
party retained considerable authority even in the midst of turmoil, quickly
reconfiguring when the worst was over.

   The Cultural Revolution period is still politically sensitive, because
issues of individual responsibility for violence and deaths have never
been settled, and because the current generation of leaders was politically socialized during that era. Nevertheless, over recent years a wealth
of historical material has become available in archives, private collections,
and memoirs, as well as on flea markets and the Internet. This chapter
primarily relies on information from local archives and from private collections, but also on documents collected by others in a similar manner.[10]
The material allows one to identify the forces of order that ultimately
prevented the People's Republic from falling apart. When the party had
ceased to function as a hierarchical organization, certain formal procedures, as well as informal party institutions, helped to preserve and restore
political order. The party's loyalty networks and its organizational repertoire, as well as the well-rehearsed subordination of the military under
the party, were key. Ostensibly, China's regime had turned personalistic,
but beneath the surface, remnants of the party continued to shape events.
China's experience of the party contributing to regime survival contrasts

sharply with conventional views, which emphasize the importance of unitary parties for avoiding elite factionalism in times of crisis and building a hard shell around their organizations.[11] In China the hard shell of the party was cracked open. Factions outside the party linked up with factions inside the party, whose leaders were driven by ideological differences as much as by career ambition. Moreover, the reaction of party leaders was characterized by judicious strategizing rather than outright opposition to the movement. The instincts of party leaders throughout the country, suddenly left to their own devices and without clear guidance from upper-level authorities, led them to tactical retreat and generous compromises. They quietly regenerated the organization and worked toward the long-term political survival of the party, whose destiny seemed bonded to their own.

This chapter consists of six parts, roughly moving from less turbulent places to more turbulent ones. The first part begins by contrasting conventional accounts of the CCP as having disappeared to a reality of a party whose institutional core survived and remained pivotal during the turmoil. The second part moves from the organization to the individuals making up the party, revealing even more continuities, with experienced party members shaping the turmoil. Third, by analyzing the forces of order in local communities, party networks turned out to be resilient and contributed to containing turmoil. Section 8.4 turns to places with more violence and shows that during the Cultural Revolution, as in other instances of violent conflict, military measures were necessary yet insufficient to cope with turmoil. Party organizations were indispensable for stabilization. Section 8.5 describes top-down efforts to pacify the most chaotic places of all, ultimately relying on Leninist methods. Finally, the quantitative Section 8.6 tests the idea that party presence was conducive to more stability. The conclusion considers whether party organizers have learned from the Cultural Revolution experience in ways that make the institution more immune to future threats, especially should the party come under attack, be torn apart by factional splits, or be led into turmoil by a revolutionary-minded leader.

8.1 INSTITUTIONS: THE PARTY IS DEAD, LONG LIVE THE PARTY

Paying scant attention to the CCP, the scholarship on the Cultural Revolution focuses either on Mao at the top, or on the masses at the bottom. At a time when Mao's power was virtually unchallenged, when the leader's cult of personality reached a climax, and when his instructions were omnipresent in the lives of people throughout the country, understanding the politics at Mao's court goes a long way in explaining the course of events.[12] Just as striking as Mao's towering presence is the political energy erupting in communities around China, making sociopolitical analysis of local conflict very fruitful.[13] Yet the existing literature is much better at illuminating the origins of conflict, rather than the means by which the turmoil could be contained and order reestablished.[14] To explain the forces of order, a study of the party is essential. Both formal (this section) and informal (following sections) party institutions were decisive for the People's Republic to survive the turmoil.

8.1.1 Securing the Institutional Core of the Party

Conventional accounts underestimate the agency of the CCP during the Cultural Revolution. China's official assessment of the Cultural Revolution laments that "it was hard for the Party and state to prevent the initiation of the 'cultural revolution' or check its development."[15] Instead, it simply describes the party and its members as victims:

運動開始後，黨的各級組織普遍受到衝突並陷於癱瘓、半癱瘓狀態，黨的各級領導幹部普遍受到批判和鬥爭，廣大黨員被停止了組織生活，黨長期依靠的許多積極份子和基本群眾受到排斥。

Once the movement began, most party organizations at all levels were beleaguered and fell into a state of paralysis or semi-paralysis; most party cadres were criticized and struggled against; party members stopped their organizational activities, activists and the masses whom the party had relied on for a long time were ostracized.[16]

Since political loyalty was owed to Mao Zedong personally and since the masses attacked cadres throughout China, the party lost its authority and could not function normally. Yet the institutional core of the party was preserved throughout the crisis. Rules were made that safeguarded the power of the center and the continuity of the party's membership base.

No party organization was safe from rebel attacks. Rebels who acted under Mao's instructions to "attack the headquarters" could hardly accept that certain party organizations would be off limits. Leaders repeatedly attempted – with varying degrees of success – to establish such restrictions. The moderate Premier Zhou Enlai sought to put the East China Office out of the rebels' reach.[17] Hierarchically situated between the central government and the provinces, the East China Office had been powerful during the pre-1949 wartime, but had turned into a somewhat obscure and redundant institution. Possibly Zhou Enlai considered reactivating this office should the situation spiral further out of control. The radical central leader Kang Sheng declared that rebel activity in the Organization Department at the central level was inadmissible.[18] His motivation was apparent: The personal information of cadres, held by the department, was Kang Sheng's political capital. Moreover, having run party purges in the past in close connection with the Organization Department, the department held material that was used against Kang Sheng himself. Such restrictions had a transient effect at best, because taboos only served to whet the rebels' ambitions.

By contrast, a small set of procedural ground rules proved extraordinarily effective. Arguably the most important of these rules emerged in early 1967 and regulated local leadership succession. In January of that year, rebels in Shanghai stormed the provincial-level party committee and publicly declared a power seizure. Mao praised this event as a shining example, thereby triggering similar power seizures throughout the country, from production brigades and factory work units to provincial authorities and central agencies. Power seizures not only removed the incumbents and destroyed the authority of local governments, they also set off violent conflict between contending rebel factions. Yet these ostensibly chaotic conditions were more structured than one might think. Mao himself declared that the organization replacing a "Party Committee" as the supreme power holders should be called a "Revolutionary Committee," thereby focusing the rebels' energy on creating such a body. Predictably, competing claims to power were clashing, so that upper-level governments could pick the winner and select the legitimate Revolutionary Committee.

The virtue of this procedure was that it incorporated rebel organizations into a system that was ultimately controlled by the central party leadership. The power of the central government over province-level authorities was formally enshrined in a regulation divulged in March 1967 and followed by similar provisions at lower levels of the hierarchy:

各省、市、自治區一級的奪權,在採取行動之前,應先要取得中央同意,派代表來京通中央商量。沒有經過中央同意,不要成立臨時權力機構（革命委員會）,不要在地方報紙上報道和廣電台上廣播奪權。

Before carrying out province-level power seizures, there should be consent from the center, rebel representative should come to Beijing for consultations. Without permission from the center, no transitional authority (Revolutionary Committee) must be established, nor be reported in local newspapers and broadcasts.[19]

This regulation defined the endpoint of local struggles, confirming what most rebels knew anyway: that they were operating in a top-down system where their own power depended on the endorsement from higher levels.

In essence, rebels were allowed to destroy local authorities, but they could not legitimately succeed the incumbent government without endorsement by the central leadership. The process by which a province transitioned from a power seizure to a new government on average took about one year, although with much variation: In Heilongjiang the rebels took over from the incumbent government without a power vacuum, whereas in Xinjiang the Revolutionary Committee was created almost two years after the turmoil had started. Party leaders could be toppled, but without consent from the center no one could hold onto power legitimately. No matter how much local upheaval there was, it was known that upper levels could veto outcomes at lower levels. Thus throughout the turmoil, the authority of the party's hierarchical system continued to operate in the background.

The second most important rule served to safeguard the integrity of the party at the grassroots level. As mass organizations questioned the legitimacy of party membership, certain party members were excluded from the party and new members joined the party, following no particular procedure. This not only threatened the composition of the party, but also confounded its boundaries and its membership. Shifting party membership undermined the CCP as a consistent organization. The "Central Government Regulation on Handling Party Membership" stipulated that – except for well-defined and rare cases – disciplinary action against party members must wait until after the movement; that mass organizations had no right to admit members into the party or to exclude anyone from the party; and that archives must be preserved.[20] This regulation was effective in achieving its primary goal to stop exclusions: From 1967 to the end of the movement, only about 50,000 party members were excluded per year, whereas in ordinary years this number was at least two or three times higher.[21] There were still many new accessions to the party, but overall the regulation helped to contain the displacement of members enough to ensure organizational continuity of the membership base. After the Cultural Revolution, local party organizations quickly moved back toward the status quo ante, through the exclusion of members and rehabilitations.

8.1.2 The Party finds Shelter in the Economy

The party served as an anchor of stability not only by defining the structure of the conflict, but also by stepping in to coordinate the Socialist economy. Since the economic system heavily depended on coordination by the state, turmoil in local governments could have had devastating consequences. Yet overall, the Chinese economy functioned relatively smoothly, even during the most destructive phase of the Cultural Revolution.[22] This was possible only because CCP leaders quickly redefined the role of party cadres in an arrangement that had benefits for the economy, for the party, and even for the rebels. In essence, experienced cadres were tasked to set up Production Headquarters as a lean bureaucracy to ensure the smooth functioning of the economy. Cadres were eager to join the Production Headquarters, because it gave them better prospects of political and physical survival. Rebel groups generally had little interest in attacking the economic sector of government. First, increasing economic output was high on the Maoist agenda, so that any action that disrupted production could be labeled "counterrevolutionary." Similarly, handling physical goods came with the risk of being accused of corruption. Moreover, Production Headquarters gave themselves the air of an apolitical technocracy, whereas rebels pursued the symbolic power of institutions with "supreme authority," such as party committees. Handling statistics and organizing logistics were simply not the kind of tasks that felt like carrying out revolution. It was precisely the most radical of the rebel groups that avoided the production sector. In the eyes of pragmatic rebels, good economic performance justified the continued activity of cadres who from the rebels' perspective had lost their revolutionary legitimacy.

The party could only be so successful with its economic rescue mission because cadres had the mental flexibility that allowed them to quickly take on a new role and the organizational aptness that allowed them to calmly maintain effective operations in the midst of civilian disorder. Premier Zhou Enlai was the engineer of the Production Headquarters. He could take advantage of a patriotic consensus according to which production was indispensable to defend China against foreign threats. He could also cite Mao's widely disseminated slogan that one must "make revolution, promote production," positing that true revolutionary activity did not hurt the economy. Zhou Enlai himself and many cadres had more practical motives. In meetings with him, the consensus was that "production cannot stop. People must eat and wear clothes. There must be a bureaucratic apparatus taking care of production."[23] This was perceived as a matter of political survival. "People need oil, salt, soy sauce, vinegar, as well as soap and towels. Women need hair pins on their heads and clothes to wear. If they do not find such things in the shops, there will be uprising. This more than anything else will make people unhappy about the government."[24] Zhou Enlai's official life chronology depicts him as tirelessly fixing the economy throughout the turmoil, securing railroad logistics and instructing cadres to organize local Production Headquarters.[25] But he could only be successful because he found many local party members experienced in handling crisis situations.

Participation in production played a pivotal role in the survival strategies of party cadres. Cadres throughout China weighed their options how to escape from persecution. The prevalence of suicides indicates how difficult it was to effectively escape. Less prominent cadres tried to escape by returning to their hometowns. Since outsiders arose suspicion, they would need families with the wherewithal to ward off rebel attacks there. The various escape routes are well described in the accusation of one woman, who was rumored to have a relationship with Shandong's top rebel leader, in her own voice: "What relationship? Could I be attracted to his pock marks for their size, or rather for their quantity?"[26] When she came under rebel attack, the rebel leader sought ways to get her out of Jinan. At first, the idea was to let her see a doctor in Shanghai or Beijing, but that did not seem safe, since competing rebel groups had set up liaison offices in these cities. They ultimately decided to place her on a big state farm in a neighboring province, justifying her presence by her desire to promote production. She carried an introduction letter saying that she was an "old cadre" and was accompanied by two high provincial leaders.[27] All this shows how difficult it was to escape, even for someone with excellent relationships to the top provincial rebel leadership.

Participation in Production Headquarters was a good if by no means risk-free strategy. In the case of Shandong, the only two Standing Committee members who maintained their position of power with almost no interruption, surviving the power seizure of the rebels as well as the fall of the rebels, had made themselves indispensable to the provincial Production Headquarters. One of them recalls:

At the time, Mao Zedong came up with a series of slogans like "Our agriculture must study Dazhai," "Our industry must study Daqing," "Grasp revolution, promote production," all of them supporting the promotion of production. These slogans turned into sharp weapons in the hands of Production Headquarters at all hierarchical levels to organize the expansion of production.[28]

The Production Headquarters provided a safe haven not only to to-most officials, but also further down in the hierarchy. If anything, the percentage of cadres working for the rebel government was higher. Twenty percent of provincial-level standing committees stayed on, compared to 21 percent at the prefectural level and 29 percent at the county level.[29] More often than not, involvement in managing production was the key to local party cadres' survival.

There were occasional attacks on the Production Headquarters. In Shandong, its bureaucratic apparatus was functional within weeks after the rebellious takeover. One attack on the Production Headquarters in April–May 1967 was easily warded off, as the top rebel leader appeased one angry rebel faction by admitting one student and one worker representative to the leadership of the Production Headquarters.[30] The situation changed only in December 1968, when the rebel leader himself decided to topple some of the leaders of the Production Headquarters. This decision was born out of a dissatisfaction with the meager economic growth rate, as well as with the perception – probably correct – that the Production Headquarters had accumulated much independent power. He had his trusted associates organize more than 1,000 workers in worker propaganda teams. They boarded trucks and drove to the provincial Production Headquarters, loudspeakers and banners declaring the goal of their mission: "Mao Zedong Thought Propaganda Team of Shandong Workers to be Stationed at the Provincial Production Headquarters." Once arrived at the Production Headquarters, they declared that henceforth, no order, no report, and no decision would be valid if it had not been made in the presence of a member of the Propaganda Team.[31] This disruption had disastrous consequences for Shandong's economy and hastened the political downfall of the rebels several months later. The Production Headquarters had become a state within the state, run by the erstwhile party elite.

8.1.3 Kindling Expectations of the Party's Return

Playing by the rules of the party was the safest tactical option for cadres, rebels, and citizens, as long as they expected the party's return. Unsurprisingly, then, the leadership worked hard to maintain such expectations. This was challenging, because on a regular basis people saw the downfall of party leaders, who had been authority figures for a long time, and might have concluded that the party itself was about to perish. The key for maintaining the belief in the party was to convince people of a distinction between the individuals making up the party vs. the party as an organization: While individuals might fall, the institution was there to stay. People needed to buy into the idea that it was acceptable to destroy innumerable party cadres deemed harmful to the Maoist cause, but that the party itself was a worthy organization serving that cause.

The Ninth Party Congress was one vehicle for kindling expectations of the party's return, especially among cadres. The congress is said to have met "under conditions of secrecy unprecedented even by the standards of the world Communist Movement" and that "the first the party and the country knew of it was when a communiqué was issued on the opening day."[32] At the same time, however, many people had a sense that the Ninth Congress was in the making long before the official opening ceremony. There were oblique references in the official newspaper, such as an article at the beginning of January 1969, reminding the public that Mao Zedong had called for a Ninth Party Congress at an "appropriate time."[33] The "secret" was out in October 1967, when a circular announced that Mao was considering the modalities for a Ninth Congress, mentioning one leader's view that it should be held soon, "before the end of 1968." This circular was issued to provincial Revolutionary Committees, many of whose members had close connections to rebel organizations. The message of this circular was that the party was to be reformed – and by implication that the party was to make a comeback.[34]

Archival material reveals just how many people knew about and were involved in preparing the Ninth Party Congress as early as the beginning of 1967. Kang Sheng in particular mentioned preparations for the Ninth Party Congress early on, for example by giving a talk about a new party constitution to be adopted at the congress,[35] but also by referring to it in passing when groups from around the country visited Beijing.[36] In the case of Hubei, there was correspondence between the central and the provincial government concerning the selection of representatives to the congress. If some representatives who came to Beijing were clueless about the purpose of their visit,[37] this speaks to the fact that some of the representatives – although by no means all – were politically nobodies,[38] of whom there were more than a few on this rubber-stamping body. As early as late 1967, a central government document summarized responses to an "opinion survey," which apparently had been sent out to collect feedback on things like how to run the congress and how to select the representatives.[39]

Knowing well the consequential nature of previous party congresses – only one had been held after the foundation of the People's Republic – the "winners" of the power struggles of 1967–1968 thought of the impending Ninth Party Congress as the decisive event that would allow them to consolidate their power. For instance, a year and a half before the meeting, the provincial leaders of Shandong province began maneuvering themselves into an advantageous positions for the upcoming congress.

In February 1968, at the time of the provincial revolutionary representative assembly, Wang Xiaoyu took Zhao Xiude and standing committee member Chen Fenglai (representing the military) aside and said: 'As soon as possible put together a team to investigate the background of [the province's] new and old political leaders, in preparation for the Ninth Party Congress.' He clarified that this team would be led by himself, Zhao Xiude, Chen Fenglai, and Qin Hongzhou (member of the provincial revolutionary committee, number one in the organization for organization [sic], representing the military), that no locals must be included and that everyone was to come from the military. This organization was not to be disclosed; only a small circle should be in the know. According to Hua Guanglong's denunciation, before that conversation, Wang Xiaoyu had also told him the same thing, asking him to transmit the message to Chen Fenglai and to instruct Chen Fenglai to organize some military men, without telling anyone, only military men, telling them to investigate the cadres of the Revolutionary Committee . . . At the end, there were altogether 18 individuals serving on the Provincial Revolutionary Committee's Personnel Files Team.[40]

Wang Xiaoyu's preparations represent local leaders' efforts to transform participation of their allies on the local Revolutionary Committee into more permanent positions in well-established institutions. Because Revolutionary Committees had been set up in the turmoil of 1967 as transitional governments, their status was much more precarious than the status of a Party Congress, which was a well-defined institution with a long historical pedigree. The prospect of the Ninth Party Congress led people who were involved in local power competition to bow to higher-level party authorities, who would sooner or later decide who was to be included in the congress. For ordinary citizens, slogans hailing the party may have been enough to lead them to expect the organization's return. For rebels, given the institutional context, it was the tactically more promising option to try to secure good positions for their allies inside the party apparatus, rather than working to replace it.

8.2 INDIVIDUALS: THE INVISIBLE OMNIPRESENCE OF PARTY CADRES

It is also important to remember that the rebel leaders usually were also party members. The party went under, but most of the time party members came out on top. Party members succeeded in securing positions partly because CCP membership remained a precondition for achieving important leadership positions, no matter how much the party was condemned for its "bureaucratism." While publicly criticizing local party leaders, Beijing often replaced publicly recognizable party leaders by less well-known figures. The stipulation to build Revolutionary Committees around "three-way alliances," including revolutionary cadres, facilitated the survival of at least some incumbents. The fact that rebels without party membership tried hard to attain membership indicates that a party affiliation still improved career prospects.[41] The lack of party membership could undermine the position of leading rebels, as in the case of the top rebel in Shandong's major port city Qingdao.[42] Moreover, party members, especially the ones in leading positions, did not have the option of retreating to the sidelines, because rebels would come to seek them out. As a result, they had little choice but to compete for power at the center of the Cultural Revolution upheaval - ending up as victims, winners, or both. The destiny of the fifteen individuals, who on the eve of the Cultural Revolution had been members of Shandong's Standing Committee, reflects these dynamics: The two members from the military remained in power throughout the period, four other members held leading positions in the Revolutionary Committee right from its start in January 1967, the other nine members were victims at least throughout 1967–1968, and one of them died as a result of his remarkable attempts to protect the province's cultural relics.[43] In short, party members and leading cadres had to compete in the power struggles of the Cultural Revolution. In the process, some lost their power and even their lives, but others managed to advance their careers.

Maybe most importantly, individuals with a long party career had access to networks, experience, and knowledge, the triple combination needed to acquire and hold onto power.[44] This is comparable to the situation in Russia after the fall of the Soviet Union, where CCP members thrived economically, even after taking into account effects of nonrandom selection into the party.[45] The triple combination was essential for an individual to maneuver in the midst of the violent struggles, even when there was high-level endorsement, as the example of Shandong's top rebel leader Wang Xiaoyu 王效禹 shows. He took control of a rebel organization in Qingdao, managed to rise to the top of the province, and remained the dominant political player throughout three years of intense Cultural Revolution turmoil from 1967 to 1969. When Wang Xiaoyu sprang into action and plunged into the unfolding Cultural Revolution in 1965, he looked back on nearly thirty years of a revolutionary career.

Prior to the Cultural Revolution, during his tenure as one of Qingdao City's vice mayors, Wang Xiaoyu had cultivated the networks that later became the basis for his success. Wang's connections were such that his success became a matter of family interests to one of China's top leaders. His most important acquaintance was the son of Kang Sheng, a preeminent leader in Mao's entourage with special responsibility for Shandong province. When rebels seized power in Shanghai, the central government through Kang Sheng's son gave Wang Xiaoyu the green light to take over power in Qingdao City. In the days leading up to his power seizure, wall posters in Qingdao informed citizens about the central government's endorsement. The wall posters summarized Wang's meetings with top leaders, including Kang Sheng, and were cosigned by Kang Sheng's son.[46] Taking advantage of the connection to Kang Sheng, Wang Xiaoyu could establish himself as one of the "little Maos," who were locally powerful leaders free-riding on Mao's personality cult. Articles in the official party press implied Mao Zedong's endorsement of Wang Xiaoyu's action.[47] Movie images showing Mao Zedong shaking hands with Wang Xiaoyu were designed to bolster Wang Xiaoyu's legitimacy.[48] Imitating the song and dance epic "East Is Red," which was at the center of Mao's personality cult, artists in Shandong composed two song and dance epics around Wang Xiaoyu's power seizures in Qingdao and Jinan, respectively.[49]

In reality, Mao Zedong had largely delegated the task of steering Shandong's Cultural Revolution to others. Mao's attitude was well captured in his short rescript on a letter by Wang Xiaoyu, just months before the power seizure: "The views of Tan Qilong and that vice-mayor are correct, I think. Please deliberate and make a decision." 譚啓龍和這個副市長的意見，我看是正確的。請你們商議一下，酌定政策。[50] This "endorsement" suggests that Mao did not care much about Wang Xiaoyu, to whom he referred not by name but as "that vice-mayor." Moreover, Tan Qilong and Wang Xiaoyu politically stood on opposite sides, making Mao's instructions highly ambiguous. It was people around Mao, especially Kang Sheng, whose support enabled Wang Xiaoyu to proceed with his revolutionary designs and in the process promote Kang Sheng's son as well. At the outset of the Cultural Revolution, his son had been working as a minor official in the education department of Qingdao City. Ten years later, he was among the top-ranked leaders of Zhejiang province. His rise was closely associated with Wang Xiaoyu's rise, although later investigations against Wang, led by Kang Sheng, carefully avoided this fact. Contrary to popular perceptions at the time, Wang Xiaoyu's rise had less to do with Mao Zedong than with Wang Xiaoyu's own cunning political maneuvers. Precisely because formal party organizations were paralyzed, informal connections between individual members became all the more important, allowing long-standing party members to remain present in the political arena.[51]

At least as important as connections was political experience gained in a long party career. Party members were better able to maneuver in the midst of complex power struggles. In times when the CCP was a party in power, its cadres were functionaries filling well-defined positions in the nomenclature.[52] When the party hierarchy disappeared during the Cultural Revolution, party members reverted to their past identity as revolutionaries in less institutionalized struggles to survive and to protect their families from persecution. Wang Xiaoyu had not only mastered the administrative side of the state, he had also encountered its revolutionary side. He had witnessed purges, first as a winner and then as a victim. During purges in 1947, he had stood with the leftists and seen the rightists dismissed from office.[53] His experience at the head of Shandong's law enforcement agencies during the party purges in the second half of the 1950s influenced his approach to governing during the Cultural Revolution. Deviating from established operating procedures, he had the provincial public security bureau report directly to him, often meeting one-on-one with its director; this allowed Wang Xiaoyu to persecute his opponents and rehabilitate allies.[54] Later on, Wang Xiaoyu created two para-police squads, which were more loyal to him personally than to the existing bureaucratic apparatus. One of the organizations, the "Attack with Words – Defend with Weapons" group, performed police functions and was known for its violence. The organization took over files from the provincial public security bureau.[55] It also ran a network of black prisons.[56] Ostensibly modeled after the Shanghai example,[57] in reality Shandong's "Attack with Words – Defend with Weapons" represented only a small section of the workers and included peasants. As a personalistic organization focused on Wang Xiaoyu, it lacked revolutionary legitimacy. When the judicial system in Shandong was dealing with the Cultural Revolution in 1979, the only death sentence carried out was against the leader of the "Attack with Words – Defend with Weapons" organization.

The public security and procuratorial organs were among Wang Xiaoyu's most potent weapons. He was able to wield them effectively because he had been learning to employ them ever since the 1950s. During the antirightist campaign, he overplayed his hand trying to protect individuals whom he believed to be innocent. He refused to serve on the team that was to single out rightists, and he refused to testify against those who had been singled out as rightists. Finally he became a victim himself. In 1959 he was classified as a rightist, his party membership was put on probation, he lost his position at the Prosecutor's Office, and he was demoted in rank.[58] His absence from the political scene during the disastrous Great Leap Forward may have helped his reputation. After his rehabilitation, a couple of years before the Cultural Revolution, Wang Xiaoyu was in charge of the Socialist Education Movement[59] in the countryside outside Qingdao, giving him practical training in precisely the type of politics that would be enacted during the Cultural Revolution.

Most tangible is the information advantage that party members such as Wang Xiaoyu enjoyed. His most important stock of information came from his time at the head of the Prosecutor's Office. At a time when denunciations were the weapon of choice, information was raw material for power and could be wielded as a weapon against political competitors. This includes what Max Weber defined as Dienstwissen (official knowledge), namely "factual knowledge acquired in the process of administrating or found 'on record'."[60] Wang had extraordinary access to personal background information on leading cadres, especially of the incriminatory kind, thanks to his past work. During his time as the vice-director of Shandong's provincial Prosecutor's Office in the 1950s, Wang Xiaoyu worked with personnel files on an everyday basis. His wife, who also played an active role in the politics of the Cultural Revolution, had easy access to all incoming cables, because the Wang family lived inside the office compound – she supposedly was an avid reader of internal documents.[61] Wang cut others off from this precious source of information by putting public security organs, procuratorial offices, and the people's courts on a tight leash. Knowledge concerning the details of people's personnel files could be used against political enemies, fueling the wrath of Red Guards. The work with personnel files also made Wang Xiaoyu particularly aware of the value of governing the provincial archives. He spent much energy cleaning the dossiers of his allies.

In sum, CCP members and incumbent power holders had a competitive advantage over newcomers and therefore could dominate the political scene even at the time of greatest turmoil. At the pinnacles of power, China's national leaders were at Mao's mercy. Being able to anticipate the chairman's mercurial wishes was by far the most important skill for career advancement at Mao's court in Beijing.[62] But at the local level, out of Mao's sight, other factors became more salient, as the example of Wang Xiaoyu shows.[63] Occasionally, the Cultural Revolution saw "showstoppers" who quickly rose to fame thanks to Mao and then disappeared from the stage just as quickly once Mao moved on to another exemplary revolutionary. Such elevator careers were not only exceptional, but also short-lived.[64] Party membership was essential for more lasting success, partly because it gave leaders legitimacy, and more importantly because their networks, experience and information made them strong contenders in the power struggles at the time.

8.3 NETWORKS: PARTY NETWORKS AND LOCAL STABILITY COALITIONS

The presence of party members ultimately contributed to stability. To be sure, power competition between factions inside the party created upheaval as well. But having participated in running the party state prior to the Cultural Revolution, either as local cadres or as rank-and-file members, party members shared a vision of how the polity could be maneuvered into calmer waters. Their informal networks allowed them to work effectively toward peace. The case of Wang Xiaoyu also demonstrates how at the top of provincial politics in Shandong, the situation quickly calmed down after the power seizure. Thanks to Wang's networks and his long experience with party affairs, he knew how to fend off competitors, thereby establishing hegemonic stability, which left Shandong in a more peaceful situation than many other provinces. Further down the hierarchy, one also sees evidence of how the long shadow of the party facilitated effective coalitions for stability.

The events surrounding the "Eight Big" 八大 in Linyi, a prefecture on the southern periphery of Shandong, epitomizes how party members formed coalitions that ultimately helped to bring about stability. Once the power struggles of the Cultural Revolutions started, factional struggles put Linyi's party unity to a hard test. Local leaders followed the trends of the movement and staged a power seizure, led by the "Eight Big," even before Shandong saw its provincial power seizure. By doing so, the local party sacrificed some of its leaders, but avoided a power vacuum. Subsequently, when Wang Xiaoyu's rebels took over the provincial center, these new leaders resented their lack of influence in Linyi, feeling that allies of the previous provincial government were left in charge. This was particularly unacceptable to the new provincial leaders, because Linyi was strategically located in the south of the province, where rebels were to be recruited for battles in Xuzhou. Xuzhou, a major city in the neighboring province of Jiangsu, fell under Shandong's jurisdiction in terms of military command and railroad management, so that Wang Xiaoyu had stakes in the struggles there. Just a week after the provincial leaders had approved Linyi's new Revolutionary Committee, they dispatched a student from Shandong Normal University to denounce the newly established Revolutionary Committee for having used methods of "white terror" against dissenting rebels.[65]

It became more and more apparent that provincial leaders were nurturing the underdog faction, referred to as the "Six Big" 六大. Some party members in Linyi saw this as an opportunity for their own advancement and defected from the local coalition for stability. As the battles in Xuzhou escalated, provincial interest in Linyi increased and the "Eight Big" came under more and more pressure. In the summer of 1967, struggles in Xuzhou costed hundreds of lives. Thus Wang Xiaoyu took great interest in the southern part of Shandong, flying there in July and returning at least one more time later in the summer.[66] According to one estimate, among the 80,000 fighters in Xuzhou were 20,000 rebels sent in from Shandong, mostly from its southern parts.[67] Linyi's neighboring prefecture of Zaozhuang contributed 9,000 men and generously provided them with vehicles and weapons, including rifles and machine guns,[68] putting pressure on Linyi to send fighters as well.

The prefectural "Eight Big" coalition was so strong that the provincial government had a hard time making its authority felt. Even when provincial authorities were determined to dislodge the local coalition, this turned out to be difficult. The student who had been sent in to "light the fire of revolution" managed to organize an opposition force, but at one point, as they were assembling in a local agricultural school, the opposition was physically attacked and nearly defeated by the incumbent "Eight Big." Provincial leaders at the time realized that Linyi's coalition was very robust. After Wang Xiaoyu's fall from power in 1969, his right-hand man Han Jinhai had to make a lengthy self-criticism, during which he recalled reporting to Wang Xiaoyu after a field visit and describing the great difficulties in undermining the local coalition in Linyi.[69]

Moreover, I talked about how difficult the task ahead was. In Linyi Prefecture, we really had to exercise a lot of pressure. Originally, the "Eight Big" had seized power, and it was a revolutionary [that is good and legitimate] power seizure. The "Six Big" seceded from the "Eight Big." We stubbornly supported the "Six Big" and smashed the "Eight Big." On the ground, popular support for the "Eight Big" stood at 70% or 80%, maybe even 80% to 90%. No matter how much pressure you exercised, they wouldn't go down. So even after we went in, we had a strong sense that the task ahead wasn't easy. If you tell us to support the "Six Big," but in every so many villages you only find one outright supporter, what can we do? The majority were "Eight Big," so we were in trouble. When Wang Xiaoyu heard my report, he didn't say a thing and his face looked rather pale.

As is often the case with self-criticism, it is not clear from the transcript what part is his actual report at the time and what part is background provided for the audience of the self-criticism meeting. But it is clear that the coalition in Linyi was thought to be extremely resilient. When, at the end of the Cultural Revolution, Han Jinhai had to spend more than ten years in prison, one of the main accusations was that as the second-in-command of the provincial government, he had brought chaos to Linyi through a series of heavy-handed interventions against the "Eight Big."

In July 1967 the "Six Big" narrowly escaped defeat thanks to Wang Xiaoyu sending in investigators; firing some members of Linyi's Revolutionary Committee; and finally dispatching an outside intervention force, which by some accounts amounted to 20,000 individuals.[70] But even in summer 1968, after the "Eight Big" had been removed from power, Wang Xiaoyu felt compelled to dispatch a squad of workers from Jinan to Linyi to defend the new power holders. An embedded journalist accompanied the crowd and later recalled the events in vivid detail. On August 20th, the rebel organization most supportive of the government, the Shandong Workers General HQ, convened for an emergency meeting, preparing to send a Workers Propaganda Team to Linyi. After a pep rally, "on August 24th, a 1,000-plus-people-strong *Workers Propaganda Team*, in several dozen small and big cars, having organized people to stand along the street and cheer them on, majestically set out for Linyi."[71] Driving for most of the day, by evening the troop arrived in Linyi and concluded the day with a parade. Over the next few days they spread out to the counties of the prefecture, then reassembled. In the process, they had mobilized at least 10,000 locals to join in the fray. Then, with new orders from Wang Xiaoyu, they went after members of the "Eight Big." They encircled a village where leading members of the group were suspected to be hiding. They also broke into a military barracks, vandalized the place, beat up 500 people, and finally chose more than forty leaders from the local coalition as targets for a public struggle meeting the following day.[72] The muscular measures that provincial authorities needed to break up Linyi's local coalition for stability speak to the resilience of this coalition. Ultimately, however, the "Eight Big" could not prevail against provincially supported rebels, who were able to seize power and replace the incumbent party leadership. In one county of Linyi, locals vividly remember the traumatic moment of takeover: The dead body of a former leader was hung from a tree at a major intersection, and people were required to shoot at it to show their loyalty to the new local leadership.[73]

After its defeat in late 1967 and its complete downfall in summer 1968, the coalition for stability helped to de-escalate an explosive situation. When the hegemonic power of the "Eight Big" broke down in the autumn of 1967, Linyi looked ripe for all-out factional warfare. Yet instead of fighting it out, the coalition for stability staged a tactical retreat with a markedly de-escalating effect. Like prior generations of refugees from Shandong escaping political turmoil of the Republican era and political campaigns of the Mao era, some people from Linyi escaped to China's Northeast, never to return. Other members of the coalition followed tactics familiar from the guerrilla warfare of the Sino-Japanese War and Civil War, which some participants had witnessed and which had taken place in exactly the same locality. They retreated to Mount Maling, patiently and confidently waiting for a good opportunity to return.[74]

Up on Mount Maling, members of the conservative faction thought of themselves as a guerrilla force, struggling in support of Mao Zedong's revolution, just as some of them had done prior to the Communist takeover. Their opponents called the group the Mount Maling Gangsters. Asked why they would be perceived as gangsters, an eyewitness recalled:[75]

We clearly had a big supply problem: What could we eat? At first we relied on the peasants, but as the older comrades remembered, a guerrilla force cannot alienate the peasants. Therefore, our leaders became more creative. For example, some of us stopped a train headed south carrying food. They used a slogan saying that food produced in Shandong should be eaten by Shandong's revolutionaries. Later I participated in a bank robbery. After taking out the very substantial sum of RMB 20.000, I still remember that we decided to leave behind two pieces of paper. One was a receipt, because after all we weren't ordinary bank robbers! The other one was a letter to Mao Zedong, explaining our action. Our thinking was that if he understood the situation on the ground, he would approve. I was so young at the time!

This quote reflects that the tactics and measures of the Mount Maling guerrilla force were geared toward survival rather than taking over government.

The defensive strategy of the Mount Maling group became most visible when under attack. The rebels in power in the county capital occasionally sent out expeditions to wipe out their political enemies in the mountains, fearing that they might one day return. In these cases the Mount Maling group chose a particularly easy-to-defend site. I visited the site of one of the most dangerous battles, comparing eyewitness accounts to the documentary evidence. The site was chosen for its steep and stony slope, which makes Mount Maling look hard to climb, even though its elevation is not great. Moreover, military barracks were located at the foot of the mountain, and the stability coalition convinced the military commander in charge to place a tank on the road up the slope. The tank signaled to rebels that they should not cross beyond that point, because of the "nearby" provincial border. The steep-looking slope in conjunction with the threatening tank let the rebels give up the pursuit of the "Eight Big" and return to the county seat without a major battle.[76] The coalition for stability found its natural partner in the military, which also sought de-escalation.

Up on Mount Maling, the coalition of stability awaited a signal to return. When Wang Xiaoyu was swept out of power and publicly denounced for his support to Linyi's "Six Big," the group thought that time was ripe for its return. On June 22nd, 1969, after receiving reassurances from their adversaries who were still in power, an advance party of forty-two former cadres, out of a group of about 200 former cadres waiting for a return, ventured back to one of Linyi's county seats. After crossing a small river close to the county border, they looked back and noticed that the river had turned into a torrent: The sluice gates had been opened. Next, they saw a threatening group of men approaching from the front. Cut off in the rear, they climbed up a mountain, were surrounded and after a long battle surrendered. They were attacked by unguided mortar artillery, leaving three dead. The killing began in earnest after the surrender, exhibiting an unusual degree of violence: Apart from fatal shootings, there were instances of a person's head being smashed, eyes poked out, and a heart dug out. Fifteen more individuals were killed, nine of them party members, some of them having held local positions of leadership before the Cultural Revolution. This was a desperate explosion of violence, committed by people who had realized that their days in government were numbered.[77] The main force of the coalition of stability had stayed behind and returned more successfully a few months later – the last slaughter helping their legitimacy as leaders restoring peace to the prefecture.

Linyi was by no means exceptional in that the local party at first managed to preserve unity, until higher-level authorities stirred up trouble to bring to power new leaders, who would be dependent on upper-level support and therefore would ensure upper-level influence. Liaocheng prefectures held out even longer than Linyi, until the province denounced its "fake" power seizure. But even then Liaocheng's leaders were able to temporize and minimize the effect of provincial intervention. In both prefectures, the early compromise between competing local rebel organizations was a formidable achievement, which was deliberately broken up by outside intervention.

The most puzzling aspect of the Cultural Revolution is not how swiftly the turmoil unfolded, but how quickly it was stopped. At the end of

1968, it was hard to envision how the People's Republic could ever overcome the violent civilian turmoil that had spread throughout the country. The establishment of transitional governments, in the form of Revolutionary Committees, was essential for the state to maintain at least a modicum of political authority. The next step toward stability was to transform the Revolutionary Committees into organs fully responsive to upper-level instructions, more permanently moving the party state out of its self-inflicted emergency mode. In China's quest for regular governance, the party made a formidable comeback and after the Ninth Congress; by mid-1969, much of its hierarchy was back in place.

The longer Wang Xiaoyu stayed in power, the more actively he created institutions that had no link to the party and were tailor-made to consolidate his power. "Attack with Words – Defend with Weapons" and the "Shandong Workers Propaganda Troop" were the two mass organizations whose chains of command were least compatible with the party state, but which were intimately linked to Wang Xiaoyu. Therefore, to destroy competing organizations and revive the party state, Wang Xiaoyu had to go. Following the Ninth Party Congress, in May 1969 the politbureau decided to "remove Wang Xiaoyu from his leadership position and to put Yang Dezhi in charge of Shandong."[78] Wang Xiaoyu and other provincial leaders from Shandong were forced to make self-criticisms, both in Beijing and in Jinan. A central official document, endorsed by chairman Mao, specifically pointed to Wang Xiaoyu's "anti-restoration movement" as a "grave mistake."[79] The "anti-restoration movement" had been carried out mainly by the "Attack with Words – Defend with Weapons" and the "Shandong Workers Propaganda Troop." Wang Xiaoyu experienced remarkable personal loyalty. One military leader was concerned about rumors alleging that a "peaceful military takeover" had ousted Wang Xiaoyu and that now "a military regime" was ruling.[80] Indeed, Wang Xiaoyu has fervent admirers even today. At the end, the frontal attack from Beijing diminished Wang Xiaoyu's authority and undermined his support base.

The violent onslaught by Red Guards and worker rebels during the Cultural Revolution had paralyzed the CCP. Yet the same Red Guards and worker rebels who had gone all-out in attacking the party often sought to attain party membership as a vehicle for political and social advancement. According to widespread perceptions at the time, party membership remained an important condition for taking up leadership positions. On his visit to Shandong, a journalist from the official People's Daily questioned Wang Xiaoyu about the director of Qingdao's Revolutionary Committee, who was a worker lacking party membership. In response to the journalist, Wang Xiaoyu picked up the phone, called the director, and, upon learning that the party membership had not been arranged yet, instructed the director to take this formality seriously. Wang Xiaoyu then turned back to the journalist, making it clear that in the absence of a party organization, party membership was meaningless, since it was merely a question of him signing off a person's membership.[81] The journalist remains outraged even today, but Wang Xiaoyu had correctly pointed to a curious phenomenon: People valued party membership even in the absence of the party.

The political salience of party membership sharply increased when it became widely known that another Party Congress was in the making. Initially, there was ambiguity over whether representatives all had to be party members. Some believed that the selection of representatives would follow the Cultural Revolution's triple formula, consisting of an even portion of military, cadres, and rebels, with rebels not necessarily being party members. In reality, the Congress turned out to be dominated by party members. The salience of party membership increased even further when local "Party Small Leading Groups" were created, which were instrumental in moving from transitional government to more permanent structures. These groups eventually were to help select participants for the Ninth Congress. In turn, these Party Small Leading Groups found themselves at the center of local power competition. The decisive difference between Revolutionary Committees and the Party Small Leading Groups was that only party members could participate in the latter, as the name suggests. At a meeting of leaders from Shandong's thirteen prefectures in June 1968, the provincial leader Wang Xiaoyu cautioned the group that going forward, party membership would once again become a decisive political asset:

Now let me highlight an extremely crucial point, especially keeping in mind the preparatory work for Party Small Leading Groups. Some comrades participate in Revolutionary Committees, but they are not yet party members. Their political consciousness may or may not conform to the party's demands. However, when we develop the party and incorporate new members, we cannot lower the standards. Thus we must increase and strengthen party education.[82]

The "Party Small Leading Groups" were the crucial focal point, as it became increasingly clear that they were the entry point for the returning Leninist hierarchy.

Notwithstanding deadly confrontations such as in Linyi Prefecture, on the whole Shandong province experienced less bloodshed than other provinces. Places where Cultural Revolution events took a more violent course also witnessed more active military involvement. Yet the high visibility of the military should not obscure the fact that civilian measures were the key for restoring order. Hubei province is an ideal case to investigate the functions of the party in a more violent context, thanks to extraordinary archival access, including to a unique set of military cables in a civilian archive.[83] Contrary to Mao's dictum that "political power grows out of the barrel of a gun," turmoil was overcome because peace-building effectively combined military and civilian measures, as one would expect in light of the literature on conflict resolution.[84] The institution at the heart of peacebuilding with Chinese characteristics was the CCP. Because force alone was insufficient, military action backed up an essentially civilian pacification process, geared toward the re-creation of Communist state institutions.

8.4.1 The Deceptive Promises of Military Force

Like soldiers engaged in peacekeeping operations around the world, People's Liberation Army (PLA) units experienced the limited use of hard military capabilities in the face of severe factional warfare. The situation around Guangji County (today: Wuxue) in 1967–1968 epitomizes the challenges.

Battles in Guangji County and other counties here continue to escalate, spreading ever more widely, now already affecting counties in three different provinces.... The two conflicting parties in Guangji County, the "Workers Association" and the "Reds," have accumulated 4,000 firearms and are engaged in fierce battle. They are already well organized; it is too late to defuse the situation, escalation is occurring and the risk of large-scale battle will without any doubt materialize, with grave consequences. Presently, Huanggang Military Subregion and Unit 8206 have dispatched people to the scene to solve the problem of Guangji. However, even after two days have passed they are still outside the county seat without being able to enter the town; because their capabilities are limited, their numbers are insufficient and there is no way to control the evolving situation.[85]

This cable reflects an awareness among PLA leaders that military force could not easily resolve the conflict. In the case of Guangji, military leaders nevertheless decided to send reinforcements. After scoring some initial successes, the units left after about two months without achieving a lasting settlement.[86]

Guangji county only received the reinforcements because it was strategically located in proximity to the provincial borders. More ordinary places could not count on the same level of support. In one county of Xianning Prefecture, fighting broke out on June 14th, 1968. Two days later military leaders came, but rebels detained them. On the 17th and 18th, eight people died, including one soldier killed by a hand grenade. Following the instincts of military men, prefectural military leaders suggested sending in one brigade, or about 500 soldiers.[87] Yet committing such a large number of soldiers to one local conflict that looked like so many other conflicts was a questionable strategy, especially since the detainment of the military leader suggested that the two parties were not interested in outside intervention. The military official in charge in the provincial capital did not endorse the idea of a military surge. Instead his instructions, scribbled on the cable, were to investigate, send a report, and take it from there.

Even to the leaders in Xianning, in hindsight, their initial strategy of sending soldiers for a robust pacification mission must have looked like a bad idea. Less than a week after Xianning's leaders had sent their report to Wuhan, a similar conflict broke out closer to the prefectural seat.[88] Another two days later, in yet another place an attack targeted the PLA itself.[89] Given this escalation, sending in enough soldiers to pacify each of these trouble spots would have overcommitted troops. Recognizing this reality, commanders in Xianning henceforth recommended softer approaches, such as making detailed investigations or outlawing certain organizations. The commanders had learned that their initial strategy of militarily robust pacification was doomed.

Military force also failed to prevent rebels from storming PLA weapon depots. In Dongfeng (today: Xiaogan) Prefecture, by May 1968 bloody battles drew supporters from as far away as the provincial capital. In a climate of rising tension, with both sides holding hostages, rebels plundered weapons depots.[90] In Xiangfan Prefecture, forty-three people had been killed by the end of June, and the death toll was quickly rising.[91] Rebels looted weapons from one county adjacent to the main battleground, probably because the PLA had removed weapons from the places that saw the most severe fighting. By doing so, however, the PLA gave the rebels a reason to attack relatively calm localities, spreading warfare to less afflicted localities. Military force was of little avail in stopping the looting – partly because commanders thought it unwise to shoot at rebels and partly because the massive onslaught of rebels had a good chance of carrying off the victory, even if shot at.

Ideology could have a disarming, if transient effect. PLA's de-escalation tactics included attempts to talk people out of looting weapons: "propagating Mao Zedong thought" and doing "ideological work," as it was called then. Experiences from revolutionary warfare presumably helped officers to engage locals in dialogue. The following report from Xianning Prefecture, after 24 hours of turmoil in May 1968, exemplifies both the potential and the limits of ideology as a weapon:

> At 8pm on May 21st plundering of the Xianning Military Region's weapons depot began.... After the incident, officers and soldiers from the subregion and brigade 8204 went out to propagate Mao Zedong thought and do ideological work, reminding people of the September 5 Directive. By dawn of May 22nd, almost all the weapons and ammunition had been returned. But around noon, the May 16 Brigade once again sent a carload of people to plunder weapons, threatening with arms and beating up officers and soldiers, who were on site carrying out propaganda work. Lots of weapons and ammunition were taken.[92]

Later that day, more groups arrived to loot weapons. At first, Mao Zedong thought proved to be literally disarming. But on second thought, rebels came to the conclusion that plundering weapons was the right thing to do after all.

It was hard to convince rebels to stop attacking military installations in an era when, according to official propaganda, it was "right to rebel." Looters cited Mao's policy of "arming the left,"[93] even when Mao had already abandoned it.[94] The military had a hard stance, because central authorities frequently vilified military leaders. Looters could also cite a precedent of August 1967, when in a matter of days rebels in the provincial capital carried off 19,361 rifles, 4,691 submachine guns, and 1,021 light machine guns.[95] Precisely because Maoist ideology was open to interpretation, forceful arguments could be more effective than interventions by force, which in and of themselves were not apt to achieve a sustainable conflict resolution.

8.4.2 Joining Hands with the Party

The PLA needed support from the party to carry out its civilian tasks, so vital for effective pacification. Only the party had the manpower with the technical expertise to lead the Socialist economy, and sufficient knowledge of local conditions to mediate at the grassroots level. At the beginning of the Cultural Revolution, the PLA insulated itself from factional struggles inside the party by appointing their own political commissioners, instead of having the local party secretary concurrently serve in this key military position.[96] Later, when the military became involved in the economy and in local power struggles, it reached out to party members and recruited them to the cause of re-creating stability under the military's watch.[97]

The goal to secure the proper functioning of the state-led economy provided the initial focal point for the military to forge a pragmatic coalition with party cadres, many of whom had been under severe rebel attack or chased out of office. In February 1967, Hubei's military established an Office for Grasping Revolution and Promoting Production with headquarters in a hotel, presumably to downplay its power and emphasize its political neutrality. A public communiqué announced the names of the office's leaders, but contrary to a draft version left out their previously held positions, to dissociate them from past policies now criticized as "rightist."[98] The military announced that for the spring sowing season, peasants and youngsters officially on duty in the countryside should return to their villages. Other professions were to support the peasants by going back to work.[99] Since Maoist discourse highly valued production and since the catastrophic famine of 1958–1961 was still a fresh memory, this call to order fell on fruitful ground.

Weary of being exposed to the onslaught of popular criticism, local party cadres were relieved to be able to go back to work under military protection. An estimated 30,000 cadres came to a mobilization meeting and listened to Hubei's generals. In conversations among themselves, they were enthusiastic: "After all these months, this was the first time that I participated in a revolutionary mass meeting. Listening to chairman Mao's words [relayed via the generals], we know that he once again solicits and trusts us cadres." Another person, with tears in his eyes, announced: "Under the lead of the military party committee and with the help of the broad revolutionary masses, I want to atone for my crimes by grasping revolution and promoting production." A flowery, but probably accurate comment of one cadre was: "Listening to the speeches was like eating watermelon in the heat of summer; it cleared up our minds."[100] Moving from Red Guard Publications and nebulous speeches on ideology to the clarity of the military project, today's reader of the archival records experiences a similar mental relief.

Thanks to support from cadres and to the military hierarchy quietly helping to set up new structures, the Office for Grasping Revolution and Promoting Production quickly established local branches throughout Hubei Province. Within weeks, 3,398 individuals throughout the province (excluding the provincial capital Wuhan) had enlisted with the military.[101] A three-level cadre conference, held at the beginning of March, was the crucial turning point when cadres rallied around the flag of the military.[102] The conference stopped cadre absenteeism, but also led hundreds of cadres to investigate the situation on the ground in the countryside, township by township and village – by village. Most importantly, in all counties and prefectures a group of leaders was identified to be in charge of production. The coalition forged around the goal of promoting production was extraordinarily stable. Maybe the "most dangerous incident" of the entire Cultural Revolution[103] in the provincial capital led to extreme political uncertainty, but the hierarchy in charge of production continued to function. In November 1967, only about one third of the counties were "C-type" counties in great turmoil. All other counties were either "B-type" with a clearly identified leadership team, but many people failing to show up for work, or even well-functioning "A-type" counties.[104] Production statistics also reflect the effectiveness of the system, some jurisdictions fulfilling their quotas, while the most turbulent places still delivered about half of the quota. Despite great turmoil, agricultural output in 1967 decreased by only 7 percent.[105]

The cooperative relationship between military leaders and party cadres is also reflected in mutual information sharing. The military was well-informed thanks to local civilian supporters, and the provincial civilian leadership was well-informed thanks to the military sharing information. From January to November 1968 Hubei Military Region received 2,855 cables.[106] Information in the headings of the cables allows the reader to infer the percentage of cables shared with civilian leaders. Between the breakdown of the party's power in January and mid-May, only about 9 percent of the cables were transmitted to the top civilian leadership; between mid-May and end of June 18 percent were shared; and in the remainder of the year 22 percent were shared. Trust between Hubei's military and its civilian leadership increased gradually over the course of 1968.

Regular information transmission through formal channels was of utmost importance. To be sure, military cables were not the only method of information transmission at the time. Local rebels were summoned to the provincial capital for consultations, as in the case of one nightly factional battle, which had resulted in more than thirty casualties.[107] Defeated factions came to the provincial capital to present their grievances and lobby for support.[108] Letters were written to high-level authorities, even straight to Mao's wife.[109] Red Guard and worker rebel organizations edited collected volumes to advance their own view-points.[110] Public denunciations and self-criticisms offered yet another method to solicit detailed information about local events. This flow of information amounted to an unenlightening cacophony of voices in the revolutionary language of angry Red Guards and rebel workers,[111] replete with ideological references and empty slogans. Military officers them-selves routinely deployed this kind of language in their outside com-munication. By contrast, following the military tradition, internal cables were written in a concise language, giving a sense of matter-of-fact accu-racy. Most importantly, sharing information in a formalized system cre-ated a common understanding among civilian and military cadres, which allowed them to act together.

8.4.3 Reproducing Leninist Structures

Even in the face of escalating violence, jointly working toward pacifica-tion, cadres could take advantage of Chinese Socialist state institutions, such as the work unit, to contain turmoil. Without intervention, violence tended to spread, as factions sought allies and provisions. In one typical case, after a series of deadly battles, a faction temporarily retreated to rob banks, plunder food, and loot weapons in neighboring areas.[112] Cadres worked hard to prevent such spillovers from one jurisdiction to another. Military cables routinely mentioned the presence of outsiders and their role in instigating violence. Looking over the shoulders of decision makers in the provincial capital, we can see from their highlighting and marginal notes scribbled on the military cables that they were most interested in that information, because it allowed them to take effective action.[113] If outside troublemakers were associated with a particular university or fac-tory, provincial leaders could order them to return home by going either through the work unit or through one of the rebel organizations, most of which were hierarchical organizations.

For military as for civilian cadres, it was intuitive to work toward institutions as they had existed before the Cultural Revolution. In this process, the creation of Revolutionary Committees was the central event that fundamentally changed political dynamics. Instead of maintain-ing their political status by displaying their fighting power, rebels now had the prospect of transforming their fighting power into political power, thanks to "permanent" seats on Revolutionary Committees. While the military was strongly represented in local Revolutionary Committees of Hubei, it did not monopolize them and occupied about one fourth of the seats.[114] In fact, Revolutionary Committees were quite pluralistic, certainly for a Leninist regime, and represented many segments of society. Students, peasants, workers, and former high-ranking county officials, such as ousted county party secretaries and mayors, each held about the same share of seats. The committee also included leaders of the main contending factions: in one case, a theater performer and a worker at the agricultural machine tool factory. Name lists of the committees are notable for bringing diverse individuals to the negotiating table. Revolutionary Committees held out the promise of political participation. This promise convinced many rebels to lay down their arms, so that the number of "troublemakers" became manageable.

Questions of representation became the most salient issue of local contention. When the distribution of seats on the Revolutionary Committee did not adequately reflect the power balance on the streets, or if factions overestimated their own strength, they challenged the committee.[115] Since representation seemed so valuable, rebels often agreed to the quid pro quo by which they had to lay down their weapons in return for seats on the committee. Province-level authorities in charge of approving Revolutionary Committees negotiated the distribution of seats while at the same time having the military proceed with disarmament. Most Revolutionary Committees had set aside a number of seats to be filled at a later date, giving additional maneuvering space for negotiating with factions whose strength had at first been underestimated.

Yet the promise of inclusive institutions was a false one. Once the inclusive institution had served its tactical goal of demobilizing rebels, it was quickly transformed into a classic Leninist organization. As the rebels' power on the streets waned, their influence on the Revolutionary Committee also faltered. Rebels failed to effectively institutionalize their gains.[116] The process in Guangji County was emblematic: An armistice was brokered and a local Revolutionary Committee established in September 1968. At the same time, extraordinary numbers of weapons were collected and rebel groups disbanded.[117] The military played a visible but largely civilian role in this process, organizing meetings with altogether 160,000 participants,[118] that is, 40 percent of the county population. As soon as the rebels were demobilized, in November, rebel representatives on the Revolutionary Committee came under political pressure and were excluded from the assembly. As a result, the erstwhile pluralist assembly morphed into a homogeneous group of cadres.

The methods for achieving this transformation followed patterns familiar from previous campaigns to consolidate Communist power in the countryside by vilifying competitors: At struggle meetings, unwelcome committee members were to make denunciations and self-criticisms, such as this one from a factional leader of Guangji:

> On August 3rd, I shot dead Zhu Xiwang 朱細旺. During the battles from August 2nd to 6th, I was a 'general'.... We believed that the battles in Guangji were between KMT Nationalists and CCP Communists. Thus beating and killing a few of the opponent KMT party members was not a big deal for us.[119]

In another case investigators looked into an incident where rebels arrested 150 people and tortured them by "hanging them up, then beating them; or having them kneel on sharp, pointy stones; giving them lime water to drink, or pulling needles through their fingertips."[120] Such information was used to purge unwanted Revolutionary Committee members, who had only been taken on board to get them off the streets. The point is not that the rebels were innocent, but that leaders could pick almost anyone as a target of criticism, thereby establishing their authority. Once the provincial authority was more firmly established, decisions were made behind closed doors following bureaucratic procedures. The selection of representatives for the momentous Ninth Party Committee essentially was a top-down decision-making process resulting in a group of well-disciplined party members with similar resumes.[121]

The military accompanied a stabilization process that was fundamentally civilian, pivoting on the establishment of local Revolutionary Committees. PLA personnel were visible at the inauguration of Revolutionary Committees and did not return to the barracks hastily. In Huanggang prefecture, as elsewhere,[122] the inauguration of the Revolutionary Committee was grand political theater. The festive meeting lasted three hours and had 20,000 participants, joined by 1,700 watchful soldiers. Any factional flags were banned; only the national flag was allowed. People were seated not according to their factional affiliation, but according to profession. The meeting was to send a signal of reconciliation, despite occasional, dissenting voices heard at the meeting: "Now clearly the proletariat and the Red Guards won't be governing." The military kept track of the discontented and political losers, some of whom continued to encourage resistance at sports competitions, film screenings, and small meetings: "The Revolutionary Committee is conservative and factional, going backward in history. We do not recognize it."[123] Occasionally, it was necessary to back up the Revolutionary Committee by force. This was a feasible task for the PLA, because the civilian process was so successful: The deployment of well-rehearsed methods of the party state by experienced cadres went a long way to appease even the more turbulent areas of China.

Last but not least, let us turn to top-down efforts at rebuilding the party hierarchy. To achieve the transition from protracted factional warfare to the establishment of revolutionary committees, or to exchange leaders on revolutionary committees, the tactical key were so-called study groups of Mao Zedong Thought 毛澤東思想學習班 (henceforth called study groups). Most of the time, the procedural rules established at the beginning of the Cultural Revolution (see Section 8.1) went a long way to enforce the central government's authority, so that the study groups were smooth sailing for China's leadership. In some exceptional cases, it was challenging to enforce authority, despite the military standing ready to back up the civilian procedures. But even in these cases the atmosphere of fear that was characteristic of study groups achieved its purpose. In essence, higher-level governments summoned factional leaders and other powerful agents at lower levels to attend study groups, in order to intervene decisively in lower-level power struggles and pick the winner. Such study groups were held also for less problematic transitions, but they were of critical importance in the places where pacification proved most challenging. This section describes the instrument of the study groups, which provided the mechanism through which the party made a political comeback. Following the proceedings of the study groups is fascinating, because they provide rare insights into the ways by which the CCP enforces authority in a top-down manner, engineering the subordination of those who had risen to local prominence.

8.5.1 What Mao Called "a Good Method"

Revolutionary Committees were the pivotal institutions around which the CCP re-created political order after the power seizures of early 1967, but it needed much social engineering to arrive at viable committees. Throughout 1967 and 1968 central leaders made great efforts to demobilize rebels and pave the way for local compromises that would allow setting up Revolutionary Committees. They negotiated with the constant stream of rebel representatives who came to Beijing. Prime Minister Zhou Enlai's work schedule reflects these work-intensive efforts.[124] For instance, in August 1967 he met with representatives from Jiangxi, reiterating that "neither military nor militia should hand out weapons at random, and instead should try to get the weapons back. Mass organizations should stop fighting, stop plundering weapons and stop encouraging peasants to join the fighting in the cities and should instead trust the PLA." Later that month he met with representatives from two competing factions, criticizing them for "plundering weapons and material from the PLA earmarked for use in Vietnam – which simply showed that they had no awareness of the enemy and were ignorant." In Beijing, the representatives of different factions met with different leaders, whose opinion was not necessarily coordinated. Just because a handful of rebels returned from Beijing with peaceful intentions, that probably would not have turned around the situation at home. It is questionable whether the Prime Minister's admonitions had any substantive and lasting effect on the ground.

To establish its authority over independently acting rebels, the CCP had better tools at its disposal. The study groups were a most powerful tool, built on well-rehearsed practices of the revolution, including infiltration and purges.[125] The study group methodology had been endorsed by Mao Zedong himself. Though his approval was expressed in unimaginative and lame language – certainly by Mao's standards – it was omnipresent at the time, even appearing on the ID cards of the participants: "The organization of study groups is a good method, study groups can solve many problems."[126] A "big push" was needed that signaled a new beginning, with a clearly identified set of actors whose authority was publicly known. Leaders in Beijing needed to collate information from varying sources, in order to conceive of a new local government that reflected power relationships enough to induce people to lay down their arms. Given the difficulties of mediating civilian conflict in other settings, it is clear that this was a challenging task. The first few transitional governments did not need this vehicle, but the later, harder-to-appease provinces relied heavily on study groups.

Study groups were a series of carefully orchestrated meetings in varying formats, stretched out over weeks if not months, that served to establish a new set of local leaders and make them subservient to the central government. At the heart of the meetings was a series of criticisms and self-criticisms, which developed a narrative of Cultural Revolution events and apportioned blame in a way that served to legitimate the new leaders. The 570 delegates participating in the study group of Shandong province were summoned to Beijing in the second half of 1969, after the central government had decided that the leader of the "rebel government" had to go. Isolated from the outside world, participants spent the first fifty days of the meeting discussing Mao's writing about party rectification, the new party constitution, and other texts related to the CCP, without touching on Shandong-related issues. During that time, party organizations were set up in the study group, creating a well-defined hierarchy. Only the second phase of the meeting broached criticisms and self-criticisms, with much information being exchanged and presumably collected by the central government. This was the phase when winners and losers became clear, with particularly unlucky individuals having to move from the conference venue into a military garrison. A third phase consolidated the gains and taught lessons on things like party discipline.[127]

Lengthy proceedings and roundabout methods cannot obscure that the essential agenda of all these meetings was straightforward. In order to revive the party, the nomenclature system had to be revived, which in turn required clarifying three closely related questions: Who counts as a party member? What is the pecking order? Who gets what position? At the outset of the study group in Beijing, one member transmitted instructions from the central leadership, raising questions about the meaning of party membership.

On July 5th we talked about the composition of our study group: How many party members? How many Youth League members? How many non-party members? You all have some ideas about these numbers. But what about those: The time when these party members and Youth League members joined? How many joined before [the Cultural Revolution]? How many have only recently joined? How many filled out the application form, but were never admitted? Those questions we don't really know much about at all, we must investigate thoroughly. If someone's application form hasn't been approved, the person certainly wouldn't count as a party member. If someone has just recently filled out an application form, the person counts even less as a party member. In his Yan'an speech, chairman Mao talked about people who entered the party organizationally, but not ideologically. In reality, such people haven't even entered organizationally either. They must have entered based on personal relationships, how could they organizationally count as party members?[128]

It was standard practice for central leaders to put local leaders on the spot and question whether the person's party membership was genuine, with the certain effect of discrediting and politically destroying that person. Day after day, the pecking order was negotiated and gradually fixed. Some participants were altogether removed from the proceedings for "lacking quality."[129] Others ran away to avoid trouble, jumping the wall of the compound. Some continued to participate as scapegoats, while others, including the various rapporteurs, turned into political victors. Repeating the central procedures at the subprovincial level, jurisdiction after jurisdiction the chains of command were fixed, once again securely fastening cadres to their hierarchical positions.

While the most powerful political actors were held in Beijing to study Mao Zedong thought, politics back in their province of origin did not stop. Quite to the contrary – new cadres were busy taking over and declaring the fall of the incumbent rebel leaders. Shandong's study group lasted from late June to late September, and precisely that period saw hectic political activity in the provincial capital. On the day after the opening of the study group, a *party small leading group* was established inside the Revolutionary Committee. It consisted of seven individuals and indicated that the party hierarchy had come back and was now in charge to supervise the work of the Revolutionary Committee. Over the following three months, similar party small leading groups were successively established in one prefectural-level Revolutionary Committee after another. Meetings brought together lower-level cadres from jurisdictions all around Shandong, demonstrating that Wang Xiaoyu had fallen and that new people were in charge. They culminated in an intense campaign to "cleanse the class ranks," which served to remove Wang Xiaoyu's closest allies from power.[130]

8.5.2 Solving the Hardest Cases: Guangxi, Xinjiang

In part the degree of difficulty depended on local leadership, but in part it depended on the extent to which local political processes were dominated by the CCP's political practices and organizational norms prior to the Cultural Revolution. Although the party's bureaucratism was their target of critique, many rebels organized themselves in ways that closely resembled the Leninist structure of the party. Certainly in Shandong, Wang Xiaoyu had come to replace the leaders, not the system. In Hubei rebels organized in hierarchical structures modeled on the party itself, which is why the provincial leaders could urge provincial rebel leaders to have their local affiliates retreat from a battle, knowing that local affiliates would listen to their rebel leaders. If Communist organizational culture had been inculcated, this helped to give the power struggles some direction, and to have power wielders coalesce around Revolutionary Committees. When rebels had a chance, they stepped right into the shoes of the CCP. Central leaders convinced or cajoled rebels into accepting the authority of local Revolutionary Committees, and the right of higher-level authorities to adjudicate on the composition of these powerful bodies. This stood at the beginning of efforts to restore order.

By the summer of 1968, five provinces still had not established a transitional government. At the time, Zhou Enlai blamed the disorder on China's foreign foes. Each enemy country allegedly gained from chaos in its own pet province: "Our enemies are happy: Taiwan says that Fujian [just across the Taiwan Strait] won't pull itself together. The Soviet Union says that Xinjiang [strategically situated in Central Asia] won't pull itself together. Indian counter-revolutionaries say that Tibet won't pull itself together. American imperialists say that Guangxi [with supply lines to Vietnam] won't pull itself together. Myanmar says that Yunnan won't pull itself together."[131] Instead of putting the blame on foreign countries, a better explanation for the unusual level of turmoil might relate to the tenuous hold of the CCP in these five provinces. With the exception of Xinjiang, the proportion of party members in the other four provinces was much below the pre–Cultural Revolution national average of 2.4 percent. In 1965, Guangxi and Tibet were the two provinces with the least party penetration, namely 1.8 percent and 1.1 percent.

Guangxi Province is known for its Cultural Revolution violence. Trying to contain the crisis, the central government had been in consultation with local military and rebel leaders throughout 1967 and 1968. In the summer of 1968, the situation in Guangxi was rapidly deteriorating: collective killings spread throughout the countryside of Guangxi, and the death toll reached new heights.[132] At that same time, military and rebel leaders were summoned to Beijing for a study group. Contrary to what the name suggests, these were intensely conflictual discussions, where the central government exercised great pressure. In the case of Guangxi, Beijing had initially supported the April 22nd faction, emboldening them to an extent that fostered violence and made the group unwilling to compromise. In the summer of 1968, central leaders had turned against the April 22nd faction.[133] The following excerpts from the transcript of a five-hour meeting in the East Auditorium of the Great Hall of the People on July 25th epitomize the way in which the top leadership brought pressure to bear on local leaders during study groups. Central leaders bullied local leaders into a peace settlement and politically destroyed those who stood in the way. References to party discipline were omnipresent. The following is an excerpt from the meeting notes of the decisive meeting that moved Guangxi province to a settlement in July 1968. The outward appearance of the material, the plausible explanation of its origins, the apparent obliviousness of the salesperson as to the document's political importance (cheap price, equivalent to a piece of Shaobing flatbread), and the accuracy of its details convince me that the document is authentic.

Kang Sheng: I heard that at a Party School in Guangxi, there is a certain instructor called Zhu Ren. Zhu Ren, are you still in your seat? (At that, Zhu Ren from the 'Red Wave Faction' of the District Party School stands up.) . . . You, party member, represent what party? The Kuomintang or Wang Gang's party? . . . What rumors did you carry to Beijing? What kind of underground meetings have you partic- ipated in? What kind of illegal activities have you been carrying out? Are you under the command of the black commando headquarters?
    Chen Boda: Fully reveal your black headquarters.
    Kang Sheng: If you still have some revolutionary language left, then speak up in front of the central government and chairman Mao's face. Where are you from? (Zhu Ren: Liucheng County in Guangxi Province.) What is your class back- ground? (Answer: Middle Peasant.) Even the landlords call themselves peasants, even the rich peasants call themselves peasants. . . .
    Premier: Are you in the 'denunciation troop'? (Answer: We are the 'report troop'.) When you set out, you might have been called 'report troop', now you are called 'denunciation troop'. Are you together with Xiong Yijun? (Answer: Haven't seen him.) Strange! Both of you came here in April.[134]

The study group was a resounding success. The military had been trying for a while to stop the bloodshed in Guangxi, but did not get very far, partly as a result of internal divisions. By contrast, one month after the July 25 meeting, on August 26, Guangxi announced the establishment of a centrally approved Revolutionary Committee. More importantly, at the same time, violence in Guangxi subsided, and by mid-autumn of 1968, mass killings had become rare events.

Out of all provinces, Xinjiang took the longest to put together a Rev- olutionary Committee. In March 1968, the province's two main factions went to Beijing for consultations, seeking to negotiate a transitional gov- ernment. But four months later, in July 1968, the two factions remained deeply divided. From the detailed records of the first meeting between the rebels and top-ranking central leaders, it is clear that the Chinese lead- ership was at a loss.[135] The meeting started with Kang Sheng explaining why he had not met with the group before: The sharp divisions among the Xinjiang group were too extreme. Zhou Enlai reproached the fac- tions: "You have been staying in the same place for four months, you are eating together and you are living side-by-side. How can you still not unite? How come you haven't reached out to each other and talked things through?" One factional leader, referred to as Hu Luanchuang (Reckless Dash) instead of by his own preferred name of Wu Julun, and who apparently was seen as a critical figure to bring stability to Xinjiang, appeared uncompromising, threatening to return to his native Shandong if his arch-enemy Wang Enmao were not removed. But since Wang Enmao had a large following, that was not an option. Mao's wife Jiang Qing, not known for being a passive listener, came in halfway through the meeting, but according to the record did not utter a word. Even as Kang Sheng reminded people that it was getting rather late, the meeting dragged on for almost five hours until 2 am. Although the discussion was inconclusive, Kang Sheng ended with an ultimatum: "Today is July 21st. I wish that within the next 10 days, that is by the end of the month, you representatives in Beijing reach a comprehensive compromise." As it turned out, Kang Sheng's deadline was overly optimistic. It took until early September for Xinjiang to set up its revolutionary committee.

8.5.3 Replicating Procedures at Sub-provincial Levels

Resembling the nested design of a Russian Matryoshka doll, operations to regain control at lower levels of the party hierarchy replicated the methods used by the central government vis-à-vis the provinces. The phrases that the central government used to denounce certain provincial leaders were repeated within that province referring to other local leaders as well. In the case of Shandong, a rapporteur orally presented a sanitized summary of the proceedings in Beijing, which was reprinted and circulated throughout the province, amounting to thirty-seven pages of implicit guidelines on the new political winds along with a new language.[136] In the cycle of violence characteristic of Leninist purges, those who had suffered emotional abuse in Beijing, including those ending up as political victors, returned to their home provinces and perpetrated abuse against representatives from lower-level jurisdictions. Ordinary people telling anecdotes about their personal suffering in the Cultural Revolution were included in study group proceedings, giving them somewhat of a local flavor. But overall the process by which top-down authority was established through the study groups was a highly standardized one.

In the case of Shandong there was a large number of study groups, following the conclusion of the proceedings in Beijing. These study groups remained the instrument of choice to regain control for a while. A full year after the Beijing meetings, the Revolutionary Committee of Qingdao established a study group.[137] The delay indicates that the party did not hastily convoke meetings, but took its time with preparatory work in the city that had been the home base of Shandong's top rebel and leader Wang Xiaoyu.[138] In addition to civilian study groups, the military also ran a series of study groups. One of these was particularly large, divided into at least four groups with up to seventeen subgroups, bringing together personnel from law enforcement agencies. Other study groups were more specialized, only including the personnel involved in the management of labor reform camps,[139] or in the prosecutor's office.[140] Cadres in the hierarchy of the judicature also organized a separate study group.[141] One goal of such study groups was to decide which local rebels should be singled out as the local villains to be destroyed along with the already-known provincial and national villains.[142]

If anything, local study groups were more fear-inspiring than central ones. Available eyewitness accounts describe such local study groups as nothing less than tortuous experiences. Organizers of local study groups could easily invite victims of rebel violence to speak bitterness. Speaking bitterness was a well-rehearsed practice to mobilize citizens against people whom they were to consider as their class enemies. In the context of the study groups, denunciations by victims served to destroy the political competitor. For instance, in Shandong's port city of Qingdao, a peasant was invited to recount in chilling detail how a group of rebels abused and murdered his sister, purposefully turning the study group into a life-threatening event for the struggle targets.[143] Sometimes participants did not know where they were held and were subject to the "five interdictions," not allowing them to communicate by letter, or take a leave, or receive visits, or link up, or run away. Remembering a study group outside a major city of Northern China, a cadre in her memoir states that "the so-called study group was entirely an atmosphere of terror."[144] Whereas central leaders were familiar figures who derived their authority directly from Mao, provincial leaders did not have the same authority built on long-standing revolutionary credentials. For them, study groups provided an opportunity to demonstrate their superiority, instill fear, and enforce party discipline in their provinces.

8.6 NUMERICAL PLAUSIBILITY CHECK

The archival record suggests that local party networks were essential to avoid a complete and lasting breakdown of political order. One would expect then that places with more party members experienced less turmoil, a claim which this section is going to test. Given the notoriously inaccurate statistical records of the Mao era, at the end of the day, empirical evidence from documents may be more convincing than any kind of quantitative test. Nevertheless, this section presents a regression analysis that serves as an additional plausibility check of the argument. The units of analysis are China's twenty-eight province-level jurisdictions.[145] Because of the small number of observations and the limits of the data, one should not expect the results to reach very high levels of statistical significance. As a supplementary piece of evidence, however, there are reasons to be confident in the results: The comparative analysis comprises the entirety of the Chinese territory with its extremely diverse Cultural Revolution experiences. Most importantly, for four distinct dimensions of upheaval – casualties, violence, fiscal decline, and duration – the results point in the same direction: The party's presence reduced the degree of turmoil.

8.6.1 The Severity of the Cultural Revolution

Casualties. The first test focuses on the number of deaths per county, reported separately for each province. The indicator captures the occurence of lethal violence, especially the deployment of military force by the government to reassert its control during campaigns in 1968.[146] In a work-intensive process, scholars have compiled the number of casualties based on official county gazetteers; the relevant data have been published.[147] Taking into account subsequent improvements of the database, the number of deaths per county varies from seven deaths per county in Qinghai to 964 deaths per county in Guangxi.[148] An important potential confounding variable is the degree to which some provincial leaders are more supportive of local efforts to write about the Cultural Revolution than others. Some provincial propaganda departments may be less willing than others to revisit the events of the Cultural Revolution, resulting in shorter accounts and fewer reported victims. As a result, partly for reasons unrelated to the severity of turmoil, some counties provide much longer accounts of the Cultural Revolution than others. To control for the not directly observable editorial guidelines at the provincial level, the number of deaths per county is best compared across provinces while controlling for the average length of the accounts as a proxy for reporting bias.

Violence. The analysis investigates the number of Cultural Revolution victims in a more broadly and more loosely defined sense. Victims of political persecution include people who were beaten, expelled from their house or their hometown, or labeled counterrevolutionaries.[149] They are also reported in the data set just described.

Fiscal decline. The third test takes the state's perspective. At a time when the top leadership abandoned the state's monopoly of using violence and left citizens to fend for their own security, the human impact is not the only standard by which one should judge the severity of the Cultural Revolution. Oftentimes, military intervention helped the state to prevent chaos, so that the number of victims says little about the breakdown of local government. Changes in fiscal revenues, defined as $\frac{revenues_{t_1+1}-revenues_{t_1}}{revenues_{t_1}}$, indicate the degree to which a local government bureaucracy was still functional. The more fiscal revenues, the further away the state was from anarchy. Data come from the widely used data source *China Data Online*,[150] complemented by another, authoritative but not yet digitized source[151] for Sichuan province, which inexplicably is omitted from *China Data Online*. Apart from this omission, the two sources are almost perfectly identical.

Duration. The duration of the crisis is calculated as the time elapsing between its start[152] and the establishment of a Revolutionary Committee, which was the most important event marking the return to order. The dates are uncontested and are taken from an influential Hong Kong–published Cultural Revolution history.[153] The timing of when a Revolutionary Committee was established was greatly influenced by partially idiosyncratic central government decisions. For strategic reasons, and as a result of personal connections as well as personal tastes, the central government focused on some provinces first and on others later. In other words, to some extent the establishment of Revolutionary Committees has less to do with structural factors than with agency by central leaders.

8.6.2 Specification and Data

Party penetration, the key explanatory variable, is defined as the number of party members per population on the eve of the Cultural Revolution in 1965, in logarithmic form. It is the last time that membership statistics were consistently reported before they experienced great confusion, which was only gradually resolved after 1971. The data are based on an internal compilation by the Central Organization Department.[154] The small number of observations requires parsimony in the use of control variables. All specifications control for the presence of minority populations. Since provinces with ethnic minorities have experienced more severe turmoil and since the party was less well established among minorities, ignoring minorities would lead to an overestimation of the party effect. A control variable accounts for the percentage of non-Han citizens in the population, as reported in the 1982 census.[155] Second, more industrialized places experienced more turmoil than rural areas and on average have more party members, given that the leadership sought to recruit the proletariat. To avoid this confounding factor, a control variable is defined as the industrial production as a share of gross provincial product, as reported in *China Data Online*. Third, the course of the Cultural Revolution in the two provincial-level cities Beijing and Shanghai[156] is not directly comparable to the situation in true provinces, because they served as experimental sites where top leaders frequently intervened to shape events. If not controlled for, the cities are blatant outliers on several variable dimensions. A dummy variable takes the value 1 if a provincial-level administrative unit is a city rather than a true province with a much larger territory.

8.6.3 Results

The correlation matrix of Table 8.1 reports the relationship between the four measures of upheaval. It reflects the fact that each measure captures distinct, if not entirely unrelated, aspects of the movement's intensity. All the measures move in the same direction: On average, more casualties come with more non-lethal victims, worse finances, and a longer duration of the turmoil. The two civilian measures of turmoil – fiscal revenues and the time to establishing a Revolutionary Committee – are most closely correlated: The state's finances were under more pressure in places where the period of upheaval lasted longer. Provinces with more casualties also experienced more violence, but this is a much weaker correlation, because the two partly function as substitutes. The reason why the prevalence of violence is only weakly correlated with fiscal decline and a shorter period of turmoil could be interpreted as the result of certain forms of violence, such as the one deployed by the military, shortening the movement and contributing to reestablishing civilian order. In short, the four severity measures fulfill their purpose to capture different aspects of the movement's severity.

TABLE 8.1 *Bivariate correlation of the four severity measures*

	Casualties	Violence	Fiscal revenues	Duration
Casualties	1			
Violence	0.39	1		
Fiscal revenues	−0.25	−0.28	1	
Duration	0.37	0.23	−0.66	1

For sources, see Table 8.2.

TABLE 8.2 *The party and the severity of turmoil*

	Casualties	Violence	Fiscal change	Duration
Party penetration [log]	−441.80*	−8,837.26^	9.57**	−181.49
	(0.050)	(0.077)	(0.003)	(0.291)
Length of account	0.04	1.44		
	(0.688)	(0.528)		
Minorities [percent of population]	461.89^	2545.26	−12.88***	163.61
	(0.064)	(0.636)	(0.000)	(0.352)
Industry [share of GRP]	276.40	8,447.72	−1.51	−76.58
	(0.496)	(0.354)	(0.816)	(0.839)
City [dummy]	317.07	10,994.47*	−3.76	−204.03
	(0.124)	(0.021)	(0.200)	(0.230)
Intercept	−1816.90*	−36,136.48^	37.47**	−289.33
	(0.043)	(0.069)	(0.005)	(0.680)

*** Significance at 0.001, ** significance at 0.01, * significance at 0.05, ^ significance at 0.1
Note: OLS estimators. 27/28 provincial observations. Casualties, violence, and length of account based on local gazetteers (Andrew G. Walder's dataset). Fiscal change from China Data Online. Duration from Bu Weihua, 2008, 中華人民共和國史，第六本，「砸爛舊世界」, pp. 731–733.

In light of the archival evidence, we expect that party penetration helped to contain the Cultural Revolution turmoil along each of the four very distinct analytic dimensions. Specifically, greater party penetration at the eve of the Cultural Revolution should be associated with fewer casualties, fewer victims, a better fiscal situation, and a shorter duration of the turmoil, controlling for other factors. The regression results of Table 8.2 are consistent with these conjectures from the archival research. The association between party penetration and fewer deaths is statistically significant at the 0.05 significance level, and with more broadly defined victims at the 0.1 level. The association with healthier finances is most robust at a 0.01 confidence level, while the relationship between party penetration and the duration of the movement remains uncertain. There is a 29 percent chance that the null hypothesis is true and that there is no relationship between party penetration and the time to establishing a Revolutionary Committee.

The effects are substantive. Holding the control variables constant, an increase in party penetration by 10 percent – corresponding only to less than half a standard deviation – is associated with 44 fewer casualties and 884 fewer victims per county, 1 percentage point greater fiscal revenues, and 18 fewer days to the establishment of a Revolutionary Committee. Despite the tenuous statistical significance of the party effect in some specifications, the result holds across four very distinct outcome variables: The party effect determined how close a locality came to anarchic disorder, no matter how exactly we define it. The analysis reinforces the finding that a local presence of the party helped to contain the Cultural Revolution turmoil and reestablish order.

8.7 CONCLUSION

Far from having become irrelevant, party institutions in fact shaped events of the Cultural Revolution down to the local level. Its institutional core was preserved. Rebel groups, instead of working against the party as an institution, sought to consolidate their power by following the rules set forth by the party, whose political comeback they expected. Party members with ample experience in leading mass movements were in charge both in rebel organizations and in transitional institutions. Informal party networks were rallying points for local coalitions of stability. In more violent areas, the military was successful precisely because it did not rely on force alone, but worked alongside the party. The party contributed to containing and overcoming the turmoil and at that time of crisis was indispensable for regime survival.

By applying Leninist methods of organizational control, the People's Republic regained control over the areas where early pacification attempts failed and where the situation was particularly difficult. Explanations for the resilience of the Chinese regime highlight strategies by which Chinese leaders maintain political legitimacy and manage interest politics.[157] Other explanations cite governance strategies and statecraft.[158] Regarding the party, scholars emphasize the ability of the party state to innovate, for instance by formalizing political succession.[159] Yet as the notion of adaptive authoritarianism suggests,[160] it is the combination of innovative governance techniques and tried-and-tested strategies of domination that makes the People's Republic resilient. The Cultural Revolution reveals how tried-and-tested Leninist techniques helped to overcome the onslaught of the popular uprising.

Arguably, the CCP came out of the Cultural Revolution stronger than ever: Forged in three decades of Communist Revolution and tempered in the Cultural Revolution, no other party in world history has had similar opportunities to build up its defensive forces. Political order, in Samuel Huntington's analysis, results from a degree of political organization that is on a par with and therefore able to cope with a society's degree of political mobilization.[161] As societies move into the modern age and political participation increases, more sophisticated political institutions are needed to deal with what Mao called "contradictions among the people."[162] Not unlike Mao, Huntington draws attention to the crucial role of political parties in cushioning antagonistic popular pressures emanating from the grassroots by shaping opinions and mediating interests,[163] an argument that is well known among Chinese political scientists.[164] A conceptual gain from Huntington's framework consists in measuring political institutions against the society surrounding them. With a linear and irreversible trend of modernization, political mobilization is a more or less steadily increasing function over time. Yet as the Cultural Revolution demonstrates, the degree of political mobilization fluctuates considerably. In ordinary times, political systems operate far below their breaking point. It is in moments of crisis that the political system may or may not be able to absorb the shock. In this view, crises can serve as a wake-up call for the political elite to strengthen state institutions.

To assess the impact of the movement, the question is what lessons individuals and institutions have learned. Mao emphasized how turmoil could provide individual cadres additional experience on how to withstand massive popular upheaval. Only party cadres who are challenged will have an opportunity to build up defenses. He famously postulated that "in our society, it is bad when groups of people make disturbances, and we do not approve of it. But when disturbances do occur, they force us to learn lessons from them, to overcome bureaucracy and educate the cadres and the people. In this sense, bad things can be turned into good things."[165] Personal memories of the Cultural Revolution are omnipresent among people in power today. All members of the Standing Committee of the Eighteenth and the Nineteenth Party Congress have lived through the Cultural Revolution in their teens and twenties and were involved in the movement. While one should not underestimate the long-lasting effects of historical events, as transmitted through individual memories, at the same time there is transmission through institutional arrangements and collective memories. For example, the role of the party as guarantor of the economy in combination with claims to legitimacy based on performance has remained an enduring characteristic of the Chinese party-state.

In the aftermath of the Cultural Revolution, the explicit lesson that Chinese leaders around Deng Xiaoping learned from the turmoil was a quasi-democratic one. In the official assessment of the Cultural Revolution, its destructiveness was blamed on Mao's leadership style, with the implication that from now on the party would practice inner-party democracy and consultation with the people: "We failed to institutionalize and legalize inner-party democracy... This meant that conditions were present for the over-concentration of Party power in individuals and for the development of arbitrary individual rule and the personality cult in the Party."[166] This democratic lesson became increasingly contested, partly because Deng Xiaoping failed to fully apply this lesson to his own leadership style, and turned into an authoritarian lesson in 1989. At the time of the Tian'anmen incident, the anarchic traits of the Cultural Revolution were used to justify violent intervention in the name of stability.

For decades China debated what exactly the Cultural Revolution lesson should be.[167] In the early 2000s, the internal magazine of the Organization Department carried an article "by a graduate student" that deplored episodes of patriarchy 家長制 (i.e., individual leaders exercizing arbitrary power) in the history of the CCP, mentioning the Cultural Revolution.[168] Later the debates in this magazine were silenced by lifting its classification, so that authors now have to follow normal censorship guidelines. Today, ostensibly, the democratic lesson is all but forgotten among propaganda officials and government historians of the People's Republic. Mao Zedong is seen uncritically, and Xi Jinping has concentrated more power in his own hands than Deng Xiaoping ever had, in the eyes of some observers being second only to Mao Zedong. The radical shift in historical interpretations suggests that more durable than the explicit, macro-historical lessons are the implicit lessons that shape the behavior of local cadres and organizations when under severe challenge in the future.

Although any future challenge to the regime will occur under very different historical circumstances, one might expect parallels. From the Cultural Revolution we know that even bereft of its hierarchical command lines, the CCP continued to be a political force to be reckoned with. The strength of the party lies in its organizational structures at the grassroots level, which can persist independent of elite splits at the top. As a formal hierarchical organization, the party had practically ceased to function in most parts of China throughout 1967–1968. The long shadow of the party was a catalyst that allowed the Chinese polity to return to peace. Does the party still possess the qualities that helped it to cope with upheaval in 1969? Or has it become an apparatus run by bureaucrats who would not know how to react to a major popular onslaught, other than by straightforward suppression? When local governments deal with small-scale protests, they at times use clumsy police-state methods, but at other times exhibit more responsive governance, amenable to compromise. The ability of local party organizations to continue to function without clear guidance from above might even have implications for what to expect if one day political change was to come to China. Even when the party is no longer in charge at the center of power, party cadres might be able to gain much influence even under a different political system, and party organizations might reemerge in some form or other. The turmoil of the late 1960s has demonstrated to what degree the party is an organization that from the grassroots up can quickly adapt to a new situation and find ways to gain influence over processes over which it seemingly has lost control.

9

Conclusion

China's authoritarian government has been successful in exercising authority over much of the vast East Asian landmass, partly because it was able to take advantage of the grassroots presence of its Leninist party organization. The one-child policy, one of the most ambitious policies of the twentieth century, could not have been so effectively implemented if it had not been for the CCP's rank and file, present in the villages and the factories throughout the country. Similarly, tax collection benefits from the presence of party members at the grassroots level. In fiscal terms, the costs of party members' informal privileges are small compared to the gains associated with the activities of local party members. In the cities and in the countryside, across various types of tax revenues, party members help to increase taxation rates, substantively contributing to the material base of the People's Republic by alleviating asymmetric information problems. Having a strong party presence at the grassroots helps enforcement.

The central claim that the party's rank and file functions as faithful implementers, deployed for tasks of the highest priority, must be refined in two respects. First, historically, the Great Leap Forward appears as an instance when, rather than enforcing central policy, the most committed party members resisted it. This was possible only because at the time the CCP had not yet entirely morphed from a revolutionary party to a party in power. Less than ten years after risking their lives for the Communist cause, some party members retained a strong revolutionary commitment, which motivated the high-risk behavior of foot-dragging. In a very limited way, revolutionary zeal allowed the party to function as a self-corrective device, although on the whole resistance was rare and could not prevent tens of millions of deaths. Second, another refinement concerns the function of the party in times of crisis, when rank-and-file members go far beyond their ordinary role of implementing policies. During the severe turmoil of the Cultural Revolution, when Mao called on ordinary people to attack the institutions of the party state, CCP members were left without clear instructions. They did not resist the Cultural Revolution, but acting on their own initiative, they eventually helped their communities to overcome local turmoil and return to order. In that sense, we can expect the party to function as an anchor of stability in times of crisis.

Going further back in time, an analysis of the Sino-Japanese War allows for uncovering the historical origins of party strength. Behind the front line inside Japanese-occupied territory, the CCP was shielded from Nationalist persecution and could recruit among populations displaced by war. Thus, geographic patterns of Communist recruitment were determined first and foremost by the front lines of Japanese occupation. After the Communist takeover in 1949, evening out the reach of the state was not high on the agenda of state-builders in the People's Republic, except for initial campaigns to grow membership in the South. Today the state continues to be strongest in areas formerly occupied by Japan, especially in the most embattled areas. Since geographic patterns of party membership are persistent, today still resembling the patterns of 1949, it is clear that only historical factors can explain why some parts of China are red with many party members, and others are pink with few members.

9.1 THE SUBNATIONAL TURN IN THE STATE-BUILDING LITERATURE

This book harnesses the analytic and empirical potential of subnational comparisons for studying the state. States do not cover their territories with a uniform blanket of governance. Most states are much stronger in some parts of their national territory than in others. The degree of political order varies not only among countries, but also within the borders of a single country, from one province to the next, from one county to the next, and arguably even from one neighborhood to the next. Differences within countries can be greater than differences between countries and are of utmost consequence for the lives of ordinary citizens, especially in non-OECD countries. In the case of China, subnational variation is particularly large not only because of the country's size and its population's diversity, but also because the traditional technique of differentiated governance takes advantage of diversity and reinforces differences, rather than seeking standardization at all costs.[1]

For a long time, political scientists have deplored that their discipline revolves around unitary nation states as points of reference, succumbing to the whole-nation bias.[2] Over the past fifteen years or so[3] comparative political scientists have become increasingly interested in the subnational.[4] In part, this trend followed other disciplines such as history, which had been moving beyond the nation state for a while.[5] In part, it was motivated by the objective to increase the number of observational units and improve empirical leverage.[6] In political science, the civil society literature spearheaded the subnational turn[7] and has been at the forefront ever since.[8] By contrast, the state-building literature has a commitment to the concept of a unitary state, with occasional attention to center–periphery divides; even subnational variation is studied through cross-country comparisons. The study of Latin America's "brown areas" that are outside the reach of the state is a good example.[9] Instead of explaining why, within the same country, some areas are more brown than others, important scholarly work explores why some countries have more "brown areas" than others.[10]

Only recently has the state-building literature moved beyond the traditional approach of comparing state-building outcomes across different countries.[11] In studies of European states, Daniel Ziblatt analyzes subnational variation in state capacity, through the lens of both election fraud[12] and public goods provision.[13] In the Africa field, Catherine Boone finds explanations for why the hold of the state over some rural communities is so much stronger than over others.[14] In the China field, an increasing number of studies analyze subnational variation in state-building outcomes and the uneven strength of the central state over different areas of its territory.[15] This book fully adopts the subnational mode of analysis, considering aspects of state strength at various levels of resolution. Fiscal revenues in urban areas are compared across provinces, Cultural Revolution outcomes across counties, and the success of implementing the one-child policy across townships. The subnational turn in the state-building literature reveals patterns that are far more complex than conventional ideas of center vs. periphery would suggest.

Influential thinkers in the service of the Chinese party state, like Western political scientists, for a long time have privileged cross-national comparisons. CCP strategic thinkers have identified crucial areas in need of reform by drawing lessons from a self-reflective comparison between the People's Republic of China and the Soviet Union.[16] Despite the leadership's vital interest in illuminating the origins of the party state's effective governance and its resilience, as far as one can tell, the party's researchers and think tankers forego the potential inherent in systematic subnational comparisons. To be sure, as Sebastian Heilmann's research shows, the adoption of policies after prior testing in experimental points[17] involves subnational comparisons between treatment and control group. But the nature of these comparisons, which as Heilmann himself emphasizes occur under hierarchy,[18] is highly politicized, since politics drive the underlying investigation and research process.[19] In short, the party state's think tanks have not begun to leverage fully the rich information contained in the variation of political outcomes within China.

Subnational analysis tends to involve political maps. In the process of constructing such maps, one is confronted with the interplay of physical topography, socioeconomic geography, and political spaces. The classic approach, adopted by scholars such as Karl A. Wittfogel, G. William Skinner, and Jeffrey D. Sachs, is somewhat of a one-way street: Topography determines socio-economic patterns, which in turn lead to particular political outcomes. This book points to ways in which geography interacts with human activities. The Chinese state is viable precisely because it breaks through physiographic regions and reshapes the political geography. In the past, while drainage basins were important, the manmade Grand Canal reshaped the topography in ways that altered the presence of the state as well as economic networks. The strength of party organization is indirectly linked to topography, because Japanese occupation to some extent followed railroads whose paths were designed with topography in mind. But human geography was just as important a factor in explaining patterns of occupation, patterns of mobilization, and later on patterns of convergence away from the initial patterns, under the lead of the Organization Department's social engineers. This book suggests that human geography rivals and sometimes supersedes physical geography.

9.2 HISTORICAL TRANSMISSION AND WATERSHED EVENTS

This book also advances the historical turn in political science.[20] To be sure, political science has never ignored history. Classic works on the origins of dictatorship and democracy by Barrington Moore,[21] on social revolutions by Theda Skocpol,[22] and on civic traditions in Italy[23] are all historically grounded. However, Gary King's move to unify methodology[24] and more stringently design social inquiry[25] at first reduced political scientists' historical imagination, because of methodological difficulties in dealing with temporal dynamics.[26] The historical turn salvages a hallmark of the discipline by bringing the historical richness of earlier studies back into today's more methodologically rigorous political science. Driving the historical turn are attempts to find more methodologically satisfying ways to deal with dynamic processes, including but not limited to path dependency and event sequencing.[27] It is easier to verify that historical legacies still have a significant impact on contemporary outcomes than to test causality or to numerically describe parameters of dynamic institutional change. The party growth model developed in Chapter 6 to study the convergence of party membership patterns is a method to test dynamic characteristics of institutional change, making use of substantive information on recruitment processes for the sake of an effective quantitative analysis.

When tracing historical causation, unless one is prepared to revisit prehuman times,[28] a fundamental question is how far back in time one should go. What criteria should one use to locate the relevant watershed event that altered the course of history enough to stand at the beginning of a consequential causal chain? Searching for the historical origins of China's crimson and pink areas, this book identified the late 1930s and early 1940s as the critical time period. The fact that the party was only founded in 1921 suggests that the origins of the uneven party presence lie in the twentieth century. Moreover, the rapid membership expansion during the Sino-Japanese War suggested that this period was the CCP's formative period. Finally, the geography of party strength is sufficiently different from the reach of the imperial Chinese state that it did not seem promising to go further back in time. Beyond the specifics of this case, and bearing in mind the freezing hypothesis according to which European party cleavages originated in the 1920s,[29] one might conjecture that it is at the time when a large share of the population is mass mobilized into a modern political system that the political map forms in a lasting way. To be sure, there is much debate as to when exactly political mobilization arrived in China, but Japanese colonization certainly is one plausible answer. In short, looking for watershed events that define the beginning of a distinct chain of events, the onset of modernity is a possible starting point, because, as Samuel Huntington argued,[30] new kinds of institutions are needed to achieve order in a highly mobilized society.

The second fundamental question in historical arguments concerns transmission mechanisms. Recognizing the importance of explanatory variables that date far back in history, such as the effect of a locality belonging to the Confederacy during the American Civil War on voting patterns today,[31] political science begins to address questions of transmission. Is the effect entirely direct, or can one identify a mediator that

clarifies the causal pathway? This book identifies the Leninist party organization as being at the heart of historical transmission mechanisms.
Recruitment procedures, information requirements, and incumbents wary
of sharing their power with newcomers tend to prevent convergence and
a more uniform presence of the party. While not ruling out other transmission mechanisms, such as the inheritance of political attitudes from
one generation to the next within families, organizational and political
dynamics of party membership recruitment forge a particularly strong
link between the present and the past. By contrast, the CCP's base area
legacy stands on much shakier ground, because revolutionary legacies are
more malleable and interpretable in ways that might even work against
the party. The book suggests that one should expect other membership-
based organizations, such as church communities, neighborhood associations, and labor unions, to forge similar links between the present and
their formative moment in the past.

9.3 PARTY-BASED AUTHORITARIANISM, PARTY-BASED DEMOCRACY?

Contrary to the gulf that today separates Western research on authoritarian parties from research on democratic parties, Chinese research routinely studies other countries' parties, searching for potential models and
governance techniques that could be useful for the CCP. For instance the
anti-corruption campaign, as Xi Jinping's signature policy, has encouraged a specialized research team at the Organization Department to look
at corruption prevention in parties abroad, including the German Social
Democratic party.[32] In search for better communication on the Internet,
the Organization Department studied how parties in Britain, Germany
and Switzerland use the Internet.[33] The CCP Central Committee's International Liaison Department has a research unit that focuses on international relations and political parties, not distinguishing between democratic and authoritarian ones.

Similarly in the 1950s and 1960s, political scientists made a point
to study authoritarian parties alongside democratic ones.[34] The insights
gained from studying the CCP are first and foremost applicable to other
authoritarian parties, including the CCP's close cousins in Vietnam and
North Korea. In democratic systems party members serve very different
functions, such as mobilizing voters at the grassroots level during election campaigns. While some parties are innovative in deploying their
party members in unusual ways, such as the environmental activism of
some Green Party members, observing the decline in traditional forms of

political participation through parties in most advanced democracies,[35] reflected in declining party membership,[36] authors have even gone so far as to ask: "Do political parties still need members?"[37] In certain countries, which until recently had been politically volatile like Brazil, party members have important mobilization functions,[38] but these are seen as exceptions. In that sense, we might be witnessing a historical reversal: Party members of authoritarian parties are becoming more significant political actors compared to party members of democratic parties.

Political parties -both authoritarian and democratic ones- strongly link political communities to their history. Not only do many citizens stick with the same party for a lifetime, but geographic patterns of party membership are stable from one generation to the next. It is an empirical question how much the political map of a country is shaped by contemporary socio-economic realities, by political attitudes transmitted from generation to generation and by historical events that are transmitted through formal institutions, especially membership-based institutions such as parties. The degree to which parties are in decline and party membership becomes more fluid, one may conjecture, is an important determinant of the degree to which historical influences on a country's political map remain strong. To test this conjecture, future work could use the empirical tools developed to quantify the half-life of history in the Chinese case, apply them to parties and other membership-based organizations in democratic countries, and gauge the disappearance of history effects and national convergence on countries' political maps.

Maybe most significantly, thinking about authoritarian parties alongside democratic ones is a conceptual choice that facilitates an analysis of political transitions. What will become of the CCP when China experiences regime change – how will the party shape the new policy? In the light of this book, one should certainly not underestimate the staying power of the party. Even if the top echelons fall into disarray, the party's rank and file are a force to be reckoned with, as seen during the Cultural Revolution. More importantly, future successors to the current leadership have much to gain from working with the party's rank and file, rather than casting them aside. Much more dysfunctional communist parties in formerly Soviet-dominated Europe have survived and exercised substantial political influence in the post-Communist era.[39]

Historically, the Chinese state has relied on nonstate intermediaries, distinct from bureaucrats, to govern at the grassroots level. In imperial times the local gentry, consisting of the numerous imperial degree holders either waiting for or having retired from official positions, along with local clerks and runners, filled the void left by a county government staffed with a handful of officials. Nowadays, although the presence of the formal bureaucracy has increased markedly, the state relies on party members to support governance at the grassroots level. If in the future the Chinese state were to cut down on its ambitions for the grassroots level, or alternatively were to expand its bureaucracy all the way down to the grassroots level, that would be a drastic break with the past. It would be comparable to the Meiji restoration when the Japanese state for the first time expanded its centralized bureaucratic power to the local level, instead of following "Confucian" ideals of self-regulating and autonomous local communities. Short of such a sharp break, this book suggests that Chinese state-builders, whether in the People's Republic or in a new political context, are likely to continue to exercise their authority at the grassroots through parties, maybe one day even democratic ones.

Appendix 1: Party-versus-Bureaucracy Model

The model establishes conditions under which it is advantageous for a principal, like China's central leadership, to employ two agencies, the state bureaucracy and the party hierarchy, instead of amalgamating the two. It builds on a multitask principal-agent model.

Orthodox Multitask Model with One Agent

Bengt Holmstrom and Paul Milgrom have formulated a principal-agent model, where the agent must work on two related tasks.[1] Their model in the simplified notation used by Bernard Salanié[2] provides the framework for the following analysis. The goal of this subsection is to specify the benefits that the principal can expect in the standard multitask scenario. In the following subsection, I derive the benefits in an alternative scenario, with two separate agents working on the related tasks. The third subsection compares costs and benefits in the two different scenarios.

The principal observes only his payoff. His payoff, apart from transfer payments made to the agent, is the sum of two random variables X_1 and X_2, with expected probability equal to the efforts a_1 exerted by the agent on task 1 and the efforts a_2 exerted by the same agent on task 2.

$$x_i = a_i + \epsilon_i \tag{A.1}$$

The asymmetric information problem occurs, because a disturbance ϵ_i obfuscates the signal. The characteristic multitask problem arises, because the disturbances are not always independent of each other, the covariance being ϵ_{12}.

317

The agent receives wages w, which are a linear function $\alpha_1 X_1 + \alpha_2 X_2 + \beta$ of the signals X_i observed by the principal. As a result of exerting efforts a_i, the agent incurs cost $C(a_1, a_2)$. The agent has an exponential utility function

$$-exp(-r(w - C(a_1, a_2)))$$ (A.2)

If the agent is rewarded for the two tasks under such a setting, the optimal wage contract is chosen so as to maximize the overall expected surplus, under the incentive constraints.

$$Overall\ Surplus_{jointly\ rewarded} = a_1 + a_2 - C(a_1, a_2) - \frac{r}{2}\alpha'\Sigma\alpha$$ (A.3)

$$\alpha_1 a_1 + \alpha_2 a_2 - C(a_1, a_2)$$ (A.4)

Multitask Model with Multiple Agents

Up to this point, the analysis has strictly followed the paradigmatic version of the multitask principal-agent model. Let us now modify the original model by introducing multiple, separately rewarded agents. The principal receives the same payoffs as in A.1. To reflect the division of labor between the agents, each agent is rewarded only for the outcome pertaining to one task. This means that the principal commits himself – through the wage contract – to ignore the outcome of task 2, even if it provides indirect information about the performance of agent 1. It is this commitment to ignore some of the signals that drives the result and improves the outcome. For agent i the linear wage function is

$$\alpha_i X_i + \beta$$ (A.5)

Notice that the optimal arrangement might be neither a complete pooling of the tasks nor a complete separation of tasks. Under certain conditions, it could be that the optimal arrangement falls in between jointly rewarding the two agents and separately rewarding the two agents, so that one would need to optimize the weights put on each signal in the linear wage function. However, since the modest goal of this analysis is to show that the separation of tasks can be more advantageous than the pooling of tasks, there is no need to study intermediate cases. The simplifying assumption is closer to the kinds of arrangements found in the real world, and it allows for straightforward, clear-cut comparisons of the conventional solution to multitask models and the multiagent solution to the multitask model. Thanks to the simplification, the exact conditions under which task separation is advantageous are much more intuitive to interpret.

The agent receives an expected payoff with certainty equivalent to

$$\alpha_i a_i + \beta - C(a_i) - \frac{r}{2}\alpha_i^2 \sigma_i^2 \qquad \text{(A.6)}$$

In terms of benefits, the agent expects a bonus in proportion to his efforts a_i and a lump sum transfer payment from the principal β. On the down-side, the agent suffers costs from investing efforts a_i, as well as losses that reflect his uncertainty: After all, the output visible to the principal might not fully reflect the agent's efforts, because of the disturbance term σ_i.

As before, the solution of the multitask model requires maximization of overall welfare under incentive constraints. The incentive constraints remain unchanged, but the overall welfare function now is

$$Overall\ Surplus_{separately\ rewarded} = a_1 + a_2 - C(a_1) - C(a_2)$$
$$- \frac{r_1}{2}\alpha_1^2\sigma_1^2 - \frac{r_2}{2}\alpha_2^2\sigma_2^2 \qquad \text{(A.7)}$$

Incentive constraints are identical to the original model.

Is It Advantageous to Employ Two Separately Rewarded Agents?

We will now compare the two maximization problems, to identify the conditions under which it is advantageous for the principal to assign the tasks to two separately rewarded agents, instead of to just one agent. Since the incentive constraints are identical for the two organizational solutions, the key is to compare the expected total surplus with joint rewards (equation A.3) to the expected total surplus with separate rewards (equation A.7). The principal prefers to reward the two agents separately if and only if

$$Overall\ Surplus_{jointly\ rewarded} < Overall\ Surplus_{separately\ rewarded}$$
$$\Longleftrightarrow\ a_1 + a_2 - C(a_1, a_2) - \frac{r}{2}\alpha'\Sigma\alpha < a_1 + a_2 - C(a_1) - C(a_2)$$
$$- \frac{r_1}{2}\alpha_1^2\sigma_1^2 - \frac{r_2}{2}\alpha_2^2\sigma_2^2 \qquad \text{(A.8)}$$
$$\Longleftrightarrow\ C(a_1) + C(a_2) - C(a_1, a_2) < \frac{r}{2}\alpha'\Sigma\alpha - \frac{r_1}{2}\alpha_1^2\sigma_1^2 - \frac{r_2}{2}\alpha_2^2\sigma_2^2$$

The right-hand side of A.8 is always positive. The left-hand side reflects synergy effects Ω between the two tasks: $C(a_1) + C(a_2) > C(a_1, a_2)$ means that the costs of two people engaging in the tasks separately are greater than the costs of one person taking care of both tasks all by himself. The greater the synergy effects from having one person take care of both tasks, the higher the bar for splitting up the task and assigning it to two different agents.

We know that the principal will assign the riskier task to the less risk-averse agent, because the principal must pay transfers and is affected by overall welfare. Without loss of generality, it is then possible to say that $\sigma_1 > \sigma_2$ and $r_1 < r_2$, to interpret the right-hand side of equation A.8, which we can rewrite as

$$\Omega < \frac{r - r_1}{2}\alpha_1^2\sigma_1^2 + \frac{r - r_2}{2}\alpha_2^2\sigma_2^2 + r\sigma_{12}\alpha_1\alpha_2 \tag{A.9}$$

As this equation shows, the added value of employing two agents increases if the two agents are of different types *and* if the two tasks are different. If the two sets of agents have the same level of risk averseness $r = r_1 = r_2$, or if the uncertainty of the signal adjusted by a scaling factor $\alpha_1\sigma_1 = \alpha_2\sigma_2$ is identical between the two tasks, then two terms on the right-hand side disappear, as shown in equation A.10. In short, the more different the two agents and the two tasks, the more likely the principal is to employ distinct agents.

Finally, even if the two agents or the tasks are identical, it might still be advantageous to employ multiple agents. To see this, assume identical agents (or alternatively identical tasks), so that the condition of equation A.9 simplifies to

$$\Omega < r\alpha_1\alpha_2\sigma_{12} \tag{A.10}$$

The remaining term in equation A.10 points to the third critical factor, namely the precise nature of the asymmetric information problem, captured by σ_{12}, the correlation of the noise of signal for task 1 and noise of the signal for task 2. If the noise is negatively correlated, the two signals are complementary and in conjunction provide the principal more reliable information for distributing rewards or meting out punishments. By contrast, if the variable $\sigma_{12} > 0$, the principal faces the characteristic challenge of strategic situations resembling the multitask model.

Appendix 2: Party Growth Model

The following model underlies the analysis of party membership convergence carried out in Chapter 6. It uses well-known mathematical tools and follows closely the notation in Robert J. Barro and Xavier Sala-i-Martin, 1995, *Economic Growth* and Angel de la Fuente, 2000, *Mathematical Methods and Models for Economists*. Consider a jurisdiction at time t with M_t party members. The number of new party members that can be won is a function of the number of existing party members $F(M_t)$. Assuming that in each period a constant fraction x of the membership dies, is purged, or otherwise exits the party, the dynamics of the growth process can be written as

$$\frac{\nabla M_t}{\nabla t} = F(M_t) - x M_t \qquad (A.11)$$

The change in members is the balance between entries and exits; if entries equal exits, the party growth has reached a plateau called steady state. Henceforth, the fraction of party members in the community $\frac{M_t}{P_t}$ is referred to as party strength. To simplify notation, we suppress subscripts and write partial derivatives to time, such as $\frac{\partial(M_t/P_t)}{\partial t}$ with a dot as $\dot{M}/P$. If population growth is linear, then the change in party strength can be written as

$$\dot{M}/P = f(M/P) - (x+n)(M/P) \qquad (A.12)$$

where $f(m_t)$ describes the increase in party strength as a function of the existing number of party members, and n is population growth. Assume that the expansion of the membership base follows a standard

321

Cobb-Douglas production function of the form

$$f(M/P) = a(M/P)^b \qquad\qquad (A.13)$$

with $0 < b < 1$. Production of new members is a strictly increasing function of the existing membership – that is, the more members a party already has, the easier it is to expand it to one additional person (first derivative positive). This increase is much steeper when a party has only a few members, but turns flatter when the party already has many members and saturation sets in (second derivative negative). These typical growth dynamics observed in accumulation processes in economics, as well as in the natural sciences, seem reasonable in the political domain as well: The more members an organization has, the easier it is to attract additional members; and these "economies of scale" are stronger with small organizations than with large ones. Methodologically, this assumption is appealing, because it allows for a broad range of possible growth dynamics. The limiting case of $lim_{b\to 0}$ describes a situation where the expansion of the party is (almost) independent of the number of existing members. The other limiting case of $lim_{b\to 1}$ describes a case where the ability to attract new members increases proportionally to the number of existing members, resulting in a rapid (almost infinite) escalation of party membership. Plugging the production function into equation A.12, and with the additional notational convention $m = ln(M/P)$, we yield

$$\dot{m} = ae^{m(b-1)} - (x + n) \qquad\qquad (A.14)$$

The party growth model possesses a steady state, defined as a situation $\dot{m} = 0$. When the steady state is reached, party strength reaches a plateau and ceases to increase. The absolute number of party members continues to grow, but only fast enough to offset population growth and the regular loss of party members. The zero growth condition implies that party strength in the steady state is a constant

$$m^* = \frac{1}{b-1} ln\left(\frac{x+n}{a}\right) \qquad\qquad (A.15)$$

The fraction $\frac{-n-e}{a}$ reflects the fact that final party strength in the steady state depends on how the speed of growth compares to the rate of exits from the party and to population growth. From this perspective, the unusually large share of party members in the population of the former German Democratic Republic could be due to demographics: Even if the Communist party grew at ordinary rates, over time a shrinking population drastically increased party membership per capita of population.[1]

The concise formulation of the party growth model in equation A.14 poses a twin analytical challenge. First, the marginal change in party strength $\dot{m}$ is a mathematical construct that cannot be directly observed; thus its parameters cannot be empirically determined. Second, it is a nonlinear differential equation, which is hard to handle. Therefore, we will linearize the equation, using Taylor series expansion "around" the steady state as an approximation. Mathematically speaking, the approximation is valid only "close to" the steady state, but for all practical intents and purposes, economists have found the approximation perfectly acceptable to analyze economic growth dynamics. In particular, after linearization, it is straightforward to transform the model into an equation that can be estimated empirically. Approximating equation A.14 with Taylor series to the first differential yields

$$\dot{m}(m) \approx \dot{m}(m^*) + \frac{\partial \dot{m}}{\partial m}(m - m^*) = \dot{m} + a(b-1)e^{m*(b-1)}(m - m^*) \quad (A.16)$$

Replacing m^* in the exponent using steady state equation A.15 yields a linear differential equation

$$\dot{m} = \lambda(m - m^*) \quad (A.17)$$

with $\lambda = (1 - b)(x + n)$. This linear differential equation can be transformed into a version whose coefficients can be empirically estimated. Rearranging terms, multiplication by $e^{\lambda t}$, and finally integration with respect to time leads to

$$\int e^{\lambda t}(\dot{m} + \lambda m)dt = \int e^{\lambda t}\lambda m^* dt \quad (A.18)$$

$$\Leftrightarrow e^{\lambda t}m = m^*e^{\lambda t} + b \quad (A.19)$$

$$\Leftrightarrow m(t) = e^{-\lambda t}b + m^* \quad (A.20)$$

This equation expresses party strength as a function of time. To specify arbitrary integration term b, we make use of an initial condition. If we know $m(0)$, this implies $b = m(0) - m^*$, so that

$$m(t) = e^{-\lambda t}m(0) + (1 - e^{-\lambda t})m^* \quad (A.21)$$

The logarithm of party membership at time t is the weighted average between initial party membership and party membership in the steady state. If $\lambda < 0$, then as time goes by, the influence of initial party membership recedes at rate λ, and the influence of the steady state increases accordingly. In other words, λ indicates the speed of convergence. The more negative λ, the greater the speed of convergence.

The conventional approach presented here is an approximation using Taylor series. An exact solution of the differential equation A.14 is possible. For notational simplification, the yearly decrease in party penetration as a result of population growth and exiting members is written as $d = n + x$. With the help of inverse functions, the solution is

$$m(t) = \frac{1}{1-b}log\left[\frac{1}{z} - (a - e^{z*(bt-t-C+bC)})\right] \qquad (A.22)$$

It would also be possible to estimate the five coefficients a, b, n, x and C contained in this equation, but interpretation would be cumbersome and – at least in the present algebraic form – of less substantive meaning: Coefficients a and b would indicate the shape of the underlying Cobb-Douglas function, but only indirectly indicate the steady state and the convergence rate. Coefficients n and x would be of little interest, because they are directly observable at the aggregate level: Between 1956 and 2010 China's population has increased more than twofold by the factor 2.13105, implying an annual population growth rate n of 0.01411. The average annual rate of exits x was 0.01157. Therefore the analysis proceeds using the approximation.

Notes

Chapter 1

1 The number of non-democracies, the number of citizens living in non-democracies, and the share of non-democracies with authoritarian regime parties is calculated as explained on pages 66 ff.

2 Huntington, Samuel P., 1970, *Social and Institutional Dynamics of One-Party Systems*. Geddes, Barbara, 1999, *What Do We Know about Democratization after Twenty Years?*

3 Schedler, Andreas, 2010, *Authoritarianism's Last Line of Defense*.

4 This group encompasses authoritarian and competitive authoritarian regimes, as long as their rule is supported by a single, or at least a dominant, party.

5 Geddes, Barbara, 1999, *What Do We Know about Democratization after Twenty Years?* and Levitsky, Steven and Way, Lucan A., 2010, *Competitive Authoritarianism*.

6 Magaloni, Beatriz, 2006, *Voting for Autocracy*. Svolik, Milan W., 2012, *The Politics of Authoritarian Rule*. Gandhi, Jennifer, 2008, *Political Institutions under Dictatorship*.

7 Zhou Zhongwei, 2000, 群眾性事件研究, p. 157.

8 Thelen, Kathleen, 2004, *How Institutions Evolve*, pp. 28–31.

9 For the technique of differentiated governance under the Qing Empire, see Koss, Daniel, 2017, *Political Geography of Empire*.

10 I owe the "reach of the state" metaphor to Shue, Vivienne, 1988, *The Reach of the State*.

11 This is reminiscent of the selection of new nuclear sites in Japan Aldrich, Daniel P., 2008, *Site Fights*.

12 Looney, Kristen E., 2012, *The Rural Developmental State*.

13 Schurmann, Franz, 1966, *Ideology and Organization in Communist China* represents the earlier scholarship; today, Bruce J. Dickson is one of only a few scholars studying the party.

14 Tsai, Lily L., 2007, *Accountability without Democracy*.

15 While using this term, I am not subscribing to the state-society dichotomy and do not participate in the "tug of war" (Perry, Elizabeth J., 1994, *Trends in the Study of Chinese Politics*) between state and society. As will become clear in the course of the book, grassroots party organization is not unambiguously part of the state. But it is more "state" than, say, solidary groups or Daoist secret societies.

16 The CCP appears as an explanatory variable in Dali Yang's analysis of agrarian radicalism. But he goes on, after just a couple of paragraphs, to conflate party presence with distance from Beijing, partly because at the time he did not have access to good data on CCP membership, Yang, Dali, 1996, *Calamity and Reform in China*.

17 Getty, J. Arch, 1983, *Party and Purge in Smolensk, 1933–1937*, p. 61.

18 Schurmann, Franz, 1966, *Ideology and Organization in Communist China* and Barnett, A. Doak, 1967, *Cadres, Bureaucracy, and Political Power in Communist China*.

19 With notable exceptions including Dickson, Bruce J., 2000, *Cooptation and Corporatism in China* and Dickson, Bruce J., 2014, *Who Wants to be a Communist? Career Incentives and Mobilized Loyalty in China*; as well as journalistic investigations McGregor, Richard, 2010, *The Party* and Asahi Shimbun Beijing Office, 2012, 紅の党.

20 The similar phrase "bringing the statesman back in" comes from an international relations scholar Byman, Daniel L. and Pollack, Kenneth M., 2001, *Let Us Now Praise Great Men*. Jaros, Kyle A., 2014, *The Politics of Metropolitan Bias in China* shows that leadership can fruitfully be analyzed to explain important local policy outcomes.

21 Lü Xiaobo, 2000, *Cadres and Corruption*.

22 Shambaugh, David L., 2008, *China's Communist Party*.

23 Dickson, Bruce J., 2016, *The Dictator's Dilemma*.

24 Walder, Andrew G., 2004, *The Party Elite and China's Trajectory of Change*.

25 McGregor, Richard, 2010, *The Party*.

26 For comparison: In 1989, before the cataclysm, the Communist Party of the Soviet Union had 19 million members (Gill, Graeme J., 1994, *The Collapse of a Single Party System*, table 5.1). This corresponded to 6.6 percent of the population, a comparable saturation rate.

27 The calculation is based on the rural portion of *China Household Income Project*, distributed by ICPSR.

28 Compare standard handbooks for party leaders at the grassroots level from 1990 to those from 2010, e.g. CCP Tianjin, 2003, 黨的基層組織工作手冊 and Ma Shizhong, 1990, 中國共產黨支部工作手冊.

29 Conversation with a journalist specializing on NGOs in Shanghai on August, 2012.

30 After translation, these blog entries have disappeared from the internet.

31 Zhang Ruihong, Li Wei and Qi Xiaojuan, 2010, 社區黨支部工作手冊.

32 CCP Organization Department, 2015, 入黨實務教程.

33 Temporarily available online in July 2012.

34 Jiang Jinquan, 2015, 怎樣正確開展批評和自我批評.

35 Ibid. p. 3.

36 One mysterious scheme, possibly Falun Gong–sponsored, consists of a telephone campaign: "Press 1 if you wish to exit the CCP. Press 2 if you wish to exit the Communist Youth League. Press 3 if you wish to exit the Young Pioneers." – conversations with former party member in Shanghai, August 2012; former party member in Shandong, November 2013; and former party member in Taipei, March 2017.

37 CCP Organization Department, 2011, 中國共產黨黨內統計資料彙編, p. 208.

38 In Taiyuan in early 2016, a seemingly much-in-demand handbook was Legal Press, 2015, 黨員領導幹部常用黨紀條規選編.

39 Jiang Jinquan, 2015, 怎樣正確開展批評和自我批評, p. 56.

40 Conversations in Shanxi and Shandong, where the author also saw banners of a meeting held a while ago in democratic format, that is, letting non-party members participate (January 2016). The Internet provides samples for self-critiques and self-summaries, confirming the impressions.

41 For details on the practical implementation see 濟南市委辦公廳文件, 關於開展2014年全市民主評議黨風政風行風工作的意義, September 28, 2014.

42 Conversation with a party member, beginning of August 2012.

43 In some places, this is called the "indispensable visits on six occasions policy."

44 Conversation with a volunteer in Harbin on August 26, 2012.

45 Perry, Elizabeth J., 2007, *Studying Chinese Politics*, p. 5ff.

46 支部會議紀錄(2010.10.29) "Protocol of party cell meeting (October 29, 2010)," http://nwpu2011.blog.163.com/blog/static/173101739201010595456694, last checked in April 2017, also available from the author.

47 CCP Organization Department, 1994, 中國共產黨黨員電化教育工作問答.

48 支部會議紀錄(2010.10.29) "Protocol of party cell meeting (October 29, 2010)," http://nwpu2011.blog.163.com/blog/static/173101739201010595456694, last checked in April 2017, also available from the author.

49 http://nwpu2011.blog.163.com, last checked April 2017.

50 Party general branches are on the same hierarchical level, but more important than party cells.

51 This document has disappeared from the site where the author had found it.

52 Roberts, Margaret, 2014, *Fear, Friction, and Flooding*.

53 In the US, the color red stands for the conservative Republican party, whereas in Europe it stands for left parties. Since the CCP is conservative as well as left, the color red is befitting by both of these definitions.

54 Material on CCP Organization, compiled on all hierarchical levels of the state, often contain membership statistics. Scholarship was handicapped by the difficulty of putting together a complete set of data. To my knowledge the best compilation so far has been Yang, Dali, 1996, *Calamity and Reform in China*.

55 CCP Organization Department, 2011, 中國共產黨黨內統計資料彙編. I could not find the volume during later visits, but now the Fairbank Center

library at Harvard University owns a copy; and according to the catalog of
the National Library of Australia, it should also be available there.

56 CCP Organization Department, 2011, 中國共產黨黨內統計資料彙編.

57 Apart from party members in central state organs (2 million people), there
are those employed in the financial system (1 million people), working for
railroad or aviation companies (1 million people) or serving in the State
Capital Committee (1 million people).

58 Compare Xu, Yong, 2016, 區域社會視角下 and Talhelm, Thomas, Zhang,
Xuemin, Oishi, Shigehiro, Chen, Shimin, Duan, Dongyuan, Lan, Xuezhao
and Kitayama, Shinobu, 2014, Large-Scale Psychological Differences.

59 This is my impression from eighteen months of field research.

60 The bookshelves of a party school archive in Harbin have absolutely no
local flavor; they might as well belong to a party school anywhere else in
China. The local newspaper archive is tucked away in dusty storage, and
poisonous fungus makes it unpleasant to use.

61 Yan Xiaojun, 2009, *Economic Reform and Political Change in Rural China*.

62 Zhang Ruihong, Li Wei and Qi Xiaojuan, 2010, 社區黨支部工作手冊.

63 Yang, Dali, 1996, *Calamity and Reform in China*, p. 141.

64 Levitsky, Steven and Way, Lucan A., 2012, *Beyond Patronage*.

65 Perry, Elizabeth J., 2012, *Anyuan*, esp. p. 5.

66 CCP Organization Department of Jingzhou City: Circular on changing the
paper format to A4. April 16, 2012.

67 In the run-up to the Eighth Party Congress in 1956, Shanghai's party grew
by 50%, but then shrunk the following year, despite active recruitment of
new members Mei, S. and Qiu X., 2001, 中共上海黨志, p. 306.

Chapter 2

1 Huntington, Samuel P., 1970, *Social and Institutional Dynamics of
One-Party Systems*.

2 Geddes, Barbara, 1999, *What Do We Know about Democratization after
Twenty Years?* Writing in the 1960s and comparing the early postcolonial
experiences of eighty-three developing countries, Fred van der Mechten
found that coups were most likely in countries without effective parties and
in democracies. Party-based authoritarian systems experienced by far fewer
coups. Within this group, two-party systems were less stable than one-party
dominant systems; one-party dominant systems were less stable than
one-party systems; and proletarian party systems were the most stable of
all, von der Mehden, Fred, 1964, *Politics of the Developing Nations*, p. 65.
This last assertion has withstood the test of time, since the same regimes
which van der Mechten had listed in this category are still in place after
fifty years: Communist China, North Korea, and North Vietnam (ibid., p.
56). Van der Mechten classified Cuba and Laos with "states that have no
parties or in which parties do not play effective governmental roles" (ibid.,
p. 54). An understandable (Cuba) or indisputable (Laos) choice at the time,
later developments in the two countries further confirm Mehden's point.

3 Levitsky, Steven and Way, Lucan A., 2012, *Beyond Patronage*.

4 Huntington, Samuel P., 2006 (1968), *Political Order in Changing Societies*.

5 Magaloni, Beatriz and Kricheli, Ruth, 2010, *Political Order and One-Party Rule*.

6 Geddes, Barbara, 1999, *What Do We Know about Democratization after Twenty Years?*

7 Brownlee, Jason, 2007, *Authoritarianism in an Age of Democratization*, p. 12.

8 Magaloni, Beatriz, 2008, *Credible Power-Sharing and the Longevity of Authoritarian Rule*.

9 Slater, Dan, 2010, *Ordering Power*.

10 Brancati, Dawn, 2014, *Democratic Authoritarianism*.

11 Magaloni, Beatriz and Kricheli, Ruth, 2010, *Political Order and One-Party Rule*, p. 125.

12 Svolik, Milan W., 2012, *The Politics of Authoritarian Rule*.

13 Boix, Carles and Svolik, Milan W., 2013, *The Foundations of Limited Authoritarian Government*.

14 O'Donnell, Guillermo A., 1982, *Transitions from Authoritarian Rule*.

15 Brownlee, Jason, 2007, *Authoritarianism in an Age of Democratization*, chapter 6.

16 Reuter, Ora J., Gandhi, Jennifer, 2011, *Economic Performance and Elite Defection from Hegemonic Parties*.

17 Svolik, Milan W., 2012, *The Politics of Authoritarian Rule*.

18 Compare Zhang Liang, 2001, *The Tiananmen Papers*, especially the introduction by Andrew J. Nathan and pp. 355ff.

19 Pye, Lucian W., 1988, *The Mandarin and the Cadre*, p. 135f.

20 Nathan, Andrew J., 2003, *Authoritarian Resilience*.

21 CCP, 1981, *Resolution on Certain Questions in the History of our Party since the Founding of the People's Republic of China*.

22 Vogel, Ezra F., 2011, *Deng Xiaoping and the Transformation of China*.

23 Manion, Melanie, 1993, *Retirement of Revolutionaries in China*.

24 Conversation with Ezra Vogel, July 2014.

25 Gilley, Bruce, 2003, *The Limits of Authoritarian Resilience*, p. 20.

26 Fewsmith, Joseph, 2013, *The 18th Party Congress*.

27 Asahi Shimbun Beijing Office, 2012, 紅の党.

28 For instance, Andrew J. Nathan writes about Xi Jinping's current term as General Secretary of the CCP that it is "expected to be the first of at least two." See: "Who Is Xi?", *The New York Review of Books*, May 12, 2016.

29 Brownlee, Jason, 2007, *Authoritarianism in an Age of Democratization*, chapter 4.

30 Ufen, Andreas, 2009, *The Transformation of Political Party Opposition in Malaysia and Its Implications for the Electoral Authoritarian Regime*.

31 Slater, Dan, 2010, *Ordering Power*, p. 8.

32 Collombier, Virginie, 2007, *The Internal Stakes of the 2005 Elections*.

33 Acemoglu, Daron and Robinson, James A., 2006, *Economic Origins of Dictatorship and Democracy*.

34 Wintrobe, Ronald, 1998, *The Political Economy of Dictatorship*.

35 United States Senate, 2004, *Money Laundering and Foreign Corruption.*
36 IMF, 2003, *Republic of Equatorial Guinea.*
37 Magaloni, Beatriz, 2006, *Voting for Autocracy.*
38 Blaydes, Lisa, 2011, *Elections and Distributive Politics in Mubarak's Egypt.*
39 Svolik, Milan W., 2012, *The Politics of Authoritarian Rule*, chapter 6.
40 Dickson, Bruce J. and Rost Rublee, Maria, 2000, *Membership Has Its Privileges.*
41 Lü Xiaobo, 2000, *Cadres and Corruption.*
42 Yang, Dali L., 2004, *Remaking the Chinese Leviathan.*
43 Pring, Coralie, 2017, *People and Corruption.*
44 Bates, Robert H., 1981, *Markets and States in Tropical Africa.*
45 Faust, Aaron, 2012, *The Ba'thification of Iraq*, pp. 138–141.
46 Connelly, John, 1996, *The Uses of.*
47 Slater, Dan, 2010, *Ordering Power* and Levitsky, Steven and Way, Lucan A., 2012, *Beyond Patronage.*
48 Reuter, Ora J., Gandhi, Jennifer, 2011, *Economic Performance and Elite Defection from Hegemonic Parties.*
49 Boix, Carles and Svolik, Milan W., 2013, *The Foundations of Limited Authoritarian Government.*
50 Slater, Dan, 2010, *Ordering Power*, p. 17.
51 Bergès, Michel, 2011, *Engagement Politique et Distanciation.*
52 Duverger, Maurice, 1958 (1951), *Les Partis Politiques [Political Parties].*
53 LaPalombara, Joseph and Weiner, Myron, 1966, *Political Parties and Political Development.*
54 Shambaugh, David L., 2008, *China's Communist Party.*
55 Shandong University, 2012, 如何認識當今世界的政黨政治.
56 Roberts, Sean P., 2012, *Putin's United Russia Party*, p. 157.
57 Levitsky, Steven and Way, Lucan A., 2010, *Competitive Authoritarianism*, p. 63.
58 For a noteworthy exception, see Svolik, Milan W., 2012, *The Politics of Authoritarian Rule.*
59 Gandhi, Jennifer, 2008, *Political Institutions under Dictatorship.*
60 Wang Yuhua, 2015, *Tying the Autocrat's Hands*, p. 158.
61 Gandhi, Jennifer, 2008, *Political Institutions under Dictatorship.*
62 Magaloni, Beatriz and Kricheli, Ruth, 2010, *Political Order and One-Party Rule*, p. 126.
63 Boix, Carles and Svolik, Milan W., 2013, *The Foundations of Limited Authoritarian Government.*
64 Brancati, Dawn, 2014, *Democratic Authoritarianism*, p. 314.
65 Carma Hinton's multifaceted and thoroughly researched documentary film on the 1989 Tian'anmen protests in Beijing makes this politically uncomfortable observation. Hinton, Carma, 1995, *Tian'an men* (video recording).
66 Wang Yongbing, 2010, 黨內民主的制度創新與路徑選擇, p. 106.
67 The best description of the petitioning reality is Zhao Liang's documentary film 上訪 *Petition.*

68 Edin, Maria, 2003, *State Capacity and Local Agent Control in China.*
69 Diamond, Larry Jay, 2002, *Thinking about Hybrid Regimes.*
70 Chestnut Greitens, Sheena, 2016, *Dictators and Their Secret Policy.*
71 Marshall, Monty G., Gurr, Ted R. and Jaggers, Keith, 2014, *Polity.*
72 These are all regimes with a Polity IV score below six.
73 Gandhi, Jennifer, 2008, *Political Institutions under Dictatorship.*
74 Hess, Hartmut, 2005, *Parteien in Äthiopien.*
75 Blaydes, Lisa, 2011, *Elections and Distributive Politics in Mubarak's Egypt.*
76 Masoud, Tarek, 2011, *The Road to (and from) Liberation Square.*
77 Elizabeth J. Perry makes a comparable argument with respect to China. Even if the CCP were to fall in the near future, political scientists still would need to explain why the regime had been able to hang on for so long. Perry, Elizabeth J., 2011, *From Mass Campaigns to Managed Campaigns.*
78 Levitsky, Steven and Way, Lucan A., 2010, *Competitive Authoritarianism,* p. 73.
79 Grzymala-Busse, Anna, 2011, *Time Will Tell? Temporality and the Analysis of Causal Mechanisms and Processes,* p. 13.
80 Reuter, Ora J., Gandhi, Jennifer, 2011, *Economic Performance and Elite Defection from Hegemonic Parties.*
81 Economists define a recession as "a period of declining real incomes and rising unemployment." Mankiw, N. Gregory, 2007, *Principles of Economics,* p. 739. According to Chinese statistics, 1989 was the only year with declining real income.
82 Wen Jiabao famously made the connection between growth and stability (see "Slowdown threatens stability, says PM," *Financial Times,* November 3, 2008). Since then the seemingly arbitrary number of 8 percent has emerged in debates as a magic threshold, but is revised downward in light of new economic realities.
83 This ideal point certainly is not 100 percent. Different authoritarian regimes take a different stance as to whether their party should be an elite organization or a mass organization. Most authoritarian parties aim for attracting about 10 percent of the population into the party.
84 Phillips, Kristen D., 2009, *Building the Nation from the Hinterlands,* chapter 5.
85 Chaligha, Amon, 2008, *The 2004 Neighbourhood, Hamlet, and Village Council Elections,* pp. 57–68
86 Colton, Timothy J., 2008, *Yeltsin,* esp. p. 408.
87 Stoner-Weiss, Kathryn, 2006, *Resistance to the Central State on the Periphery.*
88 Remington, Thomas F., 2013, *Putin, the Parliament, and the Party System,* p. 46f.
89 Roberts, Sean P., 2012, *Putin's United Russia Party,* chapter 5.
90 Ross, Cameron, 2009, *Local Politics and Democratization in Russia,* p. 156.
91 Brownlee, Jason, 2007, *Authoritarianism in an Age of Democratization,* chapter 4.

92 Smith, Benjamin B., 2007, *Hard Times in the Lands of Plenty*, p. 122.
93 Levitsky, Steven and Way, Lucan A., 2012, *Beyond Patronage*, p. 869.
94 Anecdotal accounts suggest that the number of protesters and victims might have been higher outside Beijing than inside Beijing. In the absence of reliable information, it is impossible to verify this suspicion. Police reports that have been smuggled out of the country clearly indicate that the conventional focus on Beijing does not do justice to the nationwide nature of the movement. Zhang Liang, 2001, *The Tiananmen Papers*.
95 Levitsky, Steven and Way, Lucan A., 2012, *Beyond Patronage*.
96 Zolberg, Aristide R., 1966, *Creating Political Order*, p. 95.
97 Chestnut Greitens, Sheena, 2016, *Dictators and Their Secret Policy*.
98 Magaloni, Beatriz and Kricheli, Ruth, 2010, *Political Order and One-Party Rule*, p. 125.
99 Suwa, Kazuyuki, 2004, 中国共産党の幹部管理政策.
100 Shefter, Martin, 1994, *Political Parties and the State*.
101 DeVido, Elise Anne, 1995, *The Making of the Communist Party-State in Shandong Province*.
102 Hess, Hartmut, 2005, *Parteien in Äthiopien*, p. 6. From today's perspective, these businesses have nothing to do with the state. At their historical origin, they were state monopolies, but through "privatization" ended up as a property of the party.
103 Phillips, Kristen D., 2009, *Building the Nation from the Hinterlands*, chapter 5.
104 Port, Andrew I., 2007, *Conflict and Stability in the German Democratic Republic*, p. 126.
105 Kim, Jin Ha, 2009, *Caging the Reasons of State*, chapter 4 and p. 325.
106 Zolberg, Aristide R., 1966, *Creating Political Order*, pp. 93–105.
107 Faust, Aaron, 2012, *The Ba'thification of Iraq*, p. 310.
108 Mas-Colell, Andreu, Whinston, Michael D. and Green, Jerry, 1995, *Microeconomic Theory*, section 13.D.
109 This is a finding of Mark Allinson's analysis of the official party training program. Allinson, Mark, 2013, *Das Parteilehrjahr der SED*.
110 Lingg, Anton, 1939, *Die Verwaltung der Nationalsozialistischen Deutschen Arbeiterpartei [The Administration of the German National-Socialist Workers Party]*, p. 163.
111 Zolberg, Aristide R., 1966, *Creating Political Order*, p. 96.
112 NSDAP Reichsorganisationsamt, 1935, *Partei-Statistik [Party Statistics]*, p. 22.
113 Lingg, Anton, 1939, *Die Verwaltung der Nationalsozialistischen Deutschen Arbeiterpartei [The Administration of the German National-Socialist Workers Party]*.
114 NSDAP, 1939, *Das Gesicht der Partei [The Face of the Party]*, p. 3.
115 Institut für Zeitgeschichte, 1983–1992, *Akten der Partei-Kanzlei der NSDAP*, vol. 1, no. 10443.
116 Fröhlich, Elke, 1996, *Die Tagebücher*, part II, vol. 14, p. 158.
117 Liu Shaoqi, 1950, *On the Party*, p. 3.

118 Prefectural archives that I visited in Shandong have extraordinarily detailed sociopolitical data, often village by village.

119 Luo Yanjun, 2013, 革命與秩序.

120 The central government carefully tailors its guidelines for local party leaders, depending on the social environment in which they work. CCP, 2001, 黨支部工作手冊. Similarly, in their annual reports, subordinate party organizations, like Shandong's Party Committee, report separately on party construction in education, industry, rural areas, urban neighborhoods, and government administration. CCP Shandong, 2004–2013, 中共山東年鑑.

121 Perry, Elizabeth J., 2014, *Citizen Contention and Campus Calm.*

122 Perry, Elizabeth J., 2012, *The Illiberal Challenge of Authoritarian China.*

123 CCP Organization Department, 2007, 中國共產黨組織工作教程, pp. 113f.

124 Faust, Aaron, 2012, *The Ba'thification of Iraq*, p. 10.

125 Gerth, Hans, 1940, *The Nazi Party*, p. 540.

126 The standardized procedure is known as "12388 Process," after the telephone hotline for that purpose. Nowadays, denunciations can be transmitted via the internet on specialized homepages 舉報網站, set up by the Disciplinary Inspection Commission. After leading the visitor to the right jurisdiction or government branch, the website has a prominently placed button marked: "I want to denounce!" 「我要舉報」http://www.12388.gov.cn/, last checked August 2014.

127 The last head of State Security, Erich Mielke, is said to have used this expression.

128 Zhou Zhongwei, 2000, 群眾性事件研究.

129 Zhou Zhongwei, 2000, 群眾性事件研究, p. 157.

130 The Ministry of State Security routinely and openly sends its agents to visit and interview citizens, especially ahead of sensitive events and significant anniversaries, to learn about the quickly changing attitudes among the people.

131 Marshall, Monty G., Gurr, Ted R. and Jaggers, Keith, 2014, *Polity IV Project.*

132 I use the common term "hybrid regimes." The Polity IV Project refers to this group as "anocracies."

133 This calculation combines the Polity IV data with world population data from the World Bank and for Taiwan with data from the Republic of China.

134 One count has has identified *seven* authoritarian regimes without any parties, mostly Middle Eastern oil-rich monarchies: Bahrain, Libya, Oman, Qatar, Saudi Arabia, Swaziland and the United Arab Emirates. Cheibub, José Antonio, Gandhi, Jennifer, Vreeland, James Raymond, 2010, *Democracy and Dictatorship Revisited.*

135 According to my estimate, there are 16 regimes of this type. Table 2.1 lists the 25 most populous non-democratic regimes. Out of 24 regimes that have parties, 6 regimes (or 25%) do not have regime parties. Assuming that among the remaining 39 less populous regimes with parties (not counting the ones without parties) (also 25%) are lacking a regime party, then there would be 6 regimes without regime parties in populous countries and 9.75 regimes without regime parties in less populous countries.

136   Damit, Mohamad Yusop bin Awang, 2002, *Negara Brunei Darussalam*, p. 88f.
137   This is the official count by researchers at the Central Committee of the CCP Zhou Yuyun, 2012, 如何認識當今世界的政黨政治.
138   Dagiev, Dagikhudo, 2014, *Regime Transition in Central Asia*, chapter 8.
139   Scheurig, Bodo, 1970, *Einf.*
140   Conze, Eckart, Frei, Norbert, Hayes, Peter and Zimmermann, Moshe, 2010, *Das Amt ind die Vergangenheit*, p. 695.
141   Falter, Jürgen W., 2016, *Was wissen wir.*
142   The literature on the Sozialistische Einheitspartei Deutschlands is abundant. In German, detailed studies look into the previously most secret micromechanisms of authoritarian control at the grassroots level. Kupke, Martin, 2012, *SED ind MfS im Kirchenbezirk Meissen [The Socialist Unity Party and the Ministry for State Security in the Church District of Meissen].*
143   Port, Andrew I., 2007, *Conflict and Stability in the German Democratic Republic.*
144   Montgomery, Bruce P., 2011, *Immortality in the Secret Police Files.*
145   Faust, Aaron, 2012, *The Ba'thification of Iraq.*
146   Tilly, Charles, 1975, *Reflections on the History of European State-Making*, p. 42.
147   Duverger, Maurice, 1958 (1951), *Les Partis Politiques [Political Parties].*
148   Huntington, Samuel P., 2006 (1968), *Political Order in Changing Societies*, p. 424f.
149   My translation of Manoïlescu, Mihaïl, 1937, *Le Parti Unique*, p. 161.
150   Translated from a French translation.Manoïlescu, Mihaïl, 1937, *Le Parti Unique*, p. 163, fn. 1.
151   Liu Shaoqi, 1980, 黨論.
152   Selznick, Philip, 1952, *The Organizational Weapon*, chapter 1.
153   Jowitt, Kenneth, 1992, *New World Disorder*, p. 122 and p. 314.
154   Slater, Dan, 2010, *Ordering Power.*
155   Huntington, Samuel P., 1970, *Social and Institutional Dynamics of One-Party Systems*, p. 12 and p. 14.
156   Slater, Dan, 2010, *Ordering Power.*
157   Perry, Elizabeth J., 2007, *Studying Chinese Politics*, p. 22, fn. 98.
158   Levitsky, Steven and Way, Lucan A., 2010, *Beyond Patronage*, note 29.
159   Phillips, Kristen D., 2009, *Building the Nation from the Hinterlands*, chapter 5.
160   Perry in her above-mentioned remark counts five cases. For the regression analysis, one would have to include cases both of the five surviving and the larger number of perished Communist regimes.
161   Namely during the Great Leap Forward (1958–1961) and during the early Cultural Revolution (1966–1971).
162   Jowitt, Kenneth, 1992, *New World Disorder*, p. vii.
163   Griffiths, John, 1988, *The Cuban Communist Party.*
164   Armstrong, Charles K., 2003, *The Korean Revolution 1945–1950.*
165   Pepper, Suzanne, 2004, *The Political Odyssey of an Intellectual Construct.*
166   Barro, Roberto J. and Sala-i-Martin, Xavier I., 1995, *Economic Growth.*

167 Tilly, Charles, 1986, *The Contentious French*.
168 Perry, Elizabeth J., 1992, *Introduction*.
169 Ertman, Thomas, 1997, *Birth of the Leviathan*, summarized on pp. 25–28.
170 Shefter, Martin, 1994, *Political Parties and the State*.
171 Selznick, Philip, 1952, *The Organizational Weapon*.
172 Jowitt, Kenneth, 1992, *New World Disorder*.
173 Huang Yasheng, 1996, *Inflation and Investment Controls in China*.
174 Chan, Hon S., 2004, *Cadre Personnel Management in China*.
175 Perry, Elizabeth J., 2011, *From Mass Campaigns to Managed Campaigns*.
176 An Zuozhang, 2011, 中國史部研究.
177 Pye, Lucian W., 1988, *The Mandarin and the Cadre*, esp. pp. 30–35.
178 Zheng Yongnian, 2010, *The Chinese Communist Party as Organizational Emperor*.
179 Yu, George T., 1966, *Party Politics in Republican China*.
180 Feng Yuan, 1995, *From the Imperial Examination to the National College Entrance Examination*.
181 For the relationship between Manchu rulers and Han officials, see Elliott, Mark C., 2001, *The Manchu Way*.
182 In other contexts as well, authors point out that states may strategically choose to be stronger in some places than others. Boone, Catherine, 2012, *Territorial Politics and the Reach of the State*.
183 Heilmann, Sebastian, 2011, *Policy-Making through Experimentation*.
184 Alisha Holland investigates how law is applied differently in different places, noting that governments have good reasons to practice forbearance in some places, but not others. Holland, Alisha C., 2015, *The Distributive Politics of Enforcement*, reminiscent of the Chinese approach to law enforcement. Wang Yuhua, 2015, *Tying the Autocrat's Hands*.
185 Koss, Daniel, 2017, *Political Geography of Empire*
186 Huntington, Samuel P., 1991, *The Third Wave*.
187 Levitsky, Steven and Way, Lucan A., 2010, *Competitive Authoritarianism*.
188 Based on a conversation with a Vietnamese living in Tokyo, 2015.
189 see "Bundessatzung der Freien Demokratischen Partei" [Federal Statutes of the Free Democratic Party], May 4th, 2013 version.
190 Yu, George T., 1966, *Party Politics in Republican China*, chapter 2.
191 Pak, Tu-jin, 2008, 朝鮮総連, Kim, Ch'an-juong, 2004, 朝鮮連 and Ryang, Sonia, 1997, *North Koreans in Japan*.
192 For election results, see http://www.ipu.org/parline-e/reports/arc/2085_09.htm, last checked June 25, 2014.
193 This has been a recurring topic in my conversations with Chinese students already in the United States, as well as Chinese students interested in coming to the United States.
194 For example, at Minnan Normal University in 2011, the department of foreign languages could only recruit 77 percent of the target party members, whereas most other departments at the school overfulfilled their targets. 關於制定2012年發張黨員計劃數的通知 [Circular on the Party Membership Recruitment Plan for 2012], found at http://zzb.mnnu.edu.cn/News_View.asp?NewsID=341, last checked July 2014.

195 Such an initiative is based at Hunan University, Foreign Language Institute and the School of International Education
196 We find this in Britain at Manchester University.
197 Nanjing Telecommunications University is trying out such a mixed approach.
198 Rare exceptions include Svolik, Milan W., 2012, *The Politics of Authoritarian Rule.*

Chapter 3

1 In October 2015 the Central Committee decided to henceforth allow couples to have two children.
2 Foucault, Michel, 2004, *S.*
3 Magaloni, Beatriz and Kricheli, Ruth, 2010, *Political Order and One-Party Rule*, p. 125.
4 The term is offensive, but a direct translation of the officially used Chinese technical term 超生.
5 The model itself is in the appendix.
6 Perry, Elizabeth J., 2011, *From Mass Campaigns to Managed Campaigns.*
7 Schurmann, Franz, 1966, *Ideology and Organization in Communist China.*
8 Hough, Jerry F., 1969, *The Soviet Prefects*, chapter 8.
9 Rutland, Peter, 1992, *The Politics of Economic Stagnation in the Soviet Union.*
10 Kim, Hyung-A, 2004, *Korea's Development under Park Chung Hee.*
11 Scalapino, Robert A., 1953, *Democracy and the Party Movement in Prewar Japan.*
12 Gill, Bates and Huang, Yanzhong, 2006, *Sources and Limits of Chinese 'Soft Power'* discusses China's attractiveness as a role model for non-Western countries.
13 The 2010 census counted a total of 18 million officials throughout China. This compares to 6.6 party members working as officials at the end of 2009, according to a governmental press release entitled "截至2009年底中國共產黨黨員人數達7799.5萬名" [By the end of 2009, CCP membership reached 77.99 mio members]. Since the term official does not distinguish between party agencies and government offices, and since there are more party members serving in higher-level authorities, the proportion of bureaucrats in local government would be substantively smaller than 6.6 mio/18.4 mio = 35.9 percent.
14 Compare the 2016 press release by the Organization Department entitled "2015年中國共產黨黨內統計公報" [Report on CCP Party Statistics of the Year 2015].
15 Barnett, A. Doak, 1967, *Cadres, Bureaucracy, and Political Power in Communist China.*
16 Lieberthal, Kenneth G., 1980, *Policy Making in China.*
17 See Section 3.3.2.

18 Jäger, Wolfgang, 1973, *Partei und System [Party and System]*, p. 13.

19 Ganev makes this observation and in endnote 1 gives a review of literature suggesting the interwoven nature of the two during the Communist era. Ganev, Venelin, 2001, *Separation of Party and State as a Logistical Problem.*

20 Zheng Shiping, 1997, *Party vs. State in Post-1949 China.*

21 Yang, Dali L., 2004, *Remaking the Chinese Leviathan.*

22 Schurmann, Franz, 1966, *Ideology and Organization in Communist China*, p. 111.

23 Lieberthal, Kenneth G., 1988, *Policy Making in China.*

24 Observing successful implementation is not enough, because success could also be the result of "luck" for which the agent should not be rewarded.

25 "[P]olitical institutions are unfortunately not simply the product, in a mechanical fashion, of particular social 'needs' at particular moments." Ziblatt, Daniel, 2006, *Structuring the State*, preface.

26 On the role of the militiary and its relationship to the party and the government, see Lim, Jaehwan, 2014, 人民解放軍と中国政治.

27 Vogel, Ezra F., 2011, *Deng Xiaoping and the Transformation of China.*

28 CCP, 1981, *Resolutionx on Certain Questions in the History of Our Party since the Founding of the People's Republic of China.*

29 Joseph Fewsmith has given a comprehensive analysis of post-Tian'anmen elite debates. Fewsmith, Joseph, 2001, *China since Tiananmen.*

30 Dickson, Bruce J., 2003, *Red Capitalists in China.*

31 Wan, Jiyao, 2013, 論黨的道路自信，理論自信，制度自信.

32 Chen Fangmeng, 2010, 轉型社會中的中國共產黨.

33 Kenneth Lieberthal's term. Lieberthal, Kenneth G., 1995, *Governing China* remains frequently used, even if related and attractive alternatives/complementary characterizations have emerged, such as "contentious authoritarianism." Chen Xi, 2012, *Social Protest and Contentious Authoritarianism in China*; "decentralized authoritarianism" Landry, Pierre F., 2008, *Decentralized Authoritarianism in China*; and "adaptive governance" Heilmann, Sebastian and Perry, Elizabeth J., 2011, *Mao's Invisible Hand.*

34 My rosy image of foreign investment projects comes from comparing them to indigenous investment projects.

35 For a study of the origins of this policy choice, see Greenhalgh, Susan, 2003, *Science, Modernity, and the Making of China's One-Child Policy.*

36 Short, Susan E. and Zhai, Fengying, 1998, *Looking Locally at China's One-Child Policy.*

37 Ge Guoqiang, 2009, 山東省人口和計畫生育大事記.

38 Koss, Daniel, 2017, *Political Geography of Empire.*

39 This is according to the *World Development Indicators* assembled by the World Bank.

40 What is missing is disaggregated information on the average number of births given by women in different age groups.

41 Population Census Office, 2010, 中國2010年人口檢查資料, p. 2024.

42 The survey is collected and distributed online by the Carolina Population Center at the University of North Carolina at Chapel Hill.
43 With few exceptions, these births occurred after the beginning of the one-child policy in 1979.
44 Hesketh, Therese and Zhu Weixing, 2006, *Abnormal Sex Ratios in Human Populations.*
45 This is from the last paragraph of a book which for the most part argues a more moderate view on sex ratios and violence. Hudson, Valerie M. and den Boer, Andrea M., 2004, *Bare Branches*, p. 262.
46 Ownby, David, 2002, *Approximations of Chinese Bandits*, esp. pp. 240–245.
47 Zeng Yi et al., 1993, *Causes and Implications of the Recent Increase in the Reported Sex Ratio at Birth in China.*
48 Sen, Amartya, 1990, *More Than 100 Million Women Are Missing.*
49 The gender ratio of the age cohort of children under age 1 stands in for the true sex ratio at birth.
50 The Chinese Internet can tell anyone about how to determine an embryo's gender.
51 Goodkind, Daniel M., 2004, *China's Missing Children.* Merlin, M. Giovanna and Raftery, Adrian E., 2000, *Are Births Underreported in Rural China? Manipulation of Statistical Records in Response to China's Population Policies.*
52 Shi, Yaojiang and Kennedy, John J., 2016, *Delayed Registration and Identifying the "Missing Girls" in China.*
53 This paragraph is based on Koss, Daniel, 2016, *Statistical Rebirths.*
54 Chu Junhong, 2001, *Prenatal Sex Determination and Sex-Selective Abortion in Rural Central China.*
55 Information from a diplomat with detailed knowledge on this issue, January 2007.
56 Use a binomial calculator, inputting values 0.485, 14, and 5.
57 To form a party cell, three party members are needed. Here I refer to administrative villages. Administrative villages can encompass several natural villages, many of which are lacking a party presence.
58 CCP Organization Department, 2006, 中國共產黨組織工作教程, p. 84.
59 It is hard to say to what degree the sex ratio at birth reflects abortions or hiding of baby girls. The Western literature tends to argue that the uneven sex ration at birth is a result of sex-selective abortions. By contrast, the Chinese literature emphasizes that many baby girls are hidden away. If the census data discussed above are any guide, the problem has shifted over time from hiding away female children to sex-selective abortions. Chu Junhong makes a compelling case that sex-selective abortions are an increasingly available option, despite all government prohibitions Chu Junhong, 2001, *Prenatal Sex Determination and Sex-Selective Abortion in Rural Central China.* I will follow Chu's interpretation. However, for the information-based argument, the absconding of children would even more clearly be a task for the party, rather than the government, because it is the ultimate form of uncertainty.

60 Lavely, William, 2001, *First Impressions from the 2000 Census* and Walfish, Daniel, 2000, *A Billion and Counting.*

61 Merlin, M. Giovanna and Raftery, Adrian E., 2000, *Are Births Underreported in Rural China? Manipulation of Statistical Records in Response to China's Population Policies.*

62 The British Medical Journal represents this view. Ding Qu Jian and Hesketh, Therese, 2006, *Family Size, Fertility Preferences, and Sex Ratio in China in the Era of the One Child Family Policy* and Zhu Wei Xing, Li Lu and Hesketh, Therese, 2009, *China's Excess Males, Sex Selective Abortion, and One Child Policy.*

63 Alternatively, the more balanced sex ratio in "red" areas with more party members could, counterintuitively, be interpreted as party members being particularly prone to helping their communities hide children.

64 Available from China Data Center of the University of Michigan at Ann Arbor. The data are released in various formats. I used a tool called China Geo-Explorer II, which shows a data visualization on a map and then allows the numerical data to be extracted from the map.

65 The national subsample is 9.5 percent, but the subsample for Shandong is almost exactly 10 percent of the population.

66 The comparison month is January.

67 Hershatter, Gail, 2011, *The Gender of Memory*, pp. 206–208.

68 Chu Junhong, 2001, *Prenatal Sex Determination and Sex-Selective Abortion in Rural Central China.*

69 White, Tyrene, 2000, *Domination, Resistance, and Accommodation in China's One-Child Campaign*, p. 179.

70 Zheng Yongnian argues for separating party and state precisely in order to answer such questions. Zheng Yongnian, 2010, *The Chinese Communist Party as Organizational Emperor.*

Chapter 4

1 Boix, Carles and Svolik, Milan W., 2013, *The Foundations of Limited Authoritarian Government.*

2 Levitsky, Steven and Way, Lucan A., 2010, *Competitive Authoritarianism.*

3 Slater, Dan, 2010, *Ordering Power*, pp. 35ff.

4 Note in particular the complementary information related to the analysis of China's rural finances, especially on the topography of taxation, in Koss, Daniel, 2016, *A Micro-Geography of State Extractive Power.*

5 One of the leading studies of the Chinese state during the Mao era is based on an analysis of the grain procurement system. Oi, Jean Chun, 1983, *State and Peasant in Contemporary China.*

6 Xu Yong, 2005, 村民自治的成长.

7 Manion, Melanie, 2006, *Democracy, Community, Trust.*

8 The realities in the village are worlds apart from self-contradictory regulation: In one – apparently still idealizing – speech, an official mentions a rule that village leaders should gain twice the average villager's income, noting that the actual remuneration is in fact unstable and inadequate, so

that one shouldn't expect too much effort from these individuals. He Yiting, 2015, 縣委書記談怎樣做四有縣委書記, p. 247. Many village leaders seem to engage in ordinary professional activities, and it is not uncommon to meet them on urban construction sites as seasonal migrant laborers.

9   Yang Hui, 2001, 農村稅費改革給基層黨組織建設提出的新要求.

10 Lam, Tong, 2011, *A Passion for Facts.*

11 This data point is for 2008, the last year when "agricultural and related taxes" are reported as a separate category in National Bureau of Statistics, various years, 中國統計年鑑.

12 Wong, Christine, 2010, *Fiscal Reform.*

13 Specifically, this concers the category "Agricultural and Related Tax." The 2008 tax yield in this category was the highest ever recorded since reporting started in 1978; see National Bureau of Statistics, various years, 中國統計年鑑.

14 According to guidelines by the statistical division of the IMF, the term "fees" is reserved for contributions charged for consuming an excusable government service, which households could decide not to consume.

15 Lieberman, Evan S., 2002, *Taxation Data as Indicators of State-Society Relations.*

16 For an elaboration on this point, see Koss, Daniel, 2016, *A Micro-Geography of State Extractive Power.*

17 Bernstein, Thomas P. and Lü Xiaobo, 2003, *Taxation without Representation in Contemporary Rural China.*

18 Kennedy, John J., 2007, *From the tax-for-fee reform to the abolition of agricultural taxes.*

19 These time horizons may be most apparent in dealing with tradeoffs between short-term growth and long-term environmental impacts. Eaton, Sarah and Kostka, Genia, 2014, *Authoritarian Environmentalism Undermined? Local Leaders' Time Horizons and Environmental Policy Implementation in China.*

20 Guo Gang, 2009, *China's Local Political Budget Cycles.*

21 Edin, Maria, 2003, *State Capacity and Local Agent Control in China.*

22 Fewsmith, Joseph, 2011, *The Elusive Search for Effective Sub-County Governance.*

23 Yep, Ray, 2004, *Can "Tax-for-Fee" reform reduce rural tension in China? The process, progress and limitations.*

24 Pransenjit Duara, even if he refers to China during the Republican era, clarifies the conceptual problems involved. Duara, Prasenjit, 1991 (1988), *Culture, Power, and the State.*

25 Oi, Jean Chun, 1999, *Rural China Takes Off.*

26 Perry, Elizabeth J., 1994, *Trends in the Study of Chinese Politics.*

27 Oi, Jean Chun, 1983, *State and Peasant in Contemporary China.*

28 Li Lianjiang and O'Brien, Kevin J., 1996, *Villagers and Popular Resistance in Contemporary China.*

29 Li Lianjiang and O'Brien, Kevin J., 1996, *Villagers and Popular Resistance in Contemporary China.*

30 Koss, Daniel, 2016, *A Micro-Geography of State Extractive Power.*

31 Dickson, Bruce J., 2016, *The Dictator's Dilemma.*
32 These two approaches are reflected in Boix, Carles and Svolik, Milan W., 2013, *The Foundations of Limited Authoritarian Government* versus Levitsky, Steven and Way, Lucan A., 2010, *Competitive Authoritarianism.*
33 Li Shuang, Lu Ming and Sato, Hiroshi, 2008, *The Value of Power in China.*
34 Later on, this chapter also presents a marginal calculation for the "optimal" size of the party for purposes of creating fiscal revenues.
35 For an overview of taxation issues see Brys, Bert, 2013, *Tax Policy and Tax Reform in the People's Republic of China.*
36 Liu Xijing, 2007, 中國增值稅流失研究 *[Study of VAT Losses in China].*
37 Shandong Department of Fiscal Affairs, Budget Office, 2007, 山東省以下財政體制.
38 While directly governed counties do not have to pay taxes to the prefectures any more, they must transfer some of the resources saved to the province. According to conversations with officials working in government finance, the provinces ask for much less than the prefecture, so that county-level officials find the status as a directly governed county a very desirable one indeed.
39 Liu Aiming, 2011, 企業所得稅特別納稅調整研究.
40 Local gazetteers, such as the Fiscal Gazetteer that is part of Shandong's Provincial Gazetteer, chronicle changes in tax regulations Shandong Province, 2010, 山東省志財政志.
41 Lü Xiaobo and Perry, Elizabeth J., 1997, *Danwei*, esp. introduction.
42 Walder, Andrew G., 1986, *Communist Neo-Traditionalism.*
43 Perry, Elizabeth J., 1993, *Shanghai on Strike.*
44 Perry, Elizabeth J., 2012, *Anyuan.*
45 Perry, Elizabeth J., 2007, *Masters of the Country? Shanghai Workers in the Early People's Republic.*
46 Lieberthal, Kenneth G., 1980, *Revolution and Tradition in Tientsin, 1949–1952.*
47 Dillon, Nara, 2015, *Radical Inequalities.*
48 Industrial workers without affiliation to an industrial party cell typically belong to a neighborhood-based party organization. The percentages are calculated based on CCP Shandong, 2004–2013, 中共山東年鑑, 2009 edition, p. 822.
49 CCP Shandong, 2004–2013, 中共山東年鑑, 2009 edition, p. 823.
50 中國共產黨有黨員8779.3萬名基層黨組織436.0萬個 [The CCP has 87.793 million members and 4.36 million basic-level organizations], Xinhua New Agency, June 29, 2015.
51 "甘肅會寧：三招讓失聯（管）黨員'歸隊'" [Gansu Province, Huining County: Three Welcomes Let Lost Party Members 'Return to the Troops'], Ninghua Government, published online August 14, 2015. Chen Zhenliang, 2012, 新時期黨的組織工作創新研究.
52 Solinger, Dorothy J., 1999, *Contesting Citizenship in Urban China.*
53 CCP Shandong, 2004–2013, 中共山東年鑑 [year 2009, pp. 822f.].
54 Liu Xijing, 2007, 中國增值稅流失研究 *[Study of VAT Losses in China].*

55 This is in addition to the its roots in the anticolonial and land reform movements. On this aspect of the party's history see Perry, Elizabeth J., 1993, *Shanghai on Strike.*

56 Chen Feng, 2010, *Trade Unions and the Quadripartite Interactions in Strike Settlement in China*, esp. p. 120.

57 CCP, 2001, 黨支部工作手冊, pp. 97f.

58 關於舉辦全區非公經濟黨員形勢任務報告會的通知 ["Circular on Meeting by Non-Public Sector Party Members of the District on Their Situation and Tasks"] 蘇高新非公委（2015）8號.

59 提升"走出去"企業稅收服務水平 ["Promoting better tax services for companies that are 'going out' "], interview published online by Liaocheng Prefecture, June 3, 2015.

60 The data sets, a detailed description of the study, and links to related publications are available from ICPSR, University of Michigan, www.icpsr.umich.edu, last checked on February 3rd, 2013.

61 Li Shi, Sato, Hiroshi and Sicular, Terry, 2013, *Rising Inequality in China.*

62 They are all subcategories of variable h1_615. Compare codebook DS5 of the CHIP data.

63 Variable h1_617a of DS5 and variable v3_208 of DS4. All CHIP data.

64 Variable h1_617b of DS5, CHIP data.

65 For example, the calculation breaks down in a village where party members gain 13 times more than an average villager, a scenario that lacks practical relevance.

66 The choice of this period is dictated by data availability: Given the data set described below, it is preferable to use slightly dated statistics rather than compromise on quality. Moreover, it would be inappropriate to use the yearly observations contained in the data, because of a high level of colinearity, especially under the same economic plan.

67 Kocher, Matthew A. and Monteiro, Nuno P., 2016, *Line of Demarcation.*

68 Chinese Finance Ministry, Budget Office, 2006, 中國省以下財政體制.

69 The source does not mention remittances from Tibet. It was not possible to find out with certainty whether there really are no remittances or whether the source chooses not to report them.

70 This is a well-known methodological concern with extreme counterfactuals. King, Gary and Zeng, Langche, 2006, *The Dangers of Extreme Counterfactuals.*

71 Quote from 中國共產黨有黨員8779.3萬名基層黨組織436.0萬個 [The CCP has 87.793 million members and 4.36 million basic-level organizations], Xinhua News Agency, June 29, 2015.

72 According to my own calculations based on CCP Organization Department, 2011, 中國共產黨黨內統計資料彙編, between 2010 and 2014 the party grew only by 7.5 million members, as opposed to 7.9 million between 2006 and 2010, which is 4.5% less.

73 Dinner conversation with a person familiar with party affairs in some Shanghai factories.

74 Same as above, Xinhua News Agency, June 20, 2015.

Chapter 5

1 Remarks on July 10, 1964, at the occasion of a meeting with representatives from the Social Democratic Party of Japan, led by Sasaki Kōzō and others Mao Zedong, 1969, 毛澤東思想萬歲, p. 533. While the quote is frequently cited on the internet in China, verification of the quote was not trivial. A reliable source is the archives of the Social Democratic Party of Japan, now at the National Diet Library in Tokyo. It is only a Japanese translation of the original quote, contained in the detailed meeting notes: もし、日本の皇軍が中国の大半を占領していなかったら、中国人民は団結して、これに反対して斗ろことができなかったし、中国共産党は権力を奪取することができなかったでしょう。 The best available Chinese version is found in Red Guard material, that is, confidential government documents confiscated and published by young Red Guards during the Cultural Revolution in their attempt to publicize the most "pure" version of Mao's thinking. The edition I used is available at Harvard-Yenching Library under call number 4292.11 2135.643(2) Red Guards, 1967–69, 毛澤東思想萬歲. The Japanese translation is very close to the Chinese quote in the Red Guard material, suggesting that the Red Guard material is authentic.
2 van de Ven, Hans J., 2010, *War and Nationalism in China 1925–1945*.
3 For a cutting-edge account of the Sino-Japanese War compare Mitter, Rana, 2013, *China's War with Japan, 1937–1945*.
4 Johnson, Chalmers A., 1962, *Peasant Nationalism and Communist Power*.
5 Lary, Diana, 2010, *The Chinese People at War*.
6 Pepper, Suzanne, 2004, *The Political Odyssey of an Intellectual Construct*.
7 Denton, Kirk A., 2014, *Exhibiting the Past*.
8 As of 2017, China's National Library shows in its catalogue only a 55-pages abbridged version, the more complete version has close to 1,000 pages. I found the long version at a tiny bookstore in China. It also exists in several libraries outside China. Second Historical Archives of China, 1994, 中國第二歷史檔案館指南.
9 Weiss, Jessica Chen, 2014, *Powerful Patriots*.
10 Compare the map before page 1 in CCP History Research Office, 1997, 中國革命老區.
11 CCP Gaoyou County, 1991, 中國共產黨江蘇省高郵縣組織史資料, p. 1.
12 CCP, 2000, 中國共產黨組織史資料, vol. 1 p. 39 and vol. 2 上 p. 68; in combination with CCP Organization Department, 2011, 中國共產黨黨內統計資料彙編, p. 7.
13 Perry, Elizabeth J., 2012, *Anyuan*, p. 144.
14 Esherick, Joseph W., 1987, *The Origins of the Boxer Uprising*.
15 Xianning Government, 1992, 咸寧市志, starting p. 873.
16 Schurmann, Franz, 1966, *Ideology and Organization in Communist China*.
17 Perry, Elizabeth J., 2007, *Masters of the Country? Shanghai Workers in the Early People's Republic*, p. 69.
18 CCP, 2000, 中國共產黨組織史資料, [vol. 3 上 p. 1]
19 Johnson, Chalmers A., 1962, *Peasant Nationalism and Communist Power*.

20 Mitter, Rana, 2013, *China's War with Japan, 1937–1945.*

21 Cohen, Paul A., 1997, *History in Three Keys.*

22 Pepper, Suzanne, 2004, *The Political Odyssey of an Intellectual Construct.*

23 Compare Wu Yuexing's map that overlays the Japanese occupied area and the Communist base areas, Wu Yuexing, 1999, 中國現代史地圖集, p. 201.

24 Chen Yung-fa, 1986, *Making Revolution*, p. 8.

25 Compare the party history of Yunnan CCP Yunnan, 1994, 中國共產黨雲南省組織史資料, p. 45 and of Shandong CCP Shandong, 1991, 中國共產黨山東省組織史資料, p. 83.

26 "中國共產黨為日軍進攻盧溝橋通電" [Telegram by the CCP on the Japanese attack at Marco Polo Bridge], July 8, 1937 Central Party School, Historical Research Office, 1997, 中共黨史參考資料, vol. 4, first document.

27 A detailed history of Zouping County during the Republican era reflects the gradual rise of the Communists. Shen, Zhijia, 1997, *Zouping, 1911–1949*, chapter 4.

28 CCP Organization Department, 1991, 中國共產黨上海市組織史資料, p. 85.

29 Mei, S. and Qiu X., 2001, 中共上海黨志, p. 305.

30 To be precise, between May 1937 and October 1939, party membership grew from 160 to 1610. Mei, S. and Qiu X., 2001, 中共上海黨志, p. 305.

31 Deng Xiaoping: "Recruiting Soldiers and Policies vis-à-vis New Recruits," January 12, 1938, in: Deng Xiaoping, 1989, 鄧小平文選.

32 Selden, Mark, 1995, *China in Revolution.*

33 Perry, Elizabeth J., 1980, *Rebels and Revolutionaries in North China, 1845–1945.*

34 Kataoka, Tetsuya, 1972, *Review.*

35 Pepper, Suzanne, 2004, *The Political Odyssey of an Intellectual Construct.*

36 Chen Yung-fa, 1986, *Making Revolution*, p. 8.

37 Schurmann, Franz, 1966, *Ideology and Organization in Communist China.*

38 Academia Sinica, Institute of Modern History, 2000, 中華民國史事日誌.

39 CASS 183, p. 248.

40 Wu Yuexing, 1999, 中國現代史地圖集.

41 Gordon, Andrew, 2003, *A Modern History of Japan.*

42 Internal party statisics, see: CCP Organization Department, 2011, 中國共產黨黨內統計資料彙編. This source from the national party headquarters indicates that no data exist for Tibet in 1956. However, provincial party headquarters report the number shown in the table: CCP Tibet, 1993, 中國共產黨西藏自治區組織史資料.

43 See Wu Yuexing, 1999, 中國現代史地圖集, p. 198. The original map excludes areas of the country, whose status is well-known (such as large parts of Manchuria). These areas are coded consistently with the rest of the map.

44 For the distinction between direct and indirect effects, as well as a definition of a mediator, see Acharya, Avidit, Blackwell, Matthew and Sen, Maya, 2015, *Detecting Direct Effects and Assessing Alternative Mechanisms.*

45 Acharya, Avidit, Blackwell, Matthew and Sen, Maya, 2016, *Explaining Causal Findings without Bias.*

46 This cannot be done, because the exclusionary restriction does not hold: Japanese occupation may well affect contemporary outcomes through intermediary variables other than patterns of party membership. Arguably, patterns of party membership are the most important, but not necessarily the only intermediary variable.

47 Japanese Defense Agency, 1968–1971, 北支の治安戦.

48 The boundaries of the counties changed greatly. The map defines Linyi by the boundaries of 1988.

49 Hsu Long-hsuen and Chang Ming-kai, 1971, *History of the Sino-Japanese War (1937–1945)*, p. 227.

50 CCP Linyi, 1988, 中國共產黨山東省臨沂市組織史資料, p. 119.

51 CCP Chiping, 1989, 中國共產黨山東省茌平縣組織史資料, p. 9.

52 CCP Chiping, 1989, 中國共產黨山東省茌平縣組織史資料, p. 9., CCP Linyi, 1988, 中國共產黨山東省臨沂市組織史資料, after p. 6.

53 Paulson, David Mark, 1982, *War and Revolution in North China*, p. 47.

54 CASS 181.

55 CASS 181, p. 17.

56 CASS 181, pp. 109–121.

57 CASS 181, pp. 107–108.

58 Tōyō Bunko 3, p. 33.

59 Tōyō Bunko 3, p. 33.

60 These pathways are described for numerous early organizers Civil Affairs Department of Shandong Provinces, 1984, 山東省著名革命烈士英名錄 [Name List of Outstanding Revolutionary Martyrs in Shandong]. I have the section concerning Heze, a peripheral prefecture.

61 Wang, Yu-chuan, 1940, *The Organization of a Typical Guerrilla Area in South Shantung*, p. 92.

62 Such as CASS 181.

63 Wang, Yu-chuan, 1940, *The Organization of a Typical Guerrilla Area in South Shantung*, p. 94.

64 Luo Yanjun, 2013, 革命與秩序.

65 Wu, David Mark, 2005, *The Role of Class Struggle in the Chinese Communist Party's Social Reform*, p. 54.

66 DeVido, Elise Anne, 1995, *The Making of the Communist Party-State in Shandong Province*, p. 58.

67 Shandong Archive, A121-04-21.

68 The number of "notable martyrs" is derived for each county in a standardized procedure. The Department of Civil Affairs had lists of martyrs, which have been compiled in order to determine which families deserve support as descendants from a revolutionary martyr. From this list a sample of "notable martyrs" is drawn (see endnote above), the number of "notable martyrs" being proportional to the number of all martyrs.

69 Kuwatarō, Baba, 1938, 北支八省の資源.

70 Kahoku Kōtsū Kabushiki Kaisha, 1939–1943, 北支現地編輯, vol. 1–6.

71 Tōyō Bunko 1. Such explorations were abundant, as a voluminous compilation by Japanese researchers shows. Honjō, Hisako, 2009, 戦前期華北実態調査の目録と解題.

72 Gordon, Andrew, 2003, *A Modern History of Japan* and Hall, John Whitney, 1966, *Government and Local Power in Japan, 500 to 1700*.

73 Kahoku Sōgō Chōsa Kenkyūjo, 1944, 華北農業統計調査県調査班調査要綱.

74 Tokyo Tōyō Bunko 2.

75 Kahoku Kōtsū Kabushiki Kaisha, 1939–1943, 北支現地編輯, vol. 1–6.

76 Snyder, Jack, 1991, *Myths of Empire*.

77 Pomeranz, Kenneth, 1993, *The Making of a Hinterland*.

78 Japanese Defense Agency, 1968–1971, 北支の治安戦, map.

79 Although the timing of construction was such that the trunk line was finalized only after the branch line.

80 Perry, Elizabeth J., 2007, *Studying Chinese Politics*, fn. 98.

81 Levitsky, Steven and Way, Lucan A., 2012, *Beyond Patronage*, p. 870.

Chapter 6

1 CCP History Research Office, 2011, 中國共產黨歷史, p. 90.

2 These high correlations occur despite the statistical noise resulting from shifting boundaries. Since 1956 the number of province-level jurisdictions increased from 28 to 31: Chongqing was split out of Sichuan, Ningxia out of Gansu, and Hainan out of Guangdong. The source does not report data for Tibet in 1956. Compare CCP Organization Department, 2011, 中國共產黨黨內統計資料彙編.

3 This is the R^2 of a bivariate regression model.

4 Banerjee, Abhijit V. and Duflo, Esther, 2014, *Under the Thumb of History? Political Institutions and the Scope for Action*.

5 Pierson, Paul, 2004, *Politics in Time*.

6 Wakeman, Frederic, 2007, *"Cleanup"*.

7 Vogel, Ezra F., 1969, *Canton under Communism*.

8 中央同意中央組織部關於今後接收黨員工作的意見 [The Central Committee agrees with the opinion by the Organization Department on the future admittance of party members], promulgated on December 7, 1958, found in PLA Artillery, Political Department, Organization Department, 1956, 組織工作文件匯集，機密, pp. 112–114.

9 The world of Chinese internal documents is full of seeming contradictions. In the case of this publication, the secrecy of the document is a legal fact, gives authors freedom to write more openly than in a public document, and produces unusual content. The secrecy is also enforced on the internet, where at the time of writing it was hard to find even a single leaked document. However, given 230,000 printed hard copies, the government seems to have given up on their circulation – so much so that some libraries more or less obliviously put the magazine on their shelves. Recently, the

magazine is no longer classified and has become less useful for studying the party. On the system of internal reference, see Tsai, Wen-Hsuan, 2015, *A Unique Pattern of Policymaking in China's Authoritarian Regime*.

10 CCP Organization Department, 2011, 中國共產黨黨內統計資料彙編, p. 368.
11 Shandong Government, 1984/85, 山東省行政區劃資料, p. 1.
12 CCP Organization Department, 2011, 中國共產黨黨內統計資料彙編, p. 369.
13 Dickson, Bruce J., 2003, *Red Capitalists in China*, Walder, Andrew G., 2004, *The Party Elite and China's Trajectory of Change* and Tsai, Kellee, 2006, *Adaptive Informal Institutions and Endogenous Institutional Change in China*.
14 Party document from Jinan.
15 The numbers are from Pingyao County's 平遙縣 recruitment plan for 2009. Document available from the author.
16 Zhang Shun and Yu Zhanghai, 2003, 發展指標不等於發展計劃.
17 When Organization Departments give out recruitment quotas for the coming year, they may also ask for justification of underperformance in the preceding year, e.g., Organization Department of the CCP Committee at Zhangzhou Normal Institute 中共漳州師範學院委員會組織部: "Notification Concerning the Membership Development Plan Targets for 2012" 關於制定2012年發展黨員計劃數的通知. Document found online, also available from the author.
18 Chen Fangmeng, 2010, 轉型社會中的中國共產黨 and Chen Zhenliang, 2012, 新時期黨的組織工作創新研究.
19 In general, the mixture of technocratic and Marxist jargon does not help to understand what problems on the ground the authors have in mind. Under supervision of Professor Lei Fang at Shandong University, students wrote about challenges of party building, including case studies. Ge Renshui, 2011, 城市化進程中基層電子黨務管理研究, but it is necessary to talk to Fang Lei or his students to discern the specific meanings.
20 Liu Bo, 2011, 西藏中共黨組織第一支部創建史初探.
21 Zhong Shilu, 2010, 中國共產黨在邊疆少數民族地區執政方略研究 p. 231.
22 These statistics draw from CCP Organization Department, 2011, 中國共產黨黨內統計資料彙編.
23 Report by a Western diplomat, written in 2007.
24 Zhang Yuebin, Mei Hua and Liu Gong, 2000, 實行發展黨員公示制的探索.
25 I am thinking of many volumes of investigation material, making up the bulk of the pre-1949 material in Liaocheng's Prefectural Archive.
26 This is according to a conversation with a Chinese professor and another conversation with a foreign journalist.
27 CCP Organization Department, 2011, 中國共產黨黨內統計資料彙編
28 CCP Shandong, 2004–2013, 中共山東年鑑.
29 This graph is based on data from a compilation of internal party statistics CCP Organization Department, 2011, 中國共產黨黨內統計資料彙編, pp. 78f.

30 The categorization of recruitment eras follows the one laid out in the source. CCP Shandong, 2002–2003, 中共山東年鑑 and CCP Shandong, 2004–2013, 中共山東年鑑.

31 CCP Organization Department, 2011, 中國共產黨黨內統計資料彙編, p. 22.

32 CCP Organization Department, 2011, 中國共產黨黨內統計資料彙編, p. 75.

33 CCP Shandong, 2004–2013, 中共山東年鑑, 2013 edition, p. 763.

34 CCP Shandong, 2004–2013, 中共山東年鑑, 2005 edition, p. 272.

35 A second approach consisted in redrawing district boundaries, also to dilute the problem: That is part of the reason why Qingdao abolished the districts of Sifang and Shibei.

36 Conversation in 2013 with a professor at Central China Normal University, who specializes on migrant workers and is observing efforts of the party to penetrate these migrant communities.

37 CCP Organization Department, 2015, 入黨實務教程, pp. 98–106.

38 The introduction letter was found online, properly filled and with the party's seal of approval. Only the portion to be retained by the sending party cell was missing.

39 In the traditional state-owned companies sector, the party is playing a well-rehearsed mediating labor conflict. On the role of the CCP within the history of Chinese labor politics, see Elizabeth Perry. Perry, Elizabeth J., 1993, *Shanghai on Strike*.

40 Jiang Shu, 2013, 國有企業如何應對黨員發展中存在的問題.

41 CCP Shandong, 2004–2013, 中共山東年鑑, 2013 edition, p. 738.

42 Dillon, Nara, 2011, *Governing Civil Society*.

43 Thornton, Patricia M., 2013, *The Advance of the Party*.

44 Leafing through Shandong's party organization yearbook, examples abound. CCP Shandong, 2004–2013, 中共山東年鑑. I first became aware of these penetration attempts through a conversation in 2011 with a journalist in Shanghai.

45 For a discussion of the party's presence in nongovernmental organizations and the phenomenon of Party-organized nongovernmental organizations (PONGOs), see Thornton, Patricia M., 2013, *The Advance of the Party*.

46 CCP Anhui, Task Force of the Organization Department, 2000, 法輪功向黨內滲透的主要特點及其危害.

47 PLA Artillery, Political Department, Organization Department, 1956, 組織工作文件匯集, 機密, p. 35.

48 CCP Organization Department, 1992, 組織工作文件選編，機密.

49 CCP Shandong, 2002–2003, 中共山東年鑑.

50 Since it is cumbersome, if not impossible, to collect similar statistics for all of China, this analysis is limited to Shandong Province. Until 2003 the province had only 139 counties, but Lanshan District, which was established in 2004, had already been listed separately in party membership statistics since 2001. For 2012, there are only 138 observations, because two urban districts of Qingdao, Sifang and Jiaonan were abolished during that year. The Hu era began in 2002, so that 2001 data are an ideal baseline.

51 The following localities failed to report party membership for certain years: Sishui and Taishan for 2001, Tianqiao for 2005 and 2006, Yanzhou for

2007. Since there are missing observations for the independent variables as well, additional observations will be lost depending on the specification.

52 With rare exceptions, party membership is increasing from year to year, in almost every county.

53 Investigating the extreme values, I identified one observation that did appear like a reporting error. Dongping 東平 for 2003 reports half as many party members as the year before and after; the local rectification campaign of that year does not explain such kind of variation. In two other cases the redrawing of jurisdictional boundaries distorted the statistics.

54 The China Data Center, University of Michigan at Ann Arbor, provides this data through China Geo-Explorer II.

55 This number is calculated based on exit rates of recent years in CCP Organization Department, 2011, 中國共產黨黨內統計資料彙編. This assumption implies that by the end of 2011, 24 percent of all party members in Shandong had been recruited after 2002.

56 To minimize standard deviation, recruitment should proceed in a way to equalize penetration in the 112 counties without a recruitment stop. Knowing that overall there were 923,488 new recruits penetration in these counties can be brought to 4.8 percent. In conjunction with the penetration rates in the counties with a recruitment stop, this results in the reported standard deviation of 0.784 percent.

57 Bo Yibo, 1997, 若干重大決策與事件的回顧.

58 Guo Yucai, 2000, 建國前入黨的農村老黨員教育管理情況調查.

59 Goodman, David S.G., 2000, *Revolutionary Women and Women in the Revolution*.

60 Perry, Elizabeth J., 2012, *Anyuan*.

61 Vogel, Ezra F., 1969, *Canton under Communism*, p. 41.

62 Levitsky, Steven and Way, Lucan A., 2012, *Beyond Patronage*.

63 King, Gary, 1998, *Unifying Political Methodology*, p. 167.

64 For example, one prefecture in Shandong, famous for bravery in the Sino-Japanese war, but also one of only few rural areas where the military intervened in 1989, in the wake of the Tian'anmen crisis.

65 Niemi, Richard G. and Jennings, M. Kent, 1991, *Issues and Inheritance in the Formation of Party Identification*.

66 Jennings, M. Kent and Niemi, Richard G., 1981, *Generations and Politics*.

67 Barro, Robert J. and Sala-i-Martin, Xavier I., 1992, *Convergence*.

68 For tricks to achieve this transformation, I used a standard textbook. de la Fuente, Angel, 2000, *Mathematical Methods and Models for Economists*.

69 Quah, Danny T., 1993, *Galton's Fallacy and Tests of Convergence Hypothesis*.

70 This number includes cases of readmitted party members, whose membership had previously been revoked. In the post-Mao era, such cases were on the decline and hit an all-time low of just 78 individuals in 2009. CCP Organization Department, 2011, 中國共產黨黨內統計資料彙編.

71 CCP Organization Department, 2011, 中國共產黨黨內統計資料彙編.

72 World Bank, World Development Indicators.

73 CCP Organization Department, 2011, 中國共產黨黨內統計資料彙編.

74 If we follow economists' prediction of economic convergence, there could not be such a lasting disparity.

75 Formula: $Half - Life = Initial\ Difference - \frac{Initial\ Difference - Persisting\ Disparity}{2}$, in the case of Hebei and Guangxi $HalfLife = 2.6\% - \frac{2.6\% - 0.6\%}{2}$.

76 The compound annual growth rate is computed as follows: $\sqrt[duration]{\frac{membership_t}{membership_{t-1}}} - 1$.

77 On the usefulness of simulation-based appraoches and on methodological choices involved in the calculation, compare King, Gary, Tomz, Michael and Wittenberg, Tomz, 2000, *Making the Most of Statistical Analyses*.

78 Assumption: The standard error is normally distributed with mean zero and constant standard deviation equal to the variance of the residual in the nonlinear regression.

79 Thelen, Kathleen, 2004, *How Institutions Evolve*.

80 Perry, Elizabeth J., 2012, *Anyuan*.

81 Ekiert, Grzegorz and Ziblatt, Daniel, 2012, *Democracy in Central and Eastern Europe 100 Years On*.

82 Zhao Suisheng, 1998, *A State-Led Nationalism*.

Chapter 7

1 Frank Dikötter puts the death toll at 45 million. Dikötter, Frank, 2010, *Mao's Great Famine*.

2 Mo Yan, 2001, *Shifu, You'll Do Anything for a Laugh*, "Iron Child."

3 MacFarquhar, Roderick, 1974–1994, *The Origins of the Cultural Revolution*, vol. 2, chapter 10.

4 Or two decades, depending on where in China.

5 Kung, James Kai-sing and Chen, Shuo, 2011, *The Tragedy of the Nomenklatura*.

6 Yang, Dali L., Xu Huayu and Tao Ran, 2014, *The Tragedy of the Nomenklatura? Career Incentives, Political Loyalty and Political Radicalism during China's Great Leap Forward*.

7 Yang, Dali, 1996, *Calamity and Reform in China*, pp. 58ff.

8 Dickson, Bruce J., 1997, *Democratization in China and Taiwan*, pp. 91ff.

9 Yang Kuisong, 2008, *Reconsidering the Campaign to Suppress Counterrevolutionaries*.

10 Ping Liu, 2013, *The Historical Fate of Chinese Popular Religions*.

11 Teiwes, Frederick C., 1979, *Politics and Purges in China*.

12 CCP History Research Office, 2011, 中國共產黨歷史, vol. 2, chapter 11.

13 CCP Shanghai, 2001, 中共上海黨志, p. 323.

14 CCP Organization Department, 2011, 中國共產黨黨內統計資料彙編, own calculation based on pp. 8–10 and pp. 207–208.

15 Conversation with a historian in December 2014.

16 GLF 602.

17 Bo Yibo, 1997, 若干重大決策與事件的回顧, p. 122.

18 Walder, Andrew G., 2015, *China Under Mao*, p. 162.

19 HYL 1.

20 Bo Yibo, 1997, 若干重大決策與事件的回顧, p. 111.
21 Bo Yibo, 1997, 若干重大決策與事件的回顧, p. 121.
22 CCP Shandong, 2001, 中共山東歷史大事記, pp. 310f.
23 CCP Heze, 1999, 中共山東省菏澤地區黨史大事記, p. 343.
24 Bo Yibo, 1997, 若干重大決策與事件的回顧, p. 127.
25 GLF 600.
26 CCP Linyi, 1988, 中國共產黨山東省臨沂市組織史資料.
27 CCP Shandong, 2001, 中共山東歷史大事記, p. 310.
28 The source for county-level mortality data is explained below.
29 *People's Daily*, August 27, 2957, "Rice yield jumps to over 10,000 jin, Shouzhang's Beitai Commune achieves a yield of 10,546 Jin per Mu"
30 Mu Lin, 2000, 六十年革命工作紀實, p. 341.
31 Lanshan District, 2002, 蘭山人大志.
32 Lanshan District, 2001, 蘭山區政協志.
33 CCP Liaocheng, 1998, 中共聊城歷史大事記1949.10–1998.3, p. 153.
34 CCP Liaocheng, 1998, 中共聊城歷史大事記1949.10–1998.3, p. 151.
35 GLF 603.
36 Ibid.
37 The source for county-level mortality data is explained below.
38 Walder, Andrew G., 2015, *China Under Mao*, pp. 101f.
39 The maps have been edited into a set of published maps accompanying Japanese Defense Agency, 1968–1971, 北支の治安戰.
40 Japanese Defense Agency, 1968–1971, 北支の治安戰, vol. 2, appendix 5.
41 CASS 181.
42 CCP Liaocheng, 1998, 中共聊城歷史大事記 1949.10–1998.3, p. 289f.
43 Guan County, 2001, 冠縣志.
44 Thaxton, Ralph A., 2008, *Catastrophe and Contention in Rural China*.
45 Lawson, Konrad Mitchell, 2012, *Wartime Atrocities and the Politics of Treason in the Ruins of the Japanese Empire, 1937–1953*, p. 287.
46 Vogel, Ezra F., 1969, *Canton Under Communism* and Bo Yibo, 1997, 若干重大決策與事件的回顧.
47 Himeta, Mitsuyoshi et al., 1993, 中国２０世紀史, p. 150.
48 HYL 2.
49 Mitter, Rana, 2013, *China's War With Japan, 1937–1945*, p. 374.
50 Japanese Defense Agency, 1968–1971, 北支の治安戰, accompanying map.
51 Shandong had 107 county-level jurisdictions since at least the eighteenth century until after the 1911 Revolution. By the time of the Communist takeover, the number had only marginally increased to 110 counties. By contrast, county borders had not been well-defined in the imperial era.
52 These statistics can be found in the classified volume Shandong Department of Statistics, Population Office, 1985, 山東省人口統計資料匯編, available from "Service Center of Chinese Publications."
53 Japanese Defense Agency, 1968–1971, 北支の治安戰.
54 If urban areas were systematically more embattled and less hit by the famine, this would create an overestimate the hypothesized effect of a place having been embattled.

55 Conversations in Liaocheng, fall 2012.
56 CCP, 1981, *Resolution on Certain Questions in the History of Our Party since the Founding of the People's Republic of China.*

Chapter 8

1 Author's calculations based on *China Data Online.*
2 Nathan, Andrew J., 2003, *Authoritarian Resilience*, Heberer, Thomas and Schubert, Gunter, 2006, *Political Reform and Regime Legitimacy in Contemporary China* and Cai Yongshun, 2008, *Power Structure and Regime Resilience.*
3 This does not mean, of course, that analyses of elite politics in 1967–1968 ignore questions of the regime's survival at the time. MacFarquhar, Roderick and Schoenhals, Michael, 2006, *Mao's Last Revolution* and Bu Weihua, 2008, 中華人民共和國史，第六本，「砸爛舊世界」.
4 Gourevitch, Peter Alexis, 1986, *Politics in Hard Times.*
5 Geddes, Barbara, 1999, *What Do We Know about Democratization after Twenty Years?*
6 Acemoglu, Daron and Robinson, James A., 2006, *Economic Origins of Dictatorship and Democracy*, p. 31.
7 Perry, Elizabeth J. and Li Xun, 1997, *Proletarian Power*, p. 1.
8 For more detail, see Roderick MacFarquhar's three-volume analysis of chairman Mao's decisions MacFarquhar, Roderick, 1974–1994, *The Origins of the Cultural Revolution.*
9 MacFarquhar, Roderick and Schoenhals, Michael, 2006, *Mao's Last Revolution.*
10 In particular the materials published by Song Yongyi from California State University.
11 Geddes, Barbara, 1999, *What Do We Know about Democratization after Twenty Years?*
12 MacFarquhar, Roderick and Schoenhals, Michael, 2006, *Mao's Last Revolution.*
13 Esherick, Joseph W., Pickowicz, Paul G. and Walder, Andrew, 2006, *The Chinese Cultural Revolution as History.*
14 Andrew Walder's definite analysis of the Cultural Revolution in Beijing provides penetrating detail on conflict escalation, but only spends three-and-a-half pages on the pacification of conflict. Walder, Andrew G., 2009, *Fractured Rebellion*, pp. 245–249. Classic earlier accounts provide even less of an answer to the question how it all ended. Hinton, William, 1972, *Hundred Day War.*
15 CCP, 1981, *Resolution on Certain Questions in the History of Our Party since the Founding of the People's Republic of China*, p. 47.
16 CCP, 2000, 中國共產黨組織史資料, vol. 6, pp. 1f.
17 Minutes of Zhang Chunqiao meeting with rebels at the East China Bureau. February 25, 1967. Song Yongyi, *Collection on China's Great Proletarian Cultural Revolution.*

18 Letter by Kang Sheng to all the battle groups in the Organization Department. August 24, 1967. Song Yongyi, *Collection on China's Great Proletarian Cultural Revolution.*

19 Ma Qipeng et al., 1989, 中國共產黨執政四十年, p. 292.

20 Regulation 中發(1967) 44號. February 12, 1967.

21 CCP Organization Department, 2011, 中國共產黨黨內統計資料彙編, p. 207.

22 Perkins, Dwight H., 1991, *China's Economic Policy and Performance,* pp. 480ff.

23 Mu Lin, 2000, 六十年革命工作紀實, p. 410.

24 Mu Lin, 2000, 六十年革命工作紀實, p. 424.

25 CCP Central Document Research Office, 1997, 周恩來年譜一九四九――一九七六 I also found his efforts reflected in local archives, including meeting notes in the Prefectural Archive of Weifang.

26 CRD 457.

27 CRD 457, p. 20.

28 Mu Lin, 2000, 六十年革命工作紀實, p. 411.

29 CCP Shandong, 2001, 中共山東歷史大事記, p. 551f.

30 Mu Lin, 2000, 六十年革命工作紀實, p. 412.

31 CRD 464.

32 MacFarquhar, Roderick and Schoenhals, Michael, 2006, *Mao's Last Revolution,* p. 288.

33 'Earnestly welcome the convention of a "Ninth Party Congress,"' *People's Daily,* January 2, 1969, p. 3.

34 "Circular by the Central Committee and the Central Cultural Revolution Group on soliciting opinions on the Ninth Party Congress. October 21, 1967, 中發(1967) 322號.

35 "Kang Sheng talks about preparing the new constitution of the Ninth Party Congress." November 13, 1967. Song Yongyi, *Collection on China's Great Proletarian Cultural Revolution.*

36 "Central leaders meet with representatives from Jiangsu visiting Beijing." November 18, 1967. Song Yongyi, *Collection on China's Great Proletarian Cultural Revolution.*

37 MacFarquhar, Roderick and Schoenhals, Michael, 2006, *Mao's Last Revolution,* ibid.

38 The diversity of representatives of Hubei is a case in point, including both politically powerful local leaders and political nobodies with perfect Maoist credentials including a good class background. Hubei Archive, SZ 139-6-19.

39 中發(1967) 322號, CRD 690.

40 CRD 473, p. 116f.

41 Many rebels were successful. Among the Standing Committee members of Jinan's prefectural-level Revolutionary Committee, no fewer than ten individuals joined the party during the Cultural Revolution: five students, one person formerly working for the Japanese police, one school principal, one migrant worker, one cadre, and "only" one "true" worker (CRD 462, p. 5).

42 Jin Feng, 2006, 王洪文，王效禹採訪追記.

43 This combines information on the composition of the Committee CCP Shandong, 1991, 中國共產黨山東省組織史資料, pp. 362f.; on the status of its members in 1969 CCP Shandong, 2001, 中共山東歷史大事記, p. 551; and on Li Zaiwen's death CCP Hebei, Historical Research Office, 2011, 栗再溫傳記與年譜.

44 Inborn political capability is another factor: Gaining influential positions before the Cultural Revolution indicates political capability.

45 Geishecker, Ingo and Haisken-DeNew, John, 2004, *Landing on All Fours? Communist Elites in Post-Soviet Russia.*

46 CRD 50.

47 The first article in "People's Daily" that mentioned Wang Xiaoyu, appeared on January 30, 1967, praising the power seizure in Qingdao.

48 CRD 475.

49 CRD 4.

50 Mao Zedong, 1998, 建國以來毛澤東文稿, p. 124.

51 Similarly, his fall was initiated by a group of provincial leaders, endorsed by a group of central leaders, and finally approved by Mao Zedong CCP Central Document Research Office, 1997, 周恩來年譜一九四九──一九七六, pp. 299f.

52 Schurmann, Franz, 1966, *Ideology and Organization in Communist China*, p. 107.

53 CRD 703.

54 CRD 4.

55 CRD 18.

56 These prisons are referred to in many of the testimonies used here. In one self-criticism, a group formerly involved in running the prisons estimates that there were 4,000 inmates (CRD 453). In a conversation with the author, one individual who at the time was in charge of the prisons believes that the number is exaggerated, but does not deny the existence of the system.

57 Perry, Elizabeth J., 2006, *Patroling the Revolution*, chapter 5.

58 CRD 472.

59 Baum, Richard, 1968, *Ssu-ch'ing.*

60 Weber, Max, 1922, *Wirtschaft und Gesellschaft [Economy and Society]*, p. 129.

61 CRD 457.

62 MacFarquhar, Roderick and Schoenhals, Michael, 2006, *Mao's Last Revolution.*

63 As well as Parris Chang's analysis of the political maneuvers by incumbent provincial leaders. Chang, Parris, 1972, *Provincial Party Leaders' Strategies for Survival during the Cultural Revolution.*

64 Zhang, Elya J., 2006, *To Be Somebody.*

65 CRD 401, p. 1.

66 CCP Tengzhou, 1995, 中共滕州黨史大事記, pp. 278–279.

67 Red Guards, 1967–1973, 紅衛兵資料, vol. 1:7, pp. 3285–3288.

68 CCP Zaozhuang, 1999, 中共棗莊歷史大事記, p. 333.

69 Han Jinhai's Self-Criticism, September 12, 1969, pp. 26–27.
70 The number comes from a narrative posted online, whose quality is apparent both because many other facts can be confirmed from written sources and because other users make knowledgeable comments. http://tieba.baidu.com/p/448755094. Link checked November 2013.
71 CRD 31, p. 2.
72 This account is based on the testimony by the embedded journalist Zhang Shi, summer 1969, CRD 31, pp. 34–37, and confirmed through an interview with another participant in June 2013.
73 Conversations in Linyi, summer 2013.
74 Conversation with eyewitnesses, one of whom at the time was shuttling between the mountain and the township, summer 2013.
75 Conversations in Tancheng, mid-June 2013. This paragraph is not a verbatim quote. Instead, it summarizes both the long answer and further details that the eyewitness provided in follow-up conversations.
76 It seems that there was no fatal shooting, although this is a hard-to-ascertain fact.
77 This paragraph summarizes the collective denunciation made at a struggle session in Jinan, especially CRD 401, pp. 21–23. The author also visited the site, with a former member of the Mount Maling Guerrillas.
78 CCP Central Document Research Office, 1997, 周恩來年譜一九四九—一九七六, vol. 3, p. 296.
79 CRD 11.
80 CRD 85, p. 3.
81 Jin, Feng, 2006, 王洪文, 王效禹採訪追記.
82 CRD 650.
83 The cables were available in Hubei's Provincial Archive in 2012/13. They probably underreport violence. There are incentives to underreport along the information chain, beginning with the soldier in the field, the military leaders who share the information with civilian authorities, and the archivists in charge of declassification.
84 Doyle, Michael W. and Sambanis, Nicholas, 2000, *International Peacebuilding.*
85 Hubei Archive, SZ 139-6-57, p. 24.
86 Guangji County, 1994, 廣濟縣志, chronology.
87 Hubei Archive, SZ 139-6-57, p. 16.
88 Hubei Archive, SZ 139-6-57, p. 18.
89 Hubei Archive, SZ 139-6-57, p. 20.
90 Hubei Archive, SZ 139-6-60, p. 42.
91 Hubei Archive, SZ 139-6-62, p. 36.
92 Hubei Archive, SZ 139-6-57, p. 13f.
93 Hubei Archive, SZ 139-6-20, p. 70.
94 Schoenhals, Michael, 2005, *"Why Don't We Arm the Left?" Mao's Culpability for the Cultural Revolution's "Great Chaos" of 1967.*
95 Wuhan Military Region, 1988, 武汉民兵简史, p. 261.
96 CCP Hubei, 1991, p. 842.

97 For cutting-edge research on the relationship between the military and the party during the Cultural Revolution see Lim, Jaehwan, 2014, 人民解放軍と中国政治.

98 Hubei Archive, SZ 139-1-1.

99 CCP Hubei, 2007, 中國共產黨湖北歷史大事記, p. 345.

100 Hubei Archive, SZ 139-1-1.

101 Hubei Archive, SZ 139-1-1.

102 Ibid.

103 MacFarquhar, Roderick and Schoenhals, Michael, 2006, *Mao's Last Revolution*, p. 199.

104 Hubei Archive, SZ 75-1-247.

105 CCP Hubei, 2007, 中國共產黨湖北歷史大事記, p. 353.

106 Hubei Archive, SZ 139-6-62.

107 Hubei Archive, SZ 239-6-62 pp. 89–90.

108 Hubei Archive, SZ 139-6-20.

109 CRD 321, letter to Chen Boda and Jiang Qing.

110 CRD 321 is such a set.

111 Perry, Elizabeth J. and Li Xun, 1993, *Revolutionary Rudeness*.

112 Hubei Archive, SZ 139-6-20.

113 Hubei Archive, SZ 139-6-60, p. 40.

114 Hubei Archive, SZ 139-1-494.

115 Hubei Archive, SZ 139-6-57, p. 15.

116 Elizabeth J. Perry and Li Xun note the rebels' failure to institutionalize their gains in the context of Shanghai Perry, Elizabeth J. and Li Xun, 1997, *Proletarian Power*, ch. 6.

117 Hubei Archive, SZ 139-6-62, p. 66.

118 Hubei Archive, SZ 139-6-62, p. 64.

119 Hubei Archive, SZ 139-6-20.

120 Hubei Archive, SZ 139-6-63.

121 The preliminary list of representatives, accompanied by their resumes, is in the Hubei Archive, SZ 139-6-19.

122 Hubei Archive, SZ 139-6-62, p. 68.

123 Hubei Archive, SZ 139-6-62, p. 74, report dated September 28.

124 CCP Central Document Research Office, 1997, 周恩來年譜一九四九――一九七六.

125 Those methods followed the Leninist script described by Selznick, Philip, 1952, *The Organizational Weapon*.

126 The author found such ID cards at a flea market in Hubei Province.

127 CRD 1, p. 23.

128 CRD 85, p. 9.

129 CRD 1, p. 16.

130 CCP Shandong, 2001, 中共山東歷史大事記, pp. 551–555.

131 CRD 323, p. 14.

132 Su Yang, 2011, *Collective Killings in Rural China during the Cultural Revolution*, esp. pp. 48ff.

133 Bu Weihua, 2008, 中華人民共和國史，第六本，「砸爛舊世界」, p. 706ff.

134 CRD 323.

135 The following paragraph is based on a record of central leaders meeting with representatives from Xinjiang, National Congress Hall, 20 July 1968, GX, pp. 289–295.
136 CD1 is the version of the report reprinted by a prefectural-level Revolutionary Committee.
137 Chronology of the Qingdao City Gazetteer.
138 Evidence of preparatory work dates from December 1969 (CRD 502).
139 CRD 520.
140 CRD 526.
141 CRD 528.
142 In Qingdao, as in the military study groups here, speeches often contain enumerations of the villains, provincial ones first, followed by local ones (e.g., CRD 501).
143 CRD 500.
144 Liu Xijing, 2007, 中國增值稅流失研究 *[Study of VAT Losses in China]*, pp. 105–111.
145 At the beginning of the Cultural Revolution Tianjin belonged to Hebei province, but became an independent province-level city like Beijing or Shanghai in 1967, bringing the number of province-level jurisdictions to 29.
146 Walder, Andrew G., 2014, *Rebellion and Repression in China, 1966–1971.*
147 Walder, Andrew G. and Su Yang, 2003, *The Cultural Revolution in the Countryside*, p. 91.
148 Andrew G. Walder kindly shared the expanded version of the data set, which he was able to collect thanks to National Science Foundation Grant SBS-1021134, "Political Movements in an Authoritarian Hierarchy." While the new version of the data broke new ground by including information on Tibet, like Walder, Andrew G. and Su Yang, 2003, *The Cultural Revolution in the Countryside* the analysis here does not use the victim counts from Tibet. The analysis works with the data from counties, autonomous counties, banners, and other county-level jurisdictions (jurisdiction types one to four in the data set).
149 Walder, Andrew G., 2014, *Rebellion and Repression in China, 1966–1971*, p. 526.
150 available from China Data Center at the University of Michigan.
151 National Bureau of Statistics of China, 1990, 全國各省自治區直轄市歷史統計資料匯編.
152 The Cultural Revolution began with a document released on May 16, 1966. The power seizures started at the beginning of January 1967. While the analysis works with a start date January 1, 1967, this choice is inconsequential. Choosing a different start day would be a linear transformation that makes no difference for the regression analysis. The results would only change if different start dates would be assumed for different provinces.
153 Bu Weihua, 2008, 中華人民共和國史，第六本，「砸爛舊世界」, pp. 731–733.

154 On this source, compare page 22. CCP Organization Department, ?, 中國
共產黨黨內統計資料彙編, p. 12.
155 Census data from *Harvard Geospatial Library.*
156 Perry, Elizabeth J. and Li Xun, 1997, *Proletarian Power* and Walder,
Andrew G., 2009, *Fractured Rebellion.*
157 Heberer, Thomas and Schubert, Gunter, 2006, *Political Reform and
Regime Legitimacy in Contemporary China.*
158 Cai Yongshun, 2008, *Power Structure and Regime Resilience.*
159 Nathan, Andrew J., 2003, *Authoritarian Resilience* and Heberer, Thomas
and Schubert, Gunter, 2006, *Political Reform and Regime Legitimacy in
Contemporary China.*
160 Heilmann, Sebastian and Perry, Elizabeth J., 2011, *Mao's Invisible Hand.*
161 Huntington, Samuel P., 2006 (1968), *Political Order in Changing
Societies.*
162 Mao Zedong, "On the Correct Handling of Contradictions among the
People," speech on February 27, 1957, published in *People's Daily* on June
19.
163 Huntington, Samuel P., 1965, *Political Development and Political Decay.*
164 Author's observations in Hubei, Shandong, Zhejiang. Electronic copies of
Huntington's work are very easily available on the Chinese internet,
indicating significant interest.
165 Mao Zedong, 1960, *On the Correct Handling of Contradictions among
the People*, p. 62.
166 CCP, 1981, *Resolution on Certain Questions in the History of Our Party
since the Founding of the People's Republic of China*, p. 47.
167 Esherick, Joseph W., Pickowicz, Paul G. and Walder, Andrew, 2006, *The
Chinese Cultural Revolution as History.*
168 "Graduate Student", 2001, 從蘇共執政期間腐財問題引出的思考.

Chapter 9

1 Koss, Daniel, 2017, *Political Geography of Empire.*
2 Rokkan, Stein, 1969, *Models and Methods in the Comparative Study of
Nation-Building.*
3 Richard Snyder's 2001 article marks a conscious and decisive turn to
within-country comparisons Snyder, Richard, 2001, *Scaling Down.*
4 Tsai, Lily L., 2009, *The Rise of Subnational and Multilevel Comparative
Politics.*
5 For example, one historian suggested that history is to be rescued from the
nation. Duara, Prasenjit, 1995, *Rescuing History from the Nation.*
6 King, Gary, 1994, *Designing Social Inquiry.*
7 Putnam, Robert D., Leonardi, Robert and Nanetti, Raffaella Y., 1993,
Making Democracy Work.
8 Tsai, Lily L., 2007, *Accountability Without Democracy*, Rithmire, Meg E.,
2014, *China's 'New Regionalism'* and Singh, Prerna, 2010, *Subnationalism
and Social Development.*

9   O'Donnell, Guillermo A., 1993, *On the State, Democratization and Some Conceptual problems.*
10 Soifer, Hillel D., 2006, *Authority over Distance.*
11 These include a series of subnational studies appearing in *Studies in Comparative International Development*, especially contributions to a special issue on infrastructural power (vol. 43, no. 3/4, fall/winter 2008).
12 Ziblatt, Daniel, 2009, *Shaping Democratic Practice and the Causes of Electoral Fraud.*
13 Ziblatt, Daniel, 2008, *Why Some Cities Provide More Public Goods Than Others.*
14 Boone, Catherine, 2003, *Political Topographies of the African State.*
15 Remick, Elizabeth J., 2004, *Building Local States* and Sheng, Yang, 2009, *Authoritarian Co-optation, the Territorial Dimension.*
16 Shambaugh, David L., 2008, *China's Communist Party.*
17 Heilmann, Sebastian, 2008, *Policy-Making through Experimentation.*
18 Heilmann, Sebastian, 2008, *Policy Experimentation in China's Economic Rise.*
19 Tsai, Wen-hsuan and Chung, Yen-Lin, Forthcoming, *A Model of Adaptative Mobilization.*
20 Giovanni Capoccia and Daniel Ziblatt have identified a "historical turn in democratization studies" Capoccia, Giovanni and Ziblatt, Daniel, 2010, *The Historical Turn in Democratization Studies*, but the trend might in fact be even broader.
21 Moore, Barrington, 1966, *Social Origins of Dictatorship and Democracy.*
22 Skocpol, Theda, 1979, *States and Social Revolutions.*
23 Putnam, Robert D., Leonardi, Robert and Nanetti, Raffaella Y., 1993, *Making Democracy Work.*
24 King, Gary, 1998, *Unifying Political Methodology.*
25 King, Gary, 1994, *Designing Social Inquiry.*
26 Gary King recognizes this difficulty:"The range of 'reasonable' specifications increases vastly when data have time series properties." King, Gary, 1998, *Unifying Political Methodology*, p. 167.
27 Pierson, Paul, 2004, *Politics in Time* and Mahoney, James and Rueschemeyer, Dietrich, 2003, *Comparative Historical Analysis in the Social Sciences.*
28 Fukuyama, Francis, 2011, *The Origins of Political Order.*
29 Lipset, Seymour M. and Rokkan, Stein, 1967, *Cleavage Structures, Party Systems and Voter Alignment.*
30 Huntington, Samuel P., 2006 (1968), *Political Order in Changing Societies.*
31 Valentino, Nicholas A. and Sears, David O., 2005, *Old Times There Are Not Forgotten.*
32 CCP Investigation Team, 2014, 國外一些主要政黨嚴明黨紀問題研究.
33 Gan Wudong, 2014, 德國，英國，瑞士主要政黨運用信息網絡的做法與啓示.
34 LaPalombara, Joseph and Weiner, Myron, 1966, *Political Parties and Political Development.*
35 Pharr, Susan J., Putnam, Robert D. and Dalton, Russell J., 2000, *A Quarter-Century of Declining Confidence.*

36 Scarrow, Susan E., 2000, *Parties without Members? Party Organization in a Changing Electoral Environment.*
37 Hooghe, Marc and Dassonneville, Ruth, 2014, *Party Members as an Electoral Linking Mechanism.*
38 van Dyck, Brandon, 2014, *Why Party Organization Still Matters.*
39 Grzymala-Busse, Anna M., 2002, *Redeeming the Communist Past.*

Appendix 1

1 Holmstrom, Bengt and Milgrom, Paul, 1991, *Multitask Principal-Agent Analyses.*
2 Salanié, Bernard, 1997, *The Economics of Contracts.*

Appendix 2

1 Malycha, Andreas and Winters, Peter J., 2009, *Die SED.*

Primary Material

Unless otherwise noted, documents are in the author's personal collection.

CASS 181: Kōain Kahoku Renrakubu 興亜院華北連絡部 [North China Liaison Office of the Asia Co-Prosperity Institute]. 1939. 南運河流域事情調查報告 [Report on the Situation in the River Basin of the Southern Canal]. Available at Tianjin Academy of Social Sciences.

CASS 183: Mantetsu Kitashi Jimukyoku Chōsabu 満鉄北支事務局調査部 [Research Division of the Manchurian Railway Company's North China Office]. 1938. 北支農業要覧 [Key Observations on Agriculture in North China]. Available at Tianjin Academy of Social Sciences.

CRD 1: 《濟南軍區李水清副司令員傳達中央首長重要指示和中央辦的毛澤東思想學習班山東班的總結》 "Li Shuiqing, vice-commander of Jinan military region, transmits instructions from central leaders and a summary of the Shandong section of the centrally managed Mao Zedong thought study group," October 20, 1969. 37 pages. Reproduced by the revolutionary committee of Huimin prefecture.

CRD 4: 《對王效禹在山東搞獨立王國，對抗中央，反對毛澤東思想幾個主要問題的揭發》 "Revealing some important problems concerning Wang Xiaoyu establishing an independent kingdom in Shandong, opposing the center, and opposing Mao Zedong thought," Zhu Wen, July/August 1969. This self-critique was made at the occasion of the study group of Mao Zedong thought organized by the central government for participants from Shandong.

CRD 11: 《中共中央文件，中發（69）25號，中央對王效禹、楊得志、袁升平三同志的報告的批示》 "Central Committee Document, Centrally Issued (1969) no.25, instructions by the central government on the report submitted by the three comrades Wang Xiaoyu, Yang Dezhi and Yuan Shengping," May 25, 1969. This document announces a policy reversal amounting to the downfall of Shandong's top leader Wang Xiaoyu.

CRD 18: 《徹底揭發批判王效禹派「工宣隊」進佔省生產指揮部所犯的嚴重錯誤》 "All the way reveal and criticize the serious errors committed by the

'Workers Propaganda Troupe' sent by Wang Xiaoyu to occupy the provincial Production Headquarters]. This document is a speech by 王澤恩, made at the occasion of a Mao Zedong study group organized by the central government

CRD 31: 《鋼鐵長城下的蛀蟲：從臨沂問題上看王效禹反對人民解放軍的滔天罪行》 "The moths under the strong Great Wall: From the Linyi's problem seeing the heinous crimes against the PLA committed by Wang Xiaoyu]. Zhang Shi. The author had served as an embedded journalist during an intervention in Linyi.

CRD 50: 《中央文革小組康生等三同志和我們的談話》 "Our conversation with three comrades from the Cultural Revolution Small Leading Group, including Kang Sheng]. Handbill found at a flea market, dated January 22, 1967.

CRD 85: 《中央首長接見山東班領導小組時的重要指示》 "Important instructions on the occasion of central leaders meeting with the small leading group of the Shandong section."

CRD 321: 《關於楊春亭同志的調查報告》 "Report on investigating comrade Yang Chunting," August 1967.

CRD 323: 《中央，中央文革首長接見廣西、新疆來京學習的兩派群眾組織時的重要指示》 "Important instructions at a meeting of central leaders and leaders of the central cultural Revolution Group with both camps' mass organizations from Guangxi and Xinjiang province," August 5, 1968.

CRD 401: 《憤怒控訴資產階級政客王效愚在臨沂地區瘋狂反對人民解放軍殘酷鎮壓革命群眾的滔天罪行》 "Angrily denounce the capitalist politician Wang Xiaoyu's heinous crimes in Linyi prefecture of madly opposing the PLA and brutally suppressing the revolutionary masses," January 1970, 26 pages.

CRD 453: 《王效禹、孟慶芝復辟資本主義的專政工具——"棒子隊"罪惡累累必須徹底揭發批判》 "Wang Xiaoyu and Meng Qingzhi's instrument for bringing back capitalism: The "stick troup's" crimes must be fully exposed and criticized].

CRD 457: 《揭開王效禹在省檢察院的罪惡活動看他是個什麼人》 "Understanding the type of person Wang Xiaoyu is by revealing his evil criminal activities at the Provincial Disciplinary Committee." This document, on Wang Xiaoyu's career and private life, is a joint report made on the occasion of a Mao Zedong study group organized by the central government to illuminate the situation in Shandong province.

CRD 462: 《王效禹建黨思想的要害是篡改黨的性質》 "The point of Wang Xiaoyu's ideas on party-building is to usurp and change the character of the party," Pan Zhongli, Part of a series of speeches at meetings in Beijing on rectifying and building the Shandong's party apparatus after Wang Xiaoyu's fall.

CRD 464: 《王效禹派「工宣隊」去省生產指揮部奪權的嚴重錯誤必須痛加批判》 "One must strongly criticize the severe mistake of Wang Xiaoyu sending a "Workers Propaganda Troop" to seize the power of the provincial Production Headquarters.]

CRD 472: 《從王效禹把持省檢察院看王效禹大搞獨立王國的陰謀活動》 "Looking at Wang Xiaoyu's monopolization of the provincial prosecutor's office to see his hidden scheme to build up an independent kingdom.]

CRD 473: 《徹底戳穿王效禹奪省革委組織組大權的罪惡陰謀》 "All the way expose the evil scheme behind Wang Xiaoyu's taking over the organization powers of the provincial revolutionary committee].

CRD 475: 《揭開王效禹大搞獨立王國的内幕》 "Revealing the inside story of Wang Xiaoyu's Scheme for an Independent Kingdom," Part of a set from a collector in Shandong's countryside. This document is a self-critique by rebel leader Han Jinhai made at the occasion of a Mao Zedong study group organized by the central government to illuminate the situation in Shandong province. To evaluate the document's reliability, I have checked some of the content and identified potential problems by talking to a close friend of the author.

CRD 500: 《向現行反革命分子楊保華討還血債》 "Making the active counter-revolutionary Yang Baohua pay for his blood debt," Qu Tongbao. Accusatory speech at a study group of Mao Zedong thought in Qingdao, December 1969.

CRD 501: 《憤怒聲討現行反革命分子王效禹、楊保華、鞠維信大搞特務班子，刺探軍情，陰謀篡軍復辟的滔天罪行》 "Angrily denouncing the reactionary, monstruous crimes of the acting counter-revolutionaries Wang Xiaoyu, Yang Baohua, Ju Weixin and their big-time spy gang, spying out the military, plotting to usurp the military." Multi-authored accusation made at a study group of Mao Zedong thought in Qingdao, December 1969.

CRD 502: 《對反動分子劉崇玉的揭發批判材料匯集》 "Material collection of unmasking critique against the reactionary element Liu Chongyu," by the secretariat of a study group of Mao Zedong thought in Qingdao, December 1969.

CRD 520: 《革命大批判材料選編》 "Material for Revolutionary Criticism and Self-Criticism Meetings," PLA, Military Control Commission of Shandong's Security Apparatus. December 1969.

CRD 526: 《王效禹是反革命分子劉佩俠的辯護士和保護傘》 "Wang Xiaoyu is the apologist and umbrella of the counter-revolutionary element Liu Peixia," material from the study group of Mao Zedong thought at the people's prosecutor's office of Shandong.

CRD 528: 《凡是鎮壓群衆的人都沒有好下場: 徹底清算資產階級政客王效禹在省法院鎮壓革命群衆的罪行》 "People who suppress the masses all come to a bad end: All the way clearly calculate the crime of the capitalist politician Wang Xiao suppressing the massses at the provincial court," material from the study group of Mao Zedong thought organized by the military control commission at the people's court of Shandong.

CRD 650: 《中央首長第四次接見青海代表回憶紀要》 "Minutes of Central Leaders' Fourth Meeting with Representatives from Qinghai," March 24, 1967. Source: Song Yongyi, *Collection on China's Great Proletarian Cultural Revolution.*

CRD 690: *CCP Documents of the Great Proletarian Cultural Revolution*, Hong Kong, Union Research Institute, 1968, Central Document 358 (67), November 27, 1967, pp. 609 ff.

CRD 703: Online. This account of the Cultural Revolution was written by someone with intimate knowledge of the events, as seen from Qingdao. I corresponded with the author and know his name, which must remain anonymous here.

GLF 600 《臨沂專區還有不少社員鬧退社影響春耕生產》 "In Linyi prefecture there are still many commune members clamoring to retreat from the commune, thereby affecting spring fields' production," April 8, 1967. Source: Song Yongyi, *Digital Collection on China's Great Leap/Great Famine*.

GLF 602 《中央組織部關於濟南市解決社會主義大躍進中幹部問題的通報》 "Circular by the CCP Central Organization Department concerning Jinan's solution to cadre personnel issues in the Socialist Great Leap Forward," July 7, 1958. Source: Song Yongyi, *Digital Collection on China's Great Leap/Great Famine*.

GLF 603 《山東省委、省府關於館陶縣停伙、逃荒問題的檢查報告》 "CCP Central's rescript on "Investigation report concerning the problem of meal stoppages and famine refugees from Guantao county" by Shandong's party committee and government," January 22, 1959. Source: Song Yongyi, *Digital Collection on China's Great Leap/Great Famine*.

Hubei Archive: Provincial Archive of Hubei Province in Wuhan. Numbers refer to the archival call numbers.

HYL 1: 《中共中央轉發開封、濟南發生浮腫病材料的批示》 "The Central Committee circulates material concerning the occurence of edema diseases in Kaifeng and Jinan," November 23, 1960, Central Committee Document [60] 986, secret. Source: Harvard-Yenching Library.

HYL 2: 《山東省人口統計資料匯編, 機密》 "Collection of Population Statistics of Shandong Province, Classified," 1985. Source: Harvard-Yenching Library. Shandong Archive: Provincial Archive of Shandong in Jinan. Numbers refer to call number in the archive.

Tōyō Bunko 1: 興亜院華北連絡部青島出張所 Asia Co-Prosperity Institute, North China Connection Bureau, Qingdao Branch Office]. 1940. 山東経済ノ特異性概要 "Synopsis of Shandong's economic specialties."

Tōyō Bunko 2: 興亜院華北連絡部. No year, around 1939. 農地開発株式会社設立要綱 [General plan for creating a stock company to develop agricultural land].

Tōyō Bunko 3: 華北交通株式会社裁室 [North China Transportation Company, President's Office]. 1940. 鉄路愛護村実態調査報告書 [Report Summarizing Investigations on the Attitudes in the Railway Protection Villages].

Secondary Sources

Academia Sinica, Institute of Modern History. 2000. 中華民國史事日誌 *[Historical Chronology of the Republic of China]*. Taibei: Academia Sinica.

Acemoglu, Daron and Robinson, James A. 2006. *Economic Origins of Dictatorship and Democracy*. New York, NY: Cambridge University Press.

Acharya, Avidit, Blackwell, Matthew, and Sen, Maya. 2015. Detecting Direct Effects and Assessing Alternative Mechanisms. *Unpublished manuscript*.

Acharya, Avidit, Blackwell, Matthew, and Sen, Maya. 2016. Explaining Causal Findings without Bias: Detecting and Assessing Direct Effects. *American Political Science Review*, **110**(3), 512–529.

Aldrich, Daniel P. 2008. *Site Fights: Divisive Facilities and Civil Society in Japan and the West*. Ithaca, NY: Cornell University Press.

Allinson, Mark. 2013. Das Parteilehrjahr der SED: Konfliktfeld zwischen Parteiführung und Massenbasis [The Socialist Unity Party's Training Year: Area of Conflict Between the Party Leadership and Its Mass Basis]. *Hefte zur DDR-geschichte*, **129**.

An, Zuozhang (ed). 2011. 中國吏部研究 *[Studies on China's Board of Personnel]*. Beijing: Dangjian Duwu Chubanshe.

Armstrong, Charles K. 2003. *The Korean Revolution 1945–1950*. Ithaca, NY: Cornell University Press.

Asahi Shimbun Beijing Office. 2012. 紅の党：習近平体制誕生の内幕 *[The Red Party: Behind the Scenes of the Establishment of the Xi Jinping System]*. Tokyo: Asahi Shimbun.

Banerjee, Abhijit V. and Duflo, Esther. 2014. Under the Thumb of History? Political Institutions and the Scope for Action. *Annual Review of Economics*, **6**, 951–971.

Barnett, A. Doak. 1967. *Cadres, Bureaucracy, and Political Power in Communist China*. New York, NY: Columbia University Press.

Barro, Robert J. and Sala-i Martin, Xavier I. 1992. Convergence. *Journal of Political Economy*, **100**(2), 223–251.

365

Barro, Roberto J. and Sala-i Martin, Xavier I. 1995. *Economic Growth.* Cambridge, MA: MIT Press.

Bates, Robert H. 1981. *Markets and States in Tropical Africa: The Political Basis of Agricultural Policies.* Berkeley, CA: University of California Press.

Baum, Richard. 1968. *Ssu-ch'ing: The Socialist Education Movement of 1962–1966.* Berkeley, CA: Center for Chinese Studies, University of California.

Bergès, Michel. 2011. *Engagement Politique et Distanciation: Le Cas Duverger [Political Engagement and Distancing: The Case Duverger].* Paris: http://classiques.uqac.ca/contemporains/berges_michel/cas_duverger/cas_duverger.html Last checked: June 2014.

Bernstein, Thomas P. and Lü, Xiaobo. 2003. *Taxation without Representation in Contemporary Rural China.* New York, NY: Cambridge University Press.

Blaydes, Lisa. 2011. *Elections and Distributive Politics in Mubarak's Egypt.* New York, NY: Cambridge University Press.

Bo, Yibo. 1997. 若干重大決策與事件的回顧 *[Review of Some Important Decisions and Events].* Beijing: Renmin Chubanshe.

Boix, Carles and Svolik, Milan W. 2013. The Foundations of Limited Authoritarian Government: Institutions, Commitment, and Power-Sharing in Dictatorships. *The Journal of Politics,* **75**(2), 300–316.

Boone, Catherine. 2003. *Political Topographies of the African State: Territorial Authority and Institutional Choice.* New York, NY: Cambridge University Press.

Boone, Catherine. 2012. Territorial Politics and the Reach of the State: Unevenness by Design. *Revista de Ciencia Política,* **32**(3), 623–641.

Brancati, Dawn. 2014. Democratic Authoritarianism: Origins and Effects. *Annual Review of Political Science,* **17**(3), 313–326.

Brownlee, Jason. 2007. *Authoritarianism in an Age of Democratization.* New York, NY: Cambridge University Press.

Brys, Bert and Matthews, Stephen and Herd, Richard and Wang, Xiao, 2013. *Tax Policy and Tax Reform in the People's Republic of China.* Paris: OECD Publishing

Bu, Weihua. 2008. 中華人民共和國史，第六本，「砸爛舊世界」：文化大革命動亂與活動 *[The History of the People's Republic of China, volume 6, "Smashing the Old World": Havoc of the Chinese Cultural Revolution (1966–1968)].* Hong Kong: The Chinese University Press.

Byman, Daniel L. and Pollack, Kenneth M. 2001. Let Us Now Praise Great Men: Bringing the Statesman Back In. *International Security,* **25**(4), 107–146.

Cai, Yongshun. 2008. Power Structure and Regime Resilience: Contentious Politics in China. *British Journal of Political Science,* **38**(3), 411–432.

Capoccia, Giovanni and Ziblatt, Daniel. 2010. The Historical Turn in Democratization Studies: A New Research Agenda for Europe and Beyond. *Comparative Political Studies,* **43**(8/9), 931–968.

CCP. 1981. *Resolution on Certain Questions in the History of our Party since the Founding of the People's Republic of China.* Beijing: Foreign Languages Press.

CCP. 2000. 中國共產黨組織史資料, *1921–1997 [Material on the Organizational History of the CCP, 1921–1997].* Beijing: Zhonggong Dangshi Chubanshe.

CCP. 2001. 黨支部工作手冊 *[Handbook for Party Cell Work]*. Beijing: Dangjian Duwu Chubanshe.

CCP Anhui, Task Force of the Organization Department. 2000. 法輪功向黨內滲透的主要特點及其危害 Important Characteristics of Falungong's Infiltration of the Party, and its Damage. *Dangjian Yanjiu Neican*, 4, 15–16.

CCP Central Document Research Office. 1997. 周恩來年譜一九四九－一九七六 *[Life Chronology of Zhou Enlai (1949–1976)]*. Beijing: Zhongyang Wenxian Chubanshe.

CCP Chiping. 1989. 中國共產黨山東省茌平縣組織史資料, *1927–1987 [Material on the Organizational History of the CCP in Chiping (Shandong), 1927–1987]*. Liaocheng: Shandong Sheng Xinwen Chuban Ju.

CCP Gaoyou County. 1991. 中國共產黨江蘇省高郵縣組織史資料 *[Material on the Organizational History of the CCP in Gaoyou (Jiangsu)]*. Beijing: Zhonggong Dangshi Chubanshe.

CCP Hebei, Historical Research Office. 2011. 栗再温傳記與年譜 *[Biography and Chronology of Li Zaiwen]*. Beijing: Zhonggong Dangshi Chubanshe.

CCP Heze. 1999. 中共山東省菏澤地區黨史大事記, *1921–1999 [Historical Chronology of the CCP in Heze Prefecture of Shandong Province, 1921–1999]*. Jinan: Shandong Renmin Chubanshi.

CCP History Research Office. 1997. 中國革命老區 *[China's Old Revolutionary Bases]*. Beijing: Zhonggong Dangshi Chubanshe.

CCP History Research Office. 2011. 中國共產黨歷史 *[History of the CCP]*. Beijing: Zhonggong Dangshi Chubanshe.

CCP Hubei. 1991. 中國共產黨湖北省組織史資料 1921。秋–1987.11 *[Material on the Organizational History of the CCP in Hubei 1921 (fall) - November 1987]*. Wuhan: Hubei Renmin Chubanshe.

CCP Hubei. 2007. 中國共產黨湖北歷史大事記 *1949.5–1978.12 [Historical Chronology of the CCP in Hubei: May 1949 to December 1978]*. Wuhan: Hubei Renmin Chubanshe.

CCP Investigation Team. 2014. 國外一些主要政黨嚴明黨紀問題研究 [Strict Party Discipline in Some Important Foreign Parties]. *Dangjian Yanjiu Neican*, 270(4), 14–17 and 6.

CCP Liaocheng. 1998. 中共聊城歷史大事記1949.10–1998.3 *[Historical Chronology of the CCP in Liaocheng]*. Jinan: Shandong Renmin Chubanshe.

CCP Linyi. 1988. 中國共產黨山東省臨沂市組織史資料, *1923–1987 [Material on the Organizational History of the CCP in Linyi (Shandong), 1923–1987]*. Linyi: Shandong Sheng Chuban Zongshe Linyi Fenshe.

CCP Organization Department. 1991. 中國共产黨上海市組織史資料, *1920.8–1987.10 [Material on the Organizational History of Shanghai, August 1920 to October 1987]*. Shanghai: Shanghai Renmin Chubanshe.

CCP Organization Department. 1992. 組織工作文件選編，機密 *[Selected Documents on Organization Work, Secret]*. Beijing: internally circulated.

CCP Organization Department. 1994. 中國共產黨黨員電化教育工作問答 *[Questions and Answers on the Electronic Media Education of Party Members]*. Beijing: Zhonggong Zhongyang Dangxiao Chubanshe.

CCP Organization Department. 2006. 中國共產黨組織工作教程 [*Teaching Module on Organizational Work for the CCP*]. Beijing: Dangjian Duwu Chubanshe.

CCP Organization Department. 2007. 中國共產黨組織工作教程 [*Course on CCP Organization Work*]. Beijing: Dangjian Duwu Chubanshe.

CCP Organization Department. 2011. 中國共產黨黨內統計資料彙編 1921–2010 [*Collection of CCP Statistical Material, 1921–2010*]. Beijing: Dangjian Duwu Chubanshe.

CCP Organization Department. 2015. 入黨實務教程 [*Practical Lessons on Entering the Party*]. Beijing: Dangjian Duwu Chubanshe.

CCP Shandong. 1991. 中國共產黨山東省組織史資料 1921–1987 [*Material on the Organizational History of the CCP in Shandong 1921–1987*]. Beijing: Zhonggong Dangshi Chubanshe.

CCP Shandong. 2001. 中共山東歷史大事記 [*Historical Chronology of the CCP in Shandong*]. Beijing: Zhonggong Dangshi Chubanshe.

CCP Shandong. 2002–2003. 中共山東年鑑 [*CCP Shandong Yearbook*]. Beijing: Zhonggong Dangshi Chubanshe.

CCP Shandong. 2004–2013. 中共山東年鑑 [*CCP Shandong Yearbook*]. Jinan: Huanghe Chubanshe.

CCP Shanghai. 2001. 中共上海黨志 [*Gazetteer of the CCP in Shanghai*]. Shanghai: Shanghai Shehuikexueyuan Chubanshe.

CCP Tengzhou. 1995. 中共滕州黨史大事記 [*Historical Chronology of the CCP in Tengzhou*]. Jinan: Shandong Youyi Chubanshe.

CCP Tianjin. 2003. 黨的基層組織工作手冊 [*Work Manual for Party Grassroots Organizations*]. Tianjin: Tianjin Renmin Chubanshe.

CCP Tibet. 1993. 中國共產黨西藏自治區組織史資料 [*Material on the Organizational History of the CCP in Tibet Autonomous Region*]. Lhasa: Xicang Renmin Chubanshe.

CCP Yunnan. 1994. 中國共產黨雲南省組織史資料 1926.11–1987.10 [*Material on the Organizational History of the CCP in Yunnan, November 1926–October 1987*]. Beijing: Zhonggong Dangshi Chubanshe.

CCP Zaozhuang. 1999. 中共棗莊歷史大事記 *Historical Chronology of the CCP in Zaozhuang*. Beijing: Zhonggong Dangshi Chubanshe.

CCP Zibo. 1997. 中共淄博歷史大事記, 1949–1987 [*Historical Chronology of the CCP in Zibo, 1949–1987*]. Beijing: Zhonggong Dangshi Chubanshe.

Central Party School, Historical Research Office. 1997. 中共黨史參考資料 [*Party History Reference Material*]. Beijing: Renmin Chubanshe.

Chaligha, Amon. 2008. *The 2004 Neighbourhood, Hamlet, and Village Council Elections*. Dar es Salaam: University of Dar es Salaam.

Chan, Hon S. 2004. Cadre Personnel Management in China: The Nomenklatura System, 1990–1998. *The China Quarterly*, **179**, 703–734.

Chang, Parris. 1972. Provincial Party Leaders' Strategies for Survival during the Cultural Revolution. In: Scalapino, Robert A. (ed), *Elites in the People's Republic of China*. Seattle: University of Washington Press.

Cheibub, José Antonio, Gandhi, Jennifer, and Vreeland, James Raymond. 2010. Democracy and Dictatorship Revisited. *Public Choice*, **143**(1/2), 67–101.

Chen, Fangmeng. 2010. 轉型社會中的中國共產黨 *[CCP in Transitional Society]*. Beijing: Zhongyang Bianyi Chubanshe.

Chen, Feng. 2010. Trade Unions and the Quadripartite Interactions in Strike Settlement in China. *The China Quarterly*, **201**, 104–124.

Chen, Xi. 2012. *Social Protest and Contentious Authoritarianism in China*. New York: Cambridge University Press.

Chen, Yung-fa. 1986. *Making Revolution: The Communist Movement in Eastern and Central China, 1937–1945*. Berkeley: University of California Press.

Chen, Zhenliang. 2012. 新時期黨的組織工作創新研究 *[Pioneering Research on Party Organization Work in the New Era]*. Ph.D. thesis, Nanjing University of Aeronautics and Astronautics.

Chen, Zhenliang. 2012. 新時期黨的組織工作創新研究 *[Research on the Party's Innovative Organization Work in the New Era]*. Ph.D. thesis, Nanjing University of Aeronautics and Astronautics.

Chestnut Greitens, Sheena. 2016. *Dictators and Their Secret Policy: Coercive Institutions and State Violence*. New York: Cambridge University Press.

Chinese Finance Ministry, Budget Office. 2006. 中國省以下財政體制. Beijing: Zhongguo Caizheng Jingji Chubanshe.

Chu, Junhong. 2001. Prenatal Sex Determination and Sex-Selective Abortion in Rural Central China. *Population and Development Review*, **27**(2), 259–281.

Cohen, Paul A. 1997. *History in Three Keys: The Boxers as Event, Experience, and Myth*. New York: Columbia University Press.

Collombier, Virginie. 2007. The Internal Stakes of the 2005 Elections: The Struggle for Influence in Egypt's National Democratic Party. *Middle East Journal*, **61**(1), 95–111.

Colton, Timothy J. 2008. *Yeltsin: A Life*. New York: Basic Books.

Connelly, John. 1996. The Uses of *Volksgemeinschaft*: Letters to the NSDAP Kreisleitung Eisenach, 1939–1940. *The Journal of Modern History*, **68**, 899–930.

Conze, Eckart, Frei, Norbert, Hayes, Peter, and Zimmermann, Moshe. 2010. *Das Amt ind die Vergangenheit: Deutsche Diplomaten im Dritten Reich und in der Bundesrepublik [The Office and its Past: German Diplomats in the Third Reich and in the Federal Republik]*. Munich: Karl Blessing.

Dagiev, Dagikhudo. 2014. *Regime Transition in Central Asia: Stateness, Nationalism and Political Change in Tajikistan and Uzbekistan*. New York: Routledge.

Damit, Mohamad Yusop bin Awang. 2002. Negara Brunei Darussalam: Light at the End of the Tunnel. *Southeast Asian Affairs*, 81–91.

de la Fuente, Angel. 2000. *Mathematical Methods and Models for Economists*. New York: Cambridge University Press.

Deng, Xiaoping. 1989. 鄧小平文選 *[Selected Works by Deng Xiaoping]*. Beijing: Renmin Chubanshe.

Denton, Kirk A., 2014. *Exhibiting the Past: Historical Memory and the Politics of Museums in Postsocialist China*. Honolulu: University of Hawai'i Press.

DeVido, Elise Anne. 1995. *The Making of the Communist Party-State in Shandong Province*. Ph.D. thesis, Harvard University.

Diamond, Larry Jay. 2002. Thinking About Hybrid Regimes. *Journal of Democracy*, **13**(2), 21–35.

Dickson, Bruce J. 1997. *Democratization in China and Taiwan: The Adaptability of Leninist Parties*. New York: Clarendon Press.

Dickson, Bruce J. 2000. Cooptation and Corporatism in China: The Logic of Party Adaptation. *Political Science Quarterly*, **115**(4), 517–540.

Dickson, Bruce J. 2003. *Red Capitalists in China: The Party, Private Entrepreneurs, and Prospects for Political Change*. New York: Cambridge University Press.

Dickson, Bruce J. 2014. Who Wants to Be a Communist? Career Incentives and Mobilized Loyalty in China. *Chine Quarterly*, **217**, 42.

Dickson, Bruce J. 2016. *The Dictator's Dilemma: The Chinese Communist Party's Strategy for Survival*. New York: Oxford University Press.

Dickson, Bruce J., and Rost Rublee, Maria. 2000. Membership Has Its Privileges: The Socioeconomic Characteristics of Communist Party Members in Urban China. *Comparative Political Studies*, **33**(1), 87–102.

Dikötter, Frank. 2010. *Mao's Great Famine*. New York: Walker & Co.

Dillon, Nara. 2011. Governing Civil Society: Adapting Revolutionary Methods to Serve Post-Communist Goals. Pages 138–164 of: Heilmann, Sebastian, and Perry, Elizabeth J. (eds), *Mao's Invisible Hand: The Political Foundations of Adaptive Governance in China*. Cambridge, MA: Harvard University Asia Center; Distributed by Harvard University Press.

Dillon, Nara. 2015. *Radical Inequalities: China's Revolutionary Welfare State in Comparative Perspective*. Cambridge, MA: Harvard University Asia Center; Distributed by Harvard University Press.

Ding, Qu Jian, and Hesketh, Therese. 2006. Family Size, Fertility Preferences, and Sex Ratio in China in the Era of the One Child Family Policy: Results from National Planning and Reproductive Health Survey. *British Medical Journal*, **333**, 371–372.

Doyle, Michael W., and Sambanis, Nicholas. 2000. International Peacebuilding: A Theoretical and Quantitative Analysis. *American Political Science Review*, **94**(4), 779–801.

Duara, Prasenjit. 1991 (1988). *Culture, Power, and the State: Rural North China, 1900–1942*. Stanford, CA: Stanford University Press.

Duara, Prasenjit. 1995. *Rescuing History from the Nation: Questioning Narratives of Modern China*. Chicago: University of Chicago Press.

Duverger, Maurice. 1958 (1951). *Les Partis Politiques [Political Parties]*. Paris: Colin.

Eaton, Sarah, and Kostka, Genia. 2014. Authoritarian Environmentalism Undermined? Local Leaders' Time Horizons and Environmental Policy Implementation in China. *The China Quarterly*, **218**, 359–380.

Edin, Maria. 2003. State Capacity and Local Agent Control in China: CCP Cadre Management from a Township Perspective. *The China Quarterly*, **173**(1), 35–52.

Ekiert, Grzegorz, and Ziblatt, Daniel. 2012. *Democracy in Central and Eastern Europe 100 Years On*. Harvard: Unpublished Manuscript.

Elliott, Mark C. 2001. *The Manchu Way: The Eight Banners and Ethnic Identity in Late Imperial China*. Stanford, CA: Stanford University Press.

Ertman, Thomas. 1997. *Birth of the Leviathan: Building States and Regimes in Medieval and Early Modern Europe.* New York: Cambridge University Press.

Esherick, Joseph W. 1987. *The Origins of the Boxer Uprising.* Berkeley: University of California Press.

Esherick, Joseph W., Pickowicz, Paul G., and Walder, Andrew. 2006. *The Chinese Cultural Revolution as History.* Stanford, CA: Stanford University Press.

Falter, Jürgen W. 2016. Was wissen wir über die NSDAP-Mitglieder? Ein Blick auf den Forschungsstand [What do we know about NSDAP members? Looking at the state of the field]. Pages 89–120 of: Falter, Jürgen W. (ed), *Junge Kämpfer, alte Opportunisten: Die Mitglieder der NSDAP 1919–1945 [Young fighters, old opportunists: The members of the NSDAP, 1919–1945].* New York: Campus Verlag.

Faust, Aaron. 2012. *The Ba'thification of Iraq: Saddam Hussein and the Ba'th Party's System of Control.* Ph.D. thesis, Boston University.

Feng, Yuan. 1995. From the Imperial Examination to the National College Entrance Examination: The Dynamics of Political Centralism in China's Educational Enterprise. *Contemporary China,* 4(8), 28–56.

Fewsmith, Joseph. 2001. *China Since Tiananmen: The Politics of Transition.* New York: Cambridge University Press.

Fewsmith, Joseph. 2011. The Elusive Search for Effective Sub-County Governance. Pages 269–296 of: Heilmann, Sebastian, and Perry, Elizabeth J. (eds), *Mao's Invisible Hand: The Political Foundations of Adaptive Governance in China.* Harvard University Asia Center; Distributed by Harvard University Press.

Fewsmith, Joseph. 2013. The 18th Party Congress: Testing the Limits of Institutionalization. *China Leadership Monitor,* **Winter 2013.**

Foucault, Michel. 2004. *Sécurité, Territoire, Population: Cours au Collège de France, 1977–1978 [Security, Territory, Population: A Course at the Collège de France, 1977–1978].* Paris: Seuil/Gallimard.

Fröhlich, Elke (ed). 1996. *Die Tagebücher von Joseph Goebbels [The Diaries of Joseph Goebbels].* München: K.G. Saur.

Fukuyama, Francis. 2011. *The Origins of Political Order: From Prehuman Times to the French Revolution.* New York: Farrar, Straus and Giroux.

Gan, Wudong. 2014. 德國，英國，瑞士主要政黨運用信息網絡的做法與啓示 [Methods and Revelations on how Important Political Parties in Germany, Britain, and Switzerland use Information Networks]. *Dangjian Yanjiu Neican,* **269**(3), 16.

Gandhi, Jennifer. 2008. *Political Institutions under Dictatorship.* New York: Cambridge University Press.

Ganev, Venelin. 2001. Separation of Party and State as a Logistical Problem: A Glance at the Causes of State Weakness in Postcommunism. *East European Politics and Societies,* **15**, 389–420.

Ge, Guoqiang (ed). 2009. 山東省人口和計畫生育大事記 [Chronology of Population and Family Planning in Shandong, 1949–2009]. Jinan: Shandong Renmin Chubanshe.

Ge, Renshui. 2011. 城市化進程中基層電子黨務管理研究：以青島市城陽區為例 [Urbanization and the Digitization of Managing Party Affairs: The Case of Chengyang District in Qingdao City]. Jinan: Master's Thesis of Shandong University.

Geddes, Barbara. 1999. What Do We Know about Democratization after Twenty Years? *Annual Review of Political Science*, **2**, 115–144.

Geishecker, Ingo, and Haisken-DeNew, John. 2004. Landing on All Fours? Communist Elites in Post-Soviet Russia. *Journal of Comparative Economics*, **32**, 700–719.

Gerth, Hans. 1940. The Nazi Party: Its Leadership and Composition. *American Journal of Sociology*, **45**(4), 517–541.

Getty, J. Arch. 1983. Party and Purge in Smolensk, 1933–1937. *Slavic Review*, **42**(1), 60–79.

Gill, Bates, and Huang, Yanzhong. 2006. Sources and Limits of Chinese 'Soft Power'. *Survival: Global Politics and Strategy*, **48**(2), 17–36.

Gill, Graeme J. 1994. *The Collapse of a Single Party System: The Disintegration of the Communist Party of the Soviet Union*. New York: Cambridge University Press.

Gilley, Bruce. 2003. The Limits of Authoritarian Resilience. *Journal of Democracy*, **14**(1), 18–26.

Goodkind, Daniel M. 2004. China's Missing Children: The 2000 Census Underreporting Surprise. *Population Studies*, **58**(3), 281–295.

Goodman, David S.G. 2000. Revolutionary Women and Women in the Revolution: The Chinese Communist Party and Women in the War of Resistance to Japan, 1937–1945. *The China Quarterly*, **164**, 915–942.

Gordon, Andrew. 2003. *A Modern History of Japan: From Tokugawa Times to the Present*. New York: Oxford University Press.

Gourevitch, Peter Alexis. 1986. *Politics in Hard Times: Comparative Responses to International Economic Crises*. Ithaca, NY: Cornell University Press.

"Graduate Student". 2001. 從蘇共執政期間腐財問題引出的思考 [Thoughts about Corruption among the Soviet Communists When in Power]. *Dangjian Yanjiu Neican*, **119**(9), 14–17.

Greenhalgh, Susan. 2003. Science, Modernity, and the Making of China's One-Child Policy. *Population and Development Review*, **29**(2), 163–196.

Griffiths, John. 1988. The Cuban Communist Party. Pages 155–173 of: Randall, Vicky (ed), *Political Parties in the Third World*. London: Sage.

Grzymala-Busse, Anna. 2011. Time Will Tell? Temporality and the Analysis of Causal Mechanisms and Processes. *Comparative Political Studies*, **44**(9), 1267–1297.

Grzymala-Busse, Anna M. 2002. *Redeeming the Communist Past: The Regeneration of Communist Parties in East Central Europe*. New York: Cambridge University Press.

Guan County, 2001. 冠縣志 [Guan County Gazetteer]. Jinan: Qilu Shushe.

Guangji County. 1994. 廣濟縣志 [Guangji County Gazetteer]. Shanghai: Hanyu Dacidian Chubanshe.

Guo, Gang. 2009. China's Local Political Budget Cycles. *American Journal of Political Science*, **53**(3), 621–632.

Guo, Yucai. 2000. 建國前入黨的農村老黨員教育管理情況調查 [Investigating the Administration of Training to Old Rural Party Members who Joined the CCP before 1949]. *Dangjian Yanjiu Neican*, 13–14.

Hall, John Whitney. 1966. *Government and Local Power in Japan, 500 to 1700: A Study on Bizen Province*. Princeton, NJ: Princeton University Press.

He, Yiting. 2015. 縣委書記談怎樣做四有縣委書記 *[County Party Secretaries' Speeches on How to Become a Four Haves County Party Secretary]*, Part II. Beijing: Renmin Chubanshe.

Heberer, Thomas, and Schubert, Gunter. 2006. Political Reform and Regime Legitimacy in Contemporary China. *Asien*, **99**, 9–28.

Heilmann, Sebastian. 2008. Policy Experimentation in China's Economic Rise. *Studies in Comparative International Development*, **43**(1), 1–26.

Heilmann, Sebastian. 2011. Policy-Making through Experimentation: The Formation of a Distinctive Policy Process. Pages 62–101 of: Heilmann, Sebastian, and Perry, Elizabeth J. (eds), *Mao's Invisible Hand: The Political Foundations of Adaptive Governance in China*. Cambridge: Harvard University Asia Center; Distributed by Harvard University Press.

Heilmann, Sebastian, and Perry, Elizabeth J. (eds). 2011. *Mao's Invisible Hand: The Political Foundations of Adaptive Governance in China*. Cambridge: Harvard University Asia Center; Distributed by Harvard University Press.

Hershatter, Gail. 2011. *The Gender of Memory: Rural Women and China's Collective Past*. Berkeley: University of California Press.

Hesketh, Therese, and Zhu, Weixing. 2006. Abnormal Sex Ratios in Human Populations: Causes and Consequences. *Proceedings of the National Academy of Sciences of the United States of America*, **103**(36), 13271–13275.

Hess, Hartmut. 2005. *Parteien in Äthiopien: Zwischen Ethnischer Orientierung und Programmausrichtung [Parties in Ethiopia: Between Ethnic and Programmatic Orientation]*. Addis Ababa: Friedrich Ebert Stiftung.

Himeta, Mitsuyoshi et al. (ed). 1993. 中国２０世紀史 *20th Century History of China*. Tokyo: Tōkyō Daigaku Shuppankai.

Hinton, Carma. 1995. *Tian'an men* (videorecording). San Francisco: NAATA Distribution.

Hinton, William. 1972. *Hundred Day War: The Cultural Revolution at Tsinghua University*. New York: Monthly Review Press.

Holland, Alisha C. 2015. The Distributive Politics of Enforcement. *American Journal of Political Science*, **59**(2), 357–371.

Holmstrom, Bengt, and Milgrom, Paul. 1991. Multitask Principal-Agent Analyses: Incentive Contracts, Asset Ownership, and Job Design. *Journal of Law, Economics, and Organization*, 7(Special Issue), 24–52.

Honjō, Hisako (ed). 2009. 戦前期華北実態調査の目録と解題 *[Annotated List of Fact Finding Missions to North China During the Pre-War Era]*. Tokyo: Tōyō Bunko.

Hooghe, Marc, and Dassonneville, Ruth. 2014. Party Members as an Electoral Linking Mechanism: An Election Forecasting Model for Political Parties in Belgium, 1981–2010. *Party Politics*, **20**(3), 368–380.

Hough, Jerry F. 1969. *The Soviet Prefects: The Local Party Organs in Industrial Decision-Making*. Cambridge: Harvard University Press.

Hsu, Long-hsuen, and Chang, Ming-kai (eds). 1971. *History of the Sino-Japanese War (1937–1945)*. Taipei: Chung Wu Publishing.

Huang, Yasheng. 1996. *Inflation and Investment Controls in China: The Political Economy of Central-Local Relations During the Reform Era*. New York: Cambridge University Press.

Hudson, Valerie M., and den Boer, Andrea M. 2004. *Bare Branches: The Security Implications of Asia's Surplus Male Population*. Cambridge: MIT Press.

Huntington, Samuel P. 1965. Political Development and Political Decay. *World Politics*, **17**(3), 386–430.

Huntington, Samuel P. 1970. Social and Institutional Dynamics of One-Party Systems. Pages 3–47 of: Huntington, Samuel P., and Moore, Clement H. (eds), *Authoritarian Politics in Modern Societies: The Dynamics of Established One-Party Systems*. New York: Basic Books.

Huntington, Samuel P. 1991. *The Third Wave: Democratization in the Late Twentieth Century*. University of Oklahoma Press: Norman.

Huntington, Samuel P. 2006 (1968). *Political Order in Changing Societies*. New Haven, CT: Yale University Press.

IMF. 2003. Republic of Equatorial Guinea: 2012 Article IV Consultation. *IMF Country Report*, **13**(83).

Institut für Zeitgeschichte. 1983–1992. *Akten der Partei-Kanzlei der NSDAP: Rekonstruktion eines verlorengegangenen Bestandes [Files of the NSDAP Party Chancellery: Reconstruction of a Lost Collection]*. Munich: Saur.

Jäger, Wolfgang. 1973. *Partei und System [Party and System]*. Mainz: Kohlhammer.

Japanese Defense Agency. 1968–1971. 北支の治安戦 *[North China Pacification War]*. Tokyo: Asagumo Shinbunsha.

Jaros, Kyle A. 2014. *The Politics of Metropolitan Bias in China*. Ph.D. thesis, Harvard University.

Jennings, M. Kent, and Niemi, Richard G. 1981. *Generations and Politics: A Panel Study of Young Americans and Their Parents*. Princeton, NJ: Princeton University Press.

Jiang, Jinquan. 2015. 怎樣正確開展批評和自我批評 *[How to Correctly Engage in Critique and Self-Critique]*. Beijing: Dangjian Duwu Chubanshe.

Jiang, Shu. 2013. 國有企業如何應對黨員發展中存在的問題 [How should State-Owned Enterprises Deal with the Problems of Party Member Recruitment]. *Xianfengdui [Vanguard]*, **10**, 16–19.

Jin, Feng. 2006. 王洪文，王效禹採訪追記 [Notes from Interviews with Wang Hongwen and Wang Xiaoyu]. *Yanhuang Chunqiu*, 5, 39–42.

Johnson, Chalmers A. 1962. *Peasant Nationalism and Communist Power: The Emergence of Revolutionary China*. Stanford, CA: Stanford University Press.

Jowitt, Kenneth. 1992. *New World Disorder: The Leninist Extinction*. London: University of California Press.

Kahoku Kōtsū Kabushiki Kaisha. 1939–1943. 北支現地編輯 *The North China*. Tokyo: Daiichi Shobō.

Kahoku Sōgō Chōsa Kenkyūjo. 1944. 華北農業統計調査県調査班調査要綱 *[Important Results Concerning Agricultural Statistics of Northern China from an Investigation by the County Investigation Group]*. Beijing: Mimeograph.

Kataoka, Tetsuya. 1972. Review: Communist Power in a War of National Liberation: The Case of China. *World Politics*, **24**(3), 410–427.

Kennedy, John J. 2007. From the tax-for-fee reform to the abolition of agricultural taxes: the impact on township governments in north-west China. *The China Quarterly*, **189**, 43.

Kim, Ch'an-jŏng. 2004. 朝鮮連 *[Korean General Association]*. Tokyo: Shinchōsha.

Kim, Hyung-A. 2004. *Korea's Development under Park Chung Hee: Rapid Industrialization, 1961–79*. London: Routledge.

Kim, Jin Ha. 2009. *Caging the Reasons of State: Discipline and Constitutionalism in the Bureaucratic Pursuit of National Development – Chosun, South and North Korean Cases*. Ph.D. thesis, University of Chicago.

King, Gary. 1994. *Designing Social Inquiry: Scientific Inference in Qualitative Research*. Princeton, NJ: Princeton University Press.

King, Gary. 1998. *Unifying Political Methodology: The Likelihood Theory of Statistical Inference*. Ann Arbor: The University of Michigan Press.

King, Gary, and Zeng, Langche. 2006. The Dangers of Extreme Counterfactuals. *Political Analysis*, **14**, 131–159.

King, Gary, Tomz, Michael, and Wittenberg, Tomz. 2000. Making the Most of Statistical Analyses: Improving Interpretation and Presentation. *American Journal of Political Science*, **44**(2), 341–355.

Kocher, Matthew A., and Monteiro, Nuno P. 2016. Line of Demarcation: Causation, Design-Based Inference, and Historical Research. *Perspectives on Politics*, **14**(4), 952–975.

Koss, Daniel, and Sato, Hiroshi. 2016. A Micro-Geography of State Extractive Power: The Case of Rural China. *Studies of Comparative International Development*, **51**, 389–410.

Koss, Daniel. 2016. Statistical Rebirths: A Need to Reconsider China's Missing Women Problem? Unpublished Manuscript.

Koss, Daniel. 2017. Political Geography of Empire: Chinese Varieties of Local Government. *The Journal of Asian Studies*, **76**(1), 159–184.

Kung, James Kai-sing, and Chen, Shuo. 2011. The Tragedy of the Nomenklatura: Career Incentives and Political Radicalism During China's Great Leap Famine. *The American Political Science Review*, **105**(1), 27–45.

Kupke, Martin. 2012. *SED ind MfS I'm Kirchenbezirk Meissen [The Socialist Unity Party and the Ministry for State Security in the Church District of Meissen]*. Leipzig: Leipziger Universitätsverlag.

Kuwatarō, Baba. 1938. 北支八省の資源 *[Raw Materials in the Eight Provinces of Northern China]*. Tokyo: Jitsugyō no Nihonsha.

Lam, Tong. 2011. *A Passion for Facts: Social Surveys and the Construction of the Chinese Nation State, 1900–1949*. Berkeley: University of California Press.

Landry, Pierre F. 2008. *Decentralized Authoritarianism in China: The Communist Party's Control of Local Elites in the Post-Mao Era*. New York: Cambridge University Press.

Lanshan District. 2001. 蘭山區政協志 *Lanshan People's Consultative Conference Gazetteer*. Jinan: Jilu Shushe.

Lanshan District. 2002. 蘭山人大志 *Lanshan People's Congress Gazetteer*. Beijing: Zhongyang Wenxian Chubanshe.

LaPalombara, Joseph, and Weiner, Myron (eds). 1966. *Political Parties and Political Development*. Princeton, NJ: Princeton University Press.

Lary, Diana. 2010. *The Chinese People at War*. New York: Cambridge University Press.

Lavely, William. 2001. First Impressions from the 2000 Census. *Population and Development Review*, 27(4), 755–769.

Lawson, Konrad Mitchell. 2012. *Wartime Atrocities and the Politics of Treason in the Ruins of the Japanese Empire, 1937–1953*. Ph.D. thesis, Harvard University.

Legal Press. 2015. 黨員領導幹部常用黨紀條規選編 *[Leading Party Cadres' Frequently Used Disciplinary Regulations]*. Beijing: Falü Chubanshe.

Levitsky, Steven, and Way, Lucan A. 2010. *Competitive Authoritarianism: Hybrid Regimes after the Cold War*. New York: Cambridge University Press.

Levitsky, Steven, and Way, Lucan A. 2012. Beyond Patronage: Violent Struggle, Ruling Party Cohesion, and Authoritarian Durability. *Perspectives on Politics*, 10(4), 869–889.

Li, Lianjiang, and O'Brien, Kevin J. 1996. Villagers and Popular Resistance in Contemporary China. *Modern China*, 22(1), 28–61.

Li, Shi, Sato, Hiroshi, and Sicular, Terry. 2013. *Rising Inequality in China: Challenges to a Harmonious Society*. New York: Cambridge University Press.

Li, Shuang, Lu, Ming, and Sato, Hiroshi. 2008. The Value of Power in China: How Do Party Membership and Social Networks Affect Pay in Different Ownership Sectors? *Global COE Hi-Stat Discussion Paper Series*, gd08-011.

Lieberman, Evan S. 2002. Taxation data as Indicators of State-Society Relations: Possibilities and Pitfalls in Cross-National Research. *Studies in Comparative International Development (SCID)*, 36(4), 89–115.

Lieberthal, Kenneth G. 1980. *Revolution and Tradition in Tientsin, 1949–1952*. Stanford, CA: Stanford University Press.

Lieberthal, Kenneth G. 1988. *Policy Making in China: Leaders, Structures, and Processes*. Princeton, NJ: Princeton University Press.

Lieberthal, Kenneth G. 1995. *Governing China: From Revolution Through Reform*. New York: W.W. Norton.

Lim, Jaehwan. 2014. 人民解放軍と中国政治：文化大革命から鄧小平へ *[The Emergence and Demise of Military Governance in China]*. Nagoya: Nagoya Daigaku Shuppankai.

Lingg, Anton. 1939. *Die Verwaltung der Nationalsozialistischen Deutschen Arbeiterpartei [The Administration of the German National-Socialist Workers Party]*. Munich: Zentralverlag der NSDAP.

Lipset, Seymour M., and Rokkan, Stein. 1967. Cleavage Structures, Party Systems and Voter Alignment: An Introduction. Pages 1–64 of: Lipset, Seymour M., and Rokkan, Stein (eds), *Party Systems and Voter Alignment: Cross-National Perspectives*. New York: Free Press.

Liu, Aiming. 2011. 企業所得税特別納税調整研究 *Special Tax Adjustments Rules Pertaining to the Enterprise Income Taxation*. Ph.D. thesis, Central South University.

Liu, Bo. 2011. 西藏中共黨組織第一支部創建史初探：凱松村黨支部的創建及其意義 The History of the First Communist Party Branch of Tibet: The Establishment of the Party Branch in Kasong Village and its Significance. *Journal of Tibet University*, 26(2), 28–34.

Liu, Ping. 2013. The Historical Fate of Chinese Popular Religions: Final Years of Shandong Huidaomen, 1945–1949. Unpublished Manuscript.

Liu, Shaoqi. 1950. *On the Party*. Beijing: Foreign Languages Press.

Liu, Shaoqi. 1980. 黨論 *[Party Theory]*. Beijing: Renmin Chubanshe.

Liu, Xijing. 2007. 中國增值稅流失研究 *[Study of VAT Losses in China]*. Ph.D. thesis, Xiamen University.

Looney, Kristen E. 2012. *The Rural Developmental State: Modernization Campaigns and Peasant Politics in China, Taiwan and South Korea*. Ph.D. thesis, Harvard University.

Lü, Xiaobo. 2000. *Cadres and Corruption: The Organizational Involution of the Chinese Communist Party*. Stanford, CA: Stanford University Press.

Lü, Xiaobo, and Perry, Elizabeth J. (eds). 1997. *Danwei: The Changing Chinese Workplace in Historical and Comparative Perspective*. New York: M.E. Sharpe.

Luo, Yanjun. 2013. 革命與秩序：以山東省鄆城縣鄉村社會為中心 *(1939–1956) [Revolution and Order: Focus on the Rural Society in Shandong's Yuncheng County (1939–1956)]*. Beijing: Zhongguo Shehui Kexue Chubanshe.

Ma, Shizhong. 1990. 中國共產黨支部工作手冊 *[Work Manual for a CCP Cell]*. Jinan: Shandong Renmin Chubanshe.

Ma, Qipeng et al. (ed). 1989. 中國共產黨執政四十年 *[40 Years of CCP Rule]*. Beijing: Zhonggong Dangshi Ziliao Chubanshe.

MacFarquhar, Roderick. 1974–1994. *The Origins of the Cultural Revolution*. New York: Columbia University Press.

MacFarquhar, Roderick, and Schoenhals, Michael. 2006. *Mao's Last Revolution*. Cambridge, MA: Belknap Press of Harvard University Press.

Magaloni, Beatriz. 2006. *Voting for Autocracy: Hegemonic Party Survival and its Demise in Mexico*. New York: Cambridge University Press.

Magaloni, Beatriz. 2008. Credible Power-Sharing and the Longevity of Authoritarian Rule. *Comparative Political Studies*, **41**, 715–741.

Magaloni, Beatriz, and Kricheli, Ruth. 2010. Political Order and One-Party Rule. *Annual Review of Political Science*, **13**, 123–143.

Mahoney, James, and Rueschemeyer, Dietrich (eds). 2003. *Comparative Historical Analysis in the Social Sciences*. New York: Cambridge University Press.

Malycha, Andreas, and Winters, Peter J. 2009. *Die SED: Geschichte einer deutschen Partei [The SED: History of a German Party]*. Munuch: C.H. Beck Verlag.

Manion, Melanie. 1993. *Retirement of Revolutionaries in China: Public Policies, Social Norms, Private Interests*. Princeton, NJ: Princeton University Press.

Manion, Melanie. 2006. Democracy, Community, Trust: The Impact of Elections in Rural China. *Comparative Political Studies*, 39(3), 301–324.

Mankiw, N. Gregory. 2007. *Principles of Economics*. Mason: Thomson/South-Western.

Manoïlescu, Mihaïl. 1937. *Le Parti Unique: Institutions Politiques des Régimes Nouveaux [The Single Party: Political Institutions of New Regimes]*. Paris: Les Oeuvres françaises.

Mao, Zedong. 1960. *On the Correct Handling of Contradictions among the People*. Beijing: Foreign Language Press.

Mao, Zedong. 1969. 毛澤東思想萬歲 *[Long Live Mao Zedong Thought!]*. Hong Kong: Red Guard Material.

Mao, Zedong. 1998. 建國以來毛澤東文稿 *Papers by Mao Zedong Post–1949*. Beijing: Zhongyang Wenxian Chubanshe.

Marshall, Monty G., Gurr, Ted R., and Jaggers, Keith. 2014. *Polity™ IV Project: Dataset Users' Manual*. Online: Center for Systemic Peace.

Mas-Colell, Andreu, Whinston, Michael D., and Green, Jerry. 1995. *Microeconomic Theory*. Oxford: Oxford University Press.

Masoud, Tarek. 2011. The Road to (and from) Liberation Square. *Journal of Democracy*, **22**(3), 20–34.

McGregor, Richard. 2010. *The Party: The Secret World of China's Communist Rulers*. Harvard: HarperCollins Publishers.

Mei, S., and Qiu, X. 2001. 中共上海黨志 *[Gazetteer of the CCP in Shanghai]*. Shanghai: Shanghai Shehui Kexueyuan Chubanshe.

Merlin, M. Giovanna, and Raftery, Adrian E. 2000. Are Births Underreported in Rural China? Manipulation of Statistical Records in Response to China's Population Policies. *Demography*, **37**(1), 109–126.

Mitter, Rana. 2013. *China's War with Japan, 1937–1945: The Struggle for Survival*. New York: Allen Lane.

Mo, Yan. 2001. *Shifu, You'll Do Anything for a Laugh*. New York: Arcade Publishing.

Montgomery, Bruce P. 2011. Immortality in the Secret Police Files: The Iraq Memory Foundation and the Baath Party Archive. *International Journal of Cultural Property*, **18**(3), 309–336.

Moore, Barrington. 1966. *Social Origins of Dictatorship and Democracy*. Boston: Beacon Press.

Mu, Lin. 2000. 六十年革命工作紀實 *[Record of 60 Years of Revolutionary Work]*. Jinan: Shandong Renmin Chubanshe.

Nathan, Andrew J. 2003. Authoritarian Resilience: China's Changing of the Guard. *Journal of Democracy*, **14**(1), 6–17.

National Bureau of Statistics. various years. *China Statistical Yearbook* 中國統計年鑑. Beijing: Zhongguo Tongji Chubanshe.

National Bureau of Statistics of China. 1990. 全國各省自治區直轄市歷史統計資料匯編 *1949–1989 [Collection of Provincial-level Historical Statistics 1949–1989]*. Beijing: Zhongguo Tongji Chubanshe.

Niemi, Richard G., and Jennings, M. Kent. 1991. Issues and Inheritance in the Formation of Party Identification. *American Journal of Political Science*, **35**(4), 970–988.

NSDAP. 1939. *Das Gesicht der Partei [The Face of the Party]*. Munich: Reichsorganisationsleiter.

NSDAP Reichsorganisationsamt. 1935. *Partei-Statistik [Party Statistics]*. München: internally published.

O'Donnell, Guillermo A. 1982. *Transitions from Authoritarian Rule: Tentative Conclusions About Uncertain Democracies.* Baltimore, MD: Johns Hopkins University Press.

O'Donnell, Guillermo A. 1993. On the State, Democratization and Some Conceptual Problems: A Latin American View with Glances at Some postcommunist Countries. *World Development,* 21(8), 1355–1369.

Oi, Jean Chun. 1983. *State and Peasant in Contemporary China: The Politics of Grain Procurement.* Ph.D. thesis, University of Michigan.

Oi, Jean Chun. 1999. *Rural China Takes Off: Institutional Foundations of Economic Reform.* Berkeley: University of California Press.

Ownby, David. 2002. Approximations of Chinese Bandits: Perverse Rebels, Romantic Heroes, or Frustrated Bachelors? Pages 226–250 of: Brownell, Susan, and Wasserstrom, Jeffrey N. (eds), *Chinese Femininities, Chinese Masculinities: A Reader.* Berkeley: University of California Press.

Pak, Tu-jin. 2008. 朝鮮連：その虚像と実像 *[Korean General Association: Image and Reality].* Tokyo: Chūō Kōron Shinsha.

Paulson, David Mark. 1982. *War and Revolution in North China: The Shandong Base Area, 1937–1945.* Ph.D. thesis, Stanford University.

Pepper, Suzanne. 2004. The Political Odyssey of an Intellectual Construct: Peasant Nationalism and the Study of China's Revolutionary History – A Review Essay. *The China Quarterly,* 63(1), 105–125.

Perkins, Dwight H. 1991. China's Economic Policy and Performance. Pages 475–539 of: MacFarquhar, Roderick, and Fairbank, John K. (eds), *Cambridge History of China, Volume 15: The People's Republic, Part 2: Revolutions Within the Chinese Revoltuion, 1966–1982.* New York: Cambridge University Press.

Perry, Elizabeth J. 1980. *Rebels and Revolutionaries in North China, 1845–1945.* Stanford, CA: Stanford University Press.

Perry, Elizabeth J. 1992. Introduction: Chinese Political Culture Revisited. Pages 1–14 of: Wasserstrom, Jeffrey N., and Perry, Elizabeth J. (eds), *Popular Protest and Political Culture in Modern China.* Boulder, CO: Westview Press.

Perry, Elizabeth J. 1993. *Shanghai on Strike: The Politics of Chinese Labor.* Stanford, CA: Stanford University Press.

Perry, Elizabeth J. 1994. Trends in the Study of Chinese politics: State-Society Relations. *China Q.,* 704.

Perry, Elizabeth J. 2006. *Patroling the Revolution: Worker Militias, Citizenship, and the Modern Chinese State.* New York: Rowman and Littlefield.

Perry, Elizabeth J. 2007. Masters of the Country? Shanghai Workers in the Early People's Republic. Pages 59–79 of: Brown, Jeremy, and Pickowicz, Paul G. (eds), *Dilemmas of Victory: The Early Years of the People's Republic.* Cambridge: Harvard University Press.

Perry, Elizabeth J. 2007. Studying Chinese Politics: Farewell to Revolution. *The Chicago Journal,* 57, 1–22.

Perry, Elizabeth J. 2011. From Mass Campaigns to Managed Campaigns: "Constructing a New Socialist Countryside". Pages 30–61 of: Heilmann, Sebastian, and Perry, Elizabeth J. (eds), *Mao's Invisible Hand: The Political Foundations of Adaptive Governance in China.* Cambridge, MA: Harvard University Asia Center; Distributed by Harvard University Press.

Perry, Elizabeth J. 2012. *Anyuan: Mining China's Revolutionary Tradition*. Berkeley: University of California Press.

Perry, Elizabeth J. 2012. The Illiberal Challenge of Authoritarian China. *Taiwan Journal of Democracy*, **8**(2), 3–15.

Perry, Elizabeth J. 2014. Citizen Contention and Campus Calm: The Paradox of Chinese Civil Society. *Current History*, **113**(764), 211–217.

Perry, Elizabeth J., and Li, Xun. 1993. *Revolutionary Rudeness: The Language of Red Guards and Rebel Workers in China's Cultural Revolution*. Bloomington: East Asian Studies Center at Indiana University.

Perry, Elizabeth J., and Li, Xun. 1997. *Proletarian Power: Shanghai in the Cultural Revolution*. Boulder: Westview Press.

Pharr, Susan J., Putnam, Robert D., and Dalton, Russell J. 2000. A Quarter-Century of Declining Confidence. *Journal of Democracy*, **11**(2), 5–25.

Phillips, Kristen D. 2009. *Building the Nation from the Hinterlands: Poverty, Participation, and Education in Rural Tanzania*. Ph.D. thesis, University of Wisconsin-Madison.

Pierson, Paul. 2004. *Politics in Time: History, Institutions, and Social Analysis*. Princeton, NJ: Princeton University Press.

PLA Artillery, Political Department, Organization Department. 1956. 組織工作文件匯集，機密 *[Document Collection on Organization Work, Secret]*. Beijing: internally circulated.

Pomeranz, Kenneth. 1993. *The Making of a Hinterland: State, Society, and Economy in Inland North China, 1853–1937*. Berkeley: University of California Press.

Population Census Office. 2010. 中國2010年人口檢查資料 *[Tabulation on the 2010 Population Census of the People's Republic of China]*. Beijing: Zhongguo Tongji Chubanshe.

Port, Andrew I. 2007. *Conflict and Stability in the German Democratic Republic*. New York: Cambridge University Press.

Pring, Coralie. 2017. *People and Corruption: Global Corruption Barometer*. Berlin: Transparency International.

Putnam, Robert D., Leonardi, Robert, and Nanetti, Raffaella Y. 1993. *Making Democracy Work: Civic Traditions in Modern Italy*. Princeton, NJ: Princeton University Press.

Pye, Lucian W. 1988. *The Mandarin and the Cadre: China's Political Cultures*. Ann Arbor, MI: Center for Chinese Studies.

Quah, Danny T. 1993. Galton's Fallacy and Tests of Convergence Hypothesis. *The Scandinavian Journal of Economics*, **95**(4), 427–443.

Red Guards. 1967–1973. *Red Guard Publications* 紅衛兵資料. Washington, D.C.: Association of Research Libraries, Center for Chinese Research Materials.

Red Guards. 1967–69. 毛澤東思想萬歲 *[Long Live Mao Zedong Thought!]*. Hong Kong: Yishan Shuwu.

Remick, Elizabeth J. 2004. *Building Local States: China During the Republican and Post-Mao Eras*. Cambridge: Harvard University Asia Center; Distributed by Harvard University Press.

Remington, Thomas F. 2013. Putin, the Parliament, and the Party System. Pages 53–74 of: Herspring, Dale R. (ed), *Putin's Russia: Past Imperfect, Future Uncertain*. Lanham: Rowman and Littlefield.

Reuter, Ora J., and Gandhi, Jennifer. 2011. Economic Performance and Elite Defection from Hegemonic Parties. *British Journal of Political Science*, **41**(1), 83–110.

Rithmire, Meg E. 2014. China's 'New Regionalism': Subnational Analysis in Chinese Political Economy. *World Politics*, **66**(1).

Roberts, Margaret. 2014. *Fear, Friction, and Flooding: Methods of Online Information Control*. Ph.D. thesis, Harvard University.

Roberts, Sean P. 2012. *Putin's United Russia Party*. New York: Routledge.

Rokkan, Stein. 1969. Models and methods in the comparative study of nation-building. *Acta Sociologica*, **12**(2), 53–73.

Ross, Cameron. 2009. *Local Politics and Democratization in Russia*. New York: Routledge.

Rutland, Peter. 1992. *The Politics of Economic Stagnation in the Soviet Union: The Role of Local Party Organs in Economic Management*. New York: Cambridge University Press.

Ryang, Sonia. 1997. *North Koreans in Japan: Language, Ideology, and Identity*. Boulder, CO: Westview Press.

Salanié, Bernard. 1997. *The Economics of Contracts: A Primer*. Cambridge, MA: MIT Press.

Scalapino, Robert A. 1953. *Democracy and the Party Movement in Prewar Japan: The Failure of the First Attempt*. Berkeley: University of California Press.

Scarrow, Susan E. 2000. Parties without Members? Party Organization in a Changing Electoral Environment. In: Dalton, Russell J., and Wattenberg, Martin (eds), *Parties without Partisans: Political Change in Advanced Industrial Democracies*. Oxford: Oxford University Press.

Schedler, Andreas. 2010. Authoritarianism's Last Line of Defense. *Journal of Democracy*, **21**(1), 69–80.

Scheurig, Bodo. 1970. *Einfühung in die Zeitgeschichte [Introduction to Contemporary History]*. Berlin: Walter de Gruyter.

Schoenhals, Michael. 2005. "Why Don't We Arm the Left?" Mao's Culpability for the Cultural Revolution's "Great Chaos" of 1967. *The China Quarterly*, **182**, 277–300.

Schurmann, Franz. 1966. *Ideology and Organization in Communist China*. Berkeley: University of California Press.

Second Historical Archives of China. 1994. 中國第二歷史檔案館指南 *[Guide to the Second Archives of China]*. Beijing: Zhongguo Dangan Chubanshe.

Selden, Mark. 1995. *China in Revolution: The Yenan Way Revisited*. Armonk, NJ: M.E. Sharpe.

Selznick, Philip. 1952. *The Organizational Weapon*. New York: MacGraw-Hill.

Sen, Amartya. 1990. More Than 100 Million Women Are Missing. *New York Review of Books*, **37**(20).

Shambaugh, David L. 2008. *China's Communist Party: Atrophy and Adaptation*. Washington, D.C.: Woodrow Wilson Center Press.

Shandong Department of Fiscal Affairs, Budget Office. 2007. 山東省以下財政體制 *[The Sub-Provincial Fiscal System of Shandong]*. Jinan: Internally Published.

Shandong Department of Statistics, Population Office. 1985. 山東省人口統計資料匯編 *[Compilation of Population Statistics for Shandong Province]*. Jinan: Internally Published.

Shandong Government. 1984/85. 山東省行政區劃資料 *[Material on Administrative Divisions of Shandong]*. Jinan: Internal Material of Shandong's Department for Civil Affairs.

Shandong Province. 2010. 山東省志財政志 *[Shandong Provincial Gazetteer: Fiscal Gazetteer]*. Jinan: Shandong Renmin Chubanshe.

Shandong University. 2012. 如何認識當今世界的政黨政治 *[How to Understand Contemporary Party Politics]*. Jinan: Shandong University.

Shefter, Martin. 1994. *Political Parties and the State: The American Historical Experience*. Princeton, NJ: Princeton University Press.

Shen, Zhijia. 1997. *Zouping, 1911–1949: A Social and Political History*. Ph.D. thesis, University of Chicago.

Sheng, Yang. 2009. Authoritarian Co-optation, the Territorial Dimension: Provincial Political Representation in Post-Mao China. *Studies in Comparative International Development (SCID)*, **44**(1), 71–93.

Shi, Yaojiang, and Kennedy, John J. 2016. Delayed Registration and Identifying the "Missing Girls" in China. *The China Quarterly*, **228**, 1018–38.

Short, Susan E., and Zhai, Fengying. 1998. Looking Locally at China's One-Child Policy. *Studies in Family Planning*, **29**(4), 373–387.

Shue, Vivienne. 1988. *The Reach of the State: Sketches of the Chinese Body Politic*. Stanford, CA: Stanford University Press.

Singh, Prerna. 2010. *Subnationalism and Social Development: A Comparative Analysis of Indian States*. Ph.D. thesis, Princeton University.

Skocpol, Theda. 1979. *States and Social Revolutions: A Comparative Analysis of France, Russia, and China*. New York: Cambridge University Press.

Slater, Dan. 2010. *Ordering Power: Contentious Politics and Authoritarian Leviathans in Southeast Asia*. New York: Cambridge University Press.

Smith, Benjamin B. 2007. *Hard Times in the Lands of Plenty: Oil Politics in Iran and Indonesia*. Ithaca, NY: Cornell University Press.

Snyder, Jack. 1991. *Myths of Empire: Domestic Politics and International Ambition*. Ithaca, NY: Cornell University Press.

Snyder, Richard. 2001. Scaling Down: The Subnational Comparative Method. *Studies in Comparative International Development (SCID)*, **36**(1), 93–110.

Soifer, Hillel D. 2006. *Authority over Distance: Explaining Variation in State Infrastructural Power in Latin America*. Harvard University.

Solinger, Dorothy J. 1999. *Contesting Citizenship in Urban China: Peasant Migrants, the State, and the Logic of the Market*. Berkeley: University of California Press.

Stoner-Weiss, Kathryn. 2006. Resistance to the Central State on the Periphery. Pages 87–119 of: Colton, Timothy J., and Holmes, Stephen (eds), *The State after Communism: Governance in the New Russia*. Lanham, MD: Rowman and Littlefield.

Su, Yang. 2011. *Collective Killings in Rural China during the Cultural Revolution*. New York: Cambridge University Press.

Suwa, Kazuyuki. 2004. 中国共産党の幹部管理政策:「党政幹部」と非共産党組織 [The CCP's Cadre Management Policy: Party Cadres in Non-CCP Organizations]. *Aja Kenkyū*, 50(2), 107–125.

Svolik, Milan W. 2012. *The Politics of Authoritarian Rule*. New York: Cambridge University Press.

Talhelm, Thomas and Zhang, Xuemin and Oishi, Shigehiro and Chen, Shimin and Duan, Dongyuan and Lau, Xuezhao and Kitayama, Shinobu, 2014. Large-Scale Psychological Differences Within China Explained by Rice Versus Wheat Agriculture, *Science*, 344(6184), 603–608.

Teiwes, Frederick C. 1979. *Politics and Purges in China: Rectification and the Decline of Party Norms*. New York: Sharpe.

Thaxton, Ralph A. 2008. *Catastrophe and Contention in Rural China: Mao's Great Leap Forward Famine and the Origins of Righteous Resistance in Da Fo Village*. New York: Cambridge University Press.

Thelen, Kathleen. 2004. *How Institutions Evolve: The Political Economy of Skills in Germany, Britain, the United States, and Japan*. New York: Cambridge University Press.

Thornton, Patricia M. 2013. *The Advance of the Party: Transformation or Takeover of Urban Grassroots Society?* The China Quarterly, 213, 1–18.

Tilly, Charles. 1975. Reflections on the History of European State-Making. Pages 3–83 of: Tilly, Charles (ed), *The Formation of National States in Western Europe*. Princeton, NJ: Princeton University Press.

Tilly, Charles. 1986. *The Contentious French*. Cambridge, MA: Belknap Press of Harvard University Press.

Tsai, Kellee. 2006. Adaptive Informal Institutions and Endogenous Institutional Change in China. *World Politics*, 59(1), 116–141.

Tsai, Lily L. 2007. *Accountability without Democracy: Solidary Groups and Public Goods Provision in Rural China*. Cambridge: Cambridge University Press.

Tsai, Lily L. 2009. *The Rise of Subnational and Multilevel Comparative Politics*. Unpublished paper.

Tsai, Wen-hsuan. 2015. A Unique Pattern of Policymaking in China's Authoritarian Regime: The CCP's Neican/Pishi Model. *Asian Survey*, 55(6), 1093–115.

Tsai, Wen-hsuan, and Chung, Yen-Lin. Forthcoming. A Model of Adaptive Mobilization: Implications of the CCP's Diaoyan Politics. *Modern China*.

Ufen, Andreas. 2009. The Transformation of Political Party Opposition in Malaysia and its Implications for the Electoral Authoritarian Regime. *Democratization*, 16(3), 604–627.

United States Senate. 2004. *Money Laundering and Foreign Corruption: Enforcement and Effectiveness of the Patriot Act*. Washington, DC: Permanent Subcommittee on Investigations.

Valentino, Nicholas A., and Sears, David O. 2005. Old Times There Are Not Forgotten: Race and Partisan Realignment in the Contemporary South. *American Journal of Political Science*, 49(3), 672–688.

van de Ven, Hans J. 2010. *War and Nationalism in China 1925–1945*. London: Routledge.

van Dyck, Brandon. 2014. Why Party Organization Still Matters: The Workers' Party in Northeastern Brazil. *Latin American Politics and Society*, **56**(2), 1–26.

Vogel, Ezra F. 1969. *Canton under Communism: Programs and Politics in a Provincial Capital, 1949–1968*. Cambridge, MA: Harvard University Press.

Vogel, Ezra F. 2011. *Deng Xiaoping and the Transformation of China*. Cambridge: Belknap Press of Harvard University Press.

von der Mehden, Fred. 1964. *Politics of the Developing Nations*. Englewood Cliffs, NJ: Prentice-Hall.

Wakeman, Frederic. 2007. "Cleanup": The New Order in Shanghai. In: *Dilemmas of Victory: The Early Years of the People's Republic of China*. Cambridge, MA: Harvard University Asia Center; Distributed by Harvard University Press.

Walder, Andrew G. 1986. *Communist Neo-Traditionalism: Work and Authority in Chinese Industry*. Berkeley: University of California Press.

Walder, Andrew G. 2004. The Party Elite and China's Trajectory of Change. *China: An International Journal*, **2**(2), 189–209.

Walder, Andrew G. 2009. *Fractured Rebellion: The Beijing Red Guard Movement*. Cambridge, MA: Harvard University Press.

Walder, Andrew G. 2014. Rebellion and Repression in China, 1966–1971. *Social Science History*, **38**(3-4), 513–539.

Walder, Andrew G. 2015. *China under Mao: A Revolution Derailed*. Cambridge, MA: Harvard University Press.

Walder, Andrew G., and Su, Yang. 2003. The Cultural Revolution in the Countryside: Scope, Timing and Human Impact. *The China Quarterly*, **173**, 74–99.

Walfish, Daniel. 2000. A Billion and Counting: China's Tricky Census. *Science*, **290**(5495), 1288–1289.

Wan, Jiyao. 2013. 論黨的道路自信，理論自信，制度自信 [On the Party's Confidence in its Way, Confidence in its Theory, and Confidence in its System]. *Journal of Fujian Institute of Socialism*, **95**(2), 9–13.

Wang, Yongbing. 2010. 黨內民主的制度創新與路徑選擇：基於基層和地方黨內民主試點的實證研究 *[Institutional Innovation and Choices of Inner-Party Democracy: Empirical Research of Local Experiments in Inner-Party Democracy]*. Beijing: Zhangyang Bianyi Chubanshe.

Wang, Yu-chuan. 1940. The Organization of a Typical Guerrilla Area in South Shantung. Pages 84–130 of: Carlson, Evans Fordyce (ed), *The Chinese Army: Its Organization and Military Efficiency*. New York: Institute of Pacific Relations.

Wang, Yuhua. 2015. *Tying the Autocrat's Hands: The Rise of the Rule of Law in China*. New York: Cambridge University Press.

Weber, Max. 1922. *Wirtschaft und Gesellschaft [Economy and Society]*. Tübingen: J.C.B. Mohr (Paul Siebeck).

Weiss, Jessica Chen, 2014. *Powerful Patriots: Nationalist Protest in China's Foreign Relations*. New York. Oxford University Press.

White, Tyrene. 2000. Domination, Resistance, and Accommodation in China's One-Child Campaign. Pages 171–196 of: Perry, Elizabeth J., and Selden,

Mark (eds), *Chinese Society: Change, Conflict and Resistance*. New York: Routledge.

Wintrobe, Ronald. 1998. *The Political Economy of Dictatorship*. New York: Cambridge University Press.

Wong, Christine. 2010. Fiscal Reform: Paying for the Harmonious Society. *China Economic Quarterly*, **14**(2), 20–25.

Wu, David Mark. 2005. *The Role of Class Struggle in the Chinese Communist Party's Social Reform: A Case Study of Rushan County from 1943 to 1949*. M.Phil. thesis, University of Alberta.

Wu, Yuexing. 1999. 中國現代史地圖集 *1919–1949 [Modern Chinese History, Map Collection 1919–1949]*. Beijing: Zhongguo Ditu Chubanshe.

Wuhan Military Region. 1988. 武民兵史 *[A Short History of the Wuhan Militia]*. Wuhan: Wuhan Chubanshe.

Xianning Government. 1992. 咸寧市志 *[Xianning City Gazetteer]*. Beijing: Zhongguo Chengshi Chubanshe.

Xu, Yong. 2005. 村民自治的成長：行政放權於社會發育 [On the Growth of Villagers' Self-Governance]. *Journal of Huazhong Normal University*, **44**(2), 2–8.

Xu, Yong, 2016. 區域社會視角下農村集體經營與家庭經營的根基與機理 [The Foundation and Mechanism of Rural Collective Management and Family Management from the Perspective of Regional Society], *Zhonggong Dangshi Yanjiu*, **2016**(4), 12–27.

Yan, Xiaojun. 2009. *Economic Reform and Political Change in Rural China: The Case of Qing County*. Ph.D. thesis, Harvard University.

Yang, Dali. 1996. *Calamity and Reform in China: State, Rural Society, and Institutional Change Since the Great Leap Famine*. Stanford, CA: Stanford University Press.

Yang, Dali L. 2004. *Remaking the Chinese Leviathan: Market Transition and the Politics of Governance in China*. Stanford, CA: Stanford University Press.

Yang, Dali L., Xu, Huayu, and Tao, Ran. 2014. The Tragedy of the Nomenklatura? Career Incentives, Political Loyalty and Political Radicalism During China's Great Leap Forward. *Journal of Contemporary China*, **23**(89), 864–883.

Yang, Hui. 2001. 農村稅費改革給基層黨組織建設提出的新要求 [New Tasks for Grassroots Party Building in the Wake of the Tax-for-Fee Reform]. *Dangjian Yanjiu Neican*, **119**(9), 7–8.

Yang, Kuisong. 2008. Reconsidering the Campaign to Suppress Counterrevolutionaries. *The China Quarterly*, **193**, 102–121.

Yep, Ray. 2004. Can "Tax-for-Fee" Reform Reduce Rural Tension in China? The Process, Progress and Limitations. *The China Quarterly*, **177**(1), 42–70.

Yu, George T. 1966. *Party Politics in Republican China*. Berkeley: University of California Press.

Zeng, Yi et al. 1993. Causes and Implications of the Recent Increase in the Reported Sex Ratio at Birth in China. *Population and Development Review*, **19**(2), 283–302.

Zhang, Elya J. 2006. To Be Somebody: Li Qinglin, Run-of-the-Mill Cultural Revolution Showstopper. Pages 211–239 of: Esherick, Joseph W., Pickowicz,

Paul G., and Walder, Andrew G. (eds), *The Chinese Cultural Revolution as History*. Stanford, CA: Stanford University Press.

Zhang, Liang. 2001. *The Tiananmen Papers*. New York: Public Affairs.

Zhang, Ruihong, Li, Wei, and Qi, Xiaojuan. 2010. 社區黨支部工作手冊 *[Work Manual for Party Cells in Urban Communities]*. Beijing: Zhongguo Shehui Chubanshe.

Zhang, Shun, and Yu, Zhanghai. 2003. 發展指標不等於發展計劃 [Recruitment Targets are not the same as Recruitment Plans]. 黨員之友 *[Party Member's Friend]*, 6, 27.

Zhang, Yuebin, Mei, Hua, and Liu, Gong. 2000. 實行發展黨員公示制的探索 [Experimenting with the Implementation of Public Announcements during Party Member Recruitment]. *Dangjian Yanjiu Neican*, 3, 10–11.

Zhao, Suisheng. 1998. A State-Led Nationalism: The Patriotic Education Campaign in Post-Tiananmen China. *Communist and Post-Communist Studies*, 31(3), 287–302.

Zheng, Shiping. 1997. *Party vs. State in Post-1949 China: The Institutional Dilemma*. New York: Cambridge University Press.

Zheng, Yongnian. 2010. *The Chinese Communist Party as Organizational Emperor: Culture, Reproduction and Transformation*. New York: Routledge.

Zhong, Shilu. 2010. 中國共產黨在邊疆少數民族地區執政方略研究 *[The CCP's General Plan for Policy Implementation Strategies among Ethnic Minorities in Border Areas]*. Kunming: Yunnan Renmin Chubanshe.

Zhou, Yuyun. 2012. 如何認識當今世界的政黨政治 [How to Understand Contemporary Party Politics]. Pages 8–11 of: Shandong University (ed), 第四屆中國政黨論壇：會議文集 *[Fourth Forum on Chinese Political Parties: Working Paper Collection]*. Jinan: Shandong University.

Zhou, Zhongwei. 2000. 群眾性事件研究 *[Research on Mass Incidents]*. Public Security: Internally Published.

Zhu, Wei Xing, Li, Lu, and Hesketh, Therese. 2009. China's Excess Males, Sex Selective Abortion, and One Child Policy: Analysis of Data from 2005 National Intercensus Survey. *British Medical Journal*, 338, 920–923.

Ziblatt, Daniel. 2006. *Structuring the State: The Formation of Italy and Germany and the Puzzle of Federalism*. Princeton, NJ: Princeton University Press.

Ziblatt, Daniel. 2008. Why some cities provide more public goods than others: A subnational comparison of the provision of public goods in German cities in 1912. *Studies in Comparative International Development (SCID)*, 43(3), 273–289.

Ziblatt, Daniel. 2009. Shaping democratic practice and the causes of electoral fraud: the case of nineteenth-century Germany. *American Political Science Review*, 103(1), 1–21.

Zolberg, Aristide R. 1966. *Creating Political Order: The Party-States of West Africa*. Chicago: Rand McNally.

Index